COMPARATIVE REMEDIES FOR BREACH OF CONTRACT

The book provides a comparative analysis of the law relating to remedies for breach of contract. It examines different remedies such as specific performance and damages, doing so from the viewpoint of different legal systems, principally the English, American, German, French and Israeli. Each essay is written by a recognised specialist in his or her own field. Topics covered include the relationship between substantive rights and contract remedies, the recent reforms of the law relating to breach of contract in Germany, the remedies in the context of a third party beneficiary and the extent to which a claimant can choose the remedy which he or she deems to be the most appropriate.

International Studies in the Theory of Private Law

This series of books edited by a distinguished international team of legal scholars aims to investigate the normative and theoretical foundations of the law governing relations between citizens. The context for such investigations of private law systems is set by important modern tendencies in systems of governance. The advent of the regulatory state marks the withdrawal of the state from direct control and management of social and economic activity, and the adoption instead of procedural regulation and co-regulatory strategies that promote the use of private law techniques of ordering and self-regulation in social and economic interactions between citizens. The tendency known as globalisation and the corresponding increases in cross-border trade produce the responses of transnational regulation of commerce and private governance regimes, and these new systems of governance challenge the hegemony of traditional national private law systems. Furthermore, these tendencies towards transnational governance regimes compel an interaction between different national legal traditions, with their differences in culture and philosophy as well as their differences based upon variations in market systems, which provokes questions not only about competing policy frameworks but also about the nature and adequacy of different kinds of legal reasoning.

The series encompasses a diverse range of theoretical approaches in the examination of these issues including approaches using socio-legal methods, economics, critical theory, systems theory, regulation theory, and moral and political theory. With the aim of stimulating an international discussion of these issues, volumes will be published in Germany, France, and the United Kingdom in one of the three languages.

Editors

Hugh Collins, *London School of Economics*
Christian Joerges, *European University Institute Florence*
Antoine Lyon-Caen, *Université de Paris X-Nanterre*
Horatia Muir Watt, *Université de Paris I*
Gunther Teubner, *Frankfurt University*
James Q Whitman, *Yale Law School, New Haven, CT*

Volumes published with Hart Publishing, Oxford

1. David Campbell, Hugh Collins und John Wightman (eds), *Implicit Dimensions of Contract: Discrete, Relational and Network Contracts* (2003)
2. Christian Joerges, Inger-Johanne Sand and Gunther Teubner (eds), *Transnational Governance and Constitutionalism* (2004)
3. Oren Perez, *Ecological Sensitivity and Global Legal Pluralism: Rethinking the Trade and Environment Debate* (2004)
4. Harm Schepel, *The Constitution of Private Governance* (2004)

Volumes published in German by Nomos Verlagsgesellschaft, Baden-Baden

1. Peer Zumbansen, *Ordnungsmuster im modern Wohlfahrtsstaat: Lernerfahrungen zwischen Staat, Geseelschaft und Vertrag* (2000)
2. Dan Wielsch, *Freiheit und Funktion: Zur Struktur- und Theoriegeschichte des Rechts der Wirtschaftsgesellschaft* (2001)
3. Marc Amstutz, *Evolutorisches Wirtschaftsrecht: Vorstudien zum Recht und seiner Methode in den Diskurskollisionen der Marktgesellschaft* (2001)
4. Christian Joerges and Gunther Teubner (eds), *Rechtsverfassungsrecht: Recht-Fertigungen zwischen Sozialtheorie und Privatrechtsdogmatik* (2003)
5. Gunther Teubner, Netzwerk als Vertragsverbund: *Virtuelle Unternehmen, Franchising, Just in Time in sozialwissenschaftlicher und juristischer Sicht* (2004)

Volume published with Dalloz, Paris

1. Geoffrey Samuel, *Essai d'épistémologie juridique comparative* (forthcoming)

Comparative Remedies for Breach of Contract

Edited by

NILI COHEN
AND
EWAN McKENDRICK

·HART·
PUBLISHING

OXFORD AND PORTLAND, OREGON
2005

Published in North America (US and Canada) by
Hart Publishing
c/o International Specialized Book Services
5804 NE Hassalo Street
Portland, Oregon
97213-3644
USA

Hart Publishing is a specialist legal publisher based in Oxford, England.
To order further copies of this book or to request a list of other publications please write to:

Hart Publishing, Salters Boatyard, Folly Bridge, Abingdon Rd, Oxford, OX1 4LB Telephone: +44 (0)1865 245533 Fax: +44 (0)1865 794882
email: mail@hartpub.co.uk
WEBSITE: http//:www.hartpub.co.uk

British Library Cataloguing in Publication Data
Data Available

ISBN 1-84113-453-8 (hardback)

Typeset by Olympus Infotech Pvt Ltd, India (Palatino, 10/12 pt)
Printed and bound in Great Britain by
MPG Books Ltd, Bodmin, Cornwall

List of Contributors

MAURO BUSSANI is Professor of Private and Comparative Law, University of Trieste.

DAGMAR COESTER-WALTJEN is Ordinarius Professor of Comparative Law at the Ludwig-Maximilians Universitaet, Munich; and Director of the Institute of International Law/Comparative Law.

NILI COHEN is the Pro-Rector and the Benno Gitter Professor of Comparative Contract Law at Tel-Aviv University.

DANIEL FRIEDMANN is Professor Emeritus, Tel-Aviv University and Professor of Law, The College of Management.

MARK P GERGEN is Professor of Law, University of Texas, Austin.

DAVID GILO is Lecturer, The Buchman Faculty of Law, Tel-Aviv University.

ANDREAS HELDRICH is Professor of Law Emeritus, University of Munich.

ADAM KRAMER is a Pupil Barrister, 3 Verulam Bldgs, London.

ROY KREITNER is a Lecturer in the Faculty of Law, Tel-Aviv University.

YVES-MARIE LAITHIER is Maître de Conférences at the University of Paris I (Panthéon-Sorbonne).

EWAN McKENDRICK is Professor of English Private Law, University of Oxford and a Fellow of Lady Margaret Hall.

BARAK MEDINA is Joseph H and Belle R Braun Senior Lecturer in Law, Faculty of Law, Hebrew University of Jerusalem.

VERNON VALENTINE PALMER is Thomas Pickles Professor of Law and Director of European Legal Studies, Tulane University.

GEBHARD M REHM is Lecturer in Law, University of Munich.

LIONEL SMITH is James McGill Professor of Law at McGill University.

KATHERINE WORTHINGTON is a post-graduate student at the European University Institute, Florence.

Contents

Table of Cases

AUSTRALIA

CANADA

EUROPEAN COURT OF JUSTICE

FRANCE

GERMANY

ISRAEL

NEW ZEALAND

SOUTH AFRICA

UNITED KINGDOM

UNITED STATES OF AMERICA

Table of Legislation

AUSTRIA

CANADA

EUROPEAN UNION

Directives

INTERNATIONAL

FRANCE

GERMANY

ISRAEL

NETHERLANDS

SWEDEN

UNITED KINGDOM

UNITED STATES OF AMERICA

Introduction

NILI COHEN AND EWAN McKENDRICK

The book is the product of a conference entitled 'Comparative Remedies for Breach of Contract' which took place at the Faculty of Law, Tel-Aviv University between 4 and 6 June 2002. Most, but not all of the papers in this book were presented at that conference.

The purpose of the conference and the book is to present a theoretical as well as a descriptive picture of contract remedies. This has been done by reference to various legal systems representing the common law (English, American, Canadian), some continental systems (French, German) and also a mixed system (Israeli). The sphere of inquiry has not, however, been confined strictly to claims which assume the form of a claim for breach of contract. Taking into account the blurred borderlines between contract and torts, we decided to include in the book a comparative work on economic loss, in which consideration is given both to the role of the law of contract and to the law of tort in the recovery of pure economic loss. A legal system which has a conservative law of tort may resort to the law of contract for the purpose of enabling a claimant to recover pure economic loss, and vice versa. Thus there is a need to examine the relationship between the law of contract and the law of torts.

When it is said that the law of contract can best be understood by reference to the remedies it offers, what is often meant is that the law is best examined and evaluated not by reference to its bare, black-letter rules, but rather by reference to their practical application. It is, perhaps, for this reason that the law and economics school has devoted a considerable amount of energy to the study of the law relating to remedies for breach of contract. It can also be important to appreciate that an understanding of the law of contract does not end in the courthouse. Litigation is not the only means of resolving contractual disputes (indeed, in many jurisdictions only a small percentage of contractual disputes end up in court). Today many contracting parties resort to other dispute resolution mechanisms, such as mediation, commercial arbitration and other fori which claim to offer efficiency, creativity and flexibility in the resolution of contractual disputes. Our work does not deal with these trends, nor with their impact on the understanding of contract remedies and contract theory. Rather, it examines the traditional solutions where contract disputes are dealt with by the courts, and it scrutinises the interrelationship between substantive rights and the remedies that are intended to protect these rights.

The book deals with remedies for breach but as a collection which has its origins in a set of conference papers it neither deals with the whole range of remedies (such as price reduction, set-off, or liens and other possessory security rights), nor with every major question within each remedy (restitution is mentioned in some of the chapters but is not examined separately). Further, although the book purports to serve as a comparative study of remedies for breach of contract, its framework is confined to a limited number of systems. In these senses the book does not aim to be comprehensive. But we believe that the limited picture (both in terms of the remedies and the legal systems subject to analysis) may well mirror the basic trends of the modern law of remedies in both continental and common law systems. These trends include: the efficient protection of contract rights; an increased willingness on the part of legal systems to draw from the experiences of other legal systems; a proper balance between the interests of the injured party and the party in breach; increased protection of the performance interest and a recognition of the non-pecuniary interests that may be affected by a breach of contract; the need to ensure compatibility between the various remedies on offer within a legal system; and responsiveness to the basic values of the legal system.

The book is divided into three broad parts, although these parts do not purport to be water-tight. The first part consists of three chapters which, in their different ways, are devoted to an analysis of concepts and to the basic structure and aims of the law of remedies for breach of contract. The second part, which consists of six chapters, consists of a series of comparisons. In some cases the comparison is to be found within the chapters (as in the case of the chapters by Cohen and by Bussani and Palmer). In other cases the comparison can be seen not within the chapters but between the chapters. For example, the chapters by Gergen and Laithier illustrate the contrasting perceptions of the right to terminate a contract to be found in American and French law respectively. Finally, the two chapters on the recent reforms enacted in Germany (by Heldrich and Rehm and by Coester-Waltjen) illustrate a further aspect of comparative law in that here we see the influence which other legal systems and international conventions have had on the development of the domestic law of a nation state. The third part, which consists of four chapters, deals with a number of issues relating to the remedies of specific performance and damages. We shall now introduce the various chapters and outline some of the principal issues which they raise.

The book opens with 'Rights and Remedies' by Daniel Friedmann. The author deals with the basic question underlying any discussion of remedies, namely the interrelationship between rights and remedies.

Friedmann offers four basic models which can help us to answer questions such as: can there be a legal right that is unprotected by a remedy? should the nature of a legal right be reflected in the type of remedy offered for its protection or is it the case that the type of remedy available sheds light on the nature of the right involved? The analysis of the relationship between rights and remedies also has significant implications for the debate over discretionary remedies. In the case where a remedy lies in the discretion of the court, what does this tell us about the nature of the legal right involved and of the relationship between this right and the remedy which the court, in the exercise of its discretion, decides to grant?

The four models which Friedmann identifies are as follows. The first model is the primacy of the remedy model. According to this model, it is the potency of the remedy and its availability which determines the nature of the legal right and, indeed, the very existence of the right. The second model is the primacy of the right model. The basis of this model is the assumption that the legal right precedes the remedy both in time and in importance and that remedies are merely derivative and follow from the legal right. The third model is the 'unity of the right remedy model.' This model casts doubt upon the right-remedy dichotomy and assumes that the remedy constitutes an integral part of the legal right. On this basis the remedy available for protection of the right is simply one of the many attributes of the right itself. The last model is the 'acoustic separation model.' This model was developed in the context of the criminal law and is applied by Friedmann to the law of remedies for breach of contract. According to this model legal rules can be divided into 'conduct rules' (namely rules which are intended to guide private actors) and 'decision rules' (being rules which are binding on the officials who apply the law to the conduct of others).

Friedmann evaluates the relative strengths and weaknesses of the four models and then draws his chapter to a conclusion by giving brief consideration to the role of certainty, predictability and discretion in the law of remedies. He concludes that the commitment of private law to certainty and to the non-retroactive nature of rights and obligations is not as strong as in the case of the criminal law. But it does not follow from this that certainty is not an important value in private law. On the contrary, he concludes that certainty is an important value in private law but that it is 'much less significant in the area of remedies.' The reason for this is that, while a person is entitled to know what are his primary contractual rights and obligations, she has no similar entitlement to know with certainty the consequences that will flow from a breach by her of one of her primary contractual obligations. This being the case, the rules regarding remedies have a degree of 'built-in flexibility' and 'contain many open-ended points that leave much to the court's discretion.' Friedmann maintains that this uncertainty exists even in the case where the legal right is clearly defined. In his view the fact that the right is clearly defined *ex ante* does not have the consequence that the remedy is thereby fixed because the court, when called upon to determine the remedy after the breach, has the benefit of formulating the remedy *ex post* and it may take account of circumstances and policy considerations which were not, perhaps, apparent to the parties at the moment at which they agreed on the content of the primary right. Thus, while the primary right is generally 'fixed and pre-determined,' the remedy that is applicable in the event of a breach of that right is neither fixed nor pre-determined but rather is characterised by flexibility and (a degree of) uncertainty.

In the second chapter, 'Multiplicity in Contract Remedies,' Roy Kreitner argues that the attempt to solve all of the problems of contract remedies by the application of a single, unified principle is misguided and, ultimately, futile. He argues that an adequate understanding of remedies for breach of contract must take into account the multiplicity of interests that should be protected by remedial rules. Yet in recent years there has been a proliferation of theoretical models in the common law world that attempt to give a new foundation to the law of remedies through a single, unified principle. These attempts are reviewed critically in this chapter. The critical claim made by Kreitner is that these models are 'fundamentally flawed' and are 'doomed to failure.' In his view, unification theories

> fail to explain the practice of the courts in granting diverse remedies for breach, and more importantly, they fail to account adequately for justificatory considerations that are and ought to be an inherent part of remedial rules.

Beyond the critique of unification theories, Kreitner suggests that contract scholars ought to look to contract types as a guide to the further theorisation of remedies. He offers an analysis based on contract types and employs contracts of carriage and merger agreements in order to illustrate his point.

He claims that the analysis of contract types offers two distinct advantages over unification theory. First, it provides 'a better tool for analysing and understanding the varying results of cases involving contract breaches and the remedies they entail.' Second, he asserts that contract types offer 'a research agenda that would never divorce itself from the underlying considerations that ought to govern the choice of rules governing contract breach', namely fairness between the parties, social utility and administrative concerns.

In the third chapter, 'Renegotiation, "Efficient Breach" and Adjustment: The Choice of Remedy for Breach of Contract as a Choice of a Contract-Modification Theory,' Barak Medina explores three distinct accounts of the purpose of remedies for breach of contract. The primary significance of the three accounts is said to lie in the distinct view which each gives of the contract's 'completeness.' The first account is labelled the 'traditional' approach and it is based on the notion that the purpose of remedies is to 'preserve' the contractual right by deterring violations of the contractual right and correcting the unjust consequences that flow from a violation of the right. The second account is called the 'economic' approach and it is based on the premise that the rules relating to remedies define the terms on which the parties can exit from the contract which they have concluded. The first two accounts can be distinguished on the ground that they rest on different perceptions of the contract's 'completeness'. The traditional approach is based on the perception that contractual provisions are 'all-inclusive' so that they regulate the rights and duties of the parties in all situations. The 'economic' approach by contrast recognises that the contract is not all-inclusive and provides an escape route from the contract based on the prospect of 'efficient breach.' The third account shares the perception of the 'economic' approach that parties' contract is incomplete but differs in the remedial prescription which it provides. This account is based on remedies as a 'modification mechanism', according to which the parties prefer that their contract is completed by a compelled adjustment of the contract by a third party such as a court. On this view the choice of remedy is based on considerations such as what remedy best fits as an 'adjustment mechanism' and remedies can be perceived as a means of adjusting the contract's express provisions.

This chapter underscores the need to decide what is the purpose of remedy, as a precondition to the choice of the appropriate remedy. This decision is said to be 'a choice of a theory of contract interpretation and modification'. Medina maintains that the debate between the 'traditional' and the 'economic approach' is implicitly based on the formalistic, binary model and it reflects a notion of remedies as extra-contractual. His perception that contracts are not all-inclusive leads him to the conclusion that remedies may serve not only to 'preserve' a given contractual right, but also to fill a gap in the incomplete contract in case of a substantial change in surrounding circumstances. If this is so, then a choice must be made between the concept of remedies as exit rules and of remedies as a modification mechanism.

At this point we move from the general themes of Part One into a series of comparisons to be found in Part Two. This part opens with two chapters that can usefully be read together because of the contrasting perceptions which they present of the right to exit from a contract and of the value of 'protecting' a contract (or a contractual relationship) in the event of breach. In chapter four 'The Law's Response to Exit and Loyalty in Contract Disputes' Mark Gergen examines the rules in American private law that regulate exit and loyalty in contract disputes. 'Exit' refers to the situation which arises when one party to a contract suspends or withholds performance, refuses performance or obtains substitute performance as a result of his dissatisfaction with the other party's performance or demands. 'Loyalty', by contrast, refers to the situation which arises when a party to a contract performs, accepts performance or awaits performance despite his dissatisfaction with the other party's performance or demands. The chapter is divided into two parts. In the first part Gergen examines the rules that determine when a party to a contract has the power or duty to exit in response to a clear default. He contends that the rules regulating exit and loyalty are 'much more concerned with protecting contract rights than they are concerned with promoting efficient breach.' Thus American law permits a party to exit from a contract in order to avoid suffering an uncompensated loss even though this imposes a disproportionate loss on the party in breach. The second part examines the law's response to exit and loyalty when there is a bona fide dispute regarding the adequacy of performance due, tendered, or demanded. He demonstrates that American law permits a party to perform or accept performance in a dispute, and later seek redress in a court, but only if his performance or acceptance of performance was necessary to avoid a loss. In other words, loyalty will not cut off a claim that less was owed or more was due if the performance or acceptance of performance avoids a consequential or joint loss. Thus in this area the interest in finality gives way to the goal of efficient performance.

Chapter five, by Yves-Marie Laithier, is entitled 'Comparative Reflections on the French Law of Remedies for Breach of Contract.' The chapter explores two principal issues. The first is the commitment of French law to the primacy of specific performance as a remedy for breach of contract. Laithier concludes that the rationale for the primacy of specific performance cannot be attributed to a concern for economic efficiency. Nor can it be attributed to the enforceability of the contract, notwithstanding the popularity of this theory in France. As Laithier demonstrates, the fact that the contract is enforceable does not dictate a particular remedial response. In other words, while it is the case that a breach of contract gives rise to *a* remedy, it is not necessarily the case that the remedy has to be specific performance. Yet it is the case that specific performance has a wider sphere of application in French law than it does in English and American law (on which see further the later chapter by Lionel Smith). In particular, the fact that damages are an adequate remedy does not of itself operate to deny to a French court the ability to order specific performance. The second issue examined in this is the commitment of French law to the protection or the preservation of the contract. This theme requires an examination of the law relating to the termination of a contract and, in particular, the role of the court in regulating the procedure necessary to bring about the termination of a contract. While parties to a contract can seek to escape from judicial control in France by inserting a termination clause in their contract, Laithier demonstrates that it is no easy task to exclude the jurisdiction of the courts. The courts are both omnipresent (having been 'sent out through the door' they return 'through the window') and omnipotent. The picture that is painted of French law is of a legal system that has a greater commitment than its English and American counterparts to the preservation of the contractual relationship in the face of a breach by one of the parties to the contract. It is in this respect that a contrast can usefully be drawn between the picture painted by Laithier and that painted by Gergen.

Chapters six and seven deal with aspects of the recent reform of the German Civil Code that took effect on 1 January 2002. In chapter six 'Modernisation of the German Law of Obligations: Harmonisation of Civil Law and Common Law in the Recent Reform of the German Civil Code,' Andreas Heldrich and Gebhard Rehm provide an overview of the reform. They identify the problems in German law which led to the demands for reform and demonstrate that the largely unitary approach to non-performance to be found in the new law is a symptom of the convergence between civil law and common law systems. The unitary approach to non-performance and the adoption of a clear general rule, shorn of the intricacies that plagued German law prior to the reform, that the non-performing party is liable in damages were both influenced by the common law in general and the United Nations Convention on Contracts for the International Sale of Goods in particular. The authors also demonstrate that the convergence between legal systems is not 'complete' and that differences continue to exist between German law and common law systems. While these differences are not as stark as they were in the past, they may still be important. This is particularly so given the prevalence of choice of law clauses in modern commercial contracts. The ability of contracting parties to choose the law that is to govern their contract creates a market between different legal systems. As the authors point out, the effect of the improvements that have been made to German law by the new reforms, which preserve some of the features of German law while bringing the law as a whole closer into line with what may be termed internationally accepted rules of contract law, may be to 'render German law.... a more attractive alternative for choice-of-law clauses in international transactions.'

Aspects of the recent reform of German law are considered in more detail in the next chapter by Dagmar Coester-Waltjen entitled 'The New Approach to Breach of Contract in German Law.' She focuses attention on two remedies for breach of contract (which in German law is termed 'violation of an obligation'), namely termination of the contract and damages. While the primary remedy in cases of non-performance is specific performance, in practice most creditors seek the secondary remedies of termination of the contract and damages. The scope of the right to terminate differs from many other legal systems in that it is not confined to cases of fundamental breach. Yet there do exist limits on the right to terminate, in particular the requirement that the creditor give the debtor an additional period of time for performance. Following termination the parties are freed from their obligations to perform and they are bound to restore any benefit (or its value if specific restitution is impossible) received under the contract. The right to recover damages also emanates from any breach of contract but the rules applicable to the assessment of damages differ slightly according to the following three categories of non-performance: damages for non-performance (or damages instead of performance), where the award of damages substitutes or supplements the performance; simple damages, where damages are awarded in respect of the loss suffered as a result of the violation of the obligation; and damages for expenses incurred in the expectation of performance. Liability in damages is conditioned upon fault. Though German law applies the principle of fault in general and imposes a liability in damages in cases of strict liability only under special circumstances, the difference between the German solution and those legal systems which adhere to the strict liability concept is not so great, because there is a presumption of fault in German law. Damages are limited by the principle of adequate causation (rather than forseeability), and non-pecuniary loss is recoverable in certain categories. The conclusion that is drawn from this study is that the recent reform has simplified the rules regarding remedies for breach and has achieved a fair balance between the interests of the creditor and the debtor. The concluding sentence of this chapter offers the tantalising prospect of future reform of the law of remedies. Given that the current state of German law is not perfect (and the same can be said of the law of all European states), at what level will future reform of the law of remedies take place? Will it take place at the level of the nation state or will it occur at the European level, perhaps via the Principles of European Contract Law or any successor?

Chapter eight deals with Israeli Law and the remedies it offers for breach. In 'Remedies for Breach through the Lens of the Third Party Beneficiary' Nili Cohen discusses the range of remedies for breach of contract in Israeli law through the special lens of the rights of a third party beneficiary. Since this special subject is not dealt with specifically in Israeli legislation some of the solutions are based on the experience of other jurisdictions, namely America, Germany, England and France. In employing remedies for breach a proper balance must be struck between the interests of the creditor, a contractual party but a secondary creditor, and the beneficiary, an outsider to the contract but a principal creditor. From the point of view of the beneficiary, a major concern is to guarantee her non-revocable right against any change to the contract by the contracting parties. From the point of view of the debtor the major concern is to limit his risk of enforced double liability and to guarantee that his rights against the creditor prevail also against the beneficiary. Considerations of vindicating rights, co-operation and risk avoidance play a major role in these cases.

The remedy of enforcement — the primary remedy under Israeli law — is the natural remedy available to the beneficiary. In a conflict between the beneficiary who seeks enforcement and the creditor who seeks termination, preference ought to be given to the beneficiary. When termination — a unilateral, self-help remedy — is exercised by the creditor, he should obtain the approval of the beneficiary, unless the contract cannot be performed or the court would not enforce it. Seemingly the beneficiary cannot terminate the contract, though she is not bound to accept defective performance. The scope of the beneficiary's claim for damages is likely to be limited by the nature of the transaction, for example, if the beneficiary received the benefit as a gift. The creditor could claim damages for his own loss, as long as his claim does not compete with that of the beneficiary's.

Termination of the contract by the creditor results in a mutual duty of restitution. Even though the creditor is not the recipient, the debtor would be entitled to recovery from him. Recovery from the beneficiary might be available only in limited cases. In exceptional circumstances, where the benefit was withheld from the beneficiary due to the fault of the creditor, the beneficiary might claim recovery from the debtor, though the latter has not received a benefit from the beneficiary. This again indicates the supremacy of the beneficiary's right over that of the creditor.

Part Two draws to a close with a chapter entitled 'Between Contract and Tort: Pure Economic Loss in Europe' by Mauro Bussani and Vernon Valentine Palmer. This chapter draws on the authors' extensive comparative project on the recovery of pure economic loss in thirteen European jurisdictions. The methodology used in the project was to formulate a number of hypothetical cases and then send them to experts in the various jurisdictions who would then provide the response that would be given by the courts in their jurisdiction to the facts of the particular hypothetical.

Some of the hypotheticals considered in the present chapter include cases of ricochet loss, transferred loss and reliance upon flawed data, advice or professional services. Drawing on the responses which they received from the national experts, Bussani and Palmer develop different models of the liability regimes that exist in the various European jurisdictions. They identify three regimes. The first is the liberal regime. An important characteristic of the liberal regime is the presence of a 'unitary general clause in the codified law which does not, a priori, screen out of pure economic loss.' Recovery in a liberal regime is generally allowed on the basis of extra-contractual liability rather than liability for breach of contract. The second is the pragmatic regime, in which the courts cautiously and on a case-by-case basis may recognise liability for pure economic loss. The third regime is the conservative regime which generally excludes pure economic loss from the list of interests which are protected by the law of tort. However, as the authors point out, a characteristic of the conservative regimes is that the recovery of pure economic loss 'often receives extensive lateral support from the law of contracts.' It is this 'flight to contract' which is of immediate interest to the present volume because it demonstrates that the courts (at least in Germany) have resorted to the law of contract in order to provide claimants with a remedy which in other systems would be provided via the law of tort. More fundamentally, this chapter demonstrates the importance of looking beyond the external appearance of the legal rules (the 'façade') into what the authors call 'the interior working of the system.' An examination of the rules in operation frequently requires us to break down the boundaries between contracts and torts and to examine the interplay between the two. A legal system may have a liberal tort regime which shuts out the law of contract (as in France) or it may resort to the law of contract in order to supplement a narrow law of tort (as in Germany). These are not exclusive options. A legal system may resort to tort in order to evade restrictive rules in the law of contract (as in England). In any event, this chapter demonstrates the importance of having regard to the law of civil remedies as a whole when seeking to compare and contrast the liability regimes that exist in different regimes.

Part Three deals with aspects of the law relating to specific performance and damages. In chapter ten, 'Understanding Specific Performance' Lionel Smith explores the justification for awarding specific performance, as distinct from an award of compensatory damages for a breach of contract. A promisee's performance interest (frequently called the expectation interest) is usually understood to represent the position the promisee would be in if the contract had been performed according to its terms. Often the assumption is made that specific performance and an award of compensatory damages are merely two alternative ways to protect the promisee's performance interest. However, in certain situations, specific performance may put the promisee in a better position than if the promise had been performed. Similarly, in the case where damages are awarded in lieu of specific performance, it can be seen that the 'specific performance interest' may be different from the 'performance interest' because the value of the two money awards may be quite different. It seems to follow from this that the performance interest and the specific performance interest have different objectives. Smith argues that the objective of specific performance is not simply to enforce a promise, but to prevent a defendant 'from expropriating a plaintiff's patrimonial entitlement to performance.' Further, he maintains that the wider availability of specific performance is consistent with other developments in the law, such as the protection afforded by the law to the plaintiff's right to recover the agreed contract price and the growing recognition of the plaintiff's ability to get disgorgement of the profits which the defendant has made from the breach of contract. On this basis it can be said that the wider availability of specific performance reflects a recognition of the fact that the plaintiff's right to performance is 'a patrimonial entitlement' which ought to be protected in a similar way to the way in which the law protects real rights in tangible things.

Chapter eleven turns to the remedy of damages. In 'The Deterrent Factor of Damages where Pricing is Affected' David Gilo remarks that the literature on the economic analysis of contract remedies focuses on bilateral relationships between promisors and promisees. He contends that the current literature fails to deal with the fact that many promisors are firms selling their products or services in the market place, and, moreover, that expected damages for breach are often partly passed on to the promisor's customers in the form of higher prices. In these cases, he argues that expectation damages may not suffice to make the promisor bear the full harm caused by breach, since some of the damages will ultimately be passed on to or borne by the promisor's customers. This being the case, he suggests that damages ought to be assessed at a level higher than expectation damages in order to make the promisor bear the entire harm caused by the breach and to induce the promisor to take optimal precautions to prevent breach. The difficulty with this model lies in discerning those cases in which part of the damages are expected to be passed on to the promisor's customers, in particular those cases in which the portion of damages passed on to the customers is likely to be particularly significant. Gilo does provide guidelines which could be applied by the courts when seeking to identify such cases (such as the structure of demand for the promisor's product, the effect of the promisor's cost structure and the nature of the competition between the promisor and its competitors) and, while he concedes that these guidelines 'are probably impossible to implement with precision' he nevertheless contends that they can be used by the courts as guides to assist them in the identification of cases in which part of the damages can be expected to be passed on to customers.

Chapter twelve examines the topic of remoteness of damage (which also features in other chapters, most notably by Kreitner and Gilo). Adam Kramer in his chapter entitled 'An Agreement-Centred Approach to Remoteness and Contract Damages' argues that the rules applied by the courts when deciding whether or not a loss is too remote a consequence of a breach of contract should not be seen as default rules which are applicable when the parties have not reached agreement. Rather, he contends that the allocation of responsibility for the consequences of breach is 'one of the matters that is determined by contractual agreement, even when it is not covered by the express terms of those agreements.' The argument bears a resemblance to the implied promise theory that was dominant in the latter half of the nineteenth century but it differs from the latter theory in that it draws on modern developments in the law relating to the interpretation of contracts and the implication of terms into a contract. It is therefore a much more sophisticated account than the 'implied agreement' theories of the past. Kramer argues that the contract regulates not only the primary obligations of the parties (whether express or implied) but that it can and does extend to the allocation of responsibility for the consequences of any breach of the contract. The difficulty of course is that the parties frequently do not make express provision for the consequences of breach (although provision may be made in the form of a liquidated damages clause) and so it is necessary for the courts to resort to implication in order to ascertain the allocation of responsibility that has been agreed by the parties. While the appropriateness of the implication must ultimately depend on the facts and circumstances of the individual case, Kramer nevertheless identifies a range of factors or 'norms' that can be taken into account by the courts when seeking to ascertain the expectations of the parties in relation to the allocation of responsibility for particular losses. The implications of this theory extend beyond the immediate confines of the remoteness cases. Kramer contends not only that his theory can explain the remoteness cases and provide a model with a higher predictive yield than the current rules, but that it can be applied to other issues in the law of contract, such as the recoverability of damages for mental distress and loss of amenity, and the mitigation rule.

The concluding chapter, written by Ewan McKendrick and Katherine Worthington, is entitled 'Damages for Non-Pecuniary Loss.' The authors examine the circumstances in which a claimant can recover damages for non-pecuniary loss suffered as a consequence of a breach of contract. They argue, drawing on English case law, that a distinction ought to be drawn between two categories of case. The first category consists of cases which they describe as 'positive' loss claims in which the claimant seeks to recover damages in respect of the loss of a non-pecuniary benefit to which the claimant was entitled under the contract (either because the defendant promised to confer a non-pecuniary benefit on the claimant or because the claimant attached a particular 'added value' to performance, that is to say, a value which exceeds the market value of performance). The second group consists of cases in which the breach of contract entails some form of non-pecuniary loss. Thus a party may seek to recover damages in respect of physical injury, psychiatric illness, loss of reputation, inconvenience, distress or loss of enjoyment or peace of mind suffered as a consequence of a breach of contract. Rather than attempt to articulate an over-arching general principle which can be applied to all cases, the authors have sought to identify the differences between the cases and to highlight the various factors which should be taken into account by the courts when deciding cases.

The most important part of the analysis is the recognition of the 'positive' loss category of cases. Modern cases suggest that there is growing acceptance of the fact that claimants, such as consumers and employees, do not enter into contracts simply in order to enhance their financial position. This being the case, the law of damages ought to reflect the claimant's non-pecuniary interest in the performance of the contract and not confine the claimant to the recovery of damages in respect of the financial losses which have been suffered as a result of the breach.

Finally, we would like to record our thanks to various people who have helped us in the completion of this project. Oren Bigos provided invaluable research assistance. Einat Arar was very helpful in her research assistance. We would also like to thank our publishers for their help and encouragement. The conference which generated the work was sponsored by the Benno Gitter Chair of Comparative Contract Law. We would like to express our deep gratitude to the late Benno Gitter, formerly honorary chairman of the Board of Governors of Tel-Aviv University, for his generous support.

Part One

Concepts, Coherence and Choice

1

Rights and Remedies

DANIEL FRIEDMANN*

I INTRODUCTION

THE RELATIONS OF rights and remedies are subtle and complex and raise a number of issues. These include the questions: Can there be a legal right that is unprotected by a remedy?[1] Is the nature of the legal right reflected in the type of remedy offered for its protection, or is it vice versa, namely is it the type of remedy available that sheds light upon the nature of the right involved? Another important issue, that received relatively little attention, relates to the role of discretionary remedies. Courts usually enjoy a broad discretion with regard to the type of remedy to be granted. This means that similar or even identical rights may, in certain circumstances, be accorded one type of remedy for their protection, while in other, sometimes quite similar circumstances, a different type of remedy would be offered. How does this discretion, or rather inconsistency, in the field of remedies affect our understanding of the nature of the legal right involved and the right-remedy relations?

There are four models that can explain the rights-remedies relations:

1) The primacy of the remedy model
2) The primacy of the right model
3) The unity of the right-remedy model
4) The 'acoustic separation' model.

II THE PRIMACY OF THE REMEDY MODEL

Under this model it is the potency of remedy and its availability which determines the nature of the legal right and, indeed, its very existence.

* Professor Emeritus, Tel-Aviv University, and Professor of Law, The College of Management, Tel-Aviv.

[1] Peter Birks, in his article 'Rights, Wrongs and Remedies' (2000) 20 *Oxford Journal of Legal Studies* 1, pointed out that the term 'remedy' has a number of meanings. In this chapter the

The right derives from the remedy and as a matter of sequence the remedy precedes the right. Consequently the absence of a remedy points to the non-existence of a legal right. This model is in line with the traditional approach of the common law under which 'where there is a remedy there is a right' (*ubi remedium ibi ius*), and the granting of a remedy via an action in court remains to date a major vehicle for the development of new legal entitlements and the expansion of established legal rights.[2]

This model, in its extreme form, was adopted by Holmes in whose view '[t]he primary rights and duties with which jurisprudence busies itself ... are nothing but prophesies.' A legal right (and a legal duty) 'is nothing but a prediction that if a man does or omits certain things he will be made to suffer in this or that way by judgment ot the court'.[3] This view was followed by the 'bad man' approach to the law. The 'bad man' does not worry about rights. He is concerned only with legal consequences, namely sanctions and remedies. Hence the absence of a remedy means freedom of action. In fact, freedom of action is maintained even if a remedy is available but that remedy falls short of actually preventing the specific course of action. In this type of situation it is open to the obligated party to weigh the advantages of breaching the other party's right against the 'cost' of the remedy and to decide accordingly. The famous example is that of breach of contract, which Holmes assumes entails mere liability in damages. The denial of specific enforcement leads him to the conclusion that a party to a contract may (or perhaps we should say: is entitled) to breach the contract subject to his liability to pay damages.[4]

The difficulty with this approach lies in its assumption that the remedy provides a perfect substitute[5] for the right. It is a kind of indulgence that

term 'remedy' refers to an order of the court in the plaintiff's favour on the ground that his initial entitlement has been infringed, appropriated, withheld or taken advantage of in a manner disallowed by the law.

[2] Thus the case of *Lumley v Gye* (1853) El & Bl 216, 118 ER 749 that established the modern tort of interference with contractual relations has in fact expanded the ambit of the contractual right by granting the parties to the contract a legally protected entitlement vis à vis third parties. The recent decision in *Att-Gen v Blake* [2001] 1 AC 268 (HL) that recognised the right to recover gains derived from a breach of contract has also expanded the contractual right, this time vis à vis the other party to the contract. The case of *White v Jones* [1995] 2 AC 207 (HL) provides an example of a court creating a legally protected interest via a tort action. In this case it was held by a 3–2 majority that a solicitor who was instructed to prepare a will but failed to do so within a reasonable time could be liable in negligence to the intended beneficiary. Consequently, the expectancy of the intended beneficiary was turned into a legally protected interest. Obviously this protection is fairly narrow. On the correlativity of rights and duties see generally EJ Weinrib, *The Idea of Private Law* (Harvard University Press, Cambridge, Massachusetts, 1995).

[3] OW Holmes 'The Path of the Law' 10 *Harvard Law Review* 457, 458 (1897), reprinted in *Collected Legal Papers* (Harcourt, Brace & Co, New York, 1920) 167, 168–9.

[4] OW Holmes, above n 3, at 462 (in *Collected Legal Papers* at 175); OW Holmes *The Common Law* (Little Brown, Boston, 1881) 300–1. For a criticism see D Friedmann 'The Efficient Breach Fallacy' (1989) 18 *Journal Legal Studies* 1. See also L Smith, chapter 10 below.

[5] Clearly in instances in which the legal right is specifically enforced the judgment reflects the entitlement in its initial form and does not constitute a remedial substitute.

the wrongdoer is entitled to purchase. The fact that the remedy is designed to vindicate the right, not to replace it, is disregarded.[6] Similarly disregarded is the distinction between price on the one hand and remedies and sanctions on the other.[7] A sign that provides: 'Parking Prohibited, Penalty $10' is viewed as identical to a sign: 'Parking Allowed. Price $10'.

No doubt, there are rare situations in which a party is unilaterally entitled to 'encroach and pay' or in other words to 'purchase' the right to infringe upon another's entitlement. The decision in *Vincent v Lake Erie Transportation Co* provides a conspicuous example.[8] In that case the defendant's ship unloaded cargo at the plaintiff's dock. When unloading was complete a violent storm developed and it became highly dangerous for the vessel to leave the dock. The master decided to leave the vessel moored and the wind and waves threw it against the dock. The court recognised the defence of necessity, but held the defendant liable for the damage caused to the dock on the ground that 'where the defendant prudently… avails itself of the plaintiffs' property for the purpose of preserving his own more valuable property …the plaintiffs are entitled to compensation for the injury done'.[9]

This decision provided the cornerstone for the incomplete privilege theory developed by Bohlen, under which

> an act may be so far privileged as to deprive the person whose interest is invaded … of the privilege …to terminate or prevent the invasion … but not so far as to relieve [the actor] from liability to pay for any material damage he does thereby.[10]

This approach has been adopted by the Restatement (Second) of Torts[11] and the Restatement of Restitution.[12] The question whether liability in this type of situation is in torts or in restitution has long been debated,[13] but need not concern us here. For our purposes it suffices to point out the distinction between impermissible trespass or encroachment of another's protected interest on the one hand and the use or appropriation of another's entitlement within the ambit of the incomplete privilege doctrine on

[6] Friedmann, above n 4.
[7] Cf R Cooter 'Prices and Sanctions' (1984) 84 *Columbia Law Review* 1523.
[8] 109 Minn 456; 124 NW 221 (1910).
[9] *Ibid*, 460; 222.
[10] C Bohlen 'Incomplete Privilege to Inflict Intentional Invasions of Interests of Property and Personality' (1926) 39 *Harvard Law Review* 307, 313.
[11] § 197.
[12] § 122.
[13] For the view that liability is in restitution see R Keeton 'Conditional Fault in the Law of Torts' *Harvard Law Review* (1959) 401, 72; D Friedmann 'Restitution of Benefits Obtained through the Appropriation of Property or the Commission of a Wrong' (1980) 80 *Columbia Law Review* 504, 542–3; E J Weinrib, above note 2, 196–203. For the view that liability is in tort see G Palmer *The Law of Restitution* (Little Brown, Boston, 1978) vol 1, 139–40.

the other hand. This distinction has some practical implications. Thus, in the case of impermissible trespass the owner may use self-help to resist or expel the intruder. But where the intruder's act is permissible under the incomplete privilege doctrine, the owner is required to tolerate the intrusion. In such a case an attempt by the owner to expel or resist the intruder is wrongful and constitutes a tort vis-à-vis the intruder.[14] Such practical implications may seem marginal,[15] but the basic distinction between a wrong and a permissible act remains important. In the one case the actor committed a transgression. His act was legally as well as morally wrong, and the function of the remedy is not only to compensate the victim but also to deter such conduct. In the other case the remedy is more like a price. It is a payment which the actor is required to make for having lawfully appropriated or damaged that which belongs to another.[16]

The famous article by Fuller and Perdue 'The Reliance Interest in Contract Damages'[17] appeared some 50 years after the publication of Holmes' theory. It shares Holmes' fascination with remedies, places the emphasis upon the remedy of damages and almost completely disregards the possibility of specific performance. Holmes' theory as well as Fuller and Perdue's article represent the centrality of the remedy approach and reflect an attempt to view the contractual right through the looking glass of the damages awarded for its breach.[18]

The well-known article by Calabresi and Melamed 'Property Rules, Liability Rules and Inalienability: One View from the Cathedral'[19] deviates in one aspect from the strict dominance of the remedy model. It assumes that decisions as to entitlements, namely allocation of legal rights, must precede the determination as to their protection via the law of remedies. But in other respects it follows Holmes' approach and emphasises the centrality of the remedy to the understanding of the

[14] *Prosser and Keeton on Torts*, 5th edn (West Publishing Co, St Paul, Minnesota, 1984) 147.

[15] There may be some other practical implications. Thus, where the act was privileged and no damage was caused, nominal damages will presumably not be awarded. In addition, where the act was wrongful, damages may be awarded on a more liberal scale, and the award of punitive damages in some cases is also conceivable.

[16] The availability of a remedy against a defendant who committed no wrong has recently become the focus of an extensive literature in the field of restitution; the core case being that of payment made under a mistake in which the recipient was completely innocent. See eg Birks, above n 1; K Barker 'Rescuing Remedialism in Unjust Enrichment Law: Why Remedies are Right' [1998] *Cambrige Law Journal* 301; S A Smith 'The Structure of Unjust Enrichment Law: Is Restitution a Right or a Remedy?' (2003) 36 *Loyola Law Review* 1037.

[17] (1936) 46 *Yale Law Journal* 52, 373.

[18] For a similar approach see PS Atiyah 'Holmes and the Theory of Contract' in PS Atiyah *Essays on Contract* (Clarendon Press, Oxford, 1986) 57, 61 stating that: 'it is impossible sensibly to discuss *how* binding a contract is until one knows what form of damages are likely to be awarded for its breach'. For a different approach see D Friedmann 'The Performance Interest in Contract Damages' (1995) 111 *Law Quarterly Review* 628; D Kimel 'Remedial Rights and Substantive Rights in Contract Law' (2002) 8 *Legal Theory* 313.

[19] (1972) 85 *Harvard Law Review* 1089.

nature of the legal right and its implication for the actor's freedom of action. Calabresi and Melamed assume that an entitlement can be protected either by a property rule or a liability rule (in addition it might be inalienable). When an entitlement is protected by a liability rule it means that 'someone (a 'bad man'?) may destroy the initial entitlement if he is willing to pay an objectively determined value for it'. A number of examples are offered to demonstrate the application of a liability rule. These include eminent domain and cases of nuisance for which no injunction is granted so that the plaintiff's remedy is limited to damages. Also included in this category are accidents on the ground that potential victims have no right to stop the activity that might injure them.

> If we were to give victims a property entitlement not to be accidentally injured we would have to require all who engage in activities that may injure individuals to negotiate with them before the accident, and to buy the right to knock off an arm or a leg.[20]

It is thus conspicuous that no distinction is drawn between permissible conduct and wrongful misconduct, and there is similar failure to distinguish between the price of acquisition and damages imposed for the consequences of a wrong. Eminent domain, accidents and some nuisances are all included in the same category of 'liability rules'. In the case of eminent domain, which is a permissible appropriation of property against payment, the payment to the owner is simply the price, which the public authority is required to pay for the lawful (albeit forced) taking. In the case of accidents and nuisance the payment, which the wrongdoer is liable to make, constitutes damages for the wrong. However, the tacit assumption, in line with Holmes' approach, is that this distinction makes no difference. Since mere monetary payment is involved in all these situations, they can all be included in the same category of liability rules, within which a person is allowed to appropriate or damage another's protected interest subject to the payment of money, and the question whether such payment is to be regarded as damages or price is of no moment.

At this stage I would also point out that Calabresi and Melamed disregard certain situations which do not fit neatly in their division of the subject, eg the case in which an employee, in breach of his contract, seeks to work for another employer. The former employer may sometimes get an injunction but not specific performance.[21] More problematic is the very common situation in which the court has a discretion with regard to the remedy. It may grant specific performance or an injunction, but it may deny these remedies and hold that the award of damages is the only

[20] *Ibid*, at 1108.
[21] Cf *Lumley v Wagner* (1852) 1 De Gm & G 604, 42 ER 687.

appropriate remedy. How is the plaintiff's interest to be classified beforehand or is it capable of being classified only after the court rendered its decision? The significance of discretion for the proper understanding of the rights — remedies connection is further examined below.[22]

III THE PRIMACY OF THE RIGHT MODEL

This model seems to follow naturally from any attempt systematically to organise the law. It is typical of the continental legal systems and is likely to be adopted in any systematic codification. Every comprehensive legislation in the field of private law is likely to begin by defining legal rights and duties. This approach which is often termed 'from rights to remedies' or 'where there is a right there must be remedy' assumes that the legal right precedes the remedy both in time and in importance. Remedies are merely derivative and follow from the legal rights. Under such an approach legal rights have an independent existence and it is possible to conceive of legal rights unsupported by legal remedies.

As a matter of interpretation a question sometimes arises: what is the position where the law defines a right without referring to the remedy to be granted in case of its breach? Is it to be assumed that a remedy must be available on the ground that 'where there is a right there must be a remedy',[23] and if so what kind of remedy, or should it be assumed that the whole array of remedies recognised by the legal system is to be applied? The following examples illustrate the issue:

1) Section 9 of the Israeli *Land Law 1969* deals with 'conflicting transactions'. It provides in essence that where a person undertakes to effect a transaction in land and, before this transaction is completed, he undertakes towards another person to effect a conflicting transaction 'the party to the first transaction shall prevail'. This rule does not apply if the party to the second transaction 'has acted in good faith and for consideration' and title was transferred to him 'while he is still in good faith'.

   The section thus provides an order of priority between conflicting transactions. It reflects an idea similar to the Anglo-American concept of 'equitable ownership', under which the purchaser's contractual right is stronger than a mere personal right and comes close to a real (property) right.[24] But the section says little about the remedial implications in case

[22] Text after n 54 below.

[23] This was the position adopted in the great case of *Ashby v White* 2 Raym. Ld. 938, 92 ER 126, in which the plaintiff was awarded damages for having been maliciously deprived of his right to vote, and Holt CJ stated that 'it is a vain thing to imagine a right without a remedy'. The decision is commonly regarded as illustrating the principle that the existence of a right calls for a remedy to protect it. See H Broom, *A Selection of Legal Maxims*, 10th edn (1939 by RH Kersley) 118.

[24] The purchaser as the equitable owner is entitled to specific performance. However, the precise nature of the relationship between equitable ownership and the right to specific

of a breach, except that 'the party to the first transaction shall prevail'. This obviously means that if claims for specific performance are brought against the seller both by the party to the first and the party to the second transaction, the claim of the former will be allowed while the claim of the latter will be denied (but the party to the second transaction will presumably be entitled to damages for breach of contract). It is also clear that the party to the first transaction can direct his claim for specific performance not only against the seller but also against the party to the second transaction, if the latter acquired title without consideration or without being in good faith. But what about other potential remedies? Can the party to the first transaction claim damages from the party to the second transaction, if the latter acquired title without consideration or without being in good faith, on the ground that such acquisition of title infringes the right of the party to the first transaction? And if the party to the second transaction sold the property, can the party to the first transaction claim the proceeds of the sale in restitution? The answer to these questions depends on our understanding of the nature of the right of the party to the first transaction and our assumption regarding the type of remedies available for its protection.[25]

2) A somewhat similar issue arises with regard to remedies for breach of contract. All modern legal systems offer a set of remedies for breach of contract, notably specific performance, damages and termination. A question does however arise whether the traditional remedies are exhaustive or is the injured party also entitled to restitution of the profits gained by the other party as a result of the breach? A detailed discussion of this issue will not be attempted here.[26] For our purposes it suffices to point out the approach under which the issue is to be determined in accordance with our understanding of the nature of the contractual right and the type of entitlement that it confers upon the parties to the agreement. If the contractual right is conceived as a kind of property,[27] a right that confers upon its owner an entitlement to the other party's performance,[28] then it may be concluded that the innocent party can recover the profits gained by the other party in consequence of the breach. It should however be noted that there is a great diversity among contractual rights. They differ in their content, ambit and the nature of the entitlement that they confer. It is thus clearly conceivable that some remedies, such as enforcement or

performance is somewhat obscure. The right to specific performance is sometimes predicated on the plaintiff's equitable ownership. Conversely, the plaintiff may be considered equitable owner because he is entitled to specific performance. Cf HF Stone 'Equitable Conversion by Contract' 13 *Columbia Law Review* 369, 386 (1913).

[25] These issues are discussed in N Grabelsky-Cohen 'The Nature of an Undertaking to Effect a Transaction' (1978) 4 *Tel-Aviv University Studies in Law* 33.

[26] See generally R Goff and G Jones *The Law of Restitution*, 6th edn (Sweet & Maxwell, London, 2002) 515–27, and more recently A Kull 'Disgorgement for Breach, the "Restitution Interest" and the Restatement of Contracts' (2001) 79 *Texas Law Review* 2021; J McCamus 'Disgorgement for Breach of Contract: A Comparative Perspective' (2003) 36 *Loyola of Los Angeles Law Review* 943. See also *Att-Gen v Blake*, above note 2.

[27] Friedmann, above n 13.

[28] Friedmann, above n 18.

> restitution of gains will be available for certain contractual rights but not for others.

Another issue relates to classification. It is clear that the different remedies are available to protect different rights. In fact the twofold division of property rules versus liability rules, reflects an oversimplification, since there is a whole gamut of possibilities, and the question arises to what extent does the type of remedy available or the limits upon its application affect the classification of legal rights and our understanding of their nature. This point is discussed in the following section.

IV THE UNITY OF THE RIGHT-REMEDY MODEL

This model casts doubt upon the right-remedy dichotomy and assumes that the remedy constitutes an integral part of the legal right. Each right or category of rights has a number of attributes. The remedy available for its protection, its potency or weakness or even the lack of any effective remedy is simply one of the many attributes of the legal right.

This model does not necessarily mean that a legal right does not have a 'life of its own', namely that a right cannot exist unless some remedy is available in case of its breach. Rather it assumes that the remedy or lack of it is simply one of the attributes of the legal right. Under this approach rights can be classified in accordance with their strength, ie according to the remedies available for their protection. The weakest right is the one for which no legal remedy is available in case of its breach. Section 32(a) of the Israeli *Contracts (General Part) Law 1973* offers an example of this type of legal right. It provides that 'A gambling, lottery or betting contract ... does not provide ground for enforcement or damages'.[29] The *Contracts Law* thus envisages a type of contract that is valid and binding and confers legal rights and yet no legal remedy is available to protect it. In this respect it is a very weak right. Yet, there is no denying that at least in the eyes of the legislator it is a valid and legally binding right.[30] In this respect it is similar to a legal right that cannot be enforced by virtue of a statute of limitation.[31]

Enforceable rights are in this respect 'stronger' than non-enforceable rights. But the enforceable rights category can be sub-divided according to the effectiveness of the remedies accorded to their protection. Thus,

[29] This limitation does not apply to gambling, lottery or betting contracts regulated by Law or for which a permit has been issued under any Law (section 32(b) of the *Contracts Law*).

[30] The nature of this legal right and its implications are discussed in D Friedmann and N Cohen *Contracts* (Aviram Publications, Tel-Aviv, 1991) vol 1 343–53 (Hebrew).

[31] It is assumed that under the statute the right does not expire, so that it remains valid but unenforceable.

certain contractual rights, notably those relating to the performance of personal work or personal service are not specifically enforceable, although damages are awarded for their breach.[32] The right to the personal work of another is thus 'stronger' than the right acquired by a gambling contract, but 'weaker' than the right acquired under a contract for the purchase of land for which specific performance is usually available.

This does not exhaust the possibilities of ranking of different legal rights. There is a great array of remedies and sanctions. Some are available in case of breach of certain rights at least with regard to certain breaches. Thus, punitive damages may be available in torts but are not usually granted in cases of breach of contract.[33] Does this indicate that where punitive damages are available the infringed right is 'stronger' than the right the breach of which entails merely compensatory damages? The difficulty lies in the fact that punitive damages are the exception and their award depends more on the reprehensibility of the defendant's conduct than on the nature of the plaintiff's right. But this seems to indicate a kind of separation of right and remedy and is hardly in line with the unity right-remedy model.

Finally, there arises the difficult issue of discretionary remedies, which play a highly important role in private law. In the case of a breach of a legal right the court has often a discretion either to specifically enforce the right or to award damages.[34] How is the right to be described when the remedy for its protection is not known in advance, and only *ex post facto* we can tell if it was protected by a property rule or a liability rule?[35]

The picture is further complicated by virtue of the fact that in certain situations it is the defendant who is entitled to choose the remedy. Thus, where the defendant misappropriated the plaintiff's chattel, the plaintiff could either sue in conversion, in which case he would recover the value of the chattel in monetary terms, or sue in detinue in which case it was the defendant who had a choice either to return the chattel or pay its value.[36] Moreover, even where the plaintiff elects to claim damages, his right of

[32] In Israel this is expressly provided by section 3(2) of the *Contracts (Remedies for Breach of Contract) Law 1970.*

[33] Exceptionally, courts in the United States awarded punitive damages, notably in insurance cases, for what was termed 'bad faith breach' of contract. See *Farnsworth on Contracts* 2nd edn (Aspen Law & Business New York, 1998) 788–91; JD Calamari and JM Perillo *The Law of Contracts* 4th edn (West Publishing Co, St Paul, Minnesota, 1998) 542–3.

[34] At the initial stage it is usually the plaintiff who has the choice either to demand specific performance (or injunction) or to claim damages. But while he is generally entitled to damages as a matter of right, if he chooses to demand specific performance, his claim is subjected to the court's discretion.

[35] See the terms used by Calabresi and Melamed, above n 19, and the discussion in the text after n 54 below.

[36] This was the position of the common law under which the plaintiff had actually no right to specific restitution. To prevent this possibility the plaintiff might resort to Chancery to seek a discretionary order of redelivery, but this was not always available. See JG Fleming *The Law of Torts* 9th edn (Law Book Co, Sydney, 1998) 81.

recovery is not absolute since the courts assumed a discretionary power to allow the defendant in certain circumstances to restore the chattel in lieu of damages.[37]

Hence, the nature of the legal right has some effect upon the choice of remedy, but this effect is not necessarily decisive. A great variety of other circumstances are taken into account, which indicates that the remedy, though it is in some respects closely linked to the right, is in other respects quite independent of it. This leads us to the model examined in the following section.

V THE 'ACOUSTIC SEPARATION' MODEL

The 'acoustic separation' theory was developed, in the context of criminal law, by Dan-Cohen in his article 'Decision Rules and Conduct Rules: On Acoustic Separation in Criminal Law'.[38] Dan-Cohen points out that legal rules can be divided into 'conduct rules', that are intended to guide private actors, and 'decision rules' that are binding on officials who apply the law to the conduct of others. It is customary to think that directions for conduct and directions for decisions in response to such conduct must be in complete congruity, and it has even been argued that decision rules imply or embody the corresponding conduct rules. Thus, a rule directed to the judge requiring him to 'cause to be hanged whoever … is convicted of stealing' intimates to men in general that they must not steal.[39] The opposite view focuses on conduct rules (in the above example, 'let no man steal') and concludes that the role of the courts and other officials is merely to apply or enforce the conduct rule. Common to the two approaches is the view under which there is but one set of rules. In this respect both assume the existence of a unitary system. Dan-Cohen considers that both views cannot be accepted and that their underlying unitary assumption is untenable. He advocates the separatist view under which conduct rules and decision rules constitute different categories and thus draws attention to 'the potential independence of these two sets of rules'.[40] Hence

> the distinction between conduct rules and decision rules cannot … be abolished without loss. We therefore need an account of the two kinds of rules that preserve the distinction between them and that depicts their interrelationship … .[41]

[37] Fleming, above n 36, 80.
[38] (1984) 97 *Harvard Law Review* 625, reprinted in M Dan-Cohen *Harmful Thoughts: Essays on Law, Self, and Morality* (Princeton University Press, New Jersey, 2002) 37.
[39] *Ibid*, 626. This example is taken from J Bentham *A Fragment on Government and An Introduction to the Principles of Morals and Legislation* (Blackwell, Oxford, 1948) 430.
[40] Dan-Cohen, above n 38, 629.
[41] *Ibid*, 629–30.

Complete harmony between a conduct rule and a decision rule can sometimes be maintained, but in other instances they may well diverge. The discrepancy between the two categories is likely to result from a conflict of values, which may require a broadly defined conduct rule while the decision rule needs to be more narrowly structured. In other words, the policy considerations underlying conduct rules are not necessarily identical to those underlying decision rules. Consequently, a conduct rule can prohibit a certain act, yet the decision rule may direct the official to condone it in certain circumstances. The acoustic separation model developed by Dan-Cohen envisages a situation in which the law contains two sets of messages. One is directed at the general public and provides guidelines for conduct, while the other set of messages is directed at the officials and provides guidelines for their decisions.[42] This model assumes that the private actors know the conduct rules but are unaware of the decision rules (hence the acoustic separation) which will be applied by the authorities if the conduct rule is breached. An attempt is thus made to convince the private actors to abide by the conduct rule and keep them ignorant of the decision rule that might lead the official to overlook the breach of the conduct rule. A possible example is that of duress, regarding which some maintain that the law ought to require the individual subjected to the pressure to make the socially correct choice. Others emphasise 'the unfairness of punishing a person for succumbing to pressures to which even his judges might have yielded'.[43] The acoustic separation model offers a possible way to cope with this conflict between the values of deterrence and fairness by including the defence of duress among the decision rules but excluding it from the conduct rules. Since members of the public will not be aware of the duress defence, their conduct will be guided by the criminal proscription. But since the duress defence is included in the decision rules, the person who acted under duress will not be punished.[44]

The theory as developed by Dan-Cohen concentrates on criminal law but it is of general application.[45] The idea that 'decision rules', namely rules guiding the officials who apply the law, embody the conduct rules, corresponds to the common law traditional 'from remedy to right' approach in private law.[46] The opposite view under which decision rules must follow the conduct rules so that the two set of rules will maintain complete congruity, corresponds to the centrality of the right approach under which the remedy follows the right.[47]

[42] *Ibid*, 630.
[43] *Ibid*, 633.
[44] *Ibid*, 633.
[45] Indeed Emily Sherwin, in her article 'Law and Equity in Contract Enforcement' (1991) 50 *Maryland Law Review* 253, 300–14, applied it to contract remedies.
[46] Text preceding n 4 above. There are however some differences between private law remedies and decision rules. These are examined in the text after n 47 below.
[47] Text following n 22 above.

The idea that policy considerations regarding punishment (decision rules) may differ from the considerations that underlie the definition of the crime is also applicable to private law. It means in essence that the policy considerations relating to the appropriate remedy are not necessarily identical with the considerations supporting the right, which the remedy is meant to protect. It is therefore not surprising that rights and remedies do on occasion diverge. The reason is obvious. The rules defining rights and obligations (sometimes described as 'primary' duties and obligations) provide general conduct guidelines that apply in ordinary everyday situations. The remedies deal with situations that arise after a primary duty has been breached or in which a benefit or an entitlement has been transferred or acquired in circumstances that give rise to a duty to restore it.[48] These situations are exceptional in the sense that they are not expected to occur, since the public is expected to observe the primary duties and obligations. Hence, while primary duties and obligations are concerned with everyday conduct, remedies deal with 'accidents' that occur when the everyday rules are not followed or when because of a mishap a transfer or acquisition is reversible.

A major difference between remedies in private law and criminal penalties is that criminal penalties are invariably imposed by courts or other public officials (hence their description as decision rules). But private law remedies provide rules directed at the private parties ordering them how to deal with the situation that occurred after the primary breach or after a reversible transfer or acquisition has been made. Only if they do not reach agreement is the court likely to intervene at the behest of one of the parties involved. Hence, while in criminal law there are two stages: definition of the offence (conduct rule) followed in case of breach by court imposed penalty (application of a decision rule), we have in private law three stages. First, there are the primary rights and duties (primary conduct rules). Second there are rules directed at the parties regarding the way they should deal with the event (these are usually secondary conduct rules[49]). The third stage is reached only if the second stage is not successfully concluded by the parties and the court is called upon to resolve the issue. It is only at this stage that decision rules are applied.[50]

Despite this difference between criminal law and private law, a basic similarity between remedies and penalties remain, namely that conduct

[48] See above n 16 and accompanying text.
[49] However where the defendant was completely innocent (above n 16 and accompanying text) the requirement that he restores the benefit received constitutes a primary conduct rule.
[50] Arguably, in jurisdictions in which plea-bargaining is commonly used to resolve criminal cases, the process can be compared to the second stage described above with regard to private law. The difference is that that in criminal law a court decision is generally required in order to sanction the bargain, and the court has at least in theory a measure of control over the bargain. In private law if the parties reach an agreement, there is no need to resort to the court, unless of course the agreement is not honoured.

rules (in private law: primary conduct rules) are meant to regulate normal everyday behaviour and to prevent an occurrence that will lead to the imposition of a penalty or will justify the grant of a remedy. Penalties and remedies are meant to deal with the situation after an undesired event has nevertheless occurred. In other words, primary conduct rules view the situation *ex ante*. Penalties and remedies view the situation *ex post*, and the view *ex post* is not necessarily identical to the view *ex ante*. Hence the differences in the policy considerations that apply to the two categories. *Ex ante* considerations focus on the best way to ensure that the primary conduct rule be observed, that rights are not infringed and that obligations are kept. Remedies and secondary conduct rules must deal with the situations that arise after a breach has occurred and damage has been sustained or a reversible transfer has been made. They face a situation of *fait accompli* and must therefore consider the practical way of correcting the wrong or otherwise restoring the balance between the parties. Hence rules relating to the plaintiff's duty[51] to mitigate the loss and in the case of restitution, rules relating to change of position.

Obviously, the rules on remedies and secondary conduct rules may affect the actors bound by the primary conduct rules. A person facing the possibility of breach of a primary duty may well consider the consequences. Indeed this is the cornerstone of Holmes' theory.[52] The issues involved are complex and give rise to a number of questions including the one relating to the pre-existing knowledge of the remedial consequences of the breach.[53] If it is assumed that such knowledge is lacking or deficient then we do indeed face a situation of partial acoustic separation.[54] A related question is concerned with the certainty and predictability of the remedy. It will be examined in the following section.

VI CERTAINTY, PREDICTABILITY AND DISCRETION IN THE LAW OF REMEDIES

It is a basic tenet of criminal law that the definition of every offence be made known beforehand (the non-retroactivity principle)[55] and that the

[51] The term 'duty' is a misnomer. See J Beatson (ed) *Anson's Law of Contract* 28th edn (OUP, Oxford, 2002) 615–16.

[52] Above n 4 and accompanying text.

[53] Another question which will not be explored here is: to what extent does the very existence of a legal duty, irrespective of whether a remedy is available for its breach (or its effectiveness), influence the conduct of the parties?

[54] Emily Sherwin concluded that the lack of adequate lay understanding of the complexity of contract remedies create a condition of partial acoustic separation in the area of contract law. See above n 45, 306–8.

[55] This is reflected in the well-known maxim *nullum crimen sine lege*. For a discussion see A Ashworth *Principles of Criminal Law* 4th edn (OUP, Oxford, 2003) 69–74.

offence must be clearly and strictly defined so as to create maximum certainty.[56] There is no similar commitment regarding the sanction. The court usually has a broad discretion regarding the punishment to be imposed.[57] The offender is entitled to know beforehand if the act he is about to commit constitutes an offence. But he has no vested right regarding the precise measure of punishment. All he is entitled to know is the maximum penalty (and sometimes also the minimum penalty) prescribed by the law for the offence. But this provides little guidance as to the actual punishment that will be imposed. Civil law is not committed in the same degree as criminal law to certainty and to the non-retroactivity of rights and obligations. Court decisions constantly lead to the creation of new rights and the imposition of new duties, usually with retroactive effect. Nevertheless, I would maintain the following propositions. First, certainty is an important value of private law, notably in the areas of contract and property, though less so in the areas of torts and restitution. Second, certainty is much less significant in the area of remedies. A person is entitled to know what are his property rights and his primary contractual rights and obligations. He has no similar entitlement to certainty with regard to the remedy in case of an infringement or breach. In this respect there is some similarity between criminal law and private law. Both have a strong commitment to certainty and non-retroactivity in the definition of primary conduct rules and a much weaker commitment to certainty in matters relating to the consequences of breach (sanctions and remedies).

This does not mean that there are no rules regarding remedies. But it does mean that even if they are described as non-discretionary they usually have a built-in flexibility that makes prediction of the precise result extremely difficult. Thus, damages for breach of contract are granted as a matter of right and there are rules regarding their calculation. But these rules, even if they seem clear, contain many open-ended points that leave much to the court's discretion. Thus, the rule on mitigation requires the innocent party to take reasonable steps to mitigate the loss. But what is reasonable remains a matter of appreciation, with considerable flexibility. There is similar flexibility with regard to consequential damages that are subject to the rules on remoteness. These rules focus on foreseeability from which we may perhaps deduce that the defendant who could foresee the damage that may result from the breach, is able to know in advance the extent of his liability.[58] But this is totally unrealistic. The rules

[56] Ashworth, above n 55, 75–8.
[57] This is unlike the situation under ancient law under which punishment for each offence was generally fixed. See eg Exodus 22:37.
[58] *Hadley v Baxendale* (1854) 9 Ex 341; 156 ER 145 and J Beatson *Anson's Law of Contract*, above n 51, 600–9. See further Kramer, chapter 12 below.

on remoteness are notorious for their complexity. It is extremely difficult to foresee what kind of damage the court will regard as foreseeable. In addition the foreseeability rule itself is subject to exceptions and instances of liability for unforeseeable loss are clearly conceivable.[59] Consequently, it is very difficult for the party in breach to appraise beforehand the extent of his liability in damages. He is unlikely to know if the innocent party is going to suffer consequential losses for which he may be liable and he is often unlikely to know if the innocent party is able to mitigate the loss.

Uncertainty in the application of remedies is openly admitted when the remedy is discretionary.[60] This is usually the case where the plaintiff seeks enforcement. In Anglo-American law the relevant remedies, namely specific performance and injunction, are equitable, and therefore discretionary. But why should these remedies be discretionary? Are there any reasons other than historical which call for limiting the plaintiff's right by subjecting it to the court's discretion? This leads us to the distinction between conduct rules and decision rules. A conduct rule prohibits breach of contract or the encroachment of another's right. But the law of remedies consists in the main of decision rules. Although a conduct rule was breached, the remedy is not necessarily enforcement. The court may consider that under the circumstances the mere award of damages is more appropriate.

This also offers an explanation of the inherent uncertainty in the law of remedies, an uncertainty that remains even where the legal right is clearly defined. Although the remedy is strongly linked to the right, it is applied after the event. Policy considerations *ex post* may differ from those existing *ex ante*, just as the view after the event may present a picture that differs from that seen before the occurrence. Hence also the inherent uncertainty of remedies. It is often difficult to know before the breach the kind of situation that will emerge after it is committed. The need to deal with the kind of situation that cannot always be foreseen beforehand is reflected in the flexibility of the decision rules embodied in the law of remedies.

Let me conclude by referring once more to the distinction discussed above between prices on the one hand and remedies and sanctions on the other.[61] Prices are normally fixed and pre-determined while remedies and sanctions are not.[62]

[59] Thus torts law developed the 'eggshell skull' rule (the tortfeasor takes the victim as he finds him): Fleming, above note 36, 234–6. This rule will probably also apply to cases of breach of contract causing death or bodily in injury. Cf. also the liability imposed on a shipowner for loss resulting from market fluctuation: *Koufos v C Czarnikow Ltd* [1969] 1 AC 350.

[60] See however Birks' objections to 'strong discretion' in this area (above n 1, 16–18, 22–4).

[61] Above n 7 and accompanying text.

[62] There are of course exceptions. A fine may be fixed while price may sometimes be left open to be determined by an appropriate body (as, for example, in the case of eminent domain).

2

Multiplicity in Contract Remedies

ROY KREITNER*

I INTRODUCTION

A RECURRENT THEME of contracts scholarship over recent decades has been the effort to solve the problems of contract remedies by applying a single, unified principle. The claim of this chapter is that those efforts are misguided, and distract from the more difficult, if less conceptually satisfying, work of thinking about the range of remedies appropriate to breaches of contract. Perhaps ironically, the inception of the project of unifying the remedies for breach of contract lies in one of the most powerful critiques of the idea of unification, Fuller and Perdue's 'The Reliance Interest in Contract Damages'.[1] Fuller and Perdue's article tore asunder an under-examined and unreflective conceptual unity in the law of damages for breach of contract.[2] The project of unifying remedies has often been framed as an attempt to reconstruct that lost unity. In this chapter, I argue that the attempts at reconstruction are fundamentally flawed and doomed to failure; that they exist at a level of abstraction more likely to be an obstacle to understanding contract and solving contract problems than to aid in those tasks; and that only an

*Law Faculty, Tel-Aviv University. I am grateful to Yishai Blank, Ofer Grosskopf, Sharon Hannes, Shai Lavi, Ariel Porat, and Omri Yadlin for their comments, and to the Zakheim Memorial Fund for financial support.

[1] LL Fuller and WR Perdue Jr 'The Reliance Interest in Contract Damages 1 and 2' 46 *Yale Law Journal* 52 and 373 (1936).

[2] Peter Benson has recently described *The Reliance Interest In Contract Damages* as the inauguration of twentieth-century theoretical writing on contract. In characterising the attempts of classical legal thinkers who preceded Fuller and Perdue, such as Langdell, Ames, and especially Williston, Benson holds that they were successful in bringing order and internal consistency to the law of contract, but, 'For all that, however, their work remains untheoretical: They simply presuppose the premise that the expectation remedy is a form of compensation without exploring its normative basis and they stipulate the existence of a deep connection between the expectation principle and the basic doctrines of contract formation without explaining its necessity.' P Benson 'Introduction' in P Benson (ed) *The Theory of Contract Law: New Essays* (Cambridge University Press, Cambridge, 2001) 1, 2.

understanding of contract that respects the multiplicity of interests at stake can productively link contract thinking with the practices of contracting parties and the courts.

Abandoning the search for a single unified principle to govern contract damages does not necessarily entail abandoning any search for order in the law. Contract theory should not be conducted under the threat that any deviance from coherence translates into utter chaos: the world does not divide simply into those practices that are theoretically strictly coherent, and those that are conducted on an *ad hoc*, case-by-case basis. In this chapter I suggest that some measure of order, short of logical coherence, can be brought to the law of damages for breach of contract without sacrificing a reasoned explanation for the multiplicity of remedial measures actually employed by the courts in contract disputes. Such a tentative order will be based on distinguishing among *contract types*, with the further suggestion that different purposes inherent in contract law generally take on varying levels of importance with regard to the different types of contract.

A brief chapter cannot offer a fully worked out theory of contract damages, and I will not attempt such a theory here. Instead, I would like to suggest that in some respects, contracts scholars are searching for a theory of damages in the wrong places, and to offer at least one possible direction that might help us find our way. Part I of the chapter maps out some of the leading attempts to articulate a unified principle of damages for breach of contract. It begins by describing examples of unification theory worked out in mainstream contract scholarship. It continues by examining the philosophical versions of unification theory, and concludes in a brief exploration of the economic analysis of law. For each version of unification theory, there are already built-in critiques. Part II of the chapter is an attempt to generalise some of those critiques, and to cast doubt on the appeal of unification theory generally. Finally, Part III elaborates the idea that distinguishing contracts into various types might allow us to retain a tight link among the purposes of contract enforcement and the rules governing damages for breach.

II UNIFICATION THEORIES

American legal realism had an immense impact on the understanding of remedies for breach of contract. Through critical examination of the connection between the purpose of contract enforcement and the rules governing remedies for breach, the realists succeeded in instilling the view that remedies for breach set out to vindicate a range of interests. According to this view, there was no single core principle of contracts from which the rules on remedies could be deduced. Rather, rules on remedies were to be evaluated by the success with which they advanced the relevant policy considerations. Perhaps the most elaborate extrapolation of this view was Gardner's 'An Inquiry into the Principles of the Law of Contracts',[3] published in 1932. Gardner's analysis included no less than twelve principles of decision, laid out in an elaborate ordering that included an attempted hierarchy of application. The goal was to 'examine the laws which determine the relation of the remedy to the promise, the consideration, and the breach,' and the result was first and foremost an acknowledgment of complexity:

> The task of the law of contract thus ceases to be the simple one of enforcing bargains and becomes the far more complex one of providing means for conducting a cooperative commonwealth on a voluntary basis, of reconciling group industry and economic justice with individual freedom and individual responsibility for results. To achieve this it is necessary to enforce promises to such an extent that promisees may reasonably entrust their fortunes to them, but not to an extent which will permit them to be made instruments of exploitation, multiply the chances of accidental gains or losses, or needlessly restrict the future economic initiative of promisors.[4]

Gardner's heroic grappling with complexity was much discussed in the decade following its publication, but was eventually overshadowed by a rival that offered a more workable model of accommodation for the range of purposes embodied in contract law. That rival, of course, was Fuller and Perdue's 'Reliance Interest'.[5] I will have more to say on 'Reliance Interest' later, but for now it will suffice to point out that its genuine contribution was *not* to set up reliance as the true core of contractual obligation or even of contract damages, but rather to offer a more elegant or digestible version of the claim that the purposes underlying contract enforcement were in fact multiple and complex. That claim of multiplicity and complexity became entrenched in the academic understanding of contract. However, in recent years, a growing number of contracts scholars has attempted to overcome the widespread understanding of the complexity of contract remedies and insisted that there is indeed a single unitary principle to govern the law of damages.

The attempts to unify the law of contract damages can be loosely classified into three groups. The first comprises scholars working within the mainstream of contract theory, or 'liberal pragmatism'.[6] These scholars have critiqued the vision of multiplicity underlying contract remedies

[3] GK Gardner 'An Inquiry into the Principles of the Law of Contracts' (1932) 46 *Harvard Law Review* 1.
[4] *Ibid*, 20–2.
[5] Above n 1.
[6] The appellation is borrowed from Ian Macneil. See IR Macneil 'Relational Contract Theory: Challenges and Queries' (2000) 94 *Northwestern University Law Review* 877, 882–3, especially n 28.

primarily by resorting to a reinterpretation of the case law and existing scholarship, and have offered principled visions of why remedies for breach of contract should be conceived of as unified. Their common point of departure, almost without exception, is a critique of 'Reliance Interest'. The second group comprises scholars who have offered a philosophical critique of multiplicity, relying predominantly on the role of coherence in supplying a justification for the institution of contract law. The third group consists of scholars engaged in the economic analysis of law.

It should be noted at the outset that within each of the three groups, and especially among liberal pragmatists and economists, critique of the idea of unification exists alongside unification theory, almost from its inception. Thus, there is no claim here that mainstream contract theory, philosophical contract theory, or the economic analysis of law have, as a whole, adopted a stance propounding unification theory.[7] My critique of unification theory targets a trend, but focuses on particular pieces of scholarship. Moreover, it builds on critiques first spelled out within each theoretical style, or sub-discipline. I begin with the most accessible versions of unification theory, those stemming from mainstream contract theory.

1 Liberal Pragmatist Unification Theory

Mainstream unification theories of contract remedies begin as the critique of a critique. Almost without exception, they stake their ground in a critique of Fuller and Perdue's 'The Reliance Interest in Contract Damages'. That article posited that contract damages vindicated a range of interests, including what it termed restitution, reliance, and expectation. Expectation, in Fuller and Perdue's terminology, was the interest most closely associated with what was considered the normal contract remedy, ie damages whose goal was to place the injured party in the same economic position he would have occupied had the contractual promise been performed. But the kind of compensation implied in the expectation interest was inadequate as an expression of the purposes of contract enforcement. Like Gardner's analysis that preceded them, Fuller and Perdue's goal was to emphasizse that the purposes of contract enforcement were multiple, that such multiplicity manifested itself in actual damages awards by the courts, and that contract theory should offer an explicit accounting for that multiplicity.[8]

[7] At least as far as liberal pragmatist analyses and economic analysis are concerned, unification theory is a minority position.

[8] Fuller's letter to K Llewellyn two years after the publication of *The Reliance Interest* makes this point succinctly:

> To me it seems clear that no analysis of contract law can be realistic or adequate which does not recognise that there exists a hierarchy of contract interests, which may be sloganised by saying that they extend from restitution through the reliance interest to

Unification theorists reject the proposal that contract law's basic purpose is to vindicate a range of interests. In one of the strongest statements of this position, Friedmann has claimed that 'there is but one genuine contractual interest', and whatever the nature of reliance and restitution, 'they are certainly not contractual interests'.[9] Rebelling against Fuller and Perdue's appellation of expectation, and substituting the term performance interest, Friedmann argues that 'performance is the only genuine contractual interest'.[10] The intuition behind the claim is straightforward, and Friedmann articulates it forcefully:

> The essence of contract is performance. Contracts are made in order to be performed ... This interest in getting the promised performance (hereafter the 'performance interest') is the only pure contractual interest.[11]

Friedmann's treatment of 'The Reliance Interest' is in essence a resistance to Fuller and Perdue's methodological starting point. While they sought to explain the societal purpose of contract enforcement by examining the range of remedies, Friedmann asserts that the starting point of the inquiry must be the *right*. From Friedmann's perspective, the right is necessarily a right to performance, and all remedial decisions are attempts to bridge the practical gap between the lack of performance (ie the breach) and the closest possible alternatives.[12] The argument turns on the idea that it is the nature of the right that should determine what is required of the remedy, rather than the remedies informing us about the meaning of

> the expectation interest, with a number of little midstations, disturbing to elegantia juris, along the way ... I consider the contribution made in my article on the reliance interest to lie, not in calling attention to the reliance interest itself, but in an analysis which breaks down the contract-no contract dichotomy, and substitutes an ascending scale of enforceability.

Letter from L Fuller to K Llewellyn (8 December 1938), quoted in RS Summers and RA Hillman *Contract and Related Obligation: Theory, Doctrine and Practice* 3rd edn (West Group, St Paul, Minnesota, 1997) 41.

[9] D Friedmann 'The Performance Interest in Contract Damages' (1995) 111 *Law Quartely Review* 628, 632 ('Friedmann, *Performance Interest*'). The entire article, from the title through the content, is a critique of *The Reliance Interest*. Prof Friedmann has recently reiterated the views expressed in the article in a symposium on Fuller and Perdue published as D Friedmann 'A Comment on Fuller and Perdue, the Reliance Interest in Contract Damages' *Issues in Legal Scholarship* (Berkeley Electronic Press, Berkeley, CA, 2001) vol 1, Art 3 ('Friedmann, *Comment*').

[10] Friedmann, *Performance Interest*, above n 9, 632.

[11] *Ibid*, 629.

[12] *Ibid*, 634–5. The conflicting starting points for the analysis are clearest when Friedmann ridicules Fuller and Perdue's assertion that we compensate the victim of breach 'for something he never had'. Fuller and Perdue refer to the fact that the victim of breach never had the performance or its value in hand — in that sense he is compensated for something he never had; Friedmann points out that their formulation of this point leaves out the crucial fact that while the victim did not have the performance or its value, he had a *right* or an *entitlement* to the performance, and thus he is compensated for something he did have.

the right. For Friedmann, the right is the source of answers to our questions about remedies, whereas for Fuller and Perdue, the remedies were a source of answers to a question about the possible meaning of the entitlement, a meaning that would never be divorced from our questioning about why to enforce contracts in the first place. Friedmann's position is quite nuanced. While the status of the right as the starting point for analysis is axiomatic, the content of the right is not. Indeed, he suggests that the content of the right evolves, and is still evolving, becoming more property-like.[13]

A critique of Fuller and Perdue is common to additional articulations of mainstream unification theory. Two in particular merit mention here: 'The Phantom Reliance Interest in Contract Damages'[14] and 'The Net Expectation Interest in Contract Damages'[15] both reject Fuller and Perdue's framework as more confusing than useful,[16] and both adopt a modified version of the expectation interest as the key to contract damages. In addition, both offer the reduction of complexity of damage rules as the central advance of the theories they propound.[17] In a sense, all mainstream unification theories participate in the project of reconstructing a principled core for contract doctrine, a core that was threatened, if not shattered, by the legal realists. One crucial focal point in that reconstruction is the performance or expectation principle, and thus many reconstructive attempts are based on a denial of the centrality of reliance as important to contract remedies.[18]

2 Philosophical Unification Theory

Philosophical unification theory, like its mainstream analogue, argues for a singular placement for the expectation principle in understanding and

[13] *Ibid*, 636–7; Friedmann, *Comment*, above n 9, 4.

[14] MB Kelly 'The Phantom Reliance Interest in Contract Damages' (1992) *Wisconsin Law Review* 1755.

[15] DW Barnes 'The Net Expectation Interest in Contract Damages' (1999) 48 *Emory Law Journal* 1137.

[16] 'Only the mystique surrounding the reliance interest and the confusing use of that title to describe several different approaches conceal the remarkable differences between the reliance interest in theory and the reliance interest in practice'. Kelly, above n 14, 1759. 'While most scholars agree that Fuller and Perdue's article was path-breaking, I will argue that the ultimate effect of their work was to confuse and complicate the law of contract damages.' Barnes, above n 15, 1138.

[17] 'Courts need not look backward to find the remedy; they can look forward to find the break-even point. Courts need not administer alternative remedies; a single rule covers all contract damages.' Kelly, above n 14, 1814. Similarly, David Barnes claims his theory of damages offers 'a system for calculating damages that is easier to understand, easier to implement,' and that it 'simplifies both the conceptual foundation for contract damages and the application of damage rules'. Barnes, above n 15, 1138.

[18] See eg RE Barnett 'Foreword: Is Reliance Still Dead?' (2001) 38 *San Diego Law Review* 1 ('Barnett, *Still Dead*'); RE Barnett 'The Death of Reliance' (1996) 46 *Journal Legal Education* 518; E Yorio and S Thel 'The Promissory Basis of Section 90' (1991) 101 *Yale Law Journal* 111.

applying contract remedies. But, while mainstream theories begin from a number of methodological starting points, philosophical theories are generally attempts to deduce the correct remedial principle from the nature of the contractual entitlement.[19] The most popular version of such theory is Fried's *Contract as Promise*.[20] Fried famously argues that the core of contract is promise, and that the nature of promising entails that, 'if I fail to keep my promise, it is fair that I should be made to hand over the equivalent of the promised performance'.[21] Fried goes on, not only to support the expectation principle as the proper remedial principle, but also to deny any fundamental role to reliance. The problem with Fried's position *as an argument about remedies*, as Craswell has shown, is that there is no necessary relationship between Fried's arguments about the basis for liability and the choice of any particular remedy or even remedial structure.[22]

Other scholars have stepped into the breach in order to tighten the relationship between a philosophical account of the nature of contractual entitlement and a proper understanding of remedies. Most recently, Benson has argued that the nature of contractual entitlement entails, as a matter of necessity, a justification of the expectation principle as the sole principle of contractual compensation. Benson's argument rests on the idea that the meaning of contract must be sought in the logic of a transfer of entitlement, a transfer effected by temporally sequenced assents of the parties to a contract.[23] After elaborating the logic of transfer, Benson argues that

> [i]f the law of contract can indeed be understood in terms of the logic of transfer, the expectation remedy is the natural and distinctively contractual principle of compensation.[24]

Two elements of Benson's theory are of interest here. First, the expectation principle is logically deducible from the logic of transfer, which in turn underlies the conception of contract. According to Benson, a contractual transfer of rights is precisely like a present transfer of property with the exception that what is transferred is a *right* to the property rather than the property itself. For Benson, the contractual right effects a change of ownership, and

[19] This is not to say that mainstream theories never use this procedure as well. Prof Friedmann's *The Performance Interest* uses a similar methodology.
[20] C Fried *Contract as Promise: A Theory of Contractual Obligation* (Harvard University Press, Cambridge, Massachusetts, 1981).
[21] *Ibid*, 17.
[22] R Craswell 'Contract Law, Default Rules, and the Philosophy of Promising' (1989) 88 *Michigan Law Review* 489, 517–20.
[23] P Benson 'The Unity of Contract Law' in *The Theory of Contract Law*, above n 2, 118, 128–9.
[24] *Ibid*, 137.

> [t]his change in ownership takes place at formation. Delivery neither adds to nor affects in any way this juridical situation as between the parties. By putting the promisee into actual physical possession of the thing as promised, delivery merely respects the promisee's already existing right.[25]

Significantly, Benson does not present this claim in the framework of an argument for specific performance as a primary remedy; instead, the claim is made to account for 'the expectation remedy, whether expectation damages or specific performance', the latter of which remains in its role as exceptional, and appropriate in situations where there is no market for the thing promised.[26] The contractual right, on this view, is a proprietary right, valid against a particular individual.[27] The nature of this proprietary right, according to Benson, demands that the expectation remedy be available to vindicate the right in case of breach.

The second element of Benson's theory important for our purposes is his view of the status of reliance as a basis for contract enforcement. Any theory attempting to offer a unified basis for remedies around the expectation principle must account in some way for the role of reliance, and perhaps particularly for the doctrine of promissory estoppel. Benson's response is to banish reliance from the contractual realm. He asserts that reliance-based liability is

> incompatible with an essential premise of the logic of a transfer of ownership ... Thus, there can be no intrinsic connection between reliance-based liability and the expectation principle, taken as a principle of compensation.[28]

The error of mainstream thinking about contract, on this view, is in the very attempt to view reliance-based liability as contractual at all. Instead, according to Benson, reliance-based liability generally, and promissory estoppel in particular, are actually not part of contract at all, but should be understood from the perspective of torts.[29] Together, these two elements of Benson's theory present the argument for the expectation remedy as necessary (as flowing from the nature of the entitlement) and sufficient (because other bases for enforcement are non-contractual) to explain the remedial aspect of contract.

[25] *Ibid*, 135.
[26] *Ibid*, 134.
[27] 'The right is proprietary in character ... Moreover, because this right is against a definite individual — the promisor — and, more fundamentally, because the promisee acquires it through the promisor, it is a personal right. The fact that a right is personal does not entail that it is non-proprietary but simply goes to the mode of acquiring it.' *Ibid*, 135.
[28] *Ibid*, 175.
[29] Benson, above n 23, 177.

3 Economic Analysis and Unification Theory

Today, for the most part, economic analysis of law is not amenable to unification theories of contract remedies. The initial insights of economic analysis as applied to contract damages yielded a straightforward support for expectation damages as the primary remedy for breach of contract.[30] This position grew out of the idea that expectation damages give the promisor an incentive to breach his promise if, but only if, the value of the breach (for the promisor) is greater than the value of the performance to the promisee. More important than the support for expectation damages, however, was the unified mode of questioning. Early examples of economic analysis of contract remedies seem to have assumed that there was one crucial question: how will a remedial rule affect the incentives of a promisor to perform or breach her promise?[31]

However, economic analysis soon discovered a series of additional incentive effects of remedial rules. Perhaps the most important of these problems was the fact that expectation damages would give the promisee an incentive to rely on performance of the promise as if that performance were certain, which could generate inefficient (over-) expenditure on reliance.[32] But of course, reliance expenditures are not the only concern for an economically-driven conception of contract damages.[33] Economic analysis has not been able to supply a mechanism for ranking the different areas where damages rules could generate incentives, and therefore, there are no explicit versions of unification theory in economic analysis today.[34] At the same time, various particular pieces of research are

[30] The founding article in this regard is RL Birmingham 'Breach of Contract, Damage Measures, and Economic Efficiency' (1970) 24 *Rutgers Law Review* 273, 284–6, 292.

[31] For a critique of this 'unduly narrow' vision of what economics could contribute to the analysis of contract remedies, see R Craswell 'Contract Remedies, Renegotiation, and the Theory of Efficient Breach' (1988) 61 *Southern California Law Review* 629, 630, 640.

[32] R Cooter 'Unity in Tort, Contract, and Property: The Model of Precaution' (1985) 73 *California Law Review* 1, 11–18; R Cooter and MA Eisenberg 'Damages for Breach of Contract' (1985) 73 *California Law Review* 1432, 1464–8.

[33] A partial list of choices (ie opportunities for incentives) that might be affected by the remedy for breach of contract includes: Whether to perform or to breach? How much to rely on contractual performance? How much to invest in precautions guaranteeing the ability to perform? How much information to reveal? How much effort to invest in seeking alternative deals or partners? How much effort to expend on mitigating injuries from breach? Typically, economic analysis is geared toward one particular incentive problem, or the relationship between two discrete problems, with little work having been done on integrating the diverse analyses into a single model. For comments on the diversity of incentives that the rules on contract damages could generate, see R Craswell 'Against Fuller and Perdue', (2000) 67 *University Chicago Law* Review 99, 108–9 ('Craswell, *Against Fuller*'); R Craswell 'Two Economic Theories of Enforcing Promises' in The Theory of Contract Law, above n 2, 19, 28–32; Craswell, above n 31, 630–1; Cooter and Eisenberg, above n 32, 1462; EA Posner 'Economic Analysis of Contract Law after Three Decades: Success or Failure?' (2003) 112 *Yale Law Journal* 829, 834–9.

[34] There is an ambiguity inherent in economic analysis on this point. On the one hand, economic analysis is self-consciously consequentialist and nearly anything could be relevant to

presented as if they could provide the basis for a unified view of damages, leaving the incentive questions that are not the subject of the research far off in the background. Usually, this exclusion is not accompanied by a limitation of the kinds of contracts for which the analysis is pertinent, but rather presented as a general framework for analysing remedies.[35]

III THE CRITIQUE OF UNIFICATION: RESPECTING MULTIPLICITY

Unification theories of contract remedies have been subject to critique from within the sub-disciplines in which they were generated. But the failings of unification theories can be generalised. In other words, it is possible to identify the common features of unification theories, and on that basis to offer wholesale reasons for rejecting them. That is the task of this part of the chapter.

The main problems with unification theories are two-fold. Telegraphically put, unification theories attempt too much and explain too little about contract remedies. The theories are methodologically unsound because they work on a level of abstraction too high to solve concrete problems, and they are pragmatically weak because they are too rigid, and thus force scholars to narrow the realm of contract, eliminating the consideration of too many problems that are typically considered contractual. I treat these issues in turn.

1 Methodology: The Misconceived Quest for Unifying Principle

Unification theories share an underlying methodological assumption. The assumption is that an overarching principle can yield, through a process

the consequences of legal rules, in terms of the welfare of individuals. Thus, in principle, an economic welfare function could be infinitely complex, and actually take into account a host of competing considerations according to some balancing formula. See L Kaplow and S Shavell 'Fairness versus Welfare' 114 *Harvard Law Review* 961 (2001). However, when efficiency is equated with wealth maximisation, the result is often a simplification of the factors to be considered, with the implicit claim that questions of fact can guide the normative inquiry in a manner divorced from the balancing of substantive values. This was a central theme of very early economic analysis. For a paradigmatic example, see Birmingham, above n 30. For a critique of economic analysis along these lines, see JW Singer 'Legal Realism Now' (1988) 76 *California Law Review* 465, 522–8 (reviewing L Kalman *Legal Realism at Yale: 1927–1960*) (1986)).

[35] See eg R Cooter and A Porat 'Should Courts Deduct Nonlegal Sanctions from Damages?' (2001) 30 *Journal Legal Studies* 401. A recent article on the border between mainstream and economic analysis makes a limited explicit case for unifying remedies in the expectation damages rule, arguing that when administrative concerns are taken into account, only expectation damages lead to efficient results. See MA Eisenberg and BH McDonnell 'Expectation Damages and the Theory of Overreliance' (2003) 54 *Hastings Law Journal* 1335.

of deduction, particular rules of contract law. Another way of putting this is that unification theories rely on conceptualism as their methodological basis. One extended example of the methodology should suffice to clarify the point.

Of all unification theorists, Benson is most straightforward and adamant about his conceptualism.[36] Benson claims that the proper concept of contract flows from the logic of transfer, and that once that concept is in place, it should generate by implication answers to all contract problems:

> My basic thesis is that the logic of a transfer of ownership that animates present transfers of property is also instantiated in contracts and, more specifically, in the main doctrines of the common law of contract. Indeed, it is their organizing idea.

Crucially, while Benson's essay sets out to lay down the basic structure of contract, he claims that virtually any contract rule, including

> implied terms and conditions — the law of mistake and non-disclosure, frustration, conditions antecedent and subsequent, fundamental breach, anticipatory repudiation ... interpretation ... rights of third party beneficiaries

and others are amenable to analysis through his conceptual apparatus:

> A public basis of justification aims to be complete in the sense that, through the conception of contract, it ideally is able to answer all or most of the questions that arise in relation to contract formation and breach. The contention is that the conception of contract has the necessary resources to do so. Of course, to answer these questions, it may be necessary to supplement the basic structure of this conception with various presumptions and propositions of law. However, it is important to note that, on the approach I am taking, the latter are not to be introduced *ab extra* and should not take us outside the conception of contract. Rather they are to be understood as implications of that conception when it is suitably specified to address these other questions. Essential to this approach is the idea that a contract does not admit of any gaps once it is understood in terms of the conception of contract.[37]

[36] Perhaps the clearest illustration of Benson's conceptualism could be gleaned from his treatment of consideration, where he begins with a definition and then dissects the definition in order to derive four conditions for consideration to be understood as valid, which in turn contribute to the analysis of the place of consideration in the conception of contract. See Benson, above n 23, 154ff. However, since this essay concentrates on theories of remedies, I will leave the analysis of consideration for another time. At all events, Benson is useful for purposes of illustration because he takes his conceptualism seriously: his theory has the advantage of taking conceptualism close to its logical endpoints, or to extremes, depending on one's perspective.

[37] *Ibid*, 202–3.

The analysis of the expectation principle occupies a central place in Benson's conceptualist scheme. While one goal of his essay is to justify the expectation principle in general, that very principle does the job of explaining the concept of contract. Thus:

> To begin, we should recall that from the point of view of contract law the wrong which a breach does to a promisee's right to performance consists in the promisee being deprived of the thing promised, including its value and use. This is made evident by the expectation remedy, whether expectation damages or specific performance, which aims to give the promisee physical possession of the thing promised, including its value at the time performance is due. Money damages accomplish this purpose where the thing promised is not unique but is available to the promisee on a market: Damages represent both the value of the thing promised and the means of payment by which the promisee can obtain the thing, including its value, from the market.[38]

The logic of transfer, according to Benson, entails that a promisee has a proprietary right of ownership of the thing promised, and that this right vests at formation. That Benson's view departs from traditional understandings of contractual right is unimportant. What concerns us here is that his justification of the expectation remedy as central and exclusive stems from the conceptual framework of the logic of transfer. Benson's goal is to set up an internal and single-focused examination: does a proposed remedy flow from the logic of transfer? The point of the framework is to limit the kinds of considerations that might be relevant to determining the remedy, eliminating, for instance, considerations of policy that are the bread and butter of mainstream treatments of remedies since early in the twentieth century.

The critique of this position requires, then, a justification for what has become the standard practice of thinking about remedies; in other words, the critique consists in presenting the argument for a purposive, as opposed to a conceptualist, view of contract remedies. A brief clarification of the structure of this presentation is in order. A full justification of the purposive view of remedies has two parts. The first comprises an argument for gauging various purposes when deciding whether to apply a remedy and how to measure it, in cases included in what the conceptualist views as the core of the contractual relationship. The second explains why a purposive analysis offers a better account of cases that conceptualist accounts attempt to expunge from contract. That part of the presentation is undertaken in the next section (III(2)) of this essay.

[38] *Ibid*, 134–5. It is worth noting that Benson's analysis offers no principled reason for allowing damages to be the primary remedy, since his language implies that the actual thing promised, or specific performance, is entailed by the logic of transfer. The gap opened up by the choice between specific performance and damages is only one hole in the theory.

Why then, should one adopt a purposive view of contract remedies? Answers are likely to take two forms. First, one might suggest that as long as a purposive view of remedies does not engender too much uncertainty, there is no affirmative reason to exclude the consideration of purposes when gauging remedies. The extreme conceptualist view claims that the concept simply supplies the very meaning of contract, and that any reconsideration of purposes at the level of decision-making undermines this meaning. But the meaning or meanings of contract are precisely at issue, and the bald assertion that a particular closed conceptual framework embodies *the* meaning of contract at the expense of other considerations will necessarily involve a mode of circular reasoning.[39] As Corbin put the point more than seventy years ago:

> The common law does not have any substratum of grand eternal principles on which it rests, except that judicial decision and administrative action should continually be readjusted to the needs and desires of mankind. Argument from 'principle' almost always involves a subtle begging of the question.[40]

The second answer involves a somewhat closer inspection of the context of contract remedies. Conceptualist accounts share the conception of a contractual entitlement as a right to the thing promised. And yet, all conceptualist accounts acknowledge that specific performance is not the sole remedy for breach, and indeed, in most jurisdictions, not the primary remedy. Even specific performance, coming long after the time for performance, as it must when the result of litigation, would not actually supply the thing promised *as* promised.[41] But the recognition of expectation damages is even further removed from a grant of the thing itself. The predominance of the substitutional remedy is already an indication that the law relies to a great extent on administrative concerns. When we take the investigation beyond the very existence and prevalence of damages and delve into some specific rules, we find a range of competing concerns embedded in the law of remedies.[42]

[39] Circularity is not necessarily a condemnation of the reasoning process. The defense of conceptualism embraces the form of circularity evinced in the quotations from Benson presented above, and from his exposition of the public basis of justification. P Benson 'The Idea of a Public Justification for Contract' (1995) 33 *Osgoode Hall Law Journal* 273. The idea is that any combination of justificatory considerations (for instance a possible competition among purposes) would lead to the failure of each, and thus to arbitrariness. See EJ Weinrib *The Idea of Private Law* (Harvard University Press, Cambridge, 1995) 38–42. The question of why a justificatory principle or consideration must be extended to its 'full reach' and govern a particular form of social interaction without interference or interaction with other such principles or considerations in order to maintain some justificatory power is, on my reading, never answered.

[40] AL Corbin 'The Restatement of the Common Law by the American Law Institute' (1929) 15 *Iowa Law Review* 19, 35.

[41] '[The law] never interferes until a promise has been broken, and therefore cannot possibly be performed according to its tenor.' OW Holmes Jr *The Common Law* (Little Brown & Co, Boston, 1881) 300.

[42] One clarification: the point here is not that every contract question must, as a matter of necessity, raise a number of conflicting considerations. However, almost any contract

The possibility of conflicting considerations is easily viewed when considering the rules for choosing between alternative measures of value (within expectation damages), and in the principles that limit damages. Take for instance the classic problem of deciding whether to award expectation damages based on the cost of completion of work according to the contract terms as opposed to damages based on the diminution of value of the property as a result of breach.[43] This problem is not amenable to solution by applying either the logic of transfer of entitlement or any other high-level abstraction about carrying out the parties' wills. Either result, at this level of abstraction, is a plausible interpretation of giving the injured party the value of the thing promised. To decide which interpretation to adopt, however, we must do more.

A reasonable decision-maker will take into account at least two *kinds* of considerations, each of which offer arguments in both directions. One kind of consideration deals with fairness as between the parties to the dispute: is it fair/just/right to allow the promisor to escape from performing in the manner that the promisee understood the promise? is it fair/just/right to grant the promisee a windfall money judgment that he is unlikely to use for actual restoration of the property? The second kind of consideration deals with social utility, looking as much to guiding future behaviour (primarily of non-parties) as to the dispute itself: will a rule of cost of completion generate economic waste, and in turn generate performance when neither party has an actual interest in performance? will a rule of diminution of value generate inefficient breaches, because the promisor can then discount the actual damage to the promisee? With good reason, this problem has become a staple of the first year contracts curriculum, because it forces anyone who thinks about it to grapple with different kinds of considerations, none of which are unambiguous on their own terms. The conceptualist model that counsels ignoring these considerations seems unable to move toward a solution of such a problem in concrete terms.

question might, potentially, raise such considerations, and many actual attempts to determine a rule or decide according to a rule are formulated precisely as contests among conflicting considerations. See D Kennedy 'From the Will Theory to the Principle of Private Autonomy: Lon Fuller's "Consideration and Form"' (2000) 100 *Columbia Law Review* 94, 104–6 (describing 'The Conflicting Considerations Model' of legal analysis).

[43] The classic formulation comes from *Peevyhouse v Garland Coal & Mining Co* 382 P 2d 109 (Okla 1962). More recent cases include *Schneberger v Apache Corp* 890 P 2d 847 (Okla 1994) (adopting the diminution of value award); *Meade v Kubinski* 661 NE 2d 1178, 1185 (Ill App 1996) (holding that trial court should 'compare the cost of restoring the land to its previous level of fertility with the diminution in market value at its highest and best use, and award the lesser amount'); *Willie's Construction Co v Baker* 596 NE 2d 958 (Ind App 1992) (adopting cost of completion measure where the remedial construction cost was $24,000, the diminution of value was zero, and the value of the property was $70,000).

The limitations on expectation damages offer additional examples of conflicting considerations. Again, we may focus on a classic example of damages limited to loss that is foreseeable as a result of the breach, as laid out in *Hadley v Baxendale*.[44] Is the question as to whether certain consequences of the breach are foreseeable answerable by reference to the entitlements transferred by the parties at formation, as the conceptualist analysis would assert? This might be the case where the promisor demanded a higher price for her service because of the knowledge that the promisee intended an unusual use, or was subject to unusually great injury. But that only answers the easy case where there is a concrete assumption of risk, something that is not necessary for liability. In fact, the test of foreseeability is not applied in subjective terms, but rather objectively, as a self-consciously normative inquiry. Again, decision-makers are likely to ask whether it would be fair as between the parties to assess damages;[45] and whether a default rule restricting damages would have beneficial societal effects.[46] Even the hero of conceptual analysts of contract, Williston, was willing to admit that the attempt to derive the foreseeability requirement from the parties' agreement was a fiction.[47]

A final example for this point may be drawn from the requirement of certainty for the assessment of damages. For instance, plaintiff company contracts to manage a stadium for a municipality for a period of twenty years, before the stadium is built. In fact, the stadium never gets built, and the city breaches its contract. Again, considerations of fairness to the parties and incentives to similarly situated parties will play a

[44] (1854) 9 Ex 341; 156 ER 145. See further A Kramer, chapter 12 below.

[45] This explains the recurrence of language regarding 'disproportionate' damage. The idea is that it may well be unfair, even monstrous, to hold the promisor in a contract worth next to nothing to the damages caused by its breach, even when those are easy to foresee. See Restatement (Second) of Contracts § 351(3).

[46] I Ayres and R Gertner 'Filling Gaps in Incomplete Contracts: An Economic Theory of Default Rules' (1989) 99 *Yale Law Journal* 87, 101–2.

[47] Thus Williston, in discussing limitations on damages, and in particular the implications of the doctrine of *Hadley v Baxendale*:

> To assert then, as is sometimes done expressly or impliedly, that the measure of damages for breach of a contract is based on the terms of the contract is to assert a fiction which obscures the truth and invites misapprehension which may lead to error. One who on borrowing money agrees to pay it the following month does not stipulate for the alternative right to keep the money at legal interest until the lender can get judgment and levy execution, though this is the only remedy the law can enforce. Nor can it be supposed that a seller contracts to be liable for the difference between the contract and the market price, or for consequential damages according as he does or does not know certain facts. Parties generally have their minds addressed to the performance of contracts — not to their breach or the consequences which will follow a breach. The fiction here criticised is a manifestation of the broader fiction that parties contract for whatever obligations or consequences the law may impose upon them.

Williston on *Contracts* 1st edn (New York, Baker Voorhis, 1920) vol 3 § 1357. Cf A Kramer, chapter 12 below.

central role.[48] Alongside those two types of considerations, a court will also be faced with administrative concerns.[49] In a world where prediction is not simply an art but a well developed set of sciences, reasonable certainty is primarily a question of money, or of the resources applied: will courts (and possibly juries) be competent to assess the kinds of evidence that are likely to be submitted to fulfill the certainty requirement? will such an investigation on the part of the court require resources the courts cannot or should not spare?[50]

These examples show that typical questions of contract remedies are generally not answerable, or at least generally not answered, with reference only to an overarching principle or to a commitment about the nature of a contractual right. Instead, at least in many cases, a range of purposive considerations will come into play, including fairness as between the parties; social welfare or utility, which is generally geared toward directing behaviour of similarly situated parties; and administrative considerations, generally geared toward assuring that the courts are not overwhelmed by the results of the rules they must apply. Gardner summed up the sentiment years ago:

> In short, it gradually becomes apparent, upon a broad survey of the law of remedies, that 'contracts' are not 'enforced' merely because the parties made them, but that the law affords only such remedies for breach of promise as seem most likely to promote the orderly and efficient conduct of the community's economic life.[51]

[48] Fairness considerations are likely to be central where the fact of damage is certain, and the question is what degree of proof will suffice as reasonably certain. Will it be fair, under these conditions, to impose a strict standard of proof, under which the plaintiff, though certainly damaged, remains without remedy? On the other hand, will it be fair to impose on the defendant speculative losses? The same situation implicates considerations of utility: will parties be wary of contracting in situations where losses are difficult to prove? Will potential breachers be too willing to breach because they know they can discount the injured party's losses where those are less than certain?

[49] In *Kenford Co v Erie County* 493 NE 2d 234 (NY 1986) the court noted that the plaintiff presented a massive quantity of expert proof that represented industry's most advanced and sophisticated methods for predicting results of future projects. But the nature of the proof, its very sophistication, seems to be one of the factors that led the court to the conclusion that it would be dangerous to consider such proof. The court seems to be protecting itself, or courts generally, from the prospect of facing such unfamiliar territory, or from having to take the word of experts on issues too far from its instincts and common sense. For the opposite position, ie that a court should consider evidence if it offers at least a rational basis for determination of damages, see *Perma Research and Development Co v Singer Co* 402 F Supp 881 (SDNY 1975).

[50] Some remedial rules are explicitly concerned with administrative costs, and thus require no translation into the arguments for a particular interpretation of the rule. See eg Restatement (Second) of Contracts § 366 (mandating that specific performance will not be granted where it would 'impose on the court burdens in enforcement or supervision that are disproportionate to the advantages to be gained from enforcement and to the harm to be suffered from its denial.').

[51] Gardner, above n 3, 32.

2 Narrowing Contract: The Limited Focus of Unification Theories

Unification theories tend to narrow the focus of contract, eliminating consideration of reliance-based liability from the contractual realm. Benson is particularly clear on this point, asserting that, 'Promissory estoppel is not a species of contractual liability ... Reliance-based liability, including promissory estoppel, is best understood as a species of tort, not contractual, liability'.[52] Friedmann takes a similar, though more nuanced position, claiming that often contract and tort protect the same entitlement and thus reach similar damage measures,[53] but noting that if a promise is *binding*, 'it means that the promisee is entitled to its performance (or to the performance damages)'.[54] One problem with this approach is that it assumes that the nature of the entitlement has determinate consequences upon the remedy, whereas the possibility that a *binding* promise may be binding to varying extents (varying levels of damages, for instance) is precisely the question at issue. Friedmann admits that the law does not comply with his analytical arrangement:

> In essence, the difficulty stems from an imprecise definition of the legal right and the corresponding duty or obligation. It would have been avoided if instead of defining the promise as binding, a duty of good faith in negotiation or in making promises had been imposed. In fact, § 90 [of the Restatement of Contracts] deals with different types of entitlements. In some instances in which the entitlement is indeed to performance, it may be regarded as a contractual entitlement. In other instances, in which there is a mere right not to be misled by a promise that is later broken, the remedy is limited accordingly. However, the drafting of § 90 reflects the traditional Anglo-American approach which places the emphasis upon the remedy and leaves the nature of the right in obscurity.[55]

Thus, unification theories, at least in their conceptualist form, distinguish between a genuine contractual entitlement and 'a mere right not to be misled by a promise that is later broken'. But this distinction cuts against

[52] Benson, above n 23, 177. Benson makes clear that he is demarcating two different types of liability: tort liability for certain promises, as opposed to contractual liability for others (those with actual consideration). 'The role of promise in tort is categorically different from its function in contract ... There is no intrinsic connection between tort-based promissory liability and the expectation principle.' *Ibid.*

[53] 'The *different results reached in tort and contract derive from the fact that they are usually called on to protect different rights*. Where, however, they are invoked to protect the same right, the calculation of damages, which reflect the value of this right, either in tort or in contract will be similar.' Friedmann, *Performance Interest*, above n 9, 639 (emphasis in original). It is hard to square this point, and Friedmann's ensuing detailed analysis of examples, with his earlier claim that there is only one genuine contractual interest. To this reader, at least, his examples demonstrate that contract, in many situations, embodies the tort principle.

[54] *Ibid*, 643.

[55] *Ibid*, 644.

the grain of common law thinking about contract. If, as the Restatement counsels, a contract is 'a promise… for the breach of which the law gives a remedy, or the performance of which the law *in some way* recognises as a duty',[56] then a right not to be misled by a promise that will be broken is, at least in some cases, simply a contractual right.[57] The traditional view is not limited to definitions. Instead, it manifests itself in a vision of the world of contract that includes a host of problems that conceptualists might like to see analysed under different categorical headings.[58]

The difficulty with the narrow vision of contract is two-fold. First, given current understandings of contractual liability, it is highly artificial, and leaves too many common contract situations unsolved. Second, its supposed conceptual neatness actually complicates the analysis of relatively straightforward problems. A few brief examples should clarify. In reliance on bids of various subcontractors, a general contractor calculates his bid for a tender offer, and on learning of his being granted the tender, the subcontractor claims he made a mistake in calculation, and refuses to perform.[59] A donee of real estate occupies and makes improvements on the land, and the donor's heirs refuse to finalise the transfer of title. A franchisor and a potential franchisee conduct a series of transactions, each of which is meant to fulfill conditions for the granting of the franchise. When the final condition is fulfilled, the franchisor raises the bar, making complete performance of the agreement impossible.[60] Is it conceivable that such classic problems have no place in the corpus of contracts materials, because they are 'actually' tort cases? And if so, why is part of the struggle over their solution centered on the possibility of finding consideration?[61]

The artificiality of the distinction proposed by conceptualists may not be crucial. Since the decline of the forms of action and the simplification of pleading, the drawing of boundaries between fields like contract and tort is likely to be of much more importance to the conceptualist than to someone interested in a pragmatic approach to private law.[62] However,

[56] Restatement (Second) of Contracts §1 (emphasis added).

[57] It could be argued that only the promise to engage in an undertaking will trigger contractual liability, but this would not solve the definitional problem raised by conceptualists. The obvious evidence of the mainstream view is Restatement (Second) of Contracts §90, which comes under the heading of 'Contracts without Consideration'. In other words, the common understanding is that the requirement of consideration is not a universal requirement for contractual validity of promises (see §§ 82–90), but that the situations elaborated under the topic heading are contractual.

[58] Promissory estoppel is a broad heading for some of these problems, but there are others, including firm offers, options, surety, and certain contractual claims for reliance damages.

[59] See eg *James Baird Co v Gimbel Bros Inc* 64 F 2d 344 (2d Cir 1933); *Drennan v Star Paving Co* 333 P 2d 757 (Cal 1958); *Branco Enterprises Inc v Delta Roofing Inc* 886 SW 2d 157 (Mo App 1994).

[60] *Hoffman v Red Owl Stores Inc* 133 NW 2d 267 (Wisc 1965).

[61] See R Pound 'Consideration in Equity' (1919) 13 *Illinois Law Review* 667.

[62] In fact, this issue was crucial for late nineteenth century classical theorists. They, however, could not so readily shuffle off problems of promissory estoppel to the realm of tort, because

the distinction has some ill effects on contract thinking more generally, beyond the boundary issue.[63] As far as remedies are concerned, the central problem is how to think about damages when the limitations on expectation damages are relevant. Again, two telegraphic examples: in *Kenford Co v County of Erie*,[64] the plaintiff agreed to manage a sports stadium for the county, but the stadium was never built by the county. Uncertainty and foreseeability posed insurmountable obstacles in Kenford's claim for damages. But what if there had been clear expenditures in reliance on the contract? If the 'performance interest' is the only interest protected by contract, how is the plaintiff to recover even his reliance expenditures?[65] Is it feasible or desirable to treat this case as a tort, just because of the difficulty in proving damages? The second example highlights the problem with this scenario. In *Security Stove & Manufacturing Co v American Railways Express Co*,[66] the plaintiff contracted with a carrier to send a special combination oil and gas burner to an exhibition, where he intended to display it. One package of the shipment never arrived, and the plaintiff recovered his expenses in going to the exhibition and setting up his display, or reliance damages. It is a matter of course that there was a valid contract, and relatively clear that expectation damages would raise a host of problems, ranging from causality to foreseeability and on to certainty. In addition, it is not clear that reliance damages were not considerably higher than expectation, if the latter is limited to the difference between the market value of the goods at the time of delivery and the time when they should have been delivered. But should this be a case of tort? Should the carrier be excused if he was not negligent? Should the plaintiff have to bear the burden of showing negligence? It seems clear that the answer to all of these questions is no, and that the plaintiff should be able to elect to sue for reliance damages without having to show the existence of a tort. And yet, this relatively easy contracts case becomes quite difficult if the contractual interest is narrowly and artificially defined.

they worked within a framework that suggested that the voluntary relationship or undertaking precluded the examination from the perspective of the law of torts. See JH Beale 'Gratuitous Undertakings' (1891) 5 *Harvard Law Review* 222. For a modern explanation of why the boundaries might still matter, see Barnett, *Still Dead*, above n 18, 9–11 (explaining that the determination to uphold the boundary between tort and contract is motivated by a concern for freedom of contract).

[63] The wider issue here is the extent to which all the parties' obligations should ostensibly be traced to the moment of contract formation. See D Charny 'Hypothetical Bargains: The Normative Structure of Contract Interpretation' (1991) 89 *Michigan Law Review* 1815.

[64] 73 NY 2d 312; 537 NE 2d 176; 540 NYS 2d 1 (1989).

[65] One suggestion is that courts should be willing to assume a fiction, that is, of at least a break even contract, thus awarding reliance damages as a surrogate for the difficult to prove expectation. Kelly, above n 14. This suggestion, along with its fiction, is critiqued as a 'somewhat artificial presumption' in Williston, above n 47, vol 3 §1341.

[66] 51 SW 2d 572 (Mo App 1932).

IV BEYOND UNIFICATION: TOWARD AN ANALYSIS OF CONTRACT TYPES

Unification theories of contract remedies are inadequate to explain the complexities of contractual remedies, and too rigid to guide dispute resolution in the field. By ignoring or at least minimising the importance of context and consequential analysis, they sacrifice too much to conceptual neatness. But the alternative, at least as sketched out here thus far, may leave some critics in discomfort. The realist model that takes into account a range of conflicting considerations in trying to implement the purposes of contract law through its rules offers little guidance on how to gauge the importance of various considerations or purposes. The recognition of conflicting considerations seems to throw judicial decision-making into something of a void of indeterminacy, where often, only the judge's predilections will lead her to a decision. The brave answer to this concern is that, 'certainty generally is an illusion and repose is not the destiny of man'.[67] The remainder of this chapter, in contrast, is for the faint of heart. My suggestion here is that a provisional grouping of fact situations by contract type will supply some guidance regarding the relative weight of conflicting contract principles. Such groupings will not eliminate the underlying need to consider various purposes advanced by contract law, but they might provide a few rules of thumb, or labour saving devices, which could aid in deciding contract cases according to the considerations that are typically most important in context.

I will begin by noting that classification of contract types according to fact situations is far from a new concept. In fact, it characterises both pre-classical contract law, which was arranged according to typical contractual relationships,[68] and much of the twentieth-century development of specialised fields of contract. In fact, the spinning off of certain topics from a general field of contracts was one of the pet peeves of paradigmatic conceptualist analysis:

> The law of contracts ... after starting with some degree of unity now tends from its very size to fall apart. The simplest applications of fundamental principles of contracts when found in an insurance policy or a contract of suretyship are often considered by writers on those topics as peculiarities of the law of insurance or of suretyship, controlled by no general rules. It

[67] OW Holmes Jr 'The Path of the Law' in *Collected Legal Papers* (Harcourt Brace & Co, New York, 1920) 167, 181.

[68] Until the classical scholars began to dominate the field, contract was considered the law of relations: the law of vendor and purchaser, the law of factors or of brokers, of bailor and bailee, of master and servant, of principal and agent, of landlord and tenant, of lessor and lessee, of shipper and carrier and on and on. And the content of the duties or obligations in each of these relations was supplied by law, in accordance with recognised contract types. See J Gordley *The Philosophical Origins of Modern Contract Doctrine* (Clarendon Press, Oxford, 1991) 158–60; JV Orth 'Contract and the Common Law' in HN Schreiber (ed) *The State and Freedom of Contract* (Stanford University Press, Stanford, CA, 1998) 44.

> therefore seems desirable to treat the subject of contracts as a whole, and to show the wide range of application of its principles.[69]

The existence of labour law, employment law, consumer protection law, sales law, and others, is a testament to the fact that the law is shaped by the context of its application. In what follows, I will not suggest a full-fledged return to a system of contract types, or to the primacy of classification as the most crucial lawyer's tool. Instead, I will offer two extended examples and a few brief suggestions as to why work towards a provisional (and always flexible) typology might help advance our understanding of contract remedies.

1 History: Contracts for Carriage and the Rule in *Hadley v Baxendale*

It is worthwhile to begin with a familiar case, though the analysis may undermine some of that familiarity. *Hadley v Baxendale*[70] is typically considered the leading case in laying down the rule that consequential damages are limited to the injury that the defendant could reasonably have foreseen at the time of contract formation.[71] The traditional understanding of the rule in *Hadley* is based on the idea that the consequential loss in question must be contemplated by the parties if the plaintiff is to recover. Admittedly, this understanding flows from a highly plausible, even straightforward, reading of Alderson B's speech deciding the case.[72]

[69] Williston, above n 47, v 1, iii. However, alongside this statement of purpose, Williston's first edition included chapters on agents and fiduciaries; contracts for the sale of land; contracts for the sale of personal property; contracts of employment and contracts to marry; contracts of bailment and of innkeepers; contracts of affreightment; bills of exchange and promissory notes; and contracts of suretyship. Thus, while Williston's goal was to promote a unitary view of contract, he was still tied to a tradition for which a complete treatment of the field was rooted in particular classes of contracts.
[70] (1854) 9 Ex 341; 156 ER 145.
[71] 'The fountainhead of the limitation of foreseeability is the famous English case of *Hadley v Baxendale*, which in 1854 laid down general principles that are still honored today.' Farnsworth on *Contracts* 2nd edn (Aspen Law & Business, New York, 1998) 822 .
[72] To recall the facts of the case, plaintiffs were millers, and the crankshaft of the steam engine that powered their mill was broken, and the mill was thus idle. They gave a carrier the broken shaft to deliver to the manufacturer for replacement, and the carrier delayed delivery. The miller sued for lost profits for the period of delay while the mill was stopped. Alderson B said that damages should be:

> such as may fairly and reasonably be considered either arising naturally… or such as may reasonably be supposed to have been in the contemplation of both parties, at the time they made the contract, as the probable result of the breach of it. Now, if the special circumstances under which the contract was actually made were communicated by the plaintiffs to the defendants, and thus known to both parties, the damages resulting from the breach of such a contract, which they would reasonably contemplate, would be the amount of injury which would ordinarily follow from a breach of contract under these special circumstances so known and communicated.

156 ER 145, 151.

But the connection between foreseeability or contemplation and actual awareness of special circumstances may not be as straightforward as it seems. On the one hand, there is the repeated reference to the issue of whether the special circumstances were ever communicated to the defendants, with Alderson B assuming they were not. But in direct conflict with this view is the reporter's note preceding the opinion, which explicitly states first that 'The plaintiffs' servant told the clerk that the mill was stopped, and that the shaft must be sent immediately', and second, that upon payment for carriage of the shaft, 'the defendants' clerk was told that a special entry, if required, should be made to hasten its delivery'.[73]

The real key to understanding the opinion lies not in the question of notice, but rather in the *type* of contract undertaken between the parties. The decision rests ultimately on the consideration of the damage that would 'arise generally, and in the great multitude of cases not affected by any special circumstances, from such a breach of contract'.[74] In other words, damages will typically be limited to those that arise from a particular type of contract, when both parties know they enter that type of contract, here a contract of carriage. Counsel for defendants made this point explicitly: 'A carrier has a certain duty cast upon him by law, and that duty is not to be enlarged to an indefinite extent in the absence of a special contract'.[75] *Special contract* is not merely a question of notice, but of a specific undertaking to become liable for damages beyond those typically assumed. Thus, we should pay close attention to Alderson B's statement:

> [I]f the special circumstances under which the contract was actually made were communicated by the plaintiffs to the defendants, and thus known to both parties, the damages resulting from the breach of such a contract, which they would reasonably contemplate, would be the amount of injury which would ordinarily follow from a breach of contract under these special circumstances so known and communicated ... For, had the special circumstances been known, the parties might have specially provided for the breach of contract by special terms as to the damages in that case; and of this advantage it would be very unjust to deprive them.[76]

[73] *Ibid*, 147. Further, in argument for the plaintiffs, counsel was presented by Parke B with the question: 'The defendants there [in *Waters v Towers*, 8 Ex 401] must of necessity have known that the consequence of their not completing their contract would be to stop the working of the mill. But how could the defendants here know that any such result would follow?' and he answered: 'There was ample evidence that the defendants knew the purpose for which this shaft was sent, and that the result of its nondelivery in due time would be the stoppage of the mill; for the defendants' agent, at their place of business, was told that the mill was then stopped, that the shaft must be delivered immediately, and that if a special entry was necessary to hasten its delivery, such an entry should be made.' *Ibid*, 149.

[74] *Ibid*, 151.

[75] *Ibid*, 150.

[76] *Ibid*, 151.

The *special terms* referred to here are simply a contract for extraordinary liability, or insurance. And what is at stake is the nature of a contract for carriage, which does not include such insurance. When parties desire insurance, in other words, they should contract for it specifically.[77] The concern of the court, in cases like this, is that one party should not receive a contract for insurance for the price of a contract for carriage.[78] The issue, on this reading, is not whether the parties *actually* foresee or contemplate the damage in question, but whether the *type* of relationship they undertake in the contract entails liability for such damage. Contract types entail a host of duties, among them responsibility for particular kinds of losses. The parties can contract around these duties, but to do so they must exit the typical arrangement, and more than mere notice is required for such exit.

The early development of contract doctrine regarding damages was heavily dependant on specific contract types. Leading examples include the limitation of damages for non-payment of a debt to interest,[79] and the rule limiting damages against a vendor of real estate who failed to make title to the expenses of the buyer, or what would later be termed reliance damages.[80] But these examples are only the tip of the ice-berg, prominent because they resulted in bright line rules that diverge clearly from the general formula, rather than modifying it delicately.[81] A mid-nineteenth-century

[77] This is the understanding proposed by defendants' counsel:

> Here the declaration is founded upon the defendants' duty as common carriers, and indeed there is no pretence for saying that they entered into a special contract to bear all the consequences of the non-delivery of the article in question. They were merely bound to carry it safely, and to deliver it within a reasonable time. The duty of the clerk, who was in attendance to the defendants' office, was to enter the article, and to take the amount of the carriage; but a mere notice to him, such as was here given, could not make the defendants, as carriers, liable as upon a special contract. (*Ibid*, 150.)

[78] This concern is shown in even starker terms during the argument of counsel for the plaintiffs, who relied on the case of *Borradaile v Brunton*, where the plaintiff recovered for the loss of an anchor occasioned by the breaking of a chain cable, which the defendant had warranted would last two years. Upon bringing up the case, plaintiffs' counsel was queried by Alderson B, 'Why should not the defendant have been liable for the loss of the ship?' and then by Martin B, 'Take the case of the non-delivery by a carrier of a delicate piece of machinery, whereby the whole of an extensive mill is thrown out of work for a considerable time; if the carrier is to be liable for the loss in that case, he might incur damages to the extent of £10,000'. *Ibid*, 148. The barons are suggesting that it is implausible that for the price of a contract of carriage, one could insure a huge loss in business, or for the price of a chain cable, insure an entire ship.

[79] 'Where the defendant is under a unilateral or independent obligation to pay a liquidated sum of money, the ordinary measure of damages for non-performance is the sum of money itself with the interest at the legal rate from the time when it was due. In an action by a creditor against his debtor for the non-payment of the debt, no other damages are ever allowed.' Williston, above n 47, v 3 §1410 (footnotes, citing cases, omitted).

[80] *Ibid*, §1399, citing *Flureau v Thornhill*, (1776) 2 Wm Bl 1078, and its American progeny.

[81] Williston's first edition, despite his stated desire to assert the unity of contract law, includes a short chapter on the Measure of Damages for Breach of Contract, and a chapter

writer summed up the importance of contract types for understanding damages by noting that general formulas, for instance the statement mandating that the injured party should be placed in the same situation as if the contract had been performed, are too 'vague and general' to guide practice.

> In order that rules thus expressed may be useful and available to the practitioner, they must be attentively considered by him in connection with each respectively of the *leading species* of contracts.[82]

2 Modern Remedies: The Case of Merger Agreements

The modern law of contract remedies has not abandoned contract type analysis wholesale, despite the fact that there is little discussion of types in the literature. In fact, the fields that have spun off from general contract law often engender specialised remedial principles.[83] Employment law and the law of construction contracts are often singled out for special treatment, and of course, the law of sales has generated some specialised remedial principles. The attention that these sub-fields of contracts draw to their particular contexts ought to be generalised and applied to additional fields. As an example of the possible payoff of such attention to context, I offer a brief analysis of remedies for the breach of a merger agreement.

Corporate mergers are particularly complex transactions with high stakes and many opportunities for breakdown. Buyers and sellers in the

three times as long on Application of Rules of Damages to Particular Cases, which includes treatment of contracts of employment; sale of goods; warranty of quality and of title; contracts to pay a sum of money in goods; sale of land; covenants in deeds; landlord's right to rent; covenants in leases; negative agreements; alternative contracts; promises to indemnify; contracts to pay money; contracts to lend money, and others. *Ibid*, §§1358–417.

[82] 'On the Measure of Damages Ex Contractu' (1855) 3 *American Law Register* 513, 516 (excerpting an article from (1855) 53 *London Law Magazine* 257 (emphasis added). The article goes on to analyze, among others areas, special rules of damages for: breach of a covenant to repair; hiring and service; contribution; sales, including non-delivery of goods; sale of real estate; and common carriers.

[83] See eg C Summers 'Effective Remedies for Employment Rights: Preliminary Guidelines and Proposals' (1992) 141 *University Pennsylvania Law Review* 457 (arguing that specialised remedial principles must be developed if employment rights are to be effectively guaranteed); W Kamiat 'Labor and Lemons: Efficient Norms in the Internal Labor Market and the Possible Failures of Individual Contracting' (1996) 144 *University Pennsylvania Law Review* 1953 (arguing for specialized norms for labour contracts); HC Eglit 'Damages Mitigation Doctrine in the Statutory Anti-Discrimination Context: Mitigating its Negative Impact' (2000) 69 *University Cincinnati Law Review* 7 (arguing that mitigation doctrine should be limited in the employment context). But cf G Mundlak 'Generic or Sui-generis Law of Employment Contracts?' (2000) 16 *International Journal Comparative Labor Law & Industrial Relations* 309 (arguing that contract law, and in particular the law of relational contracts, can address employment contracts while adhering to its generic premises).

market for corporate control are acutely aware of the fact that an agreement of sale is only the first step on a hazardous journey toward consummation of the deal. Directors will have to bring the proposal before the shareholders and possibly also before regulators, either of whom might reject the deal, and in the meantime, there is a significant likelihood that competing offers will be tendered. Any of these eventualities may signal the breakdown of the original transaction. Thus, the costs that the original acquirer has incurred in identifying the target company, and in legal, accounting, and financing expenses, are in jeopardy, often for significant amounts of time.

In order to protect these reliance investments, acquirers typically bargain for and obtain deal-protective measures in merger agreements. These protective measures come in many forms, ranging from stock or asset lock-ups to simple termination fees or combinations of these and other measures,[84] but all share two primary goals. The first is to ensure that if the deal is never consummated, the acquirer will receive some compensation for his efforts leading up to the agreement. The second is to make the target less attractive to potential bidders, thus increasing the chances that the deal will in fact be consummated.[85] Because of the importance of deal

[84] For a detailed description of available protective provisions, see JC Coates IV & G Subramanian 'A Buy-Side Model of M&A Lockups: Theory and Evidence' (2000) 53 *Stanford Law Review* 307 (2000). Coates and Subramanian describe the background for the increasing prevalence of lockups in the following terms:

> M&A transactions involving public company targets face a (law-derived) risk of non-consummation that is unique (or at least rare) in three respects: (1) the law requires that shareholders of the target be given some opportunity to decide for themselves whether to accept or approve the transaction; (2) compliance with disclosure and other rules regulating the process of obtaining shareholder acceptance or approval entail delay, ranging from a minimum of thirty days up to six months in some situations; and (3) shareholders may decide not to accept or approve the transaction for any reason, including a third-party bid that emerges after agreements for the initial transaction are signed. In effect, an M&A agreement gives shareholders of a public company target the option to accept the deal, and does not effectively bind the target (or its shareholders) to the deal. Lockups have emerged as a second-best way for bidders to protect their expectancy interests in the transaction. Even if bidders cannot be sure to consummate a deal for a given target, they can at least get the consolation prize of a lockup payout…
>
> Three types of lockups can be distinguished. Stock lockups give the acquirer a call option on a specified number of shares of the target at a specified strike price. Asset lockups give the acquirer a call option on certain assets of the target at a specified price. Breakup fees give the acquirer a cash payment from the target if a specified event occurs. An acquirer's rights under each type of lockup are 'triggered' by specified events that vary but usually make completion of the original deal unlikely or impossible. More than one type of lockup may be included in a deal, and in mergers both parties may obtain one or more lockups ('cross' lockups).

Ibid, 310–14 (footnotes omitted).

[85] Deal protective measures always impose a cost on the target if it does not carry out the original transaction. Since the target (or its successful late bidder) must absorb this cost, the protective measure can make the target that much less attractive to other would-be bidders.

protective provisions for shareholders, their potential to distort the market for corporate control, and because of the potential for managerial self-interest, courts have applied enhanced scrutiny in passing on the validity of such provisions.[86]

Initially, scholarly treatment of the issue confined itself to corporate law questions, and in particular, whether directors of a target corporation had violated their fiduciary duties in agreeing to the lockup or breakup fee.[87] Recently, however, several scholars have focused on the interplay between contract and corporate law in evaluating lockups and breakup fees.[88] A number of important insights may be gleaned from such an investigation. First, the specialised context of transfer of control transactions may trigger a conflict between traditional concerns of contract law, for instance protecting party expectations, and traditional concerns of corporate law, for instance safeguarding shareholders' interests in the face of managerial discretion. Second, lockups and breakup fees are analogous to stipulated damages for breach of contract, and one way for courts to weigh the validity of such provisions is through a stipulated damages analysis: in other words, if the provision corresponds to a reasonable estimate of actual damages in case of breach, it should be upheld. And for this estimation to be carried out, a method for calculating the damages must be advanced.

Combining these two points generates a particularly interesting setting for thinking about the proper damages for the breach of a merger agreement. Attention to the context of the agreement shows, along the lines of three types of considerations alluded to above, that expectation damages are particularly inappropriate in this setting. Instead, fairness, social utility, and administrative concerns all point in the direction of compensation at a level lower than expectation damages, and close to reliance damages.

(a) Fairness — An inquiry into fairness as between parties to a merger agreement must account for both the acquirer's expectations regarding the agreement, and the interests of the target's shareholders, especially in light of the possible divergence between that interest and that of its management. The concern for fairness to the interests of the shareholders

[86] See eg *Paramount Communications Inc v QVC Network Inc* 637 A 2d 34 (Del 1994); *Mills Acquisition Co v MacMillan Inc* 559 A 2d 1261 (Del 1989); *Revlon Inc v MacAndrews & Forbes Holdings Inc* 506 A 2d 173 (Del 1986).

[87] See eg I Ayres 'Analyzing Stock Lock-Ups: Do Target Treasury Sales Foreclose or Facilitate Takeover Auctions' (1990) 90 *Columbia Law Review* 682.

[88] See eg CR Taylor 'When Good Mergers Go Bad: Controlling Corporate Managers Who Suffer a Change of Heart' (2003) 37 *University Richmond Law Review* 577; JF Sneirson 'Merger Agreement, Termination Fees, and the Contract-Corporate Tension' (2002) *Columbia Business Law Review* 573; PL Regan 'Great Expectations? A Contract Law Analysis for Preclusive Corporate Lock-Ups' (1999) 21 *Cardozo Law Review* 1; CR Taylor 'A Delicate Interplay: Resolving the Contract and Corporate Law Tension in Mergers' (1999) *74 Tulane Law Review* 561.

animates the fiduciary principles that courts have traditionally used to limit the effectiveness of merger agreements. The crucial problem in this setting, for the shareholders, is that lockups or breakup fees may have the effect of preventing them from realising the true value of their shares, by precluding higher bids. If the lockup is not enforced specifically, but the original acquirer is awarded expectation damages, the same injury is inflicted on the shareholders. Thus, the obvious starting point for the inquiry is that fairness to the shareholders requires some reduction of damages, if damages are to be assessed at all. But fiduciary principles and the public policy they represent are only one side of the fairness analysis. The more difficult question is how to fairly compensate the acquirer for his investments in the transaction when the deal breaks down.[89] Granting expectation damages, as explained above, is too destructive of the protection of shareholders that corporate law demands. But does this mean that no damages should be assessed whatever? Scholars who have treated the question recently repeatedly revert to reliance damages as the proper mediation of interests, and there is some support for the position in the courts as well. Two reasons from the perspective of fairness have been advanced for the proposition: first, the merger agreement is by its nature preliminary, in that both parties know that it is likely to generate additional bids, and that there are many hurdles to overcome before the agreement takes effect. When the parties realize in advance the preliminary and tentative nature of the agreement, only reimbursements of the costs of entering the tentative agreement seem like a fair result.[90] Secondly, it has been suggested that

> reliance may be the best standard from the perspective of compensation — that is, it better approximates the real consequences of breach to an initial bidder than an expectation measure would.[91]

(b) Social Utility — Analysis of the incentives provided by rules governing damages for breach of contracts has led to a widespread

[89] This problem is especially salient from a fairness perspective since the original acquirer has often created a market for the target — the initial attempt at a takeover is what initiates an auction situation, and in fact, some targets may even lure a potential acquirer as a 'stalking horse' in order to generate the highest bid possible.

[90] When courts are faced with a breach of an agreement to negotiate in good faith, or 'an agreement to agree' they have often come to the conclusion that reliance damages are appropriate. See *Venture Assocs Corp v Zenith Data Systems Corp* 96 F 3d 275 (7th Cir 1996). For the argument about why this might be the appropriate rule even from the perspective of the party held liable when it did not agree to a binding agreement, see R Craswell 'Offer, Acceptance, and Efficient Reliance' (1996) 48 *Stanford Law Review* 481.

[91] DA Skeel Jr 'A Reliance Damages Approach to Corporate Lockups' (1996) 90 *Northwestern University Law Review* 564, 596. For an extensive, detailed analysis of the fairness of lockups and breakup fees, including an endorsement of reliance damages as the proper tool of analysis when balancing shareholder interests and acquirers' contractual interests, see Regan, above n 88. Regan's treatment of the analogy to fairness arguments in related contexts of excuse, particularly when dealing with agents and trustees, is especially illuminating.

acceptance of two propositions: first, the rule of expectation damages will normally give promisors optimal incentives in deciding whether to breach; and second, reliance damages are better suited to inducing the optimal level of reliance expenditures by the promisee.[92] A decision regarding whether to adopt the expectation or reliance measure is then sometimes framed as a question about which incentives are most important to the kind of transaction in question: incentives regarding the breach/perform decision; or incentives regarding the precaution/reliance expenditure decision. While incentives for these two decisions are often considered to be in tension, in the case of merger agreements both sides of the equation point to the efficiency of reliance damages. The promisee (the acquirer) must make significant investments in identifying the target and in legal, accounting and financial fees, all in the context of an agreement that holds a significant likelihood of falling through before consummation. Guaranteeing his profits as if the probability of consummation is one hundred per cent will give him an incentive to over-rely, and will give him a disincentive to continue to search out better opportunities.[93] Moreover, if expectation damages are assessed according to the value of a foreclosing lockup, they will actually have the effect of precluding a more efficient transaction.[94] But what of the promisor's breach or perform decision? Generally, damages set below expectation damages are thought to allow for inefficient breach, because the promisor may elect to breach by engaging in an alternative contract when the promisee's valuation is higher than the price of the alternative. In the merger context however, such a decision is always the opening parry to an auction situation, in which the original acquirer can change his offer, all the way up to his actual valuation. Thus, the 'breach' will take place only if it is efficient, in the sense that the highest value user will win the auction.[95]

[92] Technically, optimal incentives for reliance expenditures require a damage measure that is invariant with regard to actual reliance. A reliance measure that aspires to efficient incentives to rely would then have to place a limit on reliance, precisely at the optimal level. Cooter, above n 32, 14–16. In fact, 'reliance' here functions as a proxy for damages lower than expectation damages. For a classification of remedies more accurate from the economic perspective, see Craswell, *Against Fuller*, above n 33, 157–61. According to that classification, everything I have to say about 'reliance' in the merger context actually refers to 'remedies below expectation'.

[93] On the other hand, eliminating all possibility of compensation for reliance losses will discourage the acquirer from undertaking any expenses, and thus foreclose the possibility of efficient transactions.

[94] '[I]f a termination fee is excessively high, it could artificially increase the price of breaching a merger agreement such that a target is no longer able to efficiently breach a merger agreement with one acquiror to pursue a better opportunity with another.' Sneirson, above n 88, 580–1.

[95] David Skeel has argued that reliance is the better measure of damages in the context of lockups, both from the perspective of compensation, and from the perspective of incentives. Regarding incentives, his analysis is worth quotation at length:

> The principal advantage of a reliance measure, as compared to expectation, is its effect on promisee (bidder, in the lockup context) incentives. Because it assures a

(c) Administrative Concerns — In many contexts, it is believed that expectation damages are easier for a court to determine than reliance damages. In fact, this administrative concern was one of the original reasons suggested by Fuller and Perdue for why courts adopt expectation damages as the normal rule.[96] However, the relative difficulty of proving expectation and reliance varies across fact situations. In the context of merger agreements, the performance or expectation interest is notoriously difficult to prove, while most elements of reliance are easily documented. This is especially true if reliance in this context is limited to out of pocket expenses, without including opportunity costs.[97]

(d) Summary — The foregoing is far from presenting a definitive case for preferring reliance damages to expectation damages for the breach of a merger agreement. But such a definitive case is not necessary for my argument. Instead, it is enough to show that the particular fact situation implicated in merger contracts tends to yield a special balance of the conflicting considerations that should underlie any examination of remedial

> bidder the benefit of the agreement at hand, expectation gives the bidder inadequate incentives to mitigate the consequences of breach by continuing to look for other opportunities ...
>
> [T]here is little reason to be concerned about 'excessive' promisor breach in the lockup context. The agreement between an initial bidder and a target is preliminary by its very nature. If a higher valuing bidder emerges, the parties arguably contemplate — and efficient breach theory would encourage — the target's sale to the higher bidder. While a reliance-based measure might appear to give target managers an incentive to shift to another bidder even in circumstances where the new bidder does not value the target more highly, this possibility is far less problematic with respect to corporate control contests than elsewhere. In contrast to other promisees, the lockup bidder does not simply disappear if another bidder emerges. The lockup bidder still can attempt to outbid the new bidder, and it is likely to succeed unless the new bidder places a higher value on the target — precisely the context where 'breach' would be appropriate.
>
> Focusing on a bidder's reliance damages thus can be seen as providing appropriate incentives to both the bidder and the target in the lockup context. Not only does the reliance measure give the bidder an incentive to anticipate and mitigate any losses should the deal with the target fall through, but the incentive that reliance gives a target to shift to another, higher valuing bidder, should one emerge, arguably can also be seen as desirable rather than problematic.

Skeel, above n 91, 596–8.

[96] 'The difficulties in proving reliance and subjecting it to pecuniary measurement are such that the business man knowing, or sensing, that these obstacles stood in the way of judicial relief would hesitate to rely on a promise in any case where the legal sanction was of significance to him. To encourage reliance we must therefore dispense with its proof.' Fuller & Perdue, above n 1, 62.

[97] Regan, above n 88, 110–19 (arguing for such a limited reliance award to wholly innocent bidders); Sneirson, above n 88, 623–4 (arguing that expectation should never be granted, and that reliance is better from administrative and efficiency perspectives). See also Skeel, above n 91, 596 (suggesting that opportunity costs in the merger context are in any case negligible); but see Coates & Subramanian, above n 84, 332, n77 (commenting on a case in which opportunity costs were taken into account by the court, and asserting that opportunity costs are significant, even if they do not represent alternative takeover opportunities).

rules. Along the three dimensions of justification, fairness as between the parties, social utility, and administrative concerns, there is at least a prima facie case that reliance damages are better suited to the fact situation than expectation damages. The goal of my argument has little to do with merger agreements per se, and much more to do with generalising the insight provided by the exercise. Such a generalisation would encourage us as contracts scholars to search out particular fact situations and engage in the analysis of the justifications for remedies particularly suited to those situations, rather than relying on a unified principle of remedies. If persuasive, the argument should lead to a shift of the research agenda, away from the search for a unified principle to govern all contract remedies, and toward the examination of particular fact situations and contract types as guides to remedial diversity.[98]

V CONCLUSION

The dominant understanding of remedies for breach of contract takes into account the multiplicity of interests that should be protected by remedial rules. In recent years, there has been a proliferation of theoretical models that attempt to give a new foundation to the law of remedies through a single, unified principle. The argument of this chapter has been that such models are unfounded. Unification theories fail to explain the practice of the courts in granting diverse remedies for breach, and more importantly, they fail to account adequately for justificatory considerations that are and ought to be an inherent part of remedial rules. Beyond the critique of unification theories, I have suggested that contract scholars ought to look to contract types as a guide to further theorisation of remedies. The analysis of contract types offers two distinct advantages over unification

[98] For an example of recent work whose methodological starting point is the fact situation rather than the overarching principle at stake, see MP Gergen 'The Law's Response to Exit and Loyalty in Contract Disputes' (chapter 4 in this collection). An analysis of contract types would advance Gergen's arguments, particularly in regard to *Texas Assoc of Counties County Government Risk Mgmt Pool v Matagorda County* 52 SW 3d 128 (Tex 2000), the case with which Prof Gergen's article opens. On general contract principles, this case looks particularly bad — the trial court, and the dissenting opinion (in the Supreme Court), see it as quite an easy quasi-contracts case, in which someone with no obligation pays another party's debt at that party's request, and thus should have restitution. What makes the majority opinion reasonable is the fact that we are in an insurance situation, and the rule advanced by the dissent might place insurers in a position to manipulate insureds, essentially because of cash-flow issues and risk aversion, precisely the reasons they secured insurance in the first place. Put simply, this case looks bad as a piece of *general contract law* (or general quasi-contract, or unjust enrichment law); however, it begins to look more plausible as a piece of *insurance law*. Grasping for general contract law in this situation is to my mind (and to that of the Texas Supreme Court) too great a sacrifice to the goddess of conceptual neatness, or 'the unity of contract law'.

theory. First, it gives us a better tool for analysing and understanding the varying results of cases involving contract breaches and the remedies they entail. Second, contract types offer a research agenda that would never divorce itself from the underlying considerations that ought to govern the choice of rules governing contract breach: fairness between the parties; social utility; and administrative concerns. The identification and analysis of particular contract types would liberate scholars from the often sterile work of justifying particularised rules as 'exceptions' and encourage a reasoned examination of a variety of rules appropriate to the wide, but far from limitless, variety of contractual contexts.

3

Renegotiation, 'Efficient Breach' and Adjustment: The Choice of Remedy for Breach of Contract as a Choice of a Contract-Modification Theory

BARAK MEDINA*

I INTRODUCTION

A FUNDAMENTAL QUESTION in the law of contract is what should be the remedy for breach of contract. Clearly, the choice of remedy must be based on an assessment of its purpose. Contrary to how it may appear at first glance, the answer to this question is not self-evident. The aim of this chapter is to explore three distinct accounts of the purpose of remedies for breach of contract. Each reflects a distinct view of the contract's 'completeness' and results in a different set of considerations on which the choice of remedy should be based.

The choice of remedy is essentially a choice of theory about the effect of a change of circumstances which makes the contract 'inefficient'. Is this prospect left, by definition, to an *ex-post renegotiation*, or is it accounted for *ex-ante*, by either enabling each party unilaterally to purchase her way out of the contract or by setting a mechanism of compelled adjustment of the contractual provisions? More generally, the debate about the choice of remedies for breach can (and should) be reframed as a debate about the preferred 'fundamental contract law theory', rather than a debate about the implication of specific considerations and their relevancy.

Consider, first, what seems to be the obvious purpose of remedies — 'preserving' the contractual right, ie deterring violations and correcting

*Joseph H and Belle R Braun Senior Lecturer in Law, Faculty of Law, Hebrew University of Jerusalem. I am grateful to Ofer Grosskopf, Guy Mundlak, and participants in the conference on 'Remedies for Breach of Contract' (Tel-Aviv University, 2002), for their thoughtful comments and suggestions; and to Susan Kennedy for superb editorial work. I am indebted to Nili Cohen for her encouragement and support.

their unjust consequences. According to this account, the choice of remedy should be based on considerations, such as what is the conceptual content of the contractual right (ie are monetary damages a sufficient relief?), and what is the scope of the parties' autonomy (ie does a remedy of specific performance infringe the autonomy of the promisor?). However, such an account is not self-evident.

One plausible alternative is offered by the so-called 'economic approach'. It is based on Justice Holmes' famous realistic account of the remedy of expectation damages as a remedy which 'leaves [the promisor] free to break his contract if he chooses', such that 'the duty to keep a contract... means a prediction that you must pay damages if you do not keep it, and nothing else'.[1] According to this account (which reflects Holmes' broader approach of looking at the law 'as a bad man, who cares only for the material consequences'[2]), applying the expectation damages measure is equivalent to assigning the promisor the right to unilaterally 'purchase [her] way out of the contract'[3]. That is, the 'remedy' does not necessarily reflect a judicial response to correct a wrong (a 'breach' of contract); instead, it forms the legitimate way out of the contract. In other words, the remedy sets an 'exit rule'. Thus, under this account, the relevant choice is between a remedy which assigns the promisor the right to unilaterally purchase her way out of the contract (expectation damages) and one which subjects it to the promisee's consent (specific performance).

The distinction between these two approaches (which can be termed the 'traditional' and the 'economic' accounts, respectively) to the purpose of remedies emerges from their different perspectives about the 'completeness' of the contract. When a contract is formed, the parties typically face the risk that a change in the surrounding circumstances would make their contract 'inefficient' (that is, the aggregate value of breach would exceed that of performance). According to the traditional account, the choice of remedy is made irrespective of this prospect. It is based on the idea that the contractual provisions are *all-inclusive*, such that they regulate the parties' rights and duties in every possible state of the world. The prospect that the contract becomes inefficient is left to an *ex-post renegotiation*, if needed (unless otherwise explicitly provided in the contract or if specific contract law doctrines apply). As a result, the remedy is constructed, exclusively, as a *safeguard* of the contractual rights, and a unilateral exit is excluded. In contrast, the economic account, also known as the 'efficient breach theory', is founded on the premise that the parties may

[1] Justice OW Holmes 'The Path of the Law' (1897) 10 *Harvard Law Review* 457, 462.
[2] *Ibid*, 459.
[3] See eg RE Barnett 'Contract Remedies and Inalienable Rights' (1986) 4 *Social Philosophy and Policy* 179, 183: '[Under expectation damages remedy] the seller has an option to deliver or pay damages ...'.

well prefer, in some contexts, to avoid such an all-inclusive contract. In these cases, the remedy *complements* the contract, by setting, *ex-ante*, an *escape valve* out of the contract, based on the prospect of 'efficient breach'. According to this account, the choice of remedy is a result of a choice between an exit mechanism which is based on *ex-post* renegotiation (specific performance), and a unilateral exit mechanism (expectation damages).

Next, consider a third alternative, which is founded on the same premise as the economic approach — the parties' possible willingness to form an incomplete contract. However, this account focuses on the possibility that the parties prefer that their contract is completed not by enabling a unilateral exit, but by a compelled adjustment of the contract by a third party, eg the court. The court is delegated, so it is presumed, with the authority to adjust the explicit contractual provisions, as required in order to accomplish the 'purpose of the contract'. According to such an account, remedies for breach serve, primarily, as a 'modification mechanism'. This approach can explain (and justify) the practice of a compelled modification of the contract which results quite often when a remedy is applied (eg under UCC §2-716(2), 'the decree for specific performance may include such…relief as the court may deem just'). As a result, according to this account the choice of remedy is based, essentially, on considerations such as what remedy better fits as an 'adjustment mechanism'.

The premise of the contract as incomplete may therefore support two different approaches to the purpose of remedies. In order to explore the choice between these two accounts, a distinction should be made between two possible reasons for the contract's incompleteness — transaction costs and bounded rationality. In the case of the former, the parties are aware of the prospect of a possible change in the relevant circumstances which would make the contract 'inefficient', but are unable (at least not at reasonable cost) explicitly to provide in the contract all the relevant contingencies to account for this prospect. The law of remedies is aimed at completing the contract by dealing with the prospect of 'inefficient contract'. Note, however, that as far as exit rules are concerned, transaction costs cannot explain the contract incompleteness. Generally speaking, transaction costs do not constrain the parties from explicitly providing what they perceive as the optimal exit rule, since, presumably, the costs of drafting such a mechanism are trivial. In contrast, transaction costs may obstruct the parties from explicitly providing modification mechanisms, since drafting such provisions entails, among other things, an explicit definition of the purpose of the contract, which is typically ambiguous. As a result, if the reason for the contract's incompleteness is transaction costs constraints, the law's default rules regarding remedies for breach should be set based on the premise that remedies provide modification mechanisms. Parties who are interested in setting mere 'exit rules' should be able to contract around the default remedy that the law sets. Alternatively, the contract may be incomplete due to the parties' 'bounded rationality'. In this case, the parties are unaware, at the stage of the contract formation, of the prospect of a possible change of circumstances that would make the contract inefficient. Here, both alternatives — that is, remedies as exit rules and remedies as modification mechanisms — are plausible. The choice must be based on an assessment of the court's capability properly to adjust the contract.

Therefore, the fundamental choice is between three main alternatives: A view of the contract as all-inclusive, such that gaps are filled only through *ex-post* renegotiation; recognising that the contract is incomplete, and filling the gaps through exit-mechanism; and a perception of the contract as inherently incomplete, based on the prospect of compelled modification whenever needed. The choice of each of these alternatives results in a specific set of relevant considerations, according to which the choice of a specific remedy should be made.

The rest of the chapter is organised as follows: Section 2 briefly summarises the traditional account, accentuating its underlying premise of the contract as all-inclusive. Section 3 contrasts this account with the economic one, by focusing on the willingness of the former approach to acknowledge the parties' possible interest in forming an incomplete contract. Section 4 exposes the shared premise of Formalism of these two accounts. Section 5 portrays the third possible account, which is based on the premise of remedies as 'intra-contractual'. Section 6 discusses the choice between the three accounts and distinguishes between the two possible reasons for the contract's incompleteness. Section 7 is the conclusion.

II THE TRADITIONAL ACCOUNT: REMEDIES AS 'SAFEGUARDS'

A remedy for breach of contract is conventionally perceived as having two main purposes. First, to enforce the performance of contractual obligations, either directly through judicial order, or indirectly by compelling the breaching party to compensate the injured party, and thus inducing her, *ex-ante,* to fulfil her promise; and second, to compensate the injured party for the loss of her contractual right. Thus, under this traditional account, the purpose of setting a remedy for breach of contract is to 'preserve' the contractual right.

Given this definition of its purpose, the choice of remedy is based on considerations such as what is the conceptual content of the contractual right (ie are monetary damages a sufficient relief?), and what is the scope of the parties' autonomy (ie does a remedy of specific performance infringe the autonomy of the promisor?). According to one view, the promisee is fully protected if he is compensated according to the monetary value of his 'expectation interest', and thus, a remedy of expectation damages is a sufficient relief.[4] An alternative view challenges this premise, by promoting the view that the contractual right entrusts its holder with the right that the 'promise' will be fulfilled.[5] As a result, an appropriate remedy is one that secures the promisee's 'domain of autonomy', that is, primarily, specific performance, whereas the remedy of expectation damages is considered an inadequate protection of the right[6].

It is beyond the scope of this chapter to assess these competing approaches and to offer a rigid recommendation of the appropriate remedy, given the underlying account of the role of the remedy as safeguard. Clearly, the choice between the competing approaches within this account — that is, defining the essence of the contractual right — is not self-evident,[7] and must rest on some pre-defined conceptions.[8] Actually, the two prominent contract law theories — corrective justice (Fuller and Perdue[9]) and the morality of keeping promises (Fried[10]) — fail to establish persuasive support of either of these approaches, and thus cannot justify

[4] See eg Holmes, above n 1, 462.

[5] See eg Barnet, above n 3, 183: 'Persons with common sense — that is, those who have not taken a first-year contracts class (or been counseled by a lawyer who has) — would naturally assume... that when a good is purchased the purchaser obtains a right to the good. They would not assume that the seller has an *option* to deliver or pay damages ...'; D Friedmann: 'The Performance Interest in Contract Damages' (1995) 111 *Law Quarterly Review* 628, 632: '[A] person who made a payment in order to get a house, ... will be greatly surprised to learn that upon contracting to purchase a house, he acquired an interest in getting his payment back'; C Fried *Contract as Promise: A Theory of Contractual Obligation* (Harvard University Press, Cambridge Massachusetts, 1981.) 17–21; J Finnis *Natural Law and Natural Rights* (Clarendon Press, Oxford, 1980.) 320–5.

[6] JL Coleman and J Kraus 'Rethinking the Theory of Legal Rights' (1986) 95 *Yale Law Journal* 1335, 1339: '[P]art of what it means to have a (legal) right to a resource is to have a secured domain of autonomy. ... If rights entail or secure liberties, then it is hard to see how liability rules [ie the remedy of expectation damages] protect them. ... It is surely odd to claim that an individual's right is protected when another is permitted to force a transfer at a price set by third parties. Isn't the very idea of a forced transfer contrary to the autonomy or liberty thought constitutive of rights?' For such an approach see R Nozick *Anarchy, State, and Utopia* (Basil Blackwell, Oxford, 1974.) 57–75 (compensating for damages cannot justify the violation of the right); D Friedmann 'The Efficient Breach Fallacy' (1989) 18 *Journal Legal Studies* 1.

[7] See eg R Craswell 'Contract Law, Default Rules, and the Philosophy of Promising' (1989) 88 *Michigan Law Review* 489; AT Kronman 'A New Champion for the Will Theory' (1981) 91 *Yale Law Journal* 404, 412; H Dagan 'Restitutionary Damages for Breach of Contract: An Exercise in Private Law Theory' (2000) 1 *Theoretical Inquiries in Law* 115, 118–25.

[8] Coleman and Kraus, above n 6, 1369: 'Sometimes one's right requires others to seek agreement as a condition of transfer; other times not. ... [T]he choice ... depends on the purpose for which institutions are designed; and so whether rights provide autonomy or are designed purely to guarantee a level of welfare is a contingent feature of them, resolved not by appealing to *meanings* but by appeal to *justifications*'; J Raz *The Morality of Freedom* (Clarendon Press, Oxford, 1986.) 165–92; J Waldron 'Criticizing the Economic Analysis of Law' (1990) 99 *Yale Law Journal* 1441; H Dagan *Unjust Enrichment: A Study of Private Law and Public Values* (Cambridge University Press, Cambridge, 1997.) 69–70, 102–5.

[9] LL Fuller and WR Perdue 'The Reliance Interest in Contract Damages' (1936) 46 *Yale Law Journal* 52. A generalisation of this approach is the claim the contract is being absorbed into torts. See G Gilmore *The Death of Contract* (Ohio State University Press, Columbus, 1974); P Atiyah *Essays on Contract* (Clarendon Press, Oxford, 1990).

[10] Fried, above n 5.

any particular remedy for breach. Fried's theory sheds no light on which remedy is desirable, while Fuller and Perdue do not explain why the appropriate baseline for exercising corrective justice is the promisee's position prior to his reliance on the promise, and not his position after the promise was made.[11] In addition, whereas under the view that the contractual right entrusts the promisee with a 'secured domain of autonomy' the appropriate measure is clearly specific performance, the alternative view does not yield a definitive conclusion.[12]

For the purpose of the current analysis, the important aspect of the traditional approach is its implicit presumption of the contract's 'completeness'. As stated, for instance, by Epstein, 'only an infinitesimal fraction of contingencies (by probability of occurrence) are not covered [by the contract]'.[13] The premise that the purpose of the contract is to 'preserve' the contractual rights means that remedies are perceived as 'extra-contractual'. A distinction is made between the stage of the contract's interpretation — that is, of defining the content of the contractual rights and duties, and thus of a breach — and the stage of applying the remedy. Remedies are not considered a possible mechanism for filling 'gaps' in the contract. Remedies are perceived as vehicles for enforcing a given content of the contract and not as a means of shaping it. More specifically, the prospect of a possible change of circumstances, which would make the contract 'inefficient', is left to either specific contract law doctrines (such as mistake, impossibility, impracticability and frustration of the purpose of the contract), or *ex-post* renegotiation.[14] In this sense, the contract (with or without the assistance of specific contract law doctrines) is presumed to be all-inclusive, such that remedies do not serve as gap fillers.

III THE ECONOMIC ACCOUNT: REMEDIES AS 'EXIT RULES'

Following the seminal work of Calabresi and Melamed[15] (which dealt with remedies in general), the economic account (or the 'efficient breach

[11] See eg Craswell, above n 7; R Craswell 'Against Fuller and Perdue' (2000) 67 *University Chicago Law Review* 99; R Craswell 'How We Got This Way: Further Thoughts on Fuller and Perdue' Issues in Legal Scholarship, Symposium: Fuller and Perdue (2001): Article 2 <http://www.bepress.com/ils/iss1/art2>.

[12] See eg AT Kronman 'Specific Performance' (1978) 45 *University Chicago Law Review* 351; A Schwartz 'The Case for Specific Performance' (1979) 89 *Yale Law Journal* 271.

[13] RA Epstein 'Confusion about Custom: Disentangling Informal Customs from Standard Contractual Provisions' (1999) 66 *University Chicago Law Review* 821, 828.

[14] In addition, the parties may rely on unilateral adjustments, based on norms of their relationship, their industry or their social environment. See RE Scott 'Conflict and Cooperation in Long-Term Contracts' (1987) 75 *California Law Review* 2005; RE Scott 'A Relational Theory of Default Rules for Commercial Contracts' (1990) 19 *Journal Legal Studies* 597; D Charny 'Nonlegal Sanctions in Commercial Transactions' (1990) 104 *Harvard Law Review* 373.

[15] G Calabresi and DA Melamed 'Property Rules, Liability Rules, and Inalienability: One View of the Cathedral' (1972) 85 *Harvard Law Review* 1089.

theory') is based on the premise that remedies are aimed at setting 'exit' (or 'transaction') rules. These rules set the terms in which legal entitlements can legitimately be transferred. In the context of remedies for breach of contract, the remedy sets the terms in which the contract can be (practically, even if not formally) rescinded, that is, the terms in which the promisor can 'acquire' the promisee's contractual right, and thus be exempt from the duty to fulfil her promise. The distinction is between two main types of rules. The first is a so-called 'property rule', which entails that the promisor must obtain the promisee's actual consent in order to nullify the contract. Such an exit rule results from a remedy which 'preserves' the contractual right, by either enforcing the promisor to fulfil her contractual obligation (specific performance) or allowing the promisee to recover the resultant profits that the promisor has gained as a result of breaching her contractual obligation (a disgorgement remedy[16]). The alternative, a so-called 'liability rule', enables the promisor unilaterally to withdraw from the contract, subject to compensating the promisee for the monetary value of the right (his expectation interest). The remedy of expectation damages yields, so it is argued, such an exit rule.

The assessment of the alternative exit rules according to the economic account is based on both *ex-post* and *ex-ante* considerations. From an *ex-post* perspective, the analysis focuses on assessing what remedy is better suited to promoting the goal of ensuring the efficient distribution of entitlements. In the current context, the goal is to induce a breach if, and only if, the breach is 'efficient', that is, whenever the cost of performance (the value of the right to the promisor) exceeds its value to the promisee.[17] The tradeoff is between saving the 'transaction costs' incurred in order to reach an agreement to rescind the contract (including the risk of a failure to reach such an agreement), an aim that is promoted by a 'liability rule' (expectation damages), and avoiding the 'litigation costs' incurred if unilateral withdrawal is permitted, in order to assess the monetary value of the right to its holder (including the risk of inaccuracy), a goal which is induced through a 'property rule' (eg specific performance).

In addition, from an *ex-ante* perspective, the goal is to induce both parties to act such that the value of the right is maximised, referring mainly

[16] Such a remedy is available in several jurisdictions. See eg *A-G v Blake* [2001] 1 AC 268. Cf *Surrey County Council v Bredero Homes* [1993] 1 WLR 1361. For an economic analysis of this remedy see eg MC Chetwin and DK Round 'Breach of Contract and the New Remedy of Account of Profits' (2002) 38 *Abacus* 406; Dagan, above n 7; SW DeLong 'The Efficiency of a Disgorgement as a Remedy for the Breach of Contract' (1989) 22 *Indiana Law Review* 737.

[17] The term 'efficient breach' was first coined in CJ Goetz and RE Scott 'Liquidated Damages, Penalties, and the Just Compensation Principle: Some Notes on an Enforcement Model and a Theory of Efficient Breach' (1977) 77 *Columbia Law Review* 554. Earlier economic analysis of the choice of remedies for a breach of contract includes JH Barton 'The Economic Basis of Damages for Breach of Contract' (1972) 1 *Journal Legal Studies* 277; and RL Birmingham 'Breach of Contract, Damage Measures, and Economic Efficiency' (1970) 24 *Rutgers Law Review* 273.

to reliance expenditures. The exit rule allocates the contract's costs and benefits in case of an 'efficient breach'. Under specific performance, the promisor's obligation to acquire the promisee's consent vests the promisee with the opportunity to extract at least part of the benefits (or the saved-losses) that the promisor expects to achieve by rescinding the contract; while under expectation damages, the promisor is not required to share this value with the promisee. As a result, only the latter measure induces optimal reliance investment by the promisor.[18] The choice of the optimal remedy — that is, of the remedy that is expected to result in the highest expected value of the contractual right — depends on numerous additional considerations.[19] Among these are the effect of the remedy on the promisee's incentives to invest in reliance,[20] and its effect on the promisee's incentives to reveal the value of his expectation interest, in cases of asymmetric information.[21]

As with the traditional account, the economic analysis does not firmly support any particular remedy, for both theoretical and practical reasons. First, it is based on the premise that the contractual right reflects an assignment of mere monetary value.[22] Based on this premise a remedy

[18] See R Craswell 'Contract Remedies, Renegotiation, and the Theory of Efficient Breach' (1988) 61 *Southern California Law Review* 629; PA Diamond and E Maskin 'An Equilibrium Analysis of Search and Breach of Contract, I: Steady States' (1979) 10 *Bell Journal Economics* 282; PA Diamond and E Maskin 'An Equilibrium Analysis of Search and Breach of Contract, II: A Non-Steady State Example' (1981) 25 *Journal Economic Theory* 165; DT Mortensen 'Property Rights and Efficiency in Mating, Racing, and Related Games' (1982) 72 *American Economic Review* 968. See also, in a more general context, LA Bebchuck 'Property Rights and Liability Rules: The Ex Ante View of the Cathedral' (2001) 100 *Michigan Law Review* 601.

[19] For a specification of the various considerations and a review of the relevant literature see EA Posner 'Economic Analysis of Contract Law after Three Decades: Success or Failure? (2003) 112 *Yale Law Journal* 829.

[20] R Cooter 'Unity in Tort, Contract and Property: The Model of Precaution' (1985) 73 *California Law Review* 1; S Shavell 'The Design of Contracts and Remedies for Breach' (1984) 99 *Quarterly Journal Economics* 121; RA Posner *Economic Analysis of Law* 5th edn (Aspen Law & Business, New York, 1998) 130–40; TJ Muris 'Comment: The Costs of Freely Granting Specific Performance' [1982] *Duke Law Journal* 1053; W Bishop 'The Choice of Remedy for Breach of Contract' (1985) 14 *Journal Legal Studies* 299.

[21] See I Ayres and R Gertner 'Filling Gaps in Incomplete Contracts: An Economic Theory of Default Rules' (1989) 99 *Yale Law Journal* 87; I Ayres and R Gertner 'Strategic Contractual Inefficiency and the Optimal Choice of Legal Rules' (1992) 101 *Yale Law Journal* 729; JS Johnston 'Strategic Bargaining and the Economic Theory of Contract Default Rules' (1990) *100 Yale Law Journal* 615; LA Bebchuck and S Shavell 'Information and the Scope of Liability for the Breach of Contract' (1991) 7 *Journal Law, Economics and Organization* 284; EA Posner 'Contract Remedies: Foreseeability, Precaution, Causation, and Mitigation' in *Encyclopedia of Law and Economics* (Edward Elgar and University of Ghent, 1998); BE Adler 'The Questionable Ascent of Hadley v Baxendale' (1999) 51 *Stanford Law Review* 1547.

[22] This premise reflects the general conjecture in the economic analysis, that utility — and thus the entitlement, of which the utility is derived — is resembled by its monetary value. For instance, it is argued that 'property rule' is inefficient, since it protects idiosyncratic utility: 'Society does sometimes literally profit when defendants 'harm' idiosyncrasies for the sake of personal gain ... because of the community gain in wealth that derives from the 'realizing' of defendant's conversion of plaintiff's idiosyncratic values into capital assets, usable or

which sets a liability-like exit rule can be considered sufficient relief in case of a breach of contract. As discussed above, the plausibility of this premise is not self-evident.[23] In addition, a meticulous analysis of the relevant considerations according to the economic account is, inherently, indeterminate. For instance, the *ex-post* perspective, which focuses on the tradeoff between saving 'transaction costs' and avoiding 'litigation costs', may well result in support of specific performance,[24] as well as in preferring expectation damages.[25] Ultimately, the prediction is subject to an enormous amount of information, which is practically unachievable.[26] This indeterminacy may explain the failure of the economic account to gain substantial influence on positive law.[27]

My main focus is, however, on the underlying theory of each account, that is, its choices regarding the essence of the act of contract formation and about the capability of contract law doctrines. As mentioned above, the distinctive characteristic of the economic approach is its emphasis on the possible role of remedies as gap fillers. It is characterised by three underlying premises. First, the contract is assumed to be incomplete in the 'economic' sense, that is, its explicit provisions cannot *optimally* account for all the possible contingencies.[28] As a result, *ex-post* adjustments of the contract are inevitable in order to maximise the aggregate value that the parties derive from the contract. This prospect is a result of economic approach's accentuation of the likelihood of 'transaction costs'

saleable by the defendant ...': J Standen 'The Fallacy of Full Compensation' (1995) 73 *Washington University Law Quarterly* 145, 217.

[23] See eg Coleman and Kraus, above n 6.

[24] This view is based on an assessment that the 'transaction costs' that parties to a contract face if they wish to rescind the inefficient contract are not expected to be prohibitively high. See eg Schwartz, above n 12; TS Ulen 'The Efficiency of Specific Performance: Toward a Unified Theory of Contract Remedies' (1984) 83 *Michigan Law Review* 341, 369–71; Friedmann, above n 6. On the assessment of 'transaction costs' in general, as a possible obstacle to achieve a Pareto improvement see eg R Cooter 'The Cost of Coase' (1982) 11 *Journal Legal Studies* 1, 14–24; E Hoffman and ML Spitzer 'The Coase Theorem: Some Experimental Tests' (1982) 2 *Journal Law & Economics* 73; RH Coase 'Notes on the Problem of Social Cost' in *The Firm, The Market and the Law* (The University of Chicago Press, Chicago and London,1988) 157, 159–63; D Lewinsohn-Zamir 'The Choice between Property Rules and Liability Rules Revisited: Critical Observations from Behavioral Studies' (2001) 80 *Texas Law Review* 219.

[25] See eg Shavell, above n 20; Posner, above n 20.

[26] See Posner, above n 19.

[27] For a research that shows only marginal influence of economic analysis on American contract law see Posner, above n 19.

[28] A contract is incomplete in the economic sense when its provisions do not maximize the value the parties derive from it given any possible contingency. In other words, an incomplete contract is not tailored to insure that each party makes the optimal decision in each state of the world. This sense is distinguished from the formal meaning of incompleteness. See eg Ayres and Gertner (1989), above n 21, 92 (fn 29): '[A] contract may fail to specify the parties' duties for specific future contingencies [formal incompleteness]. ... A contract may also be incomplete in that it is insensitive to relevant future contingencies [economic incompleteness]' (present author's additions).

at the stage of contract formation, which are assumed to obstruct the parties from explicitly providing for every possible state of the world (or, at least, make such a provision inefficient). The parties are thus assumed to choose to form an incomplete contract. One major reason is verifiability. Arguably, contracting parties will not condition their legal obligations on nonverifiable factors, due to obstacles to enforcing them in court.[29] Another reason for contract incompleteness is information asymmetry. The better-informed party might prefer to refrain from proposing a complete contract, since she assumes that such a proposal would communicate 'private information' to the other party and would reduce her share in the contractual surplus.[30]

Second, whereas the prospect of incomplete contract is acknowledged as inescapable, the availability and the efficacy of the two 'conventional' paths of filling gaps *ex-post* — renegotiation and the application of contract law doctrines — are questioned. The economic approach reflects a fundamental mistrust in the capability of a third party, such as the court, directly to fill the gaps in the contract. In addition, as mentioned above, at the stage of performance, transaction costs are expected to impede an agreement to adjust the contract's provisions even if the contract becomes inefficient[31]. The economic approach does not exclude the possibility that these mechanisms may suffice. However, it underscores the possibility of completing the contract through a third alternative — furnishing each party with the right (or at least the practical power) unilaterally to purchase her way out of the contract. The efficacy of this path should be compared to that of its alternatives on either a case-by-case or on a more general basis. Whenever a liability-like exit rule is found to be better, it should be preferred as a gap-filling mechanism.

[29] A contract which is as complete as possible given the verification constraints is sometimes labeled as 'functionally complete'. See K Eggleston, EA Posner, and R Zeckhauser 'The Design and Interpretation of Contracts: Why Complexity Matters' (2000) 95 *Northwestern Univestiy Law Review* 91, 101. The verifiability of a fact is a result of cost-benefit analysis: A fact is verifiable if the cost of proving it to third party is less than the benefit of making this fact relevant in the contract. See eg A Schwartz 'Relational Contracts and the Courts: An Analysis of Incomplete Contracts and Judicial Strategies' (1992) 21 *Journal Legal Studies* 271. See also GG Triantis 'The Efficiency of Vague Contract Terms' (UVA Law and Economics Research Paper No 02–7, May 2002, Available from the SSRN Electronic Paper Collection); BD Bernheim and MD Whinston 'Incomplete Contracts and Strategic Ambiguity' (1998) 88 *American Economic Review* 902.

[30] See eg Johnston, above n 21; F Allen and D Gale 'Measurement Distortion and Missing Contingencies in Optimal Contracts' (1992) 2 *Economic Theory* 1; KE Spier 'Incomplete Contracts and Signaling' (1992) 23 *Rand Journal Economics* 432.

[31] See above n 24. The costs of *ex-post* renegotiations are affected by the form of the contract the parties choose *ex-ante*. See A Schwartz and J Watson 'The Law and Economics of Costly Contracting' (2004) 20 *Journal Law Economics & Organisations* 1; L Anderlini and L Felli 'Costly Bargaining and Renegotiation' 69 *Econometrica* 377 (2001); L Anderlini and L Felli 'Incomplete Contracts and Complexity Costs' 46 *Theory and Decision* 23 (1999).

The third premise of the 'economic' approach is that such exit rule can be provided not only through express contractual provision (which assigns a party the option of purchasing her way out of the contract), but also through the law of remedies. Applying the remedy of expectation damages is perceived as a choice of a liability-like exit rule. As mentioned above, this approach is based on a so-called 'realistic' view, which looks at legal rules as merely setting the price of the activities which they regulate, that is, a view which focuses exclusively on the material consequences of legal rules and not on their 'expressive' role.[32] In the current context, this view disregards the classification of the promisor's act of purchasing her way out of the contract as a 'breach' of the contract (which implies committing wrong), and considers only the material consequences of applying the remedy — the obligation to pay damages.

Thus, the economic approach entails two distinct roles of the law of remedies as 'gap filler'. The remedy completes the contract in the economic sense, by setting the appropriate exit rule, in order to deal optimally both *ex-ante* and *ex-post* with the prospect that the contract would become inefficient; and the law of remedies completes the contract by supplying the parties with the optimal exit rule.

IV THE SHARED PREMISE OF FORMALISM OF THE TRADITIONAL AND THE ECONOMIC ACCOUNTS: REMEDIES AS EXTRA-CONTRACTUAL

Over the last three decades, the notion of remedies as exit rules in general and the 'efficient breach' theory in particular, has drawn extensive academic discourse. The debate reflects opposing views regarding fundamental aspects of the law of contract. However, both sides of the debate share a common premise. Remedies for breach of contract are considered, essentially, to be extra-contractual. It is this shared premise that distinguishes these two accounts from the third one, explored below, of remedies as a modification mechanism.

Remedies are considered extra-contractual in two main aspects. One aspect, which is not explored here, is the division of the process of applying a remedy for breach into two distinct phases: The first, the 'intra-contractual' one, focuses on setting the *content* of the relevant contractual right. The second phase, the 'extra-contractual', focuses on the appropriate measure of 'preserving' the contractual right which was set in the first

[32] As mentioned above, this view can be traced back to Holmes, above n 1. For a discussion of this view see eg RP Malloy *Law and Economics — A Comparative Approach to Theory and Practice* (West Publishing Co. St. Paul Minnesota, 1990.); R Cooter 'Expressive Law and Economics' (1998) 27 *Journal Legal Studies* 585; LA Kornhauser 'The Normativity of Law' (1999) 1 *American Law & Economics Review* 3; U Gneezy and A Rustichini 'A Fine is a Price' (2000) 29 *Journal Legal Studies* 1.

phase. The possible effect of the contract's content on the choice of remedies is limited to the assessment of the essence of the contractual right — does it furnish the promisee with a secure domain of autonomy or with an entitlement to the mere monetary value of his expectation interest? In some cases, general distinctions are made, such as between contracts for sale and production contracts;[33] or between unique and market goods.[34] However, as a general rule, the choice of remedy is made only subsequent to and irrespective of the process of contract interpretation.

The other aspect of the premise of remedies as extra-contractual is the presumption that the result of intra-contractual assessment is binary: the contractual right was either fulfilled or breached. This presumption reflects a so-called 'formalistic' account. A formalistic account is characterised by restricting the role of the judiciary and enhancing that of the parties in constructing the content of the agreement. It is a conjecture which underscores the parties' *ex-ante* explicit meeting of the minds. The purpose of contract law is limited, arguably, to the enforcement of the parties' agreement. The parties need the assistance of the law in enforcing their contractual obligations, in order to induce reliance, which enhances both parties' welfare.[35] However, the law is not aimed at assisting them in forming the contract. The parties are delegated with the autonomy (as well as the onus) to draft their contract. It is assumed that the explicit rights and obligations that the parties choose best serve the purposes they were aiming at. As a result, the language of the contract, that is, the 'plain meaning' of its words, is taken seriously. The court applies clear and simple interpretive rules.[36] The parties' goal in forming the contract is assumed to be an apportioning of the relevant risks. Each party is supposed to deal on its own with the risks assigned to her, such that further co-operation is not anticipated.

As a result, according to the formalistic account, the sole role of the judiciary is to identify the content of the rights and obligations set by the parties. The court is not expected to adjust the content of the contract, based neither on 'immanent commercial practice' (as argued by anti-formalists, such as Llewellyn[37]) nor the purpose of the contract. According

[33] See eg Shavell, above n 20; Friedmann, above n 6.

[34] See eg Kronman, above n 12.

[35] See eg CJ Goetz and RE Scott 'Enforcing Promises: An Examination of the Basis of Contract' (1980) 89 *Yale Law Journal* 1261.

[36] See RE Scott 'The Rise and Fall of Article 2' (2002) 63 *Louisiana Law Review* 1 (contracting parties prefer bright-line legal rules over vague ones). See also L Bernstein 'Merchant Law in a Merchant Court: Rethinking the Code's Search for Immanent Business Norms' 144 *University of Pennsylvania Law Review* 1765 (1996) (parties that deal regularly in a given market prefer their disputes to be governed by specialized, private organizations, in large part because these institutions use more formalistic rules and procedures). However, as argued by Charny 'these institutional structures did not emerge or thrive because of efficiency advantages alone; they may have received powerful impetus from a drive towards power by some traders': D Charny 'The New Formalism in Contract' (1999) 66 *University Chicago Law Review* 842, 843.

[37] See below n 45.

to this view, commercial parties prefer to be governed under separate regimes of bright-line legal rules and flexible relational norms that are not legally enforceable.[38] The contractual right is perceived as a well-defined entitlement. Its content is strictly delineated at the stage of contract formation, such that it is not affected by a subsequent change of circumstances. Given the premise that the law's role is restricted to enforcing the parties' agreement, a firm enforcement of the contract's specified provisions, including the remedies that the parties have set, is the preferable strategy.[39] Formalism does not rule out the possibility that a substantial change in the relevant circumstances may be effective (through doctrines such as impossibility and impracticability), but even in those rare cases, the result is an expiration of the contract and not a modification or adjustment of its content. Thus, the binary outcome is strictly observed, such that remedies are regarded as 'extra-contractual'.

The formalism which is reflected by the traditional account is, basically, a result of an 'ideological' choice in the ideal of 'libertarianism', which accentuates the parties' autonomy and freedom, such that each party is assumed to be free from any obligation to which she has not explicitly agreed.[40] The economic account reflects a modified version of formalism. As we have seen above, it acknowledges that in many cases it is perfectly rational to form an (economically) incomplete contract, due to transaction cost constraints. As a result, this account is bound to recognise the need to complete the contract. However, the viable options are the two forms of exit rules, and not a compelled modification of the content of the contract.[41]

The economic account's version of formalism is a result of practical mistrust in the court's capability accurately to assess the optimal content of the contract.[42] As in numerous other contexts, 'self-enforced' mechanisms and incentive-based measures are preferred over direct regulation

[38] See Scott, above n 14; Charny, above n 14; Schwartz, above n 29. See also L Bernstein 'The Questionable Empirical Basis of Article 2's Incorporation Strategy: A Preliminary Study' (1999) 66 *University Chicago Law Review* 710 (clear 'usage of trade' and 'commercial standards' do not consistently exist; instead, the parties rely on 'weak-form customs', that is, 'a set of vaguely defined yet workable relationship-creating norms … that gradually diminish in importance as contracting relationships mature').
[39] It should be noted that there are exceptions to this strict enforcement of the words of the contract. For instance, the court is willing to depart from formalistic methodology in case of an error in transcript.
[40] See eg Epstein, above n 13.
[41] See eg V Goldberg 'Towards an Expanded Economic Theory of Contract' (1976) 10 *Journal Economics Issues* 45.
[42] See Schwartz, above n 29; RE Scott 'The Case for Formalism in Relational Contract' (2000) 94 *Northwestern University Law Review* 847; CJ Goetz and RE Scott 'The Limits of Expanded Choice: An Analysis of the Interactions between Express and Implied Contract Terms' 73 *California Law Review* 261 (1985); GK Handfield 'Judicial Competence and the Interpretation of Incomplete Contracts' 23 *Journal Legal Studies* 159 (1994).

of activities.[43] In the current context, the purpose of the law of remedies is, arguably, not to resolve failures *ex-post*, but to set the 'rules of the game' which are familiar to the parties, and which are aimed at inducing each party to act optimally *ex-ante*. For this reason, the remedy of expectation damages, which is *ex-ante* oriented, is considered, in general, to be superior. According to this measure, the relevant factor is the expectation interest as could have been perceived by the breaching party, at the stage of performance; this remedy does not require, at least not in principle, an account of the relevant circumstances at the stage of breach and its motives; and, most important, it induces each party to act optimally, by enforcing her to fully internalise the consequences of her decision whether to perform or to breach.

Therefore, both the traditional and the economic accounts reflect formalism, that is, in the current context — both are based on the premise of remedies as extra-contractual. The remedy aims at preserving the contractual right, and, according to the economic approach, it sets an exit rule, which defines the terms in which this entitlement can be reassigned. However, according to both accounts, the remedy is applied *given* a specific content of the contractual right. It is not aimed at forming or adjusting the right itself.

V CHALLENGING THE PREMISE OF REMEDIES AS EXTRA-CONTRACTUAL: REMEDIES AS 'MODIFICATION MECHANISM'

The premises of Formalism are clearly plausible, but they are not inevitable. Consider an alternative theory, under which the court is assigned a more active role in assisting the parties to form their agreement. This alternative approach shares with the economic one the presumption that the contract is inherently incomplete in the economic sense, such that the parties are practically unable optimally to account, at the stage of contract formation, for all the possible contingencies. As stated, for instance, by Kessler and Gilmore,

> only an infinitesimal fraction of [the relevant assumptions as to the state of the world] ever comes to the conscious attention of the parties; as with

[43] In the context of regulation see eg R Howse 'Retrenchment, Reform or Revolution? The Shift to Incentives and the Future of the Regulatory State' (1993) 31 *Alberta Law Review* 456; TE Malloy 'Regulating by Incentives: Myths, Models, and Micromarkets' (2002) 80 *Texas Law Review* 531; ML Cropper and WE Oates 'Environmental Economics: A Survey', (1992) 30 *Journal Economic Literature* 675; JD Hanson and KD Logue 'The Costs of Cigarettes: The Economic Case for Ex post Incentive-Based Regulation' (1997) 107 *Yale Law Journal* 1163. For a proposal to set a rule of no-retraction in contractual negotiation, which is based on the idea of inducing each party to optimally act in the negotiation without the need of a detailed ex-post assessment by the court of the parties' good faith, see O Ben-Shahar 'Against the

the iceberg, the great bulk of the contractual construct lies beneath the surface.[44]

However, unlike the economic approach, the so-called 'anti-formalistic' approach reflects a greater confidence in the court's capability to complete the contract *ex-post*, given the prevailing circumstances. It emphasises the purpose of the contract, and not necessarily the explicit obligations that the parties have set in their agreement.[45] This approach is reflected in the choice of vague contractual provisions and vague contract law rules (such as 'reasonableness', 'good faith', and 'best efforts'), which obtain much of their content from their subsequent application by courts.[46] Unlike the formalistic approach, which confines the interpreter's attention to a subset of materials (ie, the explicit language of the contract), the alternative one broadens the spectrum in an attempt to come to a more all-things-considered understanding of the contract, based on all the materials reasonably available.[47]

According to this approach, 'the contract is a skeleton-like structure upon which the relationship is built, designed to do little more than describe the general policy governing the relationship'.[48] The content of the contractual obligations is flexible. It is set *ex-post*, based on the

"Meeting of the Minds": Exploring a New Basis for Contractual Liability' (Michigan Law and Economics Research Paper No 02–015, October 2002. Available from the SSRN Electronic Paper Collection). One can find different versions of this mistrust in the ability of the court to direct activities. For a discussion of this point (in the context of contract formation doctrines) see A Katz 'When Should an Offer Stick? The Economics of Promissory Estoppel in Preliminary Negotiations' (1996) 105 *Yale Law Journal* 1249.

[44] F Kessler and G Gilmore *Contracts: Cases and Materials* 742 2nd edn (Little Brown, Boston, 1970).

[45] In this sense, this approach differs from the now 'classic' anti-formalistic account, epitomised by scholars like Corbin and Llewellyn, which is based primarily on the premise that contract law should seek guidance from the perceptions and understandings of the transactors. Llewellyn understood the 'situation sense' as the essence of contract law. See eg TD Rakoff 'Implied Terms: On Default Rules and "Situation Sense"' in J Beatson and D Friedmann (eds) *Good Faith and Fault in Contract Law* (Clarendon Press, Oxford, 1995) 191. See also RE Barnett 'The Sound of Silence: Default Rules and Contractual Consent' (1992) 78 *Virginia Law Review* 821 (default contract law rules should reflect the understanding of the inarticulate understanding of transactors).

[46] See eg A Schwartz and RE Scott 'The Political Economy of Private Legislatures' (1995) 143 *University Pennsylvania Law Review* 595, who argue that Article 2 of the UCC reflects vague rules since it was drafted by academics, and not by actual contracting parties, who prefer, arguably, 'bright line' rules.

[47] See eg PS Atiyah and RS Summers *Form and Substance in Anglo-American Law: A Comparative Study of Legal Reasoning, Legal Theory, and Legal Institutions* (Clarendon Press, Oxford, 1987); EA Posner 'The Decline of Formality in Contract Law' in FH Buckley (ed) *The Fall and Rise of Freedom of Contract* (Duke University Press, Durham, NC, 1999) 61.

[48] SW Halpern 'Application of the Doctrine of Commercial Impracticability: Searching for "the Wisdom of Solomon"' (1987) 135 *University Pennsylvania Law Review* 1123, 1129. According to this view, 'the law functions as a kind of gyroscopic monitor, keeping the parties on a more or less even course': *Ibid*, 1171.

surrounding circumstances at the time of performance, as required in order to achieve the purpose of the contract.[49] Thus, the explicit obligations that the parties agree upon in their contract are mere 'vehicles', which are aimed at delivering the main message — the purpose of the contract. Thus, the judiciary is delegated with the authority to adjust the explicit contractual provisions as required in order to accomplish (what the court perceives as) the 'purpose of the contract'.[50] As a result, according to this account the outcome of the 'intra-contractual' phase may well span a 'continuous' spectrum. The court may find that the content of the parties' explicit contractual rights and obligations should be adjusted (or that the contract was 'substantially performed'[51]), given the state of the world at the time of performance.

The contract's explicit provisions can be adjusted by applying specific contract law doctrines. However, the law of remedies is a viable — and in some senses, even a preferable — alternative for this purpose. As such, remedies are not extra-contractual, that is, they are not aimed at preserving a given contractual right. Instead, remedies are perceived as modification mechanisms. This characterisation of remedies is reflected in various doctrines of the law of remedies, such that the outcome of the application of remedies for breach is far from strict enforcement of the explicit contractual right. Under formalistic accounts, these doctrines reflect external constraints, which lead to a deviation from the underlying purpose of the remedies — to preserve the contractual right. As such, these deviations can be justified only based on extra-contractual considerations (under the traditional account) or *ex-ante* ones (under the economic approach).[52] On

[49] RA Hillman 'Court Adjustment of Long-Term Contracts: An Analysis under Modern Contract Law' (1987) Duke *Law Journal* 1 (proposes adjustments in cases of substantial unanticipated changes, and implied agreement on adjustment); RE Speidel 'Court-Imposed Price Adjustments under Long-Term Supply Contracts' (1981) 76 *Northwestern Law Review* 369 (an adjustment is justified only if the advantaged party fails to renegotiate in good faith after the change of circumstances has occurred).

[50] IR Macneil 'Contracts: Adjustment of Long-Term Economic Relations Under Classical, Neoclassical, and Relational Contract Law' (1978) 72 *Northwestern University Law Review* 854; R Gordon 'Macaulay, Macneil, and the Discovery of Solidarity and Power in Contract Law' (1985) *Wisconsin Law Review* 565; 'Relational Contract Theory: Unanswered Questions — A Symposium in Honor of Ian R Macneil', (2000) *94 Northwestern University Law Review* 737–962.

[51] *Brown-Marx Associates Ltd v Emigrant Savings Bank* 703 F 2d 1361, 1367 (11th Cir 1983): 'Substantial performance rather than exact, strict or literal performance by the first party of the terms of the contract is adequate to entitle the party to recover on it'; Restatement (Second) of Contracts, §229: 'To the extent that non-occurrence of a condition would cause disproportionate forfeiture, a court may excuse the non-occurrence of that condition unless its occurrence was a material part of the agreed exchange'. See also LA DiMatteo 'Equity's Modification of Contract: An Analysis of the Twentieth Century's Equitable Reformation of Contract Law' (1999) 33 *New England Law Review* 265, 310–12.

[52] For instance, various justifications were offered in the economic literature of the invalidation of liquidation punitive damages for a breach of contract: AS Edlin and A Schwartz 'Optimal Penalties in Contracts' (2003) 78 *Chicago-Kent Law Review* 33; P Aghion and

the other hand, the alternative account, of remedies as modification mechanisms, perceives these doctrines and the result of applying them — the deviation from preserving the explicit contractual right — as reflecting the fundamental purpose of remedies. For instance, a court's refusal to enforce a promise to give a personal service reflects, under this approach, an interpretation of the contract that it will be fulfilled only given a certain state of the world (eg the promisor's willingness to perform). The denial of specific performance due to hardship or fairness considerations reflects a change of the contract's content. This approach thus questions the premise of remedies as extra contractual. The content of the contract is defined based on the remedy which the court applies.

The relevant assessment under this account is what remedy best fits the purpose of serving as modification mechanism. Generally speaking, the remedy of specific performance is preferable. The prevailing academic discourse typically perceives this remedy as one which results in a 'strict' enforcement of contractual obligations. As such, it may well serve to 'preserve' the contractual right and to channel the parties to *ex-post* renegotiations. The endorsement of this remedy by the account of remedies as modification mechanisms is based on a different — and, to my view, a more accurate — description of the characteristics of specific performance.[53] According to this view, specific performance does not result in a strict enforcement of contractual obligations, since in issuing the remedy of specific performance the court retains a wide discretion regarding the content of the contractual obligations it enforces. The court is authorised not only to decline to enforce an obligation, but also to enforce a modified obligation and even to issue an order that modifies the obligations of both parties, including that of the injured, and may order the performance of collateral acts that are not required by the contract's explicit provisions.[54] Historically, the court's discretion resulted from the equitable nature of this remedy, which is a form of injunctive decree. As such, the court was allowed to account for various considerations in setting

B Hermalin 'Legal Restrictions on Private Contracts Can Enhance Efficiency', (1990) 6 *Journal Law Economics & Organization* 381; PH Rubin 'Unenforceable Contracts: Penalty Clauses and Specific Performance' (1981) 10 Journal *Journal of Legal Studies* 237.

[53] For a discussion of the disparity between the 'traditional beliefs' of contracts lawyers, judges, and theorists and actual contract law in general, and about remedies for breach in particular, see RA Hillman 'Contract Lore' (2003) 27 *Journal of Corporation Law*, 505.

[54] See eg *Oglebay Norton Co v Armco Inc* 52 Ohio St 3d 232, 556 NE 2d 515 (1990) (the court ordered the parties to re-negotiate, after the specific pricing mechanism failed); *Koch v Koch* 903 F 2d 1333 (10th Cir 1990). Under UCC §2–716(2), 'the decree for specific performance may include such terms and conditions as to payment of the price, damages, or other relief as the court may deem just'. As observed by Treitel, 'the remedy of specific performance is an extraordinarily flexible one. It may be granted on terms … or made conditional on the plaintiff's performing his part … or even on his assenting to a modification of the contract': GH Treitel *Remedies for Breach of Contract:A Comparative Account* (Clarendon Press, Oxford, 1988) 69.

the content of the parties' obligations, such as corrective justice, distributive justice, and efficiency. The abandoning of the distinction between equitable and common-law remedies in modern law did not abolish the court's wide discretion in setting terms in issuing specific performance, and thus to modify the content of the contractual obligations.

When issuing the remedy of specific performance the court is not called upon to assist the parties to cease their contractual relations but to revive them. When the court is called upon to enforce a party to perform, it does not find itself free to disregard the prevailing circumstances at that time. In these senses, the remedy of specific performance is, basically, *ex-post* oriented, in contrast to the remedy of expectation damages, which is *ex-ante* oriented (see section IV above).

Clearly, the court also retains wide discretion in applying the remedy of expectation damages. It is authorised to mitigate the award of damages, even below the value of the injured's expectation interest, based on several causes, such as an unusually high unrevealed value of his expectation interest,[55] unreasonably high investment in reliance, and the duty to mitigate the damage.[56] The court may also either mitigate or augment the damages awarded based on the relevant surrounding circumstances at the time of the breach, and on an appraisal of the parties' behaviour (such as, a profitable and opportunistic breach of contract). However, as a general rule, specific performance seems better suited to serve as a modification mechanism. The court's authority to adapt the parties' obligation is significantly more limited under the measure of expectation damages than under specific performance. The former remedy entrusts the judiciary with limited discretion which relates, exclusively, to the magnitude of the injured's expectation interest. Thus, the parties cannot count on an external authority that would modify their obligations, even if such an adaptation is required in order to achieve the purpose of the contract. The court may induce the parties to re-negotiate, by a threat to either mitigate or augment the magnitude of damages;[57] but it cannot dictate a concrete modification of the express terms of the contract. On the other hand, specific performance, as practically applied, entrusts the judiciary with the power substantially to alter the parties' explicitly assigned rights and obligations.

[55] Based on the rule set out in *Hadley v Baxendale* (1854) 9 Ex 341; 156 ER 145.
[56] See eg A Kull 'Disgorgement for Breach, the "Restitution Interest" and the Restatement of Contracts' (2001) 79 *Texas Law Review* 2021.
[57] For a related argument see EA Posner 'A Theory of Contract Law under Conditions of Radical Judicial Error' (2000) 94 *Northwestern University Law Review* 749 (the court can promote cooperation by providing a means that enables the aggrieved party to invoke a mutual penalty); JS Johnston 'Bargaining under Rules versus Standards' (1995) *Journal Law Economics & Organization* 256.

To sum-up: given the choice of a formalistic account, under which the court's sole role is to decide whether a specific activity should be considered a fulfillment of the contract or a breach, the premise of remedies as extra-contractual is self-evident. However, if this approach is abandoned, such that the court is entrusted with a more extensive role, the dichotomy between the 'intra-contractual' phase of contract interpretation and the phase of applying the appropriate remedy is diluted. According to such an account, remedies can be perceived as a means of adjusting the contract's express provisions, such that applying a remedy for breach is an integral part of delineating the content of the contractual right.

VI REFLECTIONS ON THE CHOICE BETWEEN THE THREE ACCOUNTS

The fundamental choice is thus between three main alternatives: A view of the contract as all-inclusive, such that gaps are filled only through *ex-post* renegotiation (the traditional account); recognising that the contract is economically incomplete, while restricting the filling of the gaps to exit-mechanism and other *ex-ante* oriented mechanisms (the economic account); and a perception of the contract as inherently incomplete, based on the prospect of compelled modification whenever needed (the account of remedies as modification mechanisms). The choice of each of these alternatives results in a specific set of relevant considerations, according to which the choice of a specific remedy should be made.

At the outset, a choice about the contract's 'completeness' is required. If the contract is assumed to be all-inclusive, unilateral withdrawal and compelled modification are both excluded, and the purpose of the remedy is to 'preserve' the contractual right. Alternatively, it may be assumed that contracts (as well as contract law doctrines) are inherently incomplete in the economic sense, that is, that the contract does not optimally account for all the possible contingencies. Clearly, this choice is not based on an empirical assessment. The parties undoubtedly cannot fully account for all possible (or even all probable) contingencies. The choice is based on a conceptual perception of the essence of the contract. The presumption that the contract is all-inclusive is a result of a view which accentuates the concept of the 'meeting of minds' as the moral basis of the contract. The alternative approach reflects an acknowledgement that the parties may prefer to agree to form an 'open-texture' mutual commitment, and thus to form an incomplete contract.

If the view of the contract as incomplete is chosen, an additional choice is required. It is the choice between two concepts of completing the contract: An 'extra-contractual' path (setting an exit rule) and an 'intra-contractual' one (adjustment of the contract). In order to explore the choice between these two accounts, a distinction should be made between two possible reasons for the contract's incompleteness — transaction costs and bounded rationality.

Consider, first, transaction costs. In this case, the parties are aware of the prospect of a possible change in the relevant circumstances which would make the contract 'inefficient'. However, they are unable (at least not at reasonable cost) explicitly to provide in the contract all the relevant contingencies to account for this prospect.[58] The law of remedies is aimed at completing the contract by dealing with the prospect of 'inefficient contract'. Note, however, that as far as exit rules are concerned, transaction costs cannot explain contract incompleteness. Generally speaking, transaction costs do not (or at least only partially) constrain the parties from explicitly providing what they perceive as the optimal exit rule, since, presumably, the costs of drafting such a mechanism are trivial. In contrast, transaction costs may obstruct the parties from explicitly providing modification mechanisms, since drafting such provisions entails, among other things, an explicit definition of the purpose of the contract, which is typically not a trivial task. As a result, if one assumes that the reason for the contract's incompleteness is transaction costs constraints, it seems that the law's default rules regarding remedies for breach should be set based on the premise that remedies provide modification mechanisms. Parties which are interested in setting mere 'exit rules' can easily contract around the default remedy that the law sets.[59] Clearly, such a conclusion can be valid only if the law does enable the parties to contract around the rule of using remedies as a modification mechanism[60] (or, as argued by Macneil, a distinction should be made between 'relational' and 'transactional'

[58] See O Hart and J Moore 'Incomplete Contracts and Renegotiations' (1988) 56 *Econometrica* 755.

[59] See Triantis, above n 29, 5: 'Article 2 [of the UCC] may provide efficient default rules even if it is more vague than most commercial parties would choose: if contracting from vague to precise terms ... is substantially cheaper than in the other direction'. See also I Ayres 'Making a Difference: The Contractual Contributions of Easterbrook and Fischel' (1992) 59 *University Chicago Law Review* 1391, 1406. In addition, if the parties are not interested in a 'flexible' contractual interpretation (that is, in a contract law which acknowledges the power of immanent practices to erode the explicit contractual provisions) the potential erosion encourages right-holders to take greater anti-erosion measures. See O Ben-Shahar 'The Tentative Case against Flexibility in Commercial Law' 66 (1999) *University Chicago Law Review* 781 (arguing that the flexibility effect and the rigidity effect of the erosion doctrines will, in theory, balance out, but flexibility-promoting doctrines affect enforcement costs, thereby indirectly affecting the value of the contractual right); I Ayres 'Eroding Entitlements as Litigation Commitment' (1999) 66 *University Chicago Law Review* 836.

[60] This condition does not necessarily hold. Under the common law, any contract can be modified by a later contract, notwithstanding explicit provisions in the contract banning renegotiation. The court may also not enforce clauses requiring modifications to be in writing. See eg B Blum *Contracts* 2nd edn (Aspen Law & Business, New York, 2001) 331. Compare UCC §2-209. For a criticism of these rules see C Jolls 'Contracts as Bilateral Commitments: A New Perspective on Contract Modification' (1997) 26 *Journal Legal Studies* 203; Schwartz and Watson, above n 31.

contract. The latter is a contract in which the parties determine, in a single joint exercise of their free choice, their respective duties to each other for the duration of the agreement; whereas the former is characterised by setting only the 'programme' of the contract at the stage of formation[61]).

Next, consider the other possible reason for the contract's incompleteness — the parties' 'bounded rationality'. In this case, the parties may account for the risk of 'opportunistic breach', but they are unaware, at the stage of contract formation, of the prospect of a possible change of circumstances that would make the contract inefficient. According to this alternative, the parties do not deliberately avoid setting a mechanism to account for cases in which the contract becomes inefficient, implicitly relying on the default remedies provided by the law. The avoidance of setting a remedy reflects the parties' ignorance of this prospect. In this case, both alternatives — that is, remedies as exit rules and remedies as modification mechanisms — are plausible. The choice must be based on an assessment of the court's capability properly to adjust the contract.

Note, however, that a choice in the latter reason for the contract's incompleteness, which may support the economic account, contradicts a fundamental presumption of this approach. Recall that the economic approach is *ex-ante* oriented. The choice of the optimal exit rule is based, so it is argued, on an assessment of each exit rule's effect on the parties' incentives and thus on their projected activities. Such analysis is based, by definition, on the presumption that the parties are fully rational. They are aware of the prospect of efficient breach and of the possible effect of a given exit rule on their payoffs. More generally, the assumption of perfectly rational parties is the basis of the economic analysis of contract law's fundamental premise that contract law default rules must be efficient. According to this argument, the parties are expected to override any default rule which is inefficient, and thus any attempt to enhance other values through contractual default rules is futile.[62] However, it is then inconsistent to assume 'bounded rationality'. As we have just seen, if the parties are perfectly rational, (default) contract law in general, and default remedies that serve as exit rules in particular, become useless. The literature on incomplete contracts shows that perfectly rational parties do not need the assistance of contract law in order to write efficient contracts. Setting complex mechanisms of contract modification and procedures of renegotiation would do the work.

In other words, in order to make contract law relevant, the economic account must assume that the parties' rationality is actually bounded. It must assume that achieving the efficient contractual provisions is costly,

[61] IR Macneil 'The Many Futures of Contracts' (1974) 47 *Southern California Law Review* 691.

[62] See eg JL Coleman *Markets, Morals, and the Law* (Cambridge University Press, Cambridge, 1988) chapter 4; RA Posner *The Economics of Justice* (Harvard University Press, Cambridge, Masachussets, 1983) chapters 3 and 4.

that is, that the parties are not perfectly rational.[63] If so, the assessment as to the optimal remedy must be modified. One possible response is to incorporate bounded rationality not only as a justification for the relevance of contract law but also in the assessment of its affect on the parties' activities, in order to choose the optimal exit rule.[64] An alternative, more radical approach is to acknowledge that bounded rationality may affect the underlying endorsement of a formalistic account. The choice between the two means of completing the contract — exit rules and compelled adjustment — depends upon empirical considerations regarding the relevant costs of *ex-ante* and *ex-post* decision-making.[65] Bounded rationality reflects high costs of *ex-ante* decision-making by the parties. The acknowledgement of bounded rationality should thus result, other things being equal, in a greater willingness to delegate authority to the court to assist the parties in drafting their contract.[66]

VII CONCLUSION

The basic argument set out above is that an essential stage in selecting a remedy for breach of contract is the choice of the appropriate theory of contract interpretation and modification. Analysis of remedies must be based on an assessment of the remedy that best fits *each* of the models of contract interpretation and, obviously, on the choice of the preferred model. The prevailing discourse, which mainly reflects the debate between the traditional and the economic approach, is implicitly based on the formalistic, binary model. It reflects a notion of remedies as extra-contractual. However, I have tried to show that such a notion is not self-evident. In particular, if one is willing to assume that the contract is not all-inclusive since the parties may prefer to form an incomplete contract, remedies may well serve not only to 'preserve' a given contractual right, but to fill a gap in the incomplete contract in case of a substantial change in surrounding circumstances. If so, a choice must be made betweenthe concept of remedies as exit rules and of remedies as a modification mechanism.

[63] Accordingly, Williamson has argued that the term 'transaction costs' is, actually, a metaphor for bounded rationality: OE Williamson *Markets and Hierarchies: analysis and antitrust implications : a study in the economics of internal organization* (Free Press, New York, 1975).

[64] See eg Posner, above n 19.

[65] L Kaplow 'Rules versus Standards: An Economic Analysis' (1992) 42 *Duke Law Journal* 557.

[66] EA Posner 'The Parol Evidence Rule, the Plain Meaning Rule, and the Principles of Contractual Interpretation' (1998) 146 *Univesity Pennsylvania Law Review* 553; K Eggleston, E Posner, and R Zeckhauser 'The Design of Interpretation of Contracts: Why Complexity Matters' (2000) 95 *Northwestern University Law Review* 91.

Part Two

Comparisons

4

The Law's Response to Exit and Loyalty in Contract Disputes

MARK P GERGEN*

THIS ESSAY SITUATES the rules in American private law that regulate exit and loyalty in contract disputes within a general theoretical framework. By exit I mean when a party to a contract suspends or withholds performance, refuses performance, or obtains substitute performance due to his dissatisfaction with the other party's performance or demands. Exit is an important self-help remedy for breach of contract. By loyalty I mean when a party performs, accepts performance, or awaits performance despite his dissatisfaction with the other's performance or demands. Exit and loyalty are regulated by rules that dictate when a person has the power or duty to exit (eg material breach, mitigation, and the law of conditions), by rules that dictate when failure to exit in a timely fashion will cause a person to lose the power to exit or other prerogatives (eg mitigation, waiver, estoppel, and election of remedies), by rules that dictate when a person who loyally performs in a dispute may recover the cost or value of performance exceeding his obligation (eg voluntary payment and restitution), and by rules that dictate when it is appropriate to threaten exit to force resolution of a dispute (eg accord and satisfaction and duress).

Section I examines the rules that determine when a party has the power or duty to exit in response to a clear default. I show that American law permits a party to act in response to a clear default to protect himself from an uncompensated loss though his action imposes a disproportionate loss on the defaulter. The rules regulating exit and loyalty are much more concerned with protecting contract rights than are they concerned with promoting efficient breach, at least when the right protected is clear. Section II examines the law's response to exit and loyalty when there is a

*I thank Hans Baade, Andrew Kull, Douglas Laycock and Alan Rau for their insights and comments. Earlier versions of this chapter were presented at the conference on 'Comparative Remedies for Breach of Contract' (Tel-Aviv, 2002) and to the Faculty of Law, University College London.

bona fide dispute about an obligation or right. I show that what may seem to be a hodgepodge of rules can be organized around what I call the goal of efficient performance. Generally the law treats performance or acceptance of performance in a dispute as final, foreclosing later assertion of an inconsistent legal position, unless the performance or acceptance of performance avoids a consequential or joint loss. In other words, the interest in finality (and the goal of remedial simplicity more generally) gives way to the goal of efficient performance when rights are unclear.[1]

The importance of the goal of remedial simplicity in American contract law is an over-arching theme. A feature of the American legal landscape looms over the law. Legal processes are very slow in the United States so parties are likely to have to act first and resolve their rights in court later when a contract demands immediate performance.[2] The cumbersomeness of civil litigation is exacerbated by the use of a civil jury to resolve factual disputes and, sometimes, to make fact-specific normative determinations. Jury trials are extraordinarily time-consuming and expensive, and there is good reason to believe that juries are erratic adjudicators of complex commercial disputes.

I THE POWER OR DUTY TO EXIT IN RESPONSE TO A CLEAR DEFAULT

The work of defining when a person has the power to withhold or refuse performance in response to default is primarily done, in American private law, by the doctrine of material breach. The concept

[1] Section II builds upon MP Gergen 'Restitution as a Bridge Over Troubled Contractual Waters' (2002) 71 *Fordham Law Review* 79, which proposed a rule that allows restitution for a disputed performance if the performance was necessary to avoid a loss. The Restatement (Third) of Restitution and Unjust Enrichment, Council Draft No 5, § 35 (24 November 2003) endorses such a rule graciously crediting my article for the suggestion.

[2] Getting a judgment in a hard fought civil case can literally take years in American courts. J Geordt et al *Examining Court Delay: The Pace Of Litigation In 26 Urban Trial Courts: 1987* National Center for State Courts Williamsburg, VA, 1989) xiii (while 7 of the 26 large urban trial courts studied disposed of felony cases within 1 year of arrest and 14 had 10% or less pending at 1 year after arrest, only two courts were close to disposing of civil cases within 2 years of filing); SK Smith et al *Bureau of Justice Statistics, Special Report, Tort Cases in Large Counties* (Department of Justice, Bureau of Justice Special Report April 1995)(available at http://www.ojp.usdoj.gov/bjs/pub/ascii/tcilc.txt) (average time to dispose of tort case in the nation's 75 largest counties was slightly more than 1 1/2 years; average time for processing of cases that were tried was 2 years). There is no preliminary declaratory judgment. See *Doran v Salem Inn* 422 US 922, 931 (1975) ('prior to final judgment there is no established declaratory remedy comparable to a preliminary injunction'). Sometimes a preliminary injunction may be sought to compel the other party to perform. In most cases where a preliminary injunction is sought in a contract setting the plaintiff seeks to prevent the defendant from acting in a way that would make performance impossible. For example, a buyer will seek an injunction to prevent a seller from disposing of property that is under contract. Courts are reluctant to grant preliminary injunctions in such cases even when the property

of material breach is nestled in the law alongside the concepts of substantial performance and total breach. A finding of material or total breach triggers several possible legal responses. They include the power to suspend performance, the power to abandon a contract and find substitute performance, and the power to rescind a contract and recover in restitution for performance already rendered.[3] The concept of substantial performance often is associated with a claim by the defaulter to be paid for work done. In most American states a defaulter who substantially performs has a right to recover the contract price less damages caused by his default (the contract remedy), otherwise he recovers in restitution.[4] In a few states a defaulter who substantially performs recovers in restitution, otherwise he forfeits compensation.[5]

An initial problem in defining material breach and the cognate concepts is distinguishing among the various functions these concepts perform. Logically, whether a default is material (or total or substantial) should depend on the specific response that follows.[6] A solution is to tie each concept to a different response and then define each to cover conduct meriting that particular response. The Restatement (Second) of Contracts takes roughly this tact. It distinguishes between material and total breach on the basis of whether the harm from the breach is curable.

is unique. The *Texaco-Pennzoil* litigation, which resulted in multi-billion verdict on a theory of tortious interference, provides a notable illustration. When Getty and Texaco announced their deal Pennzoil, the disappointed suitor for Getty, immediately sought a preliminary injunction in a Delaware chancery court. The court denied the request for an injunction though it found that Getty would probably win on the merits on the contract claim against Pennzoil and that it would suffer irreparable injury because the injunction would also implicate third parties (Gordon Getty and and Texaco) against whose Getty's claim was less certain. The unreported decision is *Pennzoil Co v Getty Oil Co* 1984 WL 15,664 (Court of Chancery of Delaware 6 February 1984). When a contract does not involve a unique asset plaintiffs run into the traditional view that loss of money, even if difficult to measure, is not irreparable injury sufficient to justify a preliminary injunction. DA Laycock *Death of the Irreparable Injury Rule* (OUP, USA, 1991) 112, 121–2.

[3] To this list might be added the right to disgorgement of profits realized by the defaulter on certain opportunistic breaches. On the distinction between restoration and disgorgement see A Kull 'Disgorgement for Default, the "Restitution Interest", and the Restatement of Contracts' (2001) 79 *Texas Law Review* 2021.

[4] *Reynolds v Armstead* 166 Colo 372, 443 P 2d 990 (1968); *Levan v Richter* 152 Ill App 3d 1082, 504 NE 2d 1373 (1987); *Plante v Jacobs* 10 Wis 2d 567, 103 NW 2d 296 (1960).

[5] *JA Sullivan Corp v Commonwealth* 397 Mass 789, 494 NE 2d 374 (1986). The New York rule on construction contracts is a variant. A contractor who substantially performs is paid on the contract (less damages) otherwise he has no claim in restitution. *Steel Storage & Elevator Construction Co v Stock* 225 NY 173, 121 NE 786 (1919). New York law has softened in other settings. *Hadden v Consolidated Edison Co of New York* 34 NY 2d 88, 356 NYS 2d 249, 312 NE 2d 445 (1974) (stating that willfulness of default is only a factor to be considered in deciding if employee substantially performed and holding that employee who had taken bribes from contractors did not forfeit his pension).

[6] Corbin is eloquent on the point. *Corbin on Contracts* 2nd edn (West Publishing Co, St Paul, Minnesota, 1962) vol 6 § 1253 9–12.

A material breach that is curable only justifies suspending performance.[7] An uncurable material breach is defined as a total breach, which discharges the non-defaulting party, justifying his withdrawal from the contract.[8] A total breach also seems to justify the optional restitution remedy.[9] Presumably cure was emphasised in the Restatement to solidify its relevance under the common law.[10] It is a mistake to emphasize cure if that derogates from other relevant considerations, such as whether damages are likely to be an adequate remedy if the non-defaulting party accepts performance or continues to perform.[11] Another problem with the Restatement's approach is that it equates the response of discharge and the response of restitution.[12]

The duty to mitigate damages performs a function similar to the doctrine of material breach when a party is faulted for not reducing his loss by continuing to do business with a defaulter after breach.[13] *Henrici*

[7] The Restatement (Second) of Contracts states that an uncured material failure to perform suspends the other party's duties and that an uncurable material failure to perform discharges the other party's duties. See Restatement (Second) of Contracts § 242, comment (a).

[8] The concept of a total breach is used to delimit when a party may sue for damages on the entire contract. Restatement (Second) of Contracts § 236. A total breach is defined as a default that discharges the other party's performance obligation or a default coupled with a repudiation. Restatement (Second) of Contracts §§ 243(1), (2). Thus an uncurable material breach is a total breach.

[9] The provision on the right to rescind and recover in restitution says that a 'total breach' is the trigger and not a 'material breach'. Restatement (Second) of Contracts § 373.

[10] That a party ought to give notice and an opportunity to cure before withdrawing from a contract is well-established in the common law. See eg *Pollard v Saxe & Yolles Dev Co* 12 Cal 3d 374, 525 P 2d 88, 92, 115 Cal Rptr 648, 652 (1974); *Sturdy Concrete Corp v Nab Constr Corp* 65 AD 2d 262, 411 NYS 2d 637, 644 (1978); *United States ex rel Cortolano & Barone Inc v Morano Constr Corp* 724 F Supp 88, 98 (SDNY 1989); *Cyclo Floor Machine Corp v National Housewares Inc* 296 F Supp 665, 682 (DUtah 1968); *McClain v Kimbrough Construction Co* 806 SW 2d 194 (Tenn App 1990).

[11] There is this danger because the seller's right to cure under the Uniform Commercial Code is understood not to excuse the seller from the obligation to provide goods that perfectly conform to the contract should the buyer demand except with regards to time of delivery.

[12] For a persuasive argument for treating the two responses differently see A Kull 'Restitution as a Remedy for Breach' (1994) 67 *Southern California Law Review* 1465, 1476. The gist of the argument is that withholding performance is a simple self-help remedy that does not require going to court. Recovering performance already rendered usually does require the assistance of a court. And restitution raises difficult problems of valuation when the performance cannot be returned in kind.

[13] RA Hillman 'Keeping the Deal Together After Material breach — Common Law Mitigation Rules, The UCC, and the Restatement (Second) of Contracts' (1976) 47 *Colorado Law Review* 553, remains a good article on the topic. Hillman writes against the many cases that state in categorical terms that there is no obligation to do further business with a defaulter. The most famous of these cases is *Canadian Industrial Alcohol Co v Dunbar Molasses Co* 258 NY 194, 200–01, 179 NE 383, 385 (1932) ('The plaintiff replied in substance that it had no longer any faith in the defendant's readiness or ability to live up to its engagements, and did not wish to add another contract to the one already broken. The law did not charge it with a duty to make such an experiment again.') See also *W-V Enterprises Inc v Federal Saving & Loan Insurance Corp* 234 Kan 354, 367, 673 P 2d 1112, 1122 (1983) ('there is no obligation to mitigate damages if the mitigation involves dealing with the defaulting party.')

v South Feather Land & Water Co[14] illustrates. South Feather assumed a long-term contract to supply water to Henrici's farm. It proposed a new pricing scheme that would have slightly increased Henrici's payments. The parties disagreed about whether South Feather had this right. Henrici refused to take water on these terms and allowed his farm to wither. He had no other source of water for irrigation. The case holds that even though Henrici was in the right on the dispute he could not recover for the damage to his farm because he should have mitigated damages by taking the water and later suing to recover the over-payment. I will use *Henrici* later for its extreme facts nicely illustrate some pivotal principles.

Under the Restatement (Second) of Contracts, five factors bear on the determination of material breach.[15] These five factors are similar to the five factors that bear on the determination of 'fundamental breach' under the UNIDROIT principles.[16] With little loss of substance the two lists of

[14] 177 Cal 442, 170 P 1135 (1918). CJ Goetz and RE Scott 'The Mitigation Principle: Toward a General Theory of Contractual Obligation' (1983) 69 *Virginia Law Review* 967, 1024 n 99 collects other cases holding that a party acted inappropriately in refusing to do business with a defaulter. The article claims that courts recognise a duty to do business with a defaulter when there are significant gains from cooperation and there is no bad faith extortion or risk of under-compensation. The cases bear the claim out only if one adds the qualification that a party may refuse to do business with a defaulter to avoid an uncompensated loss even though this imposes a significantly larger loss on the defaulter and without regard to the defaulter's good faith.

[15] Restatement (Second) of Contracts § 241. The five factors are:

(a) the extent to which the injured party will be deprived of the benefit which he reasonably expected;
(b) the extent to which the injured party can be adequately compensated for the part of the benefit of which he will be deprived;
(c) the extent to which the party failing to perform or to offer to perform will suffer forfeiture;
(d) the likelihood that the party failing to perform or to offer to perform will cure his failure, taking account of all the circumstances including any reasonable assurances;
(e) the extent to which the behavior of the party failing to perform or to offer to perform comports with standards of good faith and fair dealing.

Some decisions state a much higher standard to justify termination that 'the breach [must] destroy the entire purpose of the contract.' See eg *Peters v Blagden Homes Inc* 151 A 2d 183 (DC 1959); *Ervin Const Co v Van Orden* 125 Idaho 695, 700, 874 P 2d 506, 511 (Idaho 1993). Another version of the standard asks if 'the contract would not have been made if default in that particular had been expected or contemplated.' *Huffman v Saul Holdings Ltd* 194 F 3d 1072, 1081 (8th Cir 1999), following *Berland's Inc of Tulsa v Northside Village Shopping Ctr Inc* 378 P 2d 860, 865 (Okla1963).

[16] UNIDROIT Article 7.3.1(2): In determining whether a failure to perform an obligation amounts to a fundamental non-performance regard shall be had, in particular, to whether: (a) the non-performance substantially deprives the aggrieved party of what it was entitled to expect under the contract unless the other party did not foresee and could not reasonably have foreseen such result; (b) strict compliance with the obligation which has not been performed is of essence under the contract; (c) the non-performance is intentional or reckless; (d) the non-performance gives the aggrieved party reason to believe that it cannot rely on the other party's future performance; (e) the non-performing party will suffer disproportionate loss as a result of the preparation or performance if the contract is terminated.

five can be reduced to three general factors: (1) whether withholding performance is necessary to put the aggrieved party in the rightful position[17]; (2) the burden withholding performance imposes on the defaulter[18]; and (3) the quality of the defaulter's conduct.[19] As will be seen in a moment, the question whether the duty to mitigate prohibits refusing performance can be reduced to these same factors.

Let me say just a few words about the relevance of the quality of the defaulter's conduct for it does not bear on my central point in this section.[20] It is uncontroversial that the quality of the defaulter's conduct is relevant when the presence or absence of misconduct bears on the likelihood that the aggrieved party will suffer a loss if he does not withhold or refuse performance.[21] Further, it is well-established at least in American law that uncertainty regarding the measure of damages or the appropriateness of a response to breach is more likely to be resolved against an intentional or negligent defaulter.[22] The controversy is over cases that countenance forfeiture or unjust enrichment to punish willful or intentional breach.

[17] Restatement factors (a), (b), and (d) go to this general factor. UNIDROIT factors (a), (b), and (d) go to this general factor.

[18] Restatement factor (c) refers to forfeiture. UNIDROIT factor (e) refers to disproportionate loss.

[19] Restatement factor (e) has a standard of 'good faith and fair dealing'. UNIDROIT factor (c) refers to intentional or reckless non-performance.

[20] This factor is relevant in section II for one clear implication is that a defaulter's honest belief that he is acting within his rights weighs against allowing the other party to suspend or withhold performance.

[21] This reasoning explains why a principal need not risk his affairs with an agent who has shown himself to be untrustworthy. *Kershentsev v Mascotte Prods Inc* 781 F Supp 339, 352 (ED Pa 1991) (exclusive booking agent failed to keep records, failed to procure bookings, lost funds, and lied), rev'd 981 F 2d 1247 (3d Cir 1992). It explains why a buyer of goods or services must continue to work with a seller who has shown himself to be willing and able to make good any defect in his performance. *Kiriakides v United Artists Communications Inc* 312 SC 271, 440 SE 2d 364 (1994)(finding no material breach where tenant tries to ascertain amount due and paid it as soon as it was established); *Smaldino v Larsick* 90 Ohio App 3d 691, 630 NE 2d 408 (finding no material breach where seller of furnace declined to accept full payment until work was completed and the defect was reparable). UCC § 2–508(2) codifies this by conditioning the right of the seller to cure a defect after the time of performance on the seller reasonably believing that the goods would be acceptable as tendered with a cash allowance. And it explains why a party need not await cure from someone who is consistently dilatory. *Associated Lathing and Plastering Co v Louis C Dunn Inc* 286 P 2d 825, 828, 135 Cal App 2d 40, 51 (1955) (A general contractor need not give the subcontractor an opportunity to do curative work costing $3,500 on a contract of $139,808 where the 'subcontractor has already indicated that he intends to delay, hedge and refuse to cooperate'). This reasoning also explains why even an extraordinary effort will not protect a contractor from termination when the effort is not adequate to protect the buyer from what would be an irredeemable loss. *Milner Hotels Inc v Norfolk and Western Railway Co* 822 F Supp 341, 346, 347, aff'd 19 F 3d 1429 (4th Cir1994) (railroad was justified in terminating lodging contract with hotel where best efforts of hotel could not ensure compliance with health and safety code after fire).

[22] Corbin accepted that in cases where harm caused by a default was uncertain 'neither court nor jury can not be influenced by the moral aspects of the case and the quality of the conduct of the parties'. *Corbin on Contracts* § 1124.

Corbin, who strongly condemned such cases,[23] gave *McNeal-Edwards Co v Frank L Young Co*[24] as a particularly troublesome example. The seller delivered defective oil causing the buyer $10,730 in damages. In response the buyer retained possession of drums belonging to the seller causing the seller $100 in damages. The court held that this was wrong (and indeed that the buyer committed the tort of conversion) and as a consequence it denied the buyer's larger claim for damages. The law has softened somewhat. Recent authority treats intentional breach as only one factor to be considered in deciding if default is material[25] and condemns bad faith breach rather than intentional breach.[26] This authority offers little guidance on what constitutes bad faith or how it weighs in the balance.

It is useful to distinguish two reasons why we might care about the burden withholding or refusing performance imposes on the defaulter. We might care about the resulting inefficiency when withholding or refusing performance imposes a loss on the defaulter without providing a corresponding gain to the aggrieved party. And we might care about the resulting unjust enrichment when withholding or refusing performance imposes a loss on the defaulter while providing a gain in the nature of a windfall to the aggrieved party. While there is contrary authority,[27] the

[23] *Corbin on Contracts* § 1254.

[24] 35 F 2d 829 (1st Cir 1929).

[25] *Hadden v Consolidated Edison Co* 34 NY 2d 88, 356 NYS 2d 249, 312 NE 2d 445 (1974); Restatement (Second) of Contracts, § 241, illustration 7, based on *Mathis v Thunderbird Village* 236 Or 425, 389 P 2d 343 (1964). *Nolan v Sam Fox Publishing Co* 499 F 2d 1394, 1398–99 (2d Cir 1974), affirms a trial court's refusal to grant rescission of license agreement where defendant failed to pay 74 per cent of the royalties due under a contract but failure to pay was due to negligence.

[26] *Vincenzi v Cerro* 186 Conn 612, 442 A 2d 1352, 1354 (1982). One change made between the First and Second Restatement of Contracts was eliminating the willfulness of the default as a consideration in the analysis of materiality and substituting the element of bad faith. The term willful was rejected as 'less precise.' Restatement (Second) of Contracts § 241, comment (f). A problem with the term willful is it tends to be equated with intentional or knowing. Not all intentional defaults are inappropriate. For a non-controversial example see *Vines v Orchard Hills Inc* 181 Conn 501, 435 A 2d 1022 (1980), which holds that a vendee who defaulted on a contract to purchase a condominium because his employer transferred him to a distant location did not default willfully in a way that would bar a claim for restitution of the down payment.

[27] For a recent case so stating see *Hoosier Rural Energy Electric Co-op Inc v Amoco Tax Leasing IV Corp* 34 F 3d 1310, 1320 (7th Cir 1995)('Hoosier Energy's inability to claim additional compensation is not a forfeiture but rather is "he loss of an anticipated bargain".') This is also implicit in the rule that a defaulter is limited to recovering the lesser of the benefit conferred and contract price on a restitution claim. The effect of this rule is to cast a loss from the aggrieved party's bad bargain on the defaulter. Restatement (Second) of Contracts § 374 illustrations 2 and 4 make this point giving as an example where a contractor who defaults is promised $10,000 to do work that once properly completed is worth only $9,000 to the owner. The latter figure is used to determine the compensation due the contractor for the part-completed work.

It is difficult to find cases that employ the rule in the Restatement in a way that clearly penalize a defaulter and gives the other a windfall. Usually the rule is invoked to justify denying recovery to a defaulter who does not present evidence that his part performance

better view is that withholding or refusing performance results in unjust enrichment when it puts the aggrieved party in a position better than he bargained for while putting the defaulter in a position worse than his bargain. In other words, unjust enrichment is measured against the rightful positions of the aggrieved party and the defaulter under the contract and not their starting positions. Thus, countless insurance cases invoke the principle opposing forfeiture to protect the right of an insured to collect on what is in effect a winning bet notwithstanding his default on a technical term of the bet. Sales cases that prevent a buyer from rejecting goods because of a minor defect to get out of a losing bargain are similar.[28] Forfeiture is a subcategory of unjust enrichment that results from denying the defaulter his agreed return on a contract after he has performed.[29]

Withholding or refusing performance is inappropriate when an aggrieved party does not need to so act to vindicate his rights and the action would impose a significant loss on the defaulter. *Henrici v South Feather Land & Water Co* illustrates. By taking the water and paying the price requested under protest Henrici could have avoided an enormous loss with no sacrifice of rights. Withholding or refusing performance also is inappropriate when it would provide a windfall to the aggrieved party while imposing a substantial loss on the defaulter. This is so even if there is a small sacrifice in the rights of the aggrieved party. The famous case of *Jacobs & Young v Kent* [30] illustrates. Kent had to pay for Cohoes pipe in his home though his contract with Jacobs & Young specified that Reading pipe would be used because the cost of replacing the pipe was grossly disproportionate to Kent's loss. The case is fairly easy because the two brands of pipe were the exact same so the court could be sure that the substitution caused no harm. The doctrine of material breach can require a party to pay for sub-par performance when that leaves him with a small

was of value to the other. In *United States Pipe & Foundry Co v City of Waco* 100 SW 2d 1099, 1112 (Tex Civ App Waco 1936), affirmed on other grounds, 130 Tex 126, 108 SW 2d 432 (1937), the rule was invoked to deny a seller that delivered defective pipe from offering evidence that some of the buyer's difficulties were attributable to faulty installation by a contractor. Corbin poses the hypothetical of defective work that is destroyed in a fire that is not attributable to the defect. He thought that in this situation the contractor should be paid for the value of the work unless the defendant presented evidence that tied the loss to the defect. 5A *Corbin on Contracts* § 1124, n 19.

[28] See JJ White and RS Summers *Uniform Commercial Code* 3rd edn (West, St Paul, Minn, 1988) 355–7 (concluding that 'relatively little is left' of the UCC perfect tender rule because courts have used a variety of devices to prevent sellers from rejecting goods in bad faith to escape a disadvantageous bargain).

[29] The Restatement defines forfeiture as 'the denial of compensation that results when the obligee loses his right to the agreed exchange after he has relied substantially'. Restatement (Second) of Contracts § 227 comment (b). The Restatement's definition of forfeiture suggests two baselines for measuring forfeiture. The reference to 'reliance' and 'the denial of compensation' suggests a baseline of the defaulter's pre-contractual position. The reference to the defaulter's 'right to the agreed exchange' suggests a baseline of the defaulter's position on performance.

[30] *Jacob and Youngs v Kent* 230 NY 239, 129 NE 889 (1921).

uncompensated loss.[31] *Plante v Jacobs*[32] is a commonplace illustration. A contractor misplaced a living room wall narrowing the room by one foot. The case holds that the Jacobs had to pay the balance due on the contract for the work done and that they could not recover the price of moving the wall (around $4,000) or other damages for the wall's misplacement because narrowing the room did not lower the house's market value. The Jacobs' loss from a having a smaller living room was uncompensated.

Plante v Jacobs illustrates the unremarkable proposition that the law does not enforce rights to the hilt, though non-enforcement may impose a small loss on the right-holder, when enforcement to the hilt would result in significant unjust enrichment. Even property rights can give way if an infringement is minor and enjoining the infringement would inflict an undue hardship on the infringer.[33] The result may also depend on Plante having misplaced the wall inadvertently. Had Plante knowingly disregarded the plans to reduce construction costs a court might find a material breach on the ground that he acted willfully or in bad faith. This finding could justify the court either relieving the Jacobs from the obligation to pay the balance of the contract price or awarding the Jacobs the cost of moving the wall. Again the treatment of property rights is similar. Typically the doctrine of undue hardship protects only innocent infringers.[34]

[31] *Peevyhouse v Garland Coal and Mining Co* 382 P 2d 109 (Okl 1962), cert den 375 US 906 (1963), is a famous and troublesome illustration on the related problem of choosing between loss in market value and remedial cost as a measure of damages for defective performance. Garland failed to fulfill its promise to restore seven acres of farmland that it had strip mined. The Peevyhouses were left with a large water-filled pit that barred access to other land they owned and leased. The cost of restoring the land was estimated as $29,000 while the market value of the seven acres taken by the pit was only $350 at the time. The jury had awarded $5,000. The Oklahoma Supreme Court reduced the award to $350 reasoning that damages were limited to loss in market value when remedial cost was grossly disproportionate. Peevyhouse is often paired with *Groves v John Wunder* 205 Minn 163, 286 NW 235 (1939), which holds that a defendant who willfully fails to perform must pay the remedial cost though it is far in excess of loss in market value.

Decisions such as *Peevyhouse* and *Groves* might seem a striking testament to the value placed on remedial simplicity in American law. In many of these cases the loss to the aggrieved party is between remedial cost and loss in market value. The law requires choosing one or the other objective measure of damages though we are confident one over-compensates and the other under-compensates. A difficulty with this justification for the rule is that the aggrieved party is entitled to put on evidence that he has abnormal interests or preferences that justify an award of remedial costs. If we are going to allow a judge or jury to evaluate this sort of evidence in choosing one or the other measure of damages it is a small additional burden to ask them to choose an intermediate amount. A possible explanation is that setting an intermediate amount is, under American law, inevitably a question for the jury. On the other hand, choosing one or the other objective measures can be done by a judge if the evidence is such that the judge can honestly conclude that no reasonable person could disagree that one or the other objective measures is the better approximation.

[32] 10 Wis 2d 567, 103 NW 2d 296 (1960).

[33] *Mannillo v Gorski* 54 NJ 378, 255 A2d 258 (1969) (innocent encroacher is made to pay only the market value of what he has taken).

[34] *Ariola v Nigro* 16 Ill 2d 46, 156 NE 2d 536 (1959) (relying on rule that an intentional encroachment will always be enjoined).

Cases like *Jacob & Youngs v Kent* and *Plante v Jacobs* are the exception and not the rule. American law permits a party to refuse non-conforming performance to avoid suffering an uncompensated loss though the refusal imposes a disproportionate loss on the defaulter. Sales law on the power to revoke acceptance provides an example. Revocation is more troublesome than rejection because the seller is likely to incur a loss when it must recover and resell goods that have been used by the buyer. Under the Uniform Commercial Code, a buyer may revoke acceptance for a hidden defect only if the defect 'substantially impairs' the value of the goods to him.[35] Commentators who have looked closely at the cases have found that courts are very protective of buyer's rights in applying this seller-friendly standard.[36]

Colonial Dodge Inc v Miller[37] nicely illustrates. Miller bought a station wagon with special ordered extra wide tyres. The car was delivered without a spare extra wide tyre. Miller discovered the tyre was missing within a day but after he had driven the car four hundred miles. He demanded a spare from the dealer and was told that it could not be supplied because of a strike at the factory. Miller immediately parked the car in front of his house and demanded that the dealer retrieve it. Eventually the car was towed from the street by the police where it was impounded for a number of years as the case passed through the courts. The dealer sued for the price. He won in the trial court, lost on appeal, won on rehearing, and finally lost at the state supreme court by a vote of six to three. The expected loss to the Miller from the temporary lack of a spare was small but, perhaps, meaningful to him.[38] Much of the loss would have been in worrying while driving without a spare. There was also a small chance that Miller would be stranded without a spare. None of these losses were compensable in damages. Returning the car imposed a large loss on the dealer for it could no longer be sold as new. That the case was thought close despite this imbalance between Miller's likely loss and the loss to the dealer — the thirteen judges who heard the case split seven to six with one switching — is telling evidence of the unwillingness of judges to require a party to take and pay for clearly defective performance when that would leave him with an uncompensated loss.

[35] UCC 2-608(1). The CISG has a fundamental default standard.
[36] JA Sebert Jr 'Rejection, Revocation, and Cure Under Article 2 of the Uniform Commercial Code: Some Modest Proposals' (1990) 84 *Northwestern University Law Review* 375, 399–408, is a good review of the case law. DW Garland 'Determining Whether a Nonconformity Substantially Impairs the Value of Goods: Some Guidelines' (1993) 26 *Uniform Commercial Code Law Journal* 129 comes to much the same conclusions.
[37] 420 Mich 452, 362 NW 2d 704 (1984).
[38] The dealer and the manufacturer thought Miller was returning the car on a pretext. Local newspaper and television had reported that dealers were delivering new cars without spares because of the auto strike. This being Detroit it was understandably big news. MacCauley, Kidwell and Whitford *Contracts Law in Action: The Concise Course* (Lexis-Nexis 2003) 130–1.

American contract law also permits a party to withhold performance to avoid suffering an uncompensated loss though this action inflicts a disproportionate loss on the defaulter. *Parker v Twentieth-Century Fox Film Corp*[39] illustrates. Shirley MacLaine Parker had a contract with Twentieth-Century Fox to play the female lead in *Bloomer Girl*, a musical about gender and racial conflict in the antebellum south with a precociously progressive female lead. The studio cancelled plans for *Bloomer Girl* and offered MacLaine as a substitute the female lead in *Big Country, Big Man*, a dramatic western, with the same base compensation, $750,000 for fourteen weeks work. MacLaine turned down the second part and sued for the base compensation. In its defence, the studio argued that MacLaine failed to mitigate damages by not taking the second role. The trial court rejected this defence on a motion for summary judgment. The fighting issue in the case was whether the question of the comparability of the roles (framed as whether the second role was 'different and inferior' to the first) should have gone to the jury. The California Supreme Court said no affirming the trial court.[40] Allowing MacLaine to refuse the second role probably is inefficient in the narrow sense that the studio's expected gain from the switch of the films exceeded her expected loss.[41] She was idled for fourteen weeks when she 'was one of the biggest female stars in Hollywood'.[42] Awarding her the base salary may well have given her a windfall at the studio's expense. She was paid for fourteen weeks while

[39] 3 Cal3d 176, 86 Cal Rptr 737, 474 P 2d 689 (1970). As often happens to cases in the canon, *Parker* has been used to make a variety of points. See V Goldberg '*Bloomer Girl* Revisited Or How to Frame an Unmade Picture' [1998] *Wisconsin Law Review* 1051 (explaining that the decision should have been rested on the ground that base price in the contract was paid by the studio to have an option on Parker's time); WJ Woodward Jr 'Clearing the Brush for Real-Life Contracting' (1999) 24 *Law & Social Inquiry* 99, 105 (explaining that the case is a good vehicle for exploring the difference between book law and real life); MJ Frug 'Re-reading Contracts: A Feminist Analysis of a Contracts Casebook' (1985) 34 *American Universities Law Review* 1065, 1114–25 (discussing feminist issues raised by the case).

[40] *Parker* is representative of the case law. A survey of recent contract and Title VII cases concludes that courts require that two positions be 'virtually identical' before they will require a terminated employee to take another position to mitigate damages. RJ Gonzales 'Satisfying the Duty to Mitigate in Employment Cases: A Survey and a Guide' (1991) 69 *Mississippi Law Journal* 749, 760–2. The author adds that courts have been more willing to require an employee to relocate when his line of work and past behavior indicated he was not averse to relocating. In Title VII cases (but not breach of contract claims), an employee may be denied full back wages past a certain time on the theory that he should take less desirable and lower paying work to mitigate damages.

[41] I express no view on whether the law's response in *Parker* is efficient in a larger perspective after we consider the possibility of re-negotiation or effects on contracting and reliance. Performance is efficient in the very restricted sense that I use the term when the joint expected return to the parties is positive.

[42] Goldberg (above n 38) 1052. I take the facts not found in the opinion from Goldberg's excellent article. Goldberg argues that there was an alternative basis for decision because the contract had a 'play or pay' provision that required the studio to pay MacClaine if it cancelled the project. Goldberg argues this was an easier basis. I think it was an easy mitigation case as well.

she took what may have been a much-needed break. But the result saved her from suffering what would otherwise have been an uncompensated loss. There is good reason to believe that MacLaine genuinely preferred the role in *Bloomer Girl* to the role in *Big Country, Big Man*. The court could not compensate her loss through damages because it was too speculative. Apparently the judges thought it better that a defaulter suffer a large loss than an aggrieved party suffer a smaller uncompensated loss.

The answer is the same in American law when the question is whether an aggrieved party must halt performance in response to default when he thinks it is in his interest to continue and collect the contract price. American law students are taught otherwise for a case often used to teach the mitigation doctrine, *Rockingham County v Luten Bridge Co*[43] holds that a contractor acted inappropriately in completing a bridge after the contract was cancelled. The treatment of *Luten Bridge* in the casebooks and teaching manuals suggests most teachers do not appreciate how exceptional the result is.[44] There are only a handful of cases like *Luten Bridge* in which a person hired to do work that is uniquely of value to another continues to do work after the other says stop and then sues for the contract price.[45] In this situation, the aggrieved party will recover the contract price if he can show he had to continue work to avoid suffering an uncompensated loss.[46] Indeed, an aggrieved party may continue work to

[43] 35 F 2d 301 (4th Cir 1929). English law is, at least nominally, even more protective of the contractor giving him a right to complete performance and recover the contract price unless, perhaps, he has no legitimate interest in performing the contract. *White & Carter (Councils) Ltd v McGregor* [1962] AC 413 (defendants cancelled contract to have plaintiff place advertisements on its litterbins on the day contract was made, plaintiffs went ahead and placed the advertisements for the three-year period of the contract and recovered the contract price). A Burrows *Remedies for Torts and Breach of Contract* 2nd edn (Butterworths, London, 1994) 317–22, surveys the inroads on the case. Continued performance is not allowed if it requires the cooperation of the other or if continuing is 'wholly unreasonable' (which is distinguished from being 'merely unreasonable'), meaning, I think, that continuing resulted in damages greatly increasingly and was unnecessary to protect the plaintiff's interests under the contract.

[44] For example, Farnsworth, Young and Sanger *Contracts* 6th edn (Foundation, New York, 2001) 494, present it as unexceptional 'that the injured party cannot recover for cost that could have been avoided by simply *stopping performance*' and poses as the difficult case where avoiding loss requires 'taking *affirmative steps*'.

[45] The classic case is *Clark v Marsiglia* 1 Denio (NY) 317, 43 Am Dec 670 (1845) (holding that a painter who completed painting after stop order could not recover contract price). Corbin cites four other cases. *Corbin on Contracts* § 1039 n 18.

[46] *O'Hare v Peacock Dairies Inc* 26 Cal App 2d 345, 79 P 2d 433 (1938) (holding that farmer could continue to produce and deliver milk to defendant under long-term contract because he ought not be obliged to sell his herd to stop production); *Southern Cotton-Oil Co v Heflin* 99 Fed 339 (1900) (holding that manufacturer of cotton seed who contracted to sell manufacturing by-products to defendant could continue production after stop order and recover difference between contract price and market price); *Northern Helix Co v United States* 19 Ct Cl 118, 455 F 2d 546 (1972), 207 Ct Cl 862, 524 F 2d 707 (1975), cert den 429 US 866 (1976) (holding that manufacturer could continue to produce and deliver helium under long-term contract where production was inter-related with other operations, manufacturer had no storage facilities, and there were no other buyers).

avoid an uncompensated loss even if this imposes a disproportionate loss on the other. As in *Parker*, courts do not try to balance interests except in the grossest sense.

Bomberger v McKelvey[47] illustrates. McKelvey bought a lot from Bomberger agreeing to pay Bomberger $3,500 to demolish a building on the lot. McKelvey planned to build a large drug store on several lots. McKelvey decided to delay construction of the store and ordered Bomberger not to proceed with demolition. Bomberger demolished the building anyway claiming that he needed skylights salvaged from the building, which were worth around $540, to fulfill another construction contract. The demolished building was worth around $26,000 and was generating $300 monthly rent. The case holds that Bomberger acted reasonably because getting substitute skylights may have delayed completion of his other project by several months. The court made no effort to quantify or to balance the parties' respective losses.

Of course, the right to perform and collect the contract price in the face of a repudiation is not absolute. English judges, who start from the premise that there is a right to perform and collect the contract price upon repudiation, have struggled to define when this right gives way. One judge summed it up this way: 'How one defines that point is obviously a matter of some difficulty, for it involves drawing a line between conduct which is merely unreasonable and conduct which is *wholly* unreasonable.'[48] This seems to me an apt description of the balance the courts struck in *Parker v Twentieth Century Fox* and *Bomberger v McKelvey*. In countenancing 'merely unreasonable' behaviour the English judge is saying that an aggrieved party may act to avoid an uncompensated loss though his action imposes a significantly larger loss on the defaulter.

The general principle is that a party may act in response to default by rejecting performance, withholding performance, or continuing to perform to protect himself from an uncompensated loss though his action inflicts a disproportionate loss on the defaulter. The theory of efficient breach misdescribes American contract law. This principle is not absolute, but when it gives way it is to avoid unjust enrichment — an outcome that would give the aggrieved party a significant windfall at the expense of the defaulter — and not in the interest of efficient performance.

II EXIT AND LOYALTY IN A BONA FIDE DISPUTE

This section examines the rules that regulate exit and loyalty when there is a bona fide dispute regarding the adequacy of performance due, tendered,

[47] 35 Cal 2d 607, 220 P 2d 729 (1950).
[48] *Clea Shipping Corp v Bulk Oil International Ltd* [1984] 1 All ER 129.

or demanded. It shows that the law permits a party to perform or accept performance in a dispute, and later seek redress in a court through a claim that he was obligated to do less or he was entitled to receive more, but only if his performance or acceptance of performance was necessary to avoid a loss. The goal of efficient performance is central to understanding this area of law.

This insight, while novel, should not be a surprise. Picture a contract as two people undertaking to row a boat across a river. In the middle of the river a dispute arises over whether one is pulling his weight. The law has two different sets of rules of engagement for the dispute. If the river is placid and the day is clear, the law encourages the rowers to resolve the dispute themselves in the boat as best they can. The law permits one rower to stop rowing until the other concedes, and if the rowers manage to make it across the river, the law treats this as the end of the matter and will not allow either rower to seek redress in court unless both rowers clearly agreed to stay their dispute until they got to shore. If the river is dangerous the law encourages the rowers to put their dispute to the side and row to safety where a court will hear their dispute and try to set matters right. If a rower stops, he is likely to be held responsible for the resulting loss even if he was in the right on the dispute. The law discourages threats to stop. And in extreme circumstances the law permits a rower to lie by pretending to submit to a threat in order to induce the rower making the threat to continue rowing.

The rules of engagement we are about to look at presuppose an honest dispute. Quite different rules kick in if a person makes a dishonest demand for performance or refuses to perform an obligation that he knows is due. Thus a note given to settle a dishonest claim or a release given by a creditor in return for part payment of an undisputed debt may be unenforceable for lack of consideration.[49] Unjustified non-payment of a debt will strip a debtor of contract rights. For example, it will give the creditor the right to accelerate future payments.[50] As we have seen, bad

[49] Lack of consideration was the argument eventually adopted in *Hackley v Headley* 50 Mich 43, 14 NW 693 (1883), to excuse a creditor from a release extracted by the debtor by a threat to withhold money that was not in dispute. For a more recent case along the same lines see *Wickman v Kane* 136 Md App 554, 766 A 2d 241, 246–7 (2001) (finding no valid accord and satisfaction where undisputed sum was paid to obtain release of a disputed claim on grounds of lack of consideration). The weight of authority is that refusal to pay money even in bad faith is not economic duress. *Selmer Co v Blakesell-Midwest Co* 704 F 2d 924 (7th Cir 1983). For an exceptional case to the contrary see *Capps v Georgia Pacific Corp* 253 Or 248, 453 P 2d 935 (1969).

[50] *Couch on Insurance* 3rd edn, (by Lee R Russ, St Paul, Minn, 1995) § 232:43. See *Williams v Mutual Benefits Health & Accident. Assoc* 100 F 2d 264, 265 (5th Cir 1938) (When one who is obligated by contract to make money payments to another, absolutely repudiates and abandons the obligation without just excuse, the obligee is entitled to maintain his action in damages at once for the entire default)(Texas law); *Needham v American National Insurance Co* 97 SW 2d 1016 (Tex Civ App Dallas 1936), writ dismissed.

faith breach may give the aggrieved party the power to withhold performance though it results in forfeiture by the defaulter. And there is the late twentieth century innovation of the tort of bad faith breach of contract. This tort exposes an insurer who unjustifiably denies a claim to liability for emotional distress damages and sometimes punitive damages. Dangerous legal shoals these but they do not threaten if a refusal to perform or a demand for performance is honest. So non-payment of insurance is a tort only if it is in bad faith. The tort of bad faith breach permits an insurer to test a questionable claim in court no matter how hard the decision to fight may be on the insured and no matter how small the claim.[51]

The voluntary payment doctrine is a good place to start. It is an exemplar of the rules that encourage immediate resolution of a dispute when withholding performance will not have ruinous consequences. The doctrine cuts off the claim of a debtor who pays a disputed debt.[52] Its rationale is to ensure 'that those who desire to assert a legal right do so at the first possible opportunity; this way, all interested parties are aware of that position and have the opportunity to tailor their own conduct accordingly'.[53] Other rules cut off the claim of a creditor who accepts part payment. The rules on accord and satisfaction permit what has been described as 'an exquisite form of commercial torture'.[54] They enable a debtor to tender part payment of a disputed debt that the creditor can take only if he relinquishes his claim for the balance.[55] And a creditor has little hope of avoiding a release on ground of duress because of a precept foreclosing claims of financial distress.[56]

[51] WT Barker 'Evidentiary Insufficiency in Insurance Bad Faith Suits' (1999) 6 *Connecticut Insurance Law Journal* 81, 110.

[52] Restatement (Third) of Restitution and Unjust Enrichment, Tentative Draft No 1, § 6, comment (e) (stating that voluntary payment rule will bar recovery of payment of disputed claim) and illustration 18. Reporter's Note (e) provides authority.

[53] *Randazo v Harris Bank Palatine* 262 F 3d 663, 668 (7th Cir 2001).

[54] J White and RS Summers *Handbook of the Law under the Uniform Commercial Code* 2nd edn (St Paul, Minn, West Publishing, 1980) §13–21, 544. This sentiment is echoed in *Horn Waterproofing Corp v Bushwick Iron & Steel Co* 66 NY 2d 321, 326, 488 NE 2d 56, 59, 497 NYS 2d 310, 313 (1985).

[55] The history of former Uniform Commercial Code § 1-207 (now § 1-308) attests to the strength of this practice. The statute allows a party to reserve his rights while accepting performance offered by the other party. Though the statute made no exception many courts held this provision did not apply to an accord and satisfaction. Courts had split on whether the statute changed the common law doctrine of accord and satisfaction. *Air Van Lines Inc v Buster* 673 P 2d 774 (1984), is a leading case holding that the statute did not alter the common law rule. For a contrary case that reviews the arguments and authority on both sides see *Horn Waterproofing Corp v Brunswick Iron & Steel Co Inc* 66 NY 2d 321, 497 NYS 2d 310, 488 NE 2d 56 (1985). An explicit exception was added in 1990.

[56] An often-litigated question involves the effectiveness of a release given by a creditor to settle a disputed debt when in exchange for the release the debtor pays a sum that was not in dispute. The weight of the authority is that a release is valid in these circumstances if there is a single debt or closely related debts. *Kilander v Blickle Co* 280 Or 425, 428–9, 571 P 2d 503,

The voluntary payment doctrine has the familiar stickiness of an interpretive presumption. Payment is final unless the parties' state clearly that this was not their intent. The rule is sticky in another more unusual way. Under the traditional rule, a debtor cannot avoid the voluntary payment doctrine by saying when he pays that he reserves his right to recover the money.[57] The rules on accord and satisfaction (and the precept foreclosing a duress claim) are similar in that they prevent the creditor from unilaterally reserving his right to sue for the balance if he takes part payment. The upshot of these rules is that avoiding finality on payment requires both parties' expressed assent.

Another body of rules permits a party to perform or accept performance in a dispute and still have his day in court. *Henrici v South Feather Land & Water Co*[58] illustrates these rules. One will recall that Henrici and South Feather disagreed about South Feather's right to increase the price of water. The decision holds that Henrici was responsible for the damage to his farm when he refused to take the water and pay the price South Feather demanded.[59] This was so even though Henrici was in the right on

504–5 (Or 1977). However there is authority that 'circumstances of unfair pressure or economic coercion' cut in the other direction: *Flagel v Southwest Clinical Physiatrists* 157 Ariz 196, 202, 755 P 2d 1184, 1190 (Ariz App 1988).

[57] For clear statements that a reservation of rights does not avoid the voluntary payment doctrine see *Rowe v Union Central Life Insurance Co* 194 Miss 328, 12 So 2d 431, 433–4 (1943), and 75 ALR 658 (stating that a payment may not be recovered 'though the payer makes the payment with an express reservation of his right to litigate the claim'.) This rule is codified in Georgia. OCGA §13–1–13. The Restatement (Third) of Restitution will take this position.

A handful of cases hold that a reservation of rights avoids the bar of the voluntary payment doctrine. See *Community Convalescent Center Of Naperville Inc v First Interstate Mortgage Company Of Illinois* 181 Ill App 3d 996, 999, 537 NE 2d 1162, 1164, 130 Ill Dec 833, 835 (1989) ('since plaintiff paid the 30 days' interest 'under protest,' plaintiff is not barred from recovery under the voluntary-payment doctrine.'); *Avianca Inc v Corriea* 1992 WL 93128 (DDC 1992) ('The voluntary payment doctrine does not generally apply, however, when a party has expressly reserved a right to take some legal action or when the party has paid under protest.') A few other cases state in *dicta* that a debtor could have reserved his rights. *Prenalta Corp v Colorado Interstate Gas Co* 944 F 2d 677 (10th Cir 1991); *Randazzo v Harris Bank Palatine NA* 262 F 3d 663, 671 (7th Cir 2001); *Getto v City of Chicago* 86 Ill 2d 39, 49, 55 Ill Dec 519, 426 NE 2d 844 (1981); *Putnam v Time Warner Cable of Southeastern Wisconsin* 274 Wis 2d 41, 59, 663 NW 2d 254, 263 (2001); *City of Miami v Keton* 115 So 2d 547, 552 (Fla 1959).

The older cases tend to treat a protest as evidence of duress. This comes from framing the issue as a problem in restitution. If the issue is framed as a problem in contract, then the question is what it takes to establish an agreement by the payee that the payment is conditional upon the validity of his claim. Such an agreement avoids the bar of the voluntary payment doctrine. See Restatement of Restitution §45, comment (e) ('The rule stated in this Section does not apply if the parties have agreed that the payment is conditional upon the validity of the transferee's claim.') The general principle that the offeror is master of the offer supports the conclusion that if the payor conditions payment on a reservation of rights than the payee acquiesces in that when he accepts the payment. *Prenalta Corp* approaches the issue on this basis.

[58] 177 Cal 442, 170 P 1135 (1918).

[59] As we shall see, Henrici had another option. He might have tendered the old price pending resolution of the dispute. Had South Feather responded to this tender by cutting off the water supply that would be a material breach by it and it would be responsible for the damage to Henrici's farm. Henrici's tender of the old price would not be a material breach by

the underlying issue of price. Crucial to the decision is the court's assumption that Henrici would not have waived his right to challenge price had he taken the water and paid what South Feather asked. While the court did not explain presumably it would have allowed a restitution claim by Henrici to recover the over-payment. I will say more about this restitution claim shortly.

Changing the facts in *Henrici* brings to the fore several rules that encourage cooperation in a dispute when non-cooperation would be harmful. What would have happened had South Feather told Henrici that taking the water constituted acceptance of the new price and a waiver of his claim to the old price? This is the accord and satisfaction gambit. It is clear that Henrici could recover for his losses if he refused the water and was in the right on price. His duty to mitigate would not require him to relinquish his claim of a right to pay less.[60] By casting the loss back on South Feather the rule punishes South Feather for escalating the dispute.

Moreover, under UCC §1-308[61] Henrici might still be able to take the water and reserve his rights by saying he was doing so notwithstanding South Feather's insistence that taking the water means he relinquishes the claim.[62] This response enables Henrici to test South Feather's resolve because South Feather would have to follow through on its threat to stop delivery of water. The law might even allow Henrici to deceive South Feather to defuse the conflict. If Henrici agreed to South Feather's demand to get water he desperately needed he might be able to avoid the contract by claiming duress. South Feather's threat to withhold water is border-line extortion and a core instance of bad faith because the threatened act would inflict a large loss on Henrici while yielding a small benefit

him justifying suspension of performance by South Feather because any loss from underpayment is easily compensated should South Feather be in the right. Further, Henrici's tender of the old price is in good faith. In sum, Henrici had two choices in the case — he could pay either the new or the old price pending resolution of the dispute — between which the law is indifferent. This is sensible for, putting issues like insolvency and collection to the side, there is no reason to prefer one party over the other when we ask who should hold money in dispute pending resolution of the dispute.

[60] Restatement (Second) of Contracts §350, comment (e) ('If the party in default offers to perform the contract for a different price, this may amount to a suitable alternative. But this is not the case if the offer is conditioned on surrender by the injured party of his claim for default.'), and Illustration 15, which is based on *Gilson v FS Royster Guano Co* 1 F 2d 82 (3rd Cir 1924). See also *Corbin on Contracts* §1043, 274–5 (stating that there is no duty to take substitute performance from defaulting party if it would involve a surrender of rights, compromise, or accord and satisfaction).

[61] This is former §1-207. It provides: 'A party that with explicit reservation of rights performs or promises performance or assents to performance in a manner demanded or offered by the other party does not thereby prejudice the rights reserved. Such words as "without prejudice", "under protest" or the like are sufficient.'

[62] UCC §1-308. This is implicit in the line of cases holding that a creditor could use §1-308 (formerly § 1-207) to take payment offered in satisfaction and then sue for the balance. See n 55.

to South Feather.[63] The doctrine of duress and UCC §1–308 in effect allow a party unilaterally to dictate that performance is not final to preserve a claim of right.

There is more. Even if South Feather was in the right in the underlying dispute, its refusal to deliver the water unless Henrici relinquished his claim of a right to the old price would likely be considered a material breach by South Feather. It would have no right to withhold the water though Henrici persisted in paying the old price because the slight under-payment would not be a material breach by Henrici. Often when a contractual relationship breaks down it is a result of reciprocal escalation of a dispute. In this situation a court may assign the entire loss from the break-down to one party by holding that he was the first materially to breach the contract. This will be whoever the court believes inappropriately escalated the dispute. As *Henrici v South Feather Land & Water Co.* illustrates, it need not be the party who is in the wrong in the underlying dispute.

K&G Construction Co v Harris[64] shows how the doctrine of material breach enables a court to assign the loss from a breakdown to the party who the court believes inappropriately escalated a dispute. Harris had a contract with K&G to excavate and move dirt in K&G's multi-house construction project. Harris' bulldozer damaged a house and Harris and his insurer denied liability. In response, K&G withheld progress payments totalling less than the amount of its claim. Harris in turn stopped work and K&G hired another company to finish the job. Both parties suffered a loss. K&G paid the substitute more than it would have paid Harris; Harris lost the profit he would have made completing the job. If the court thought that K&G acted inappropriately in withholding progress payments, then it could hold this was a material breach. Harris would then have been in the right in leaving the job and he would recover his lost profits. Instead the court concluded that Harris materially breached the contract when it withdrew from the job. K&G recovered the additional cost of the substitute. In a moment I will explain why the court was right in assigning fault to Harris.

Cases like *K&G Construction* raise the question whether a party's honest but incorrect belief that he is acting within his rights is relevant to determining the quality of his breach. Two apparently contradictory propositions bracket the answer. One is from the Restatement (Second) of

[63] Restatement (Second) of Contracts §176(2)(a) defines a threat as improper 'if the resulting exchange is not on fair terms' and 'the threatened act would harm the recipient and would not significantly benefit the party making the threat'. *Silsbee v Webber* 171 Mass 378, 50 NE 555 (1898) (threat by employer directed at employee's mother to tell his ill-father of his theft if mother did not pay off the loss), is an example in the blackmail vein. J Dawson 'Economic Duress — An Essay in Perspective' (1947) 45 *Michigan Law Review* 253, proposes disproportionality as an organising principle.

[64] 223 Md 305, 164 A 2d 451 (1960).

Contracts: 'Generally, a party acts at his peril if, insisting on what he mistakenly believes to be his rights, he refuses to perform his duty'.[65] The other is from *Corbin on Contracts*: 'Disputes often arise as to what performance the contract requires; and the plaintiff's default is not willful if he performs in accordance with his own honest interpretation, even though he knows the other party holds a different one'.[66] Each proposition is true to a point. The apparent contradiction largely disappears once you realise they are speaking of different responses to breach.[67] The Restatement speaks to whether a defaulter's belief that he performed his

[65] Restatement (Second) of Contracts §250 (When a Statement or an Act Is a Repudiation), comment (d). Illustration 9 states that A's good faith belief that he is not obligated to deliver a deed until August 1 does not protect A when he threatens not to deliver the deed at all unless B agrees to accept it on August 1 rather than July 30, the date the deed is actually due to be delivered. The example misfires. The threat may be inappropriate even if A is correct in his belief that the deed is not due until August 1.

[66] 5A *Corbin on Contracts* §1123, 9 (1964). Corbin does not cite case authority. For some see *WJ Walker v Shasta Minerals & Chemical Co* 352 F 2d 634, 638 (10th Cir 1965); *Golf Carts Inc v Mid-Pacific Country Club* 493 P 2d 1338, 1340 (Haw 1972); *Hanson v Duffy* 106 Ill App 3d 727, 62 Ill Dec 401, 435 NE 2d 1373, 1378 (1982); *Berke & Co v Griffin Inc* 116 NH 760, 765, 367 A 2d 583, 586–7 (1976); *Kiriakides v United Artists Communications Inc* 440 SE 2d 364, 367 (SC 1994). *New York Life Insurance Co v Viglas* 297 US 672, 676–7 (1936) famously holds than an insured cannot accelerate payments due under an insurance policy when the insurer fails to make a payment in the honest belief it is not due. Cardozo explains:

> Repudiation there was none as the term is known to the law. Petitioner did not disclaim the intention or the duty to shape its conduct in accordance with the provisions of the contract. Far from repudiating those provisions, it appealed to their authority and endeavored to apply them. ... If it made a mistake, there was a breach of a provision of the policy with liability for any damages appropriate thereto. We do not pause at the moment to fix the proper measure. Enough in this connection that at that stage of the transaction there had been no renunciation or abandonment of the contract as a whole.

The converse proposition is that bad faith in an offer of performance is a reason for treating the offer as a material breach. For authority see *Peter Kiewit Sons' Co v Summit Construction Co* 422 F 2d 242, 257 (8th Cir 1969) ('Kiewit's meager offer of $143,000 on June 29 as compensation for all the extra backfill work is so lacking in good faith as to constitute a repudiation of the Subcontract. ... Kiewit's lack of good faith is evident from its $143,000 offer, which was but 10 per cent of Summit's estimate.'); *Pacific Coast Engineering Co v Merritt-Chapman & Scott Corp* 411 F 2d 889 (9th Cir 1969) (holding that persistent assertion of position party had been told by third parties was unjustified is a repudiation).

[67] Corbin's proposition should be distinguished from the proposition that the presentation of a claim or demand in bad faith standing alone is not a breach of contract. The difference, if there is one, is between words and deeds. *Reiss v Murchison* 503 F 2d 999 (9th Cir 1974), cert den 420 US 993 (1975) (holding that the filing of a claim of total breach does not give the party against whom the claim is asserted the right to halt performance); *Oak Ridge Construction Co v Tolley* 351 Pa Super 32, 504 A 2d 1343, 1348 (1985); *Dixie Roof Decks Inc v Borggren/Dickson Construction Inc* 195 Ga App 881, 395 SE 2d 19 (1990); *In re Chateaugay Corp* 104 BR 637 (SDNY 1989). Relatedly, it is not a breach of contract or a tort to use legal process to resolve a dispute or to protect one's position pending resolution even though the use of process harms the other party at least so long as the process is used in good faith. *Wachter v Gratech Co Ltd* 608 NW 2d 279, 288–9 (ND 2000) (holding that it is not abuse of process to file a mechanic's lien that turned out to be grossly excessive in amount if the filing was done in good faith). (*Note continues overleaf.*)

obligation saves him from liability to the other for damages. The answer generally is no. Corbin speaks to whether a defaulter's belief that he performed his obligation is relevant to deciding whether his breach was material giving the other the power to exit. The answer is yes, but it is only one factor among several.

The boundaries between these different rules of engagement for contract disputes are not well defined. There is little in the voluntary payment rule to preclude its application had Henrici paid what South Feather demanded.[68] The best argument is that Henrici's payment is not voluntary, but this argument runs into the counter-arguments that South Feather did nothing improper in demanding a payment it thought within its rights and that Henrici had other options that would have adequately protected his interests. One court has drawn a boundary between the rule in UCC §1-308,[69] which allows a party to perform or accept performance in a dispute while reserving his rights, and the common law rule of accord and satisfaction, which does not. The case holds that §1-308 applies in a continuing dispute on an executory contract.[70] This is a bit over-broad. It means that Henrici could not try to force a settlement on his terms by tendering a cheque for the old price in satisfaction, which seems right.[71] But it also means that a lessee could never rely on payment in satisfaction to resolve a dispute over past rent on a continuing lease. A concern with threats that would inflict disproportionate harm if carried out is an important strand in the law of duress.[72] As you shall see, this gets at the crucial

Two of these propositions clash in *Woodar Investment Development Ltd v Wimpey Construction UK Ltd* [1980] 1 WLR 277 (HL). Lord Wilberforce echoes the proposition from Corbin: 'it would be a regrettable development of the law of contract to hold that a party who bona fide relies on an express stipulation in a contract in order to rescind or terminate a contract should, by that fact alone, be treated as having repudiated his contractual obligations if he turns out to be mistaken as to his rights'. Lord Salmon, quoting Lord Denning in an earlier case, echoes the Restatement: 'I have yet to learn that a party who breaks his contract can excuse himself by saying that he did it on advice of his lawyers; or that he was under an honest misapprehension. Nor can he excuse himself on these grounds from the consequences of a repudiation.'

[68] Palmer argues that doubt about a debt should not always bar recovery of a payment. He cites *Pilot Insurance Co v Cudd* 208 SC 6, 36 SE 2d 860 (1945), where an insurer was allowed to recover death benefits paid for a sailor missing at sea after the government issued a certificate stating the insured 'is presumed to have died'. A policy favoring quick payment of insurance claims is said to support such decisions. As important is the war-time setting, which makes it impractical for the insurer to investigate the claim to resolve the uncertainty. Palmer adds that the result should be otherwise if the insurer paid less than in full for that would suggest the payment was a compromise of a disputed claim. GE Palmer *Law of Restitution* (Little Brown, Boston, 1978) §14.7.

[69] Former § 1-207. This section permits a party to perform or assent to performance in a manner demanded or offered by the other party while reserving his rights by stating that he acts 'under protest' or like words.

[70] *Air Van Lines Inc v Buster* 673 P 2d 774 (1984).

[71] The concern is that after rightfully rejecting the cheque South Feather would halt delivery of water for total non-payment.

[72] Restatement (Second) of Contracts §176(2)(a), defines a threat as improper 'if the resulting exchange is not on fair terms' and 'the threatened act would harm the recipient and would

factor. But the law of duress is quite fuzzy once one gets beyond a few core cases of classically wrongful threats, and there are cases stating categorically that 'it is not duress for a party to insist upon what he believes to be his legal rights'.[73]

A rule proposed in a draft of the Restatement (Third) of Restitution and Unjust Enrichment identifies the key factor. The rule addresses the case where a party renders a performance he disputes he owes and later brings a restitution claim to recover its cost or value. The rule allows the restitution claim but only if nonperformance by either party would impose consequential harm.[74] In cases covered by the voluntary payment rule, which cuts off the restitution claim, withholding payment or the counter-performance imposes no such harm. This rule supplies a basis for the restitution claim in *Henrici v South Feather Land & Water Co.* An article I published in 2002 proposes such a rule and makes a doctrinal and policy argument for it.[75] That article also shows that the rule is an alternative basis for many cases that allow a party to rescind a contract on breach and recover damages for the cost of his performance when such cost is in excess of the contract price, including the notorious *Boomer v Muir*.[76] In a substantial majority of the cases in which the optional restitution claim is used to recover costs exceeding the contract price the cost overrun is attributable to the other's breach.

Whether a party's decision to withhold or refuse performance imposes a consequential loss is important in the assignation of fault under the rules of material breach and mitigation when parties escalate an honest dispute. Recall *K&G Construction*. A subcontractor damaged the general contractor's property and denied legal responsibility. The general contractor withheld progress payments totalling less than the amount of its claim. The subcontractor then stopped work forcing the general contractor to hire another firm to do the work. The court cast the loss on the subcontractor. The rules on material breach and mitigation compel the result. In the absence of bad faith, the rules on material breach and mitigation ask a court to balance a party's need to withhold or refuse performance to avoid suffering an uncompensated loss with the resulting burden on the other party. Neither the subcontractor's denial of responsibility for the damage to the property nor the general contractor's withholding of money due was a material

not significantly benefit the party making the threat'. Comment (f) misfires by suggesting the concern is with malice or vindictiveness rather than with coercion. Illustration 12 gives as an example an employer's threat to prevent an employee from working elsewhere if he does not release a claim. The employer makes the threat for his own gain and not out of malice. If he carries out the threat he probably does it to back up the threat and not out of malice.

[73] *Jacobs v Atlantco Ltd Partnership No 1* 36 Md App 335, 347, 373 A 2d 1255, 1261 (1977).
[74] Restatement (Third) of Restitution and Unjust Enrichment, Council Draft No 5, §35, comment (b).
[75] MP Gergen 'Restitution as a Bridge Over Troubled Contractual Waters' (2002) 71 *Fordham Law Review* 79.
[76] 24 P 2d 570 (Cal App 1933).

breach because there was no net loss from the delay in payment and each party's individual loss could easily be compensated. The subcontractor's abandonment of the job was both a failure to mitigate damages and a material breach because it caused a significant joint net loss.

That a party avoids a loss by accepting deficient performance is also relevant to the determination that acceptance is not a waiver of his right not to pay the contract price for the defective performance. Judge Posner has made the general point.[77] Sales law rules that define the effects of a buyer's acceptance of defective goods also serve the goal of efficient performance. A buyer may revoke his acceptance if he takes goods with assurances that a defect will be cured so long his interim use of the goods does not greatly diminish their value.[78] More generally, when performance is such that it cannot be returned without a material loss — the classic example is an improvement to property — its retention does not trigger waiver or estoppel.[79] The consequence is that an owner may refuse to pay the contract price while keeping a defective improvement.[80] The rule eliminates the incentive an owner of property otherwise would have to destroy unsatisfactory work done to his property in order to avoid having to pay the contract price for the work.

The common principle is that performance or acceptance of performance in a dispute is not final — loyalty will not cut off a claim that less was owed or more was due — if the performance or acceptance of performance avoids a consequential or joint loss. It is difficult to find authority for what may seem a logical corollary to this principle. This is a principle countenancing exit as the preferred response when a contract is uncertain and exit does not impose a consequential or joint loss.

A rare exception is a 1995 decision by Judge Posner. The case is *CL Maddox Inc v Coalfield Services*.[81] Maddox subcontracted with Coalfield to

[77] *McElroy v BF Goodrich* 73 F 3d 722 (7th Cir 1996) (declining to find waiver or estoppel where the plaintiff 'was simply making the best of a bad deal — and incidentally mitigated his damages'.) This point was unnecessary to reach the holding for the decision goes on to find the plaintiff's claim of default was unfounded.

[78] UCC §2-608.

[79] Restatement (Second) of Contracts §246(1) and (2). Comment (d) explains that this is so because it would be unfair to put the obligor to the choice between incurring the expense of restoring the property to its original condition or paying for the defective improvements.

[80] Most American states give the contractor a restitution claim if he can prove the value of his work to the owner. Giving the owner the upper hand in litigation on the contractor's claim for restitution encourages the owner not to demolish unsatisfactory work in order to avoid having to pay more than its worth to him. Some states (and English law) go even further and give the contractor no claim for the value of his work. For American law see above nn 4 and 5. *Sumpter v Hedges* [1898] 1 QB 673 (CA) illustrates the position of English law. A contractor who abandoned an uncompleted project recovered for materials left on site used by the owner but not for work done. The Law Commission for England and Wales advocated allowing a restitution claim in its Report No 121 'Pecuniary Restitution on Breach of Contract' (1983).

[81] 51 F 3d 76 (7th Cir 1995).

do underground mine demolition work at a price of $230,000. Coalfield faxed a contract stating that it would do the work in three weeks provided it could work day and night seven days a week. Maddox asked for and got a change in a term that was irrelevant to the eventual dispute and said that it would sign and return the contract. This it never did despite repeated requests by Coalfield. Coalfield worked for over two weeks and found the work going much slower than expected partly because it was not allowed to work Sundays. Coalfield estimated the job was 45 percent complete at this point and submitted its first bi-weekly bill. At the same time it pulled its men off the site. It is not clear how much this stoppage would have delayed work.[82] Maddox offered to pay the amount requested less 10 per cent but asked Coalfield to sign a letter agreeing to extend the deadline by one week and to pay $1,000 liquidated damages per day after this deadline.[83] Coalfield refused to go back to work on these terms telling Maddox that the job would take five to six more weeks to finish. The trial judge initially concluded that Coalfield broke the contract, but he got qualms about this conclusion and passed the case over to a magistrate, who decided that Maddox broke the contract. The court of appeals affirmed with Judge Posner writing the opinion. His specific arguments do not stand up, but unreported facts may well explain the decision.[84]

A striking feature of the case is Judge Posner's refusal to decide who was in the right on the underlying dispute. This turned on whether

[82] Coalfield argued that it could have put men back to work immediately. Judge Posner inferred that the stoppage entailed at least an eight day delay based on a Coalfield fax. 51 F 3d 80.

[83] It is not clear from the opinion how strongly Coalfield insisted upon this. On this potentially crucial point the opinion says: 'he appeared to condition this promise [to pay the invoice] on Coalfield's signing an "acceptance letter" that Maddox enclosed'. 51 F 3d 78.

[84] Judge Posner concluded 'that the most plausible interpretation of Maddox's action is that it was seeking excuses for not paying Coalfield anything'. 51 F 3d 80. Maddox's failure to sign and return the contract hardly suggests this. Given Maddox's acquiescence in Coalfield starting no one could reasonably question that there was some sort of contract under which Maddox would pay for the work that was done. Nor does the letter 'demanding' that Coalfield agree to pay liquidated damages support Judge Posner's conclusion. Maddox offered to pay for the work done less 10 percent of the contract price. Liquidated damages were only $1,000 per day. Had the job taken the eight weeks predicted by Coalfield liquidated damages would have been $28,000 on a $230,000 contract. The decision is on weak legal grounds as well. Judge Posner was forced to rest on UCC §2-609 because he reasoned that the stoppage occurred before the demand letter. That section allows a party to suspend performance if he asks for and does not get adequate assurances when he has reasonable grounds for insecurity regarding the other party's performance. The difficulty with this argument is that the only basis for insecurity was Maddox's failure to sign and return the form contract and the only demands for assurances were Coalfield's requests that the contract be signed. This puts a great deal of weight on nonperformance of an act that is often a formality. The opinion does not disclose the contents or tenor of Coalfield's repeated requests that the contract be signed. Perhaps those requests made it clear that getting the signed contract was important to Coalfield, which it might well have been because the contracts had terms, such as an indemnity clause, protecting Coalfield from significant risks of doing underground mine work. The decision would be very understandable if Coalfield warned Maddox that it was going to stop work if it did not get a signed contract.

Coalfield had promised to do the work in three weeks and whether Coalfield had a legal excuse for falling behind. Maddox raised the general issue by arguing that Coalfield seized upon the demand letter to get out of what it knew was a losing contract. Judge Posner rejected the argument reasoning that how litigation under the contract would have come out was uncertain.[85] Another striking aspect of the case is Judge Posner's argument that Coalfield was justified in halting work once litigation loomed because of the risk of a screwy result in litigation.[86] This reasoning treats parties to a contract who dispute a material term in good faith as if they had no contract. The upshot is that a party has no duty to incur substantial costs in the face of legal uncertainty. This reasoning goes against the grain of modern contract law, which holds parties to indefinite agreements.[87] But, as we shall see, Judge Posner is on to something important.

The more common response in the situation where there is a mutual falling out over a contract and the parties go to court is that the court will determine who was in the right in the dispute and then assign damages on that basis. Courts do not do what Judge Posner did, which is to say it was right to walk from the contract because it was uncertain. *Hope's Architectural Products Inc v Lundy's Construction Inc*[88] illustrates the more common response. Lundy's hired Hope's to manufacture custom-build window fixtures for a school construction project. The contract price was $55,000. Production was to take twelve to fourteen weeks but it was delayed for reasons that Hope's claimed were outside its control. In late September Lundy's requested that installation begin by October 19. Lundy's repeated this demand on October 14 and threatened to charge liquidated damages for delay though the contract did not provide for liquidated damages. Hope's shipped the windows on October 28 to be delivered on November 4. On November 1, Lundy's again called Hope's asking where the windows were and warning that there might be a

[85] 51 F 3d 81–2.
[86] 51 F 3d 80 ('Every day that Coalfield continued working, it put itself further in Maddox's power. Had it finished the job it would have found itself owed $230,000 with no leverage over Maddox to extract the money short of a suit to enforce what, depending on Mr. Maddox's testimony and its reception by a jury, might be merely a vague oral contract.')
[87] UCC §1–204(3).
[88] 781 F Supp 711 (D Kans 1991). The prologue to the opinion says a fair amount about the judge's approach:

> This case presents a familiar situation in the field of construction contracts. Two parties, who disagreed over the meaning of their contract, held their positions to the brink, with litigation and loss the predictable result of the dispute. What is rarely predictable, however, (and what leads to a compromise resolution of many construction disputes when cool heads hold sway) is which party will ultimately prevail. The stakes become winner-take-all.

781 F Supp 711–12.

substantial back-charge.[89] Hope's responded by refusing to deliver the windows unless the contract price was first paid in full, placed in escrow, or given to the architect. Lundy's refused saying it could not get the money on short notice from the school district. Hope's did not deliver the windows and Lundy's bought substitutes elsewhere. Hope's sued for the contract price.[90] Hope's disputed the delivery date, whether time was of the essence, and excuse. The court resolved each point against Hope's.[91] A decision for Lundy's followed with two more steps. The court reasoned that Hope's default gave Lundy's the right to withhold damages[92] and that this made Hope's demands for pre-payment in full unreasonable.[93] One can imagine a different result had Hope's been in the right in the claim that the two-week delay in delivering the window's was not a breach of contract or at least not a material breach. Then Lundy's would have been acting unreasonably in threatening to charge liquidated damages (which it would have no right to do) making Hope's demands for pre-payment more reasonable.

CL Maddox and *Hope's Architectural Products* appear irreconcilable.[94] *CL Maddox* stands for the proposition that uncertainty about one's rights and obligations justifies withholding performance in a dispute. *Hope's Architectural Products* stands for the opposite proposition. The premise is that a party who stands on uncertain rights to justify withholding performance gambles. If he is found to be wrong on the underlying dispute, he will be made to bear the resulting loss. Other cases pointing in these and other directions could be recited,[95] but there is little value in this exercise. These two decisions fairly represent the state of the law. *Hope's Architectural Products* is a thoughtful decision by a trial judge who conscientiously works

[89] Hope's said a 20 per cent back-charge was threatened. Lundy's said a back-charge of an unspecified amount was discussed. 781 F Supp 712.

[90] It is mistake to infer from the absence of a counter-claim by Lundy's that Lundy's suffered no loss from having to purchase the windows from another source. Lundy's might not have filed a counter-claim fearing that would raise the issue of whether it should have mitigated damages by taking the windows from Hope's.

[91] 781 F Supp 714–15.

[92] UCC §2-717 gives a buyer this right. There is no case law explicitly addressing whether this provision protects a buyer who withholds payment wrongly but in good faith.

[93] The court analyzed the demand as a demand for reasonable assurances under UCC §2-609. There is authority that a party in default cannot invoke §2-609. See *Palmco Corp v American Airlines Inc* 983 F 2d 681 (5th Cir 1993).

[94] The two cases have one feature in common. In both cases the law left the parties where it found them.

[95] A recent California case points in a third and radically different direction. It holds that in a dispute where a contract is so indefinite that it is not fair to say that either party was in the wrong a court should be flexible and try to fashion a remedy that will 'effect justice under the circumstances' to both parties. *Denver D Darling Inc v Controlled Environments Construction Inc* 89 Cal App 4th 1221, 1238, 108 Cal Rptr 2d 213, 224–5 (2001). This approach seems feasible only when the parties do work together and the issue is how to split the risks and rewards of cooperation.

through the arguments. *CL Maddox* is a typically bold and argumentative decision by Judge Posner.

I think there are few decisions like *CL Maddox* because courts have not had directly to confront the question whether it is appropriate to walk away from an uncertain contract. Under the common law, a court could avoid the question by ruling that uncertainty about the making or terms of a contract meant there was no contract. The Uniform Commercial Code (UCC) makes these outs more difficult. Before the UCC, Judge Posner could have found no contract by invoking the mirror image rule or by ruling that the contract was conditioned upon Maddox returning Coalfield's form.[96] With the relaxation of these rules we are likely to see more decisions like *CL Maddox* that explicitly countenance exit in the face of uncertainty to avoid the costs and hazards of litigation. This is the important thing that Judge Posner is on to.

Once this possibility is on the table the question will arise what makes exit an inappropriate response in the face of legal uncertainty? The natural answer is when exit imposes a consequential loss. Once the decision is made to hold parties to an uncertain contract because of the gains from cooperation, then determining who is in the right in the underlying dispute is relevant to determining who is in the wrong when a dispute ends in a total breakdown. That determination will be decisive even if the parties are equally obdurate. But it is not always decisive. A party cannot exit from a contract, even though the other party is in the wrong, if exit imposes a consequential loss and is unnecessary to protect his interests in the contract.[97]

III CONCLUSION

The cases and rules examined in this chapter show the common law method at its best and worst. I know of few areas in the common law that are so muddled. It is easy to think of reasons for the muddle. The common law got off on a very bad foot in dealing with these problems.[98] Much of the relevant law is organised around the law's response — eg restitution,

[96] UCC §2–207(3) clearly forecloses the first argument and probably forecloses the second.

[97] In this light one fact is crucial to the outcome in *Hope's Architectural Products*. In proposing that the full purchase price be put in escrow or in the hands of the architect Hope's offered Lundy's a way out of the impasse that would have addressed the concerns of both parties. It is apparent that neither party trusted the other to hold the money in dispute. But Lundy's responded with good reason for rejecting this solution — it could not get the money on short notice from the school district.

[98] Consider Williston's qualms over allowing a claim to be brought on a repudiated contract before the time of performance. Williston 'Repudiation of Contracts' (1901) 14 *Harvard Law Review* 421, 428. Or the odd response of implying a subsidiary promise not to do anything inconsistent with the obligation. *Hochester v de la Tour* (1853) 2 E&B 678, 118 ER 922, 926.

estoppel, discharge, and waiver — rather than the conduct that provokes that response.[99] And we are uncomfortable with some of the underlying issues raised in these cases. We are uncomfortable sacrificing rights to prudential concerns. And we are uncomfortable with the idea of uncertain rights.[100] Still judges seem to do a fine job despite the clumsy doctrinal tools. They do a better job than theoreticians who come to the cases with larger points to make. Perhaps they do a fine job because the relevant goals — to execute the bargain with the least cost and fuss — are intuitive.

[99] P Birks 'Unjust Enrichment and Wrongful Enrichment' (2001) 79 *Texas Law Review* 1767 makes a related but more general point that the general headings of private law should be organised around the causative event (Contract, Wrong, Unjust Enrichment, and Miscellany) and not the law's response (not Restitution).

[100] It might be better if we could purge the term rights from the analysis and speak instead of relevant interests. P Westen 'The Rueful Rhetoric of Rights' (1986) 33 *University California Los Angeles Law Review* 977, 996–1008, explores how the confusion between the two distinct meanings of rights — rights as entitlements and rights as legally protected interests — confounds the analysis of unconstitutional conditions.

5

*Comparative Reflections on the French Law of Remedies for Breach of Contract**

YVES-MARIE LAITHIER

IN A TREATISE that remains, a century after its first publication, a standard reference work for French civil lawyers, [1] Planiol wrote: the debtor must devote to the performance of his contractual obligations, 'the entirety of his work force, at the risk of ruining his health and endangering his life.' [2] The tone was set. And this was in striking contrast with the opinion defended, at that same time, in the United States by Judge Sloss, in a well-known case which contributed to the recognition of the notion of impracticability:

> a thing is impossible in legal contemplation when it is not practicable; and a thing is impracticable when it can only be done at an excessive and unreasonable cost. We do not mean to intimate that the defendants could excuse themselves by showing the existence of conditions which would make the performance of their obligation more expensive than they had anticipated, or which would entail a loss upon them. But, where the difference in cost is so great as here, and has the effect, as found, of making performance impracticable, the [defendant should be excused from performing]. [3]

What is most remarkable is that, at the dawn of the twenty-first century, the gap between these traditionally different legal systems has hardly been bridged. While the concept of impracticability was introduced in the

* The author would like to express sincere thanks to Horatia Muir Watt for her guidance and to Audrey Benguira and Alessandro Nolet for their translation.

[1] For an explanation of this phenomenon which is not indifferent to a comparison between French law and the common law, see, P Jestaz, C Jamin, *La doctrine*, (Paris, Dalloz, 2003) 150 *et seq*. Planiol's Treaty (first volume) was published in October 1899.

[2] M Planiol, G Ripert, *Traité pratique de droit civil français, Obligations*, (Paris, LGDJ, 1931) n° 382, 582.

[3] *Mineral Park Land Co v Howard*, (1916) 156, 458, at 460.

Uniform Commercial Code[4] and the Restatement (Second) of Contracts[5], one can still read from the pen of French authors that 'even if the debtor must ruin himself in performing his obligation, there is no *force majeure*, so long as performance remains physically possible.' [6] Money isn't everything! In fact, many decisions have refused to release the debtor from his obligation simply on the ground that his performance had become more onerous following a change in circumstances.[7] However, case law is not as straightforward as textbooks may suggest. Indeed the courts have not always given in to the will of the parties, who are presumed to have foreseen the future and allocated their risks when entering into a contract. In any event little attention will, here, be drawn to these cases.

This example reveals the strong attachment of French law — and even more of French lawyers — to specific performance of contractual obligations. There are at least two explanations for this.

The first one stems from the very concept of contract. Briefly, under French law, a contract is conceived as an act of free will. Indeed, no one denies that a contract allows an exchange,[8] but that is merely one of its roles and not its substance. The contract is conceived of as a meeting of the minds, which materialises through an exchange of assents. [9] Nothing compels the parties to enter into the contract. But from the moment that they have bound themselves, they must loyally perform their obligations. The most elementary liberal philosophy dictates, in effect, that he who has freely committed himself ought to keep his commitments. This philosophy is corroborated by the moral precept demanding that one who makes a promise ought to keep it. Indeed, French law is frequently imbued with morality,[10] and in the French general theory of contracts, the distinction between contractual obligations and promises is never a clear one. As a result of this conception, the court's role cannot be to modify what the parties have willingly agreed to. Its function is to compel them

[4] § 2-615 comment 4.

[5] § 261: Where, after a contract is made, a party's performance is made impracticable without his fault by the occurrence of an event the non-occurrence of which was a basic assumption on which the contract was made, his duty to render that performance is discharged, unless the language or the circumstances indicate the contrary. For further information see eg, J M Perillo, *Calamari and Perillo on Contracts*, 5th edn, (St Paul, West, 2003), § 13.9

[6] F Terré, P Simler, Y Lequette, *Droit civil. Les obligations*, 8th edn, (Paris, Dalloz, 2002) n° 582. See also P Malaurie, L Aynès, P Stoffel-Munck, *Les obligations*, (Defrénois, Paris, 2003), n° 760.

[7] Soc, 8 mars 1972, *D* 1972, p 340 ; Com, 31 octobre 1978, *GP* 1979, I, pan 38; Soc, 20 février 1996, *Bull* V, n° 59.

[8] V J Ghestin, 'Le contrat en tant qu'échange économique', *Revue d'économie industrielle* 2000, 81.

[9] In relation to the disctinction between will and assent see, M-A Frison-Roche, 'Remarques sur la distinction de la volonté et du consentement en droit des contrats', *Revue trimestrielle de Droit civil* 1995, 573.

[10] The standard reference work being G Ripert, *La règle morale dans les obligations civiles*, 4th edn, (Paris, LGDJ, 1949). The author makes clear in his foreword that it is Christian morality that is here in question.

to perform their obligations, however circumstances may have evolved. For the contract is at the same time an (autonomous) act of free will and of anticipation.[11]

This brings us to the second explanation, which consists of the function ascribed to the contract. The contract is a bridge towards the future, a means of managing risks, and of exercising control over the facts; security of business transactions and stability are principles that govern the subject. Accordingly, the contract must be immutable. Neither party is allowed to modify the contract unilaterally if that power had not been previously provided for in the agreement itself. Nor is the judge allowed to modify the contract, either by adding obligations or by reviewing the contract in order to restore an economic balance.[12] This would be insulting for the parties' will and, according to some, would be putting at risk the *'force obligatoire'* or enforceable nature of the contract.

This conception of the contract is not a purely theoretical construction. For many, it corresponds to the rule enacted in Article 1134 para 1 of the Civil Code. This fundamental text states that: 'agreements legally formed have the force of law for those who have agreed to them.' The expression, borrowed from Domat,[13] is the French version of the Latin maxim *pacta sunt servanda*, itself being the translation of a 'principle of natural law.'[14] In reality the meaning of Article 1134 para 1 of the Civil Code is not as rich. As we shall see,[15] this provision merely prescribes the French rule, known as the *'force obligatoire'*, designed to include contracts within the category of positive legal obligations, thus making contracts legally enforceable. This rule simply means that the debtor and the creditor are bound by an obligation that is subject to the sanction of the law.[16] In other words, it is the basis of all remedies for breach of contract, whether they are provided for by legislation, case law or the agreement itself. The list of remedies available to the creditor, as the victim of the other party's failure

[11] See generally, H Lécuyer, 'Le contrat, acte de prévision' *L'avenir du droit. Mélanges en hommage à François Terré*, (Paris, Dalloz, PUF, Juris-Classeur, 1999) 643.

[12] The decision *Canal de Craponne* is the most famous illustration for that purpose, Civ, 6 mars 1876, *D* 1876, I, 193. This decision is generally cited as the symbol of the judge's deference before the parties. A subtler analysis, inspired by North-American work, would be to maintain that the decision contains a penalty default rule, that is a rule that is deliberately detrimental in order to bring the parties, who are in a better position to determine their interests, to provide for the specific adjustment mechanisms that they find suitable. See for that matter, C Pérès-Dourdou, *La règle supplétive*, foreword G Viney, (Paris, LGDJ, 2004) n° 588.

[13] J Domat, *Les loix civiles dans leur ordre naturel*, (éd Durand, Paris, 1777) Part I, Book I, Title I, Section II, n° VII, 17 : 'agreements being formed, all that has been agreed to has the force of law for those who have agreed to it.' Domat, who here intends to rationalise Roman law, is the one who, along with Pothier, has provided the greatest inspiration for the drafters of the Civil Code.

[14] A Sériaux, *Droit des obligations*, 2nd edn, (Paris, PUF, coll Droit fondamental, 1998) n° 42.

[15] See text below, at n 48.

[16] See more generally, Y-M Laithier, *Etude comparative des sanctions de l'inexécution du contrat*, foreword H Muir Watt, (Paris, LGDJ, 2004).

to perform, is well established. On the other hand, the way in which French authors still present and understand this list is extremely heterogeneous. This is why some have suggested that the study of English law in particular, and the common law in general, would be very instructive.

In an influential article published in 1994, the French comparatist Denis Tallon sharply criticised the way in which French scholars categorise remedies for breach of contract, and in particular for failing to provide this field with the consistency which it had not been given by the Civil Code.[17] Professor Tallon deplores the fragmented presentation of remedies, which results in practical inconvenience for the creditor — who must 'explore the four corners of textbooks to discover the various options that the law provides him with'[18] — and which hinders the growth of a general theory of breach of contract.[19] Moreover, the author stresses the inappropriateness of the treatment given to bilateral contracts, dealt with separately as if they were less common; the conceptualisation of damages as a form of liability and erroneously paralleled with tortious liability; and the lack of detailed analysis relating to the compatibility or incompatibility of the various remedies as between one another. After observing that English law was established through *remedies*,[20] Professor Tallon suggests that it could provide valuable inspiration in reorganising and clarifying the state of French law, in order to set up a complete and consistent system, shedding light on the remedies available to the creditor, the defences open to the debtor, and the powers of the court.

This article had the great merit of provoking much thought in France about a subject that is ultimately concerned with the practical aspects of contract. This indeed was what the author wished[21] and, in that sense, his objective has been fulfilled. The grounds for his position are nevertheless debatable. Admittedly, the often-used notion of *remedy* is seldom rigorously analysed by common lawyers.[22] Neither the typology of remedies,[23] nor the meaning of the notion, have been perfectly determined. Save for its medical meaning, similar in both the English and French languages,[24] which suggests that the word refers to something

[17] D Tallon, 'L'inexécution du contrat: pour une autre présentation', *Revue trimestrielle de Droit civil* 1994, 223.
[18] D Tallon, *ibid.*
[19] In relation to French authors persistent trend to establish 'general theories' see P Jestaz, C Jamin, *La doctrine*, n 1 above, 150 *et seq*, 230 *et seq*.
[20] D Tallon, n 17 above, 223 *et seq*: '(...) it is the common law system that could help us. For some, it might seem unexpected, the common law not being, in essence, famous for its logical constructs. And yet, it is in England that contract law was established, on the basis of the remedies available to the contracting party who is the victim of the breach : *remedies precede rights*. Thus, it provides a global understanding of what the creditor may do when there is *breach of contract*.
[21] D Tallon, n 17 above, 237
[22] P Birks (ed), *English Private Law*, (Oxford, OUP, 2000) § 18.01.
[23] S M Wadddams, 'Remedies as a Legal Subject' (1983) 3 *Oxford Journal of Legal Studies* 113.
[24] The word, of Latin origin, is composed of the prefix *re* and the verb *mederi* (to attend, treat).

other than punishment, we could enumerate, more or less accurately, no less than five possible legal meanings, which tend to overlap with closely related notions, including (but not limited to) actionable 'rights'.[25] Besides, the confusion is such that Professor Birks has expressed the wish to see this expression disappear from English legal vocabulary.[26] Furthermore, the fragmentation of the formal presentation of remedies is no less within the common law than it is in France. Thus some time ago Sir Guenter Treitel observed:

> One of the most perplexing problems in the English law of contract concerns the remedies which one contracting party has in the event of the other's failure to perform in accordance with the contract. One reason for the difficulty is that discussions of this problem are often widely scattered in the books, with the result that very different solutions are proposed for problems which appear to be basically similar.[27]

For example, the chapters dealing with remedies do not mention rescission of contract nor clauses limiting or excluding liability; equitable remedies (among which is specific performance) are only dealt with briefly in contract law textbooks and a serious review requires one to turn to specialised material, either completely devoted to remedies, or to Equity. This scattering occurs within every area of the law of obligations. Hence, for want of establishing a connection between contract law and tort law, the breach of a contractual obligation by the debtor with the help of a third party requires that one examine a contract law textbook in order to determine the remedies which may be available against the former, and a tort law textbook in order to determine the remedies which may be available against the latter. Similarly, the implementation of the rules preventing the defaulting debtor's unjust enrichment are to be found within the law of restitution, which again, is treated as an entirely separate subject within the common law.

The above does not of course deprive the proposed comparative exercise of its use. Yet, the comparative study of French, English and American law has more to offer than a new taxonomy of remedies for breach of contract. A first approach would consist in pointing out the similarities (for example, the use and usefulness of clauses limiting liability, the significance of actions for an agreed sum etc) and the differences (for example, the existence of a daily fine for delay in the performance of a contract [*astreinte*] under French law, mitigation of damages and restitutionary damages in English and American law). This first stage of the analysis is both indispensable and fertile. Yet, one can go beyond it in

[25] P Birks, 'Rights, Wrongs, and Remedies' (2000) 20 *Oxford Journal of Legal Studies* 1 at 9 *et seq.*
[26] P Birks, *ibid*, 3, 19 *et seq.*
[27] G H Treitel, 'Some Problems of Breach of Contract' (1967) 30 *Modern Law Review* 139.

questioning what, in substance, distinguishes these two major legal traditions given that, in our view, the function of comparative law is to complete the understanding of law.[28] The aim of this analysis is to discover, sometimes hidden[29] similarities, and bring to light true differences; these differences must be considered for what they are and not as legitimate or illegitimate barriers to the harmonisation or unification of the law.[30] What, therefore, should be the chief lesson to be drawn from the comparative study of remedies for breach of contract? The answer is twofold. On the one hand, the understanding of the enforceable nature of contracts is not identical under French, English and American law, knowing, however, that the meaning given to it by most French lawyers is inaccurate. On the other hand, English and American law grant economic considerations far greater importance than does French law. Both aspects are interconnected: the French understanding of enforceability explains its relative, but certain, disregard of the economic efficiency of remedies for breach of contract.[31] We shall try to illustrate this by showing in the next part of this chapter (Part I) the way in which French law favours specific performance of contractual obligations and, even more importantly, in Part II, by demonstrating the commitment of French law to the continuation of the contract despite the breach.

I A LAW FAVOURABLE TO SPECIFIC PERFORMANCE OF CONTRACTUAL OBLIGATIONS

If French law favours specific performance, it is not in the name of the supposedly underlying economic efficiency of this remedy. The rationale claimed for it is that of enforceability. The following criticism of this rationale (in Part A) will naturally bring us to question the primacy attributed to that remedy (in Part B).

A The Alleged Rationale for Specific Performance's Primacy Under French Law

The role attributed to specific performance in France is, above all, the expression of an ideal. For many years, specific performance had been

[28] R Sacco, *La comparaison juridique au service de la connaissance du droit*, (Paris, Economica 1991,) 8 *et seq*.
[29] R Sacco 'Droit commun de l'Europe, et composantes du droit' in M Cappelletti (dir), *New Perspectives for a Common Law of Europe — Nouvelles perspectives d'un droit commun de l'Europe, foreword Kohnstamm*, (Leyden, Boson Sijthoff, 1985,) 95, at 105.
[30] See P Legrand, *Le droit comparé*, (Paris, PUF, 1999,) 37.
[31] This thesis is the one developed in Y-M Laithier, *Etude comparative des sanctions de l'inexécution du contrat*, n 16 above.

considered for what it is, namely, a means among others to grant the creditor, who is the victim of a breach of contract, satisfaction in the form of the expected benefit, available when an award of damages only seemed unfair. However, a radical change of view occurred around the second half of the nineteenth Century. Specific performance ceased to be a means and became an end in itself. Appealing to reason, it seems correct to state that it is in the very nature of contractual obligations to be specifically performed, this being the only remedy capable of 'fulfilling' both the subjective rights of the creditor and the objective rights created by the contract. It follows that acceptance of the proposition that the debtor may legally be released by paying damages instead of providing the promised performance would amount to allowing him unilaterally to alter the content of the obligation, to transforming any contractual obligation into an alternative obligation and, finally, to denying the very existence of a civil obligation. The pecuniary remedy is therefore not only unfair, but above all 'illogical.'[32] Under this approach, performance of the contract can only mean specific performance. Considered as an ideal remedy, justified by the power of each individual to bind himself voluntarily under the contract, specific performance thus bears no limits. If its scope is still in fact limited in certain instances, the reasons lie in the means available to implement that remedy — that is, the fact that measures of enforcement may only affect the debtor's property and not his person. Consequently, nothing prevents the judge from ordering that the debtor of a 'personal' obligation perform what he had promised. Believing the opposite would be to confuse the end with the means; it would also tarnish the idyllic image of the contract's enforceability.

This is no doubt the critical point but lawyers could not content themselves with expressing an ideal. To use Gény's words, they had to 'build' a form of reasoning capable of justifying the solution sought. This reasoning rests on Article 1134 para 1 of the Civil Code. Since Demolombe the relationship between specific performance and enforceability has been explicitly established:

> (...) the fundamental principle for the matter is that, agreements legally formed have the force of law for those who have agreed to them (Article 1134); and it is, consequently, the right of the creditor to require, against the debtor, the actual performance of the obligation that he has contracted.[33]

The twentieth century has therefore been, with respect to French general contract law theory, that of specific performance. Legal scholars, as a whole, have acknowledged and confirmed the primacy of this remedy, which is

[32] C Demolombe, *Traité des contrats ou des obligations conventionnelles en général*, vol 24, 2nd edn, (Paris, Durand et Hachette, 1870) n° 488, 486.
[33] C Demolombe, *ibid.*

perceived as the necessary extension of the principle of enforceability. The existence of a right to specific performance is initially affirmed through the courts, before asserting that in the case of a breach of contract any judicial action would, as a matter of principle, have no other purpose than the implementation of this right. Article 1134 para 1 of the Civil Code is then put forward as a reference, considered both satisfactory and sufficient.[34] Even then, no further explanation or discussion is provided, since all this seems so obvious.[35] The reasoning draws its strength from its apparent simplicity, which is supposed to make any additional explanation superfluous. Is it not 'obvious' that keeping one's word commands, in principle, specific performance of one's commitments? It is, however, unfortunate that this same obviousness could let us forget that general contract law did not contain any explicit provision raising specific performance to the rank of a principal remedy.

In these circumstances, could the 'legal doctrine' have relied on the leading cases and decisions of the *Cour de cassation*? Of course, examples of specific enforcement in casebooks are numerous. Thus one can find orders to: ensure the right of possession of rented property;[36] re-do construction work;[37] enter into a legal transaction;[38] close down a business;[39] return the promised subject-matter;[40] re-instate a lessee[41] or an employee;[42]

[34] Amongst past authors, see, for example, A Colin, H Capitant, *Cours élémentaire de droit civil français*, t. 2, 7th edn, (Paris, Dalloz, 1932) n° 67, 65; L Josserand, *Cours de droit civil positif français*, t II, *Théorie générale des obligations*, 3rd edn, (Paris, Sirey, 1939) n° 590, 370; M Planiol, G Ripert, *Traité pratique de droit civil français*, *op cit*, n° 776, 74 ; amongst contemporary authors, see J Flour, J-L Aubert, Y Flour, E Savaux, *Le rapport d'obligation*, 3rd edn, (Paris, A Colin, 2004) n° 160, 163 *in fine* ; A Sériaux, *Droit des obligations*, *op cit*, n° 62; F Terré, P Simler, Y Lequette, *Les obligations*, *op cit*, n° 1110, 1113 ; G Viney, P Jourdain, *Traité de droit civil* (dir J Ghestin), *Les effets de la responsabilité*, 2nd edn, (Paris, LGDJ, 2001) n° 19, 43. *Contra* F Bellivier, R Sefton-Green, 'Force obligatoire et exécution en nature du contrat en droits français et anglais : bonnes et mauvaises surprises du comparatisme', *Etudes offertes à Jacques Ghestin, Le contrat au début du XXIe* siècle, (Paris, LGDJ, 2001) 91.

[35] The allusion is made just as quickly in doctoral theses, see V Lonis-Apokourastos, *La primauté contemporaine du droit à l'exécution en nature*, foreword J Mestre, Aix-en-Provence, PUAM, 2003, n° 2, 17, n° 9, 24; M–E Roujou de Boubée, *Essai sur la notion de réparation*, foreword P Hébraud, (Paris, LGDJ, 1974) 159; P Wéry, *L'exécution forcée en nature des obligations contractuelles non pécuniaires (essai). Une relecture des articles 1142 à 1144 du Code civil*, foreword I Moreau-Margrève, (Liège, Kluwer, 1993) n° 71, 93, 150, 206.

[36] Com, 23 mai 1964, *Bull* III, n° 260.

[37] Civ 1ère, 18 janvier 1956, *Bull* I, n° 34 ; Civ 1ère, 5 juillet 1956, *D* 1956, 719 ; Civ 1ère, 14 janvier 1959, *Bull* I, n° 26 ; Civ 1ère, 18 octobre 1965, *Bull* I, n° 546 ; Civ 3e, 10 janvier 1990, *Bull* III, n° 6.

[38] Com, 31 mars 1952, *Bull*, n° 155.

[39] Req, 24 février 1862, *S* 1862, 241 (in an *obiter dictum*); Req, 7 juillet 1898, *S* 1898, I, 520 ; Soc, 24 janvier 1979, *Bull* V, n° 67 ; *adde*, M Planiol, note under Paris, 14 janvier 1889, *D* 1890, II, 289.

[40] Civ 1ère, 20 janvier 1953, D1953 222.

[41] Soc, 8 juin 1956, *Bull* IV, n° 535.

[42] Soc, 14 juin 1972, *JCP* 1972, II, 17275, note G Lyon-Caen. (The solution is now enacted.)

demolish work;[43] overhaul a place;[44] transfer shares;[45] end an activity;[46] and deliver the subject-matter[47] etc. However, the *Cour de cassation* has never entirely backed up the academic reasoning, according to which Article 1134 para 1 of the French Civil Code commands specific performance. More generally, the *Cour de cassation* refuses to state that specific performance is, as a matter of 'principle', available to a creditor who is the victim of a breach of contract. This is why it approved the decision of a court of appeal which refused to order the demolition of buildings constructed in breach of contract, on the ground that 'it rests with the judge to decide whether the works built in breach of a contract, must or must not be destroyed'. Yet the claim relied solely on Article 1134 of the Civil Code, maintaining that this provision precluded the judge from deciding in equity and that, in rejecting the demolition claim, the appeal court judges had changed the content of the contract and were thus exposed to the censure of the *Cour de cassation*.[48] That is to say that this well known 'principle' of French law, that is meant to distinguish it from the common law, is, in practice, only didactic, conjured up by academics in order to categorise and influence case law, and is in no way normative. The principle of specific performance, and in particular its primacy, therefore has a purely academic existence. It was created and shaped with the aim to preserve a certain understanding of the enforceability of contracts and, if need be, to strengthen the principle of party autonomy. This justification was supported by the majority of academics. After all, no-one would claim to be 'against' the principle of the *force obligatoire* or the enforceability of contracts. Yet, the reasoning is none the less fragile.

The fundamental mistake of French theory in this area lies in confusing a rule with one of its possible remedies. Article 1134 para 1 of the Civil Code enacts the concept of *force obligatoire* or 'enforceability' of the contract. It means that the connection established between the debtor and the creditor is legally enforceable. The debtor who does not abide by his contractual obligations is subject to a sanction, in the same way as any other person who does not respect the law. Because his conduct does

[43] Civ 1ère, 13 mars 1963, *D* 1963, somm, p 79; Civ 3e, 5 février 1974, *Bull* III, n° 56; Civ 3e, 15 février 1978, *D* 1978, IR, p 414; Civ 3e, 23 mai 1978, *Bull* III, n° 213; Civ 3e, 18 février 1981, *Bull* III, n° 38; Civ 3e, 19 mai 1981, *Bull* III, n° 101; Civ 3e, 13 octobre 1981, *Bull* III , n° 152; Civ 3e, 26 novembre 1986, *RD imm* 1987, p 236; Civ 3e, 27 mars 1991, *Bull* III, n° 106; Civ 3e, 30 juin 1993, *Bull* III, n° 105.

[44] Civ 1ère, 14 octobre 1964, *D* 1964, p 710; Civ 1ère, 26 juin 1967, *D* 1967, p 673; Civ 3e, 9 décembre 1970, *Bull* III, n° 683; Civ 3e, 18 novembre 1980, *Bull* III, n° 177; Civ 3e, 25 janvier 1995, *Bull* III, n° 29; Civ 3e, 3 avril 1996, *Bull* III, n° 91.

[45] Civ 3e, 19 février 1970, *GP* 1970, 1, p 282.

[46] Com, 23 avril 1985, *Bull* IV, n° 123.

[47] Colmar, 18 octobre 1972, *D* 1973, p 496, note M Cabrillac, A Seube.

[48] Req, 18 juin 1883, *D* 1884, V, p 353.

not comply with the norm, the debtor in breach of contract shall be liable to accept the consequences of the infringement.[49] This is where confusion usually arises, since the rule starts to blend with the remedy. Since contracts are meant to be performed, specific performance is naturally considered to be the primary remedy, which is no longer distinguished from Article 1134 para 1 of the Civil Code. The distinction between the two dimensions fades away as they blend artificially into a single one. Thus, the obligation to perform and the remedy of specific performance appear to follow from the same rule: Article 1134 para 1 of the Civil Code. This confusion is unfortunate. Even if the sanction is inseparable from the legal rule, one cannot deny that it exists in its own right. This is true both as a matter of logic and as a matter of law. The existence of a rule (for example, Article 1134 of the Civil Code) is not dependant upon the efficiency or inefficiency, the perfection or imperfection, the strictness or mildness, or the effectiveness or ineffectiveness of the remedy. Everyone agrees that the nature of a rule does not change according to whether it is complied with or not. How then can one coherently maintain that any remedy which is not specific performance is a failure to recognise Article 1134 para 1 of the Civil Code? Let us stress again that this provision states that the contracting parties are bound under the sanction of the law. This means that, when a breach of contract occurs, *a* remedy is provided. Yet, the applicable remedy is determined by a separate rule, for example, under general principles of contract law, and concerning specific performance, by Article 1184 para 2 of the Civil Code. One cannot infer from the rule which lays down the enforceability of contract (Article 1134 para 1 of the Civil Code), the kind of remedy applicable when the contract is broken. In other words, to state that non-performance of a contractual obligation is the subject of a legal sanction, is not to suggest that it must always, nor even in principle, be specifically enforced. A statement to the contrary is theoretically incorrect. Let us add that the study of the common law shows that this theoretical distinction is perfectly feasible. English law provides for the enforceability of a contract in a way similar to French law, and specific performance is (rightly) analysed as one of the possible remedies for non-performance; its domain varies according to a multiplicity of considerations, which however, do not include the enforceability of contracts for the reasons enunciated above. This conclusion, however, does not mean that the domain of specific performance is identical in these two legal systems.

[49] These are defined by Virally, as 'any harm affecting the legal status of an individual, either by creating new obligations or by forfeiture, as a consequence of the infringement of an obligation'; M Virally, *La pensée juridique*, Paris, [LGDJ, Montchrestien, 1960], ed Panthéon-Assas, (LGDJ, 1998) 71.

B The Reach of Specific Performance's Admitted Primacy Under French Law

The scope of specific performance is certainly greater under French law than it is under English or American law. The barrier which Article 1142 of the Civil Code might have raised to specific performance has been circumvented. This text provides that 'every obligation to do or not to do resolves itself into damages in case of non-performance by the debtor.' It seems at first sight to echo Holmes' famous words about liability in contract. In practice, the debtor would have a choice between performing his obligations and offering compensation to the creditor for the damage resulting from the breach.[50] This result appeared unacceptable or at least unfortunate. The nature of the contractual obligation would be modified and the notion of contract altered. If, as we say, the contract truly binds the debtor to the promised performance, then an obligation to do, or to refrain from doing, something, should not become, through its remedy, an alternative or optional obligation. The contract would be 'distorted'. As a result, after denouncing the legislator's uneasy drafting, scholars have, since the 19th century, undertaken to rectify the meaning of Article 1142 of the Civil Code and to restore it to the rank of an exception to the rule. The 'real' reading would be that the creditor must always be able to claim specific performance. Article 1142 would from now on be read as applying exclusively to 'personal' obligations to do something, defined as those which involve the 'inmost depths of one's personality.'[51]

Nevertheless, case law is simply not as plain. For example, a petition before the *Cour de cassation*, claiming that a court of appeal had not properly taken into account the creditor's right to demolition and the closing down of a business opened in breach of contract by providing only pecuniary compensation, has been dismissed on the ground that 'the judges of first instance examining the factual situation, have full authority to determine whether specific performance may be granted to the creditor under Article 1143.'[52] A similarly enlightened decision was rendered with respect to a breach of a contract for construction work, in which the *Cour*

[50] Compare G Rouhette, *Encyclopædia Universalis*, V° Contrat, (Paris, 1995,) 469 at 472 : '(...) more profoundly, the two legal families [civil law systems and the common law] converge on this issue: in case of non-performance imputable to the debtor, the appropriate remedy in principle consists in a corresponding compensation, in an allowance of damages that releases the defaulting debtor. So much, that one could affirm without exaggerating that any contractual obligation is alternative in nature: the debtor has a choice between performing on the one hand, and compensating his failure by paying a sum of money, on the other hand. There is a clear contrast between these individualistic and lucrative views and a social perspective according to which the strength of the contractual bond depends on the interest it represents for the community.'

[51] A Sériaux, *Droit des obligations*, n 14 above, n° 62.

[52] Civ 1ère, 24 mai 1960, *Bull* I, n° 283.

de cassation approved the court of appeal's refusal to grant specific performance and to award only damages instead. The Court stated that in finding

> that the defects were not significant, and that it could not be envisaged to carry out a rebuilding of these works because of the great disturbance it would cause in the premises, [the court of appeal] has, regarding the obligation to do something, justly determined that the building contractor could avoid specific performance, consistently with Article 1142 of the Civil Code, and substitute a pecuniary compensation for the specific performance.[53]

It is wrong to assert that specific performance is, 'in principle', the primary remedy only because it is feasible and requested by the victim. French case law is far less straightforward than this. To sum up therefore, if the scope of specific performance is more extensive in France than it is in common law systems, this is not as a result of the alleged normative principle.

If the scope of specific performance is greater, this results inter alia[54] from the fact that under French law an order for specific performance is not ruled out on the sole ground that damages would be an appropriate remedy. Leaving aside the historical reasons (the separation of the courts of Common law and Equity), the basis for this difference lies in the extent of the duty to mitigate damages and therewith, more fundamentally, in the importance granted to economic considerations in the implementation of remedies for breach of contract. According to English or American law, when the good or service which is the object of the contractual obligation is available and reasonably accessible on the market, the creditor, who is the victim of the breach of contract, has the ability, in practice, and usually the legal duty to obtain substitute for performance. Traditionally, common law courts consider that, in this case, damages constitute an 'appropriate remedy', since the creditor finally obtains, as rapidly as possible, that which he had originally contracted for, plus, as the case may be, the pecuniary compensation for any resulting loss. The natural result of this approach is that, the courts reject, on the same ground (the appropriateness of damages) any claim for specific performance. Deciding otherwise would amount to an exemption for the creditor from his duty to mitigate,[55] and at the same time, significantly undermine the practical reach of the doctrine of mitigation.[56] So for example, the claim of an

[53] Civ 3e, 24 juin 1971, *Bull* III, n° 411.
[54] For a more detailed comparison see, Y-M Laithier, *Etude comparative des sanctions de l'inexécution du contrat*, n 16 above, n° 280 *et seq*.
[55] See also, D Harris, D Campbell, R Halson, *Remedies in Contract & Tort*, 2nd edn, (London, Butterworths, 2002) 168. But contrast L Smith, chapter 10 below.
[56] See especially, G H Treitel, *The Law of Contract*, 11th edn, (London, Sweet & Maxwell, 2003) 1020.

advertiser requiring the court to, firstly, order the editor of a woman's magazine to reproduce an advertisement on the back cover, and secondly, to forbid publication of any other announcement in the same space, must naturally be rejected when the advertiser, who is under a duty to mitigate loss, does not demonstrate either that this magazine is unique due to its readership, or that there would be no other advertisement space available.[57] The scope of specific performance is further limited by the strict approach that is sometimes taken by the courts in determining what can reasonably be expected of the victim of a breach of contract. At times the court will reject the creditor's argument that, at the time of the breach, there were no similar or appropriate goods on the market,[58] while in other cases the court will reject the argument that the replacement, if ever possible, was unreasonably expensive, justifying such strictness on the ground that damages would compensate the loss sustained by the creditor for any expenditure of additional money.[59]

Conversely, there are some situations where the replacement is impossible or so difficult that it is not conceivable. The creditor is then exempted from the duty to reduce the loss suffered. Damages would not constitute an appropriate remedy and specific performance would then be ordered.[60] This will be the case if all the other conditions for specific performance are satisfied, since we do not contend that the scope of mitigation of loss strictly overlaps that of specific performance. The overlap is only partial. If specific performance is dismissed when the duty to mitigate loss exists, the reverse is not true: notwithstanding the absence of such a duty, specific performance may be dismissed for other reasons, for example, on grounds relating to the blameworthy behaviour of the creditor or because of the disproportionate cost of the remedy.

The difference with French law is striking. Indeed, according to the Civil Code, replacement is only an optional possibility that the creditor must, in principle, request before the court. At present, no French judge would claim to have the power, even with the aid of Article 1134 para 3 of the Civil Code (requiring performance in good faith), to dismiss a claim for specific performance on the sole ground that the creditor had the possibility, and therefore, the duty to find a replacement for himself; or, following the technique used by English and American judges, on the sole ground that damages constitute an appropriate and sufficient remedy. Introducing a general duty to mitigate damages in contract law would

[57] *American Brands, Inc v Playgirl, Inc*, 498 F 2d 947 at 950.
[58] *Klein v Pepsico, Inc*, 845 P 2d 76 at 80.
[59] *Duval & Company v Malcom*, 214 SE 2d 356, at 359.
[60] See eg, *Restatement (Second) of Contracts* § 360: 'In determining whether the remedy in damages would be adequate, the following circumstances are significant: (b) the difficulty of procuring a suitable substitute performance by means of money awarded as damages (…)', and *comment c*. In English law, G H Treitel, *The Law of Contract*, n 56 above.

lead to the reverse solution. The court could order specific performance against the debtor, only after having checked that the creditor had, at the date of the breach, no reasonable means to find a replacement for himself; if the replacement was not reasonably feasible, he would at best be awarded damages, thus ensuring that he does not use specific performance as a means to avoid his duty. Legally, the change would be remarkable since it would consist in adding another condition to access this remedy as well as in restricting its scope. All other obstacles are a matter of legal policy, and in particular they touch on the question of the room to be allocated to arguments of economic efficiency within the area of remedies for breach of contract. The answer depends, in part, on the practical consequences of each alternative. From this standpoint, it is not absolutely certain that the results reached by common law courts are manifestly fairer than the mechanism provided by Article 1144 of the Civil Code, pertaining to preliminary judicial authorisation.[61]

The French understanding of enforceability does not only explain the favoured position of specific performance. If one considers that the rule prescribed in Article 1134 para 1 of the Civil Code means that the contract must be performed, then it is also opposed to the termination of the contract. Under such an approach, as a matter of logic and of law, the contract must be upheld, even in cases of non-performance.

II A LAW FAVOURABLE TO THE UPHOLDING OF THE CONTRACT

French law is attached to the 'protection of the contract'. Its performance is 'its fate; it must be accomplished.'[62] A series of provisions aim at preserving the contract in spite of the debtor's faulty or accidental failure to perform. This policy becomes apparent through the omnipresence,[63] indeed the omnipotence[64] of the court, which presides over the destiny of the contractual bond.

A The Court's Omnipresence

The omnipresence of the judge is the direct result, on one hand, of the general rule enacted in the Civil Code and, on the other hand, of the relative weakness of the exceptions to that rule. Under French law, in order to terminate a contract a party is generally required to bring an action before

[61] As amended by the 9 July 1991 Act, and made more flexible by case law
[62] C Demolombe, *Traité des contrats, op cit*, n° 490, 471.
[63] See Part A below.
[64] See Part B below.

the court for that purpose. The creditor cannot, however severe the breach, unilaterally declare that the contract is terminated by addressing a notice to the other contracting party to that effect. Only the judge has the power to terminate the contract. An action in court is thus indispensable. This process results from Article 1184 of the Civil Code. This text does not provide for any exception, to the point that its almost obsessive repetition of the judicial nature of the termination has been pointed out and denounced by numerous academics.[65]

Through this Article, the drafters of the Civil Code wished to pay tribute to the principle of the enforceability of contracts, by giving preference to the specific performance of contracts over termination.[66] In practice, many legal scholars argue that, since specific performance affects the strength of enforceability, the circumstances for terminating contracts must be reduced. Termination must be judicial so that, once bound, the parties may not set themselves free from the obligations that the contract prescribes. Under the cover of neutrality, it is clear that termination is seen as remedy of last resort. Through its intervention, the court favours performance; 'it tries, in a word, to save the contract'.[67]

However, the theoretical explanation of Article 1184 of the Civil Code is hardly convincing. The reasoning can be split up into the following syllogism: enforceability requires spontaneous or forced performance; termination is opposed to performance; therefore, termination goes against enforceability. Nevertheless this premise is clearly wrong. As mentioned above,[68] enforceability must not be confused with the remedies for breach of contract. The reverse position is the result of the willingness — concealed behind the use of Article 1134 of the Civil Code — to extend the scope of specific performance as far as possible. In reality, there is no conflict between the principle of enforceability of contracts and termination of the contract. The interaction between Articles 1134 and 1184 is perfectly harmonious. The former allows legally formed agreements to penetrate the sphere of the law; the contract thus becomes legally enforceable. The latter states two of its remedies: specific performance and termination. But Article 1134 is not concerned with determining the scope of either of these remedies.

If the strength of the enforceability principle can be questioned, it is not possible, on the other hand, to deny the importance of the rule set out in

[65] D Tallon, 'L'article 1184 du Code civil. Un texte à rénover ?', in *Université Panthéon-Assas, Clés pour le siècle*, (Paris, Dalloz, 2000) 253 at 258.
[66] See eg J Ghestin, C Jamin, M Billiau, *Traité de droit civil* (dir J Ghestin), *Les effets du contrat*, 3rd edn, (Paris, LGDJ, 2001) n° 429; C Jamin, 'Les conditions de la résolution du contrat : vers un modèle unique?' in M Fontaine, G Viney (dir), *Les sanctions de l'inexécution des obligations contractuelles, Etudes de droit comparé*, (Bruxelles, Paris, Bruylant, LGDJ, 2001) n° 1, 451 *et seq.*
[67] G Ripert, *La règle morale dans les obligations civiles*, n 10 above, n° 76
[68] See above, n 49.

Article 1184 of the Civil Code. The *Cour de cassation* has ruled on several instances that the mere failure to bring a claim before the court constitutes *in se* and *per se* fault on the part of the creditor.[69] The contrast with American and English law is indisputable. It must, however, be put into perspective, because the procedure under Article 1184 is not considered mandatory.

There are, under French law, two ways to escape the judicial nature of the termination of contracts. The first, and most traditional, consists of agreeing on a termination clause. The validity of such clauses has been acknowledged by the *Cour de cassation* since 1860.[70] Through such a clause the creditor may unilaterally put an end to the contract in case of non-performance. Indeed, the judge will intervene if a dispute arises, but his power is then limited: while under Article 1184 of the Civil Code, it is the judge who actually pronounces the termination of the contract, here, all he can do is take notice of it.[71] This withdrawal of the judge allows the creditor to be released immediately, so that he may create new bonds with third parties and potentially limit his loss. In addition to improving foreseeability, the termination clause allows the creditor to put an end to the contract for the non-performance of any obligation and not merely for certain severe breaches. In other words, the termination clause is not only a means to overcome the judicial nature of termination in French law; it is also a means to extend the scope of termination, which explains why such clauses are present in countries where termination is a unilateral remedy.[72] These benefits, which greatly outweigh those provided by the procedure under Article 1184 of the Civil Code, explain how (or why) the termination clause gradually became a standard clause.[73]

The second way to overcome the rule in Article 1184 is a more recent practice and follows directly from a number of decisions of the first civil division of the *Cour de cassation*.[74] As Professor Sacco has justly noted, 'the

[69] See eg, Com, 25 mars 1991, *CCC* 1991, n° 162, note: L Leveneur: 'Re article 1184 of the Civil Code'; Whereas in the case a party to a bilateral contract does not perform her obligations, the party against which the promise has not been performed must, if she demands the termination of the agreement, petition before the court for that purpose; Whereas, to dismiss the company *Panel de France*'s claim (*Panel*), which requested damages against the company governed by American law *Performax Systems International* (*Performax*) to which she reproached to have fraudulently terminated, by means of a unilateral statement, the franchise that it had granted her to sell her products ; the court of appeal has found that such a termination was justified by the serious contractual default on the part of *Panel* with respect to the failure to pay the price of the products, as well as the failure to keep other commitments; Whereas in deciding so, when *Performax*, not having filed a petition for that purpose, could not unilaterally terminate the franchise agreement that had been entered into for three years, the court of appeal has infringed the text referred to above.'

[70] Civ, 2 juillet 1860, *D* 1860, I, 284.

[71] See eg, P Malaurie, L Aynès, P Stoffel-Munck, *Les obligations*, n 6 above, n° 888.

[72] See in English law, G H Treitel, *The Law of Contract*, n 56 above, 778.

[73] See P Malaurie, L Aynès, P Stoffel-Munck, *Les obligations*, n 6 above, n° 886.

[74] For other cases of departure from article 1184 of the Civil Code see Y-M Laithier, *Etude comparative des sanctions de l'inexécution du contrat*, n 16 above, n° 186 *et seq*.

necessity to address a judge is not considered, in France and in Italy, as the application of logic and indisputable principle, and as such, is not fully exercised'.[75] The creditor may immediately terminate the contract when the conduct of the debtor has become so bad that the continuation of the contractual relationship has become impossible or unbearable. Many decisions have been justified by a state of 'emergency'. This notion was supposed to justify the unilateral termination of the contract and overcome the excessively laborious mechanism contained in Article 1184 of the Civil Code. Nevertheless, a unilateral termination of the contract was justified only if immediately declared. At present, the *Cour de cassation* has dissociated the issues of timing and substance, in order to allow the unilateral termination of a contract in circumstances where neither emergency nor necessity are sufficiently present. Thus in a well-known decision, the *Cour de cassation* dismissed the claim brought by an anaesthetist against the clinic which employed him, which had unilaterally brought an end to his contract of employment with a six month notice period, as a result of the accumulation of 'faults' during fifteen years of practice. The doctor's conduct included consultations outside of the clinic, refusal to practice certain operations which were within his qualifications, lack of availability liable to result in serious consequences for the patients' health, exasperation and brutal treatment of certain patients. The court of appeal was criticised for having, inter alia, considered this termination as contrary to Article 1184 of the Civil Code. The *Cour de cassation* stated that 'the seriousness of a contracting party's behaviour may justify the unilateral termination of the agreement by other party, at its own risk and peril, and this seriousness (...) is not necessarily dependant upon there being a sufficient notice period.'[76] This ruling has recently been reaffirmed by the same division of the *Cour de cassation*.[77]

These two methods of circumventing Article 1184 do not entirely remove the judge's role in the procedure leading to the termination of a contract. Indeed, a line of strict case law requires absolute compliance with both formal and substantive legal conditions in order for termination clauses to be valid, in the absence of which judicial termination under Article 1184 regains control. Moreover, the scope of these clauses is subject to a restrictive reading by the court. The *Cour de cassation* requires that the termination clause be applied only to obligations that have been expressly listed within it, and denies lower courts the power to

[75] R Sacco, 'Le contrat inexécuté. Conférence introductive', in L Vacca (dir), *Il contratto inadempiuto*, Torino, G. Giappichelli, 1999, 16.
[76] Civ 1ère, 13 octobre 1998, *Bull* I, n° 300; *D* 1999, 197 note C Jamin.
[77] Civ 1ère, 28 octobre 2003, *Bull* I, n° 211: 'Whereas the seriousness of a party's behaviour may justify the unilateral termination of the contract by the other party, at her own risk, regardless of whether the contract has a fixed term or not.'

acknowledge, particularly at the stage of a preliminary interpretation, the contractual termination of the agreement for non-performance of obligations not formally connected to (or listed in) the clause. In addition to analysing the content of the termination clause, the court will also proceed to review the creditor's conduct when he avails himself of the clause. Indeed, termination clauses may be binding on the court, but they remain subject to the principle of good faith. This phenomenon has been much discussed, to the extent that it is now considered as the typical illustration of the role of Article 1134 para 3 of the Civil Code in contemporary case law.[78] The creditor's bad faith paralyses the working of the termination clause if he avails himself of it when he is partly or entirely to blame for the breach or, more widely, when he has not facilitated the performance of the contract. A judicial assessment of the equities of termination is surreptitiously introduced at this point, in addition to a review of the legal conditions necessary for termination. This is why one could say that the court is omnipresent: sent out by the door, it comes back in through the window! Case law considers that a brutal change in attitude of a creditor who, suddenly and unpredictably, claims what he is owed, after a long period of inactivity during which he tolerated the extended non-performance of the other party, ultimately reveals his bad faith. The damaging inconsistency of his conduct is thus stigmatised through the requirement of good faith: the creditor cannot avail himself of the termination clause because he invokes it in a way which is contrary to the legitimate expectations of the other contracting party, induced as a result of his own behaviour. This explains the outcome of decisions which have refused to grant the advantage of termination clauses to certain creditors, such as a lessor who had not received rents for eleven years,[79] a creditor recipient of an allowance who refrained from claiming the payment of an annuity for more than ten years,[80] or again a banker who requested payment of interest and delay penalties more than six years after the sum was due.[81] As for the unilateral and non-contractual termination of contracts, this does not constitute, at present, a serious limitation to the judge's omnipresence, as in practice the *Cour de cassation* has admitted it only in very few cases. From the standpoint of judicial practice, French law remains extremely distant from American and English law, which allow for unilateral termination of the contract by the creditor, even without a termination clause. This difference explains another one, which is related to the extent of the powers of the court.

[78] See *eg*, D Mazeaud, 'Loyauté, solidarité, fraternité : la nouvelle devise contractuelle ?' *L'avenir du droit. Mélanges en hommage à François Terré*, n 11 above, 603 at 613 *et seq*.
[79] Com, 7 janvier 1963, *Bull* III, n° 16.
[80] Civ 3e, 8 avril 1987, *Bull* III, n° 88; Civ 1ère, 16 février 1999, *Bull* I, n° 52.
[81] Civ 1ère, 31 janvier 1995, *D* 1995, 389, note C Jamin.

B The Court's Omnipotence

The more the court intervenes at an early stage, the greater its power to protect the unperformed contract. The means at its disposal are of two sorts, according to whether or not it involves a modification of the terms and conditions of the contract.

First of all, the judge may simply dismiss the claim on the ground that the alleged non-performance does not exist, that it has not been established, that it is not serious enough, or that it is actually imputable to the creditor. To this extent, the lower courts merely exercise the fact-finding powers that the *Cour de cassation* has granted them since the 19th century. This dismissal may, depending on the facts, be joined with an order for compensation of the creditor, corresponding to the damage resulting from the breach of contract. Indeed, it is for the court to decide, according to the circumstances of the case, whether or not the non-performance was significant enough for termination to be ordered immediately or whether it would more appropriately be addressed by an order for damages. As Professor Sériaux notes, 'Hence, the judge is provided with an important power to maintain the contractual bond, where there is, in return, pecuniary compensation for the damage incurred by a contracting party as a result of the faulty non-performance of the other'.[82] This judicial power is all the more efficient if one considers that it is exercised in advance of termination, and that the courts may favour the award of damages rather than the termination of the contract, even if the latter was the only remedy requested by the creditor.[83]

Secondly, the court can preserve the contractual bond by modifying the content of the agreement. This readjustment may be temporal. In the interests of fairness, Article 1184 para 3 of the Civil Code confers on the judge the power to grant the debtor an additional delay for performance, depending on the circumstances of the case. Since this results in the dismissal of the claim for termination in a case where there may be a serious breach, the judge must ensure that the debtor, to whom he will grant the extension of time, is in good faith and examine the extent of the damage sustained by the creditor as a result. The court will mostly have to ascertain whether performance is still useful. In this respect, it is true that, under domestic French law,[84] there is no obligation to give 'adequate assurance of due performance,'[85] it is, however, certain that there is a correlation between the probability that an additional delay be granted and the prospects for effective performance. Finally, in order to protect

[82] A Sériaux, *Droit des obligations*, n 14 above, n° 49, at 198.
[83] See eg Req, 21 octobre 1913, *S* 1914, I, 182.
[84] See, the Vienna Convention on Contracts for the International Sale of Goods, Art 71.
[85] Compare UCC § 2-609 ; Restatement (Second) of Contracts § 251.

the creditor's interests, the *Cour de cassation* has stressed that an extended delay granted under Article 1184 para 3 of the Civil Code is not renewable[86] and it allows the court order to provide for the termination of the contract if the debtor's failure to perform continues, so as to spare the creditor the need to bring a fresh petition to the court.

These readjustments can be substantial; in effect, the contract is 'remade'. Instead of terminating the contract, the judge remakes it by reviewing its price. Such re-assessment of the price is not the same thing as imposing contractual liability: it is not the result of a judicial trade-off between damages and the stated price. Each remedy has a specific purpose: compensating the foreseeable loss resulting from non-performance, in the case of contractual liability; and restoring the economic balance, when the court remakes the contract. Indeed, there is no necessary correlation between the readjustment of the value of the benefits resulting from the contract and the compensation of the loss sustained. This explains and justifies how the two remedies may be combined. The study of their respective conditions confirms that this distinction is not purely academic. Firstly, judicial remaking of the contract does not depend on the reasons for non-performance, whereas the order to pay damages implies, like any other kind of liability, a failure to perform which is imputable to the debtor. Secondly, as has been mentioned above, the rules respectively applicable to the evaluation of the price reduction and to damages clearly differ. The latter are assessed in respect of the injuries for which the law allows compensation, whereas the former is proportionate to the decrease in value of the agreed benefit. Again, French law is different from American[87] and English[88] law, which do not include price reduction among their remedies. But this gap is frequently bridged, both in international sales, which are governed by the Vienna Convention, and in certain domestic sales, through the effect of European law. Indeed, the recent English *Sale and Supply of Goods to Consumers Regulations* 2002, which transpose the 1999 Directive, introduce the possibility of 'remaking' the contract to the benefit of consumers. The new section 48C (1)(a) of the Sale of Goods Act 1979 states: '[the buyer may] require the seller to reduce the purchase price of the goods in question by an appropriate amount (...).' The issue is whether English courts will distinguish this from the usual method of assessing damages.[89] Comparative lawyers may well provide them with a helping hand.

[86] Civ 1ère, 19 décembre 1984, *Bull* I, n° 343.
[87] E A Farnsworth, *Contracts*, 4th edn, (New York, Aspen Publishers, Inc, 2004) § 12.9 at 765.
[88] G H Treitel, *The Law of Contract*, n 56 above, 952.
[89] G H Treitel, *ibid*.

6

Modernisation of the German Law of Obligations: Harmonisation of Civil Law and Common Law in the Recent Reform of the German Civil Code

ANDREAS HELDRICH AND GEBHARD M REHM*

I INTRODUCTION

ON 1 JANUARY 2002, the German Statute on the Modernisation of the Law of Obligations became law.[1] If we disregard family law for a moment, this statute changes the German Civil Code more radically than any previous reform since 1 January 1900, when the Civil Code initially entered into force.[2]

The preparatory works of this reform date back to 1978, when the then Federal Minister of Justice, Mr Hans-Jochen Vogel, announced plans to modernise the law of obligations and asked a group of renowned experts to make concrete suggestions for changes deemed necessary. The expert reports were published in 1981 and 1983[3] whereupon the Ministry of

*Prof Heldrich presented this paper at the conference in Tel Aviv University in 2002; Dr Rehm participated in drafting it.

[1] Art 9 (1) Gesetz zur Modernisierung des Schuldrechts, Bundesgesetzblatt/Federal Gazette 2001 I 3138. An English translation of the provisions affected by the reform is available at www.iuscomp.org/gla/index.html. A detailed documentation of law review articles commenting upon the reform can be found at http://www.lrz-muenchen.de/~Lorenz/schumod/index.htm. Many relevant articles are contained in Ernst/Zimmermann (eds) *Zivilrechtswissenschaft und Schuldrechtsreform* (Mohr Siebeck, Tübingen, 2001) and in Schulze/Schulte-Nölke (eds) *Schuldrechtsreform vor dem Hintergrund des Gemeinschaftsrechts* (Mohr Siebeck, Tübingen, 2001). For a brief English introduction to the changes see P Schlechtriem, (2002) *Oxford University Comparative Law Forum* 2 at http://ouclf.iuscomp.org/articles/schlechtriem2.shtml.

[2] *Däubler* NJW 2001, 3729.

[3] Bundesministerium der Justiz/Federal Ministry of Justice (ed) *Gutachten und Vorschläge zur Überarbeitung des Schuldrechts* (Bundesanzeiger, Köln, 1981, 1983).

Justice constituted a commission on the reform of the law of obligations. This commission sat until 1991 and presented its final report in 1992.[4] Its conclusions and proposals — to a great deal inspired by the United Nations Convention on Contracts for the International Sale of Goods (CISG) — were one of the main subjects of the German Lawyers' Convention in Münster 1994, where they received general approval.[5] This brief historic overview suggests that the reform was more thoughtfully prepared than frequently claimed.[6]

Due to a number of circumstances, among them the pending groundwork on the EU directive on the sale of consumer goods,[7] whose results the legislator intended to include in the reform, but also the legislative attention on the legal prerequisites and consequences of German unity, however, the plans to modernise the law of obligations then lay dormant. In August 2000, the German Federal Government wakened them and announced its intention to combine the reform with the transformation of the EU directive on the sale of consumer goods.[8] The government's decision to pursue such a 'comprehensive solution' instead of a 'small solution'[9] that would have merely transformed the EU directives into German law, and its admittedly imperfect initial draft, alarmed the members of the legal profession. After a number of conferences on the topic during which we witnessed some unusually vitriolic attacks against the supporters of the reform and the federal government,[10] and after an expert commission appointed by the former Federal Minister of Justice, Mrs Hertha Däubler-Gmelin, had suggested substantial changes to the initial draft,[11] parliament debated the reform and the German Bundestag finally passed the statute on 11 October 2001.

[4] Bundesministerium der Justiz/Federal Ministry of Justice (ed) *Abschlußbericht der Kommission zur Überarbeitung des Schuldrechts* (Bundesanzeiger, Köln, 1982). See also *Rolland*, NJW 1992, 2376.

[5] Gutachten und Verhandlungen des 60. Juristentages, Vol 1 (Suggestions), Vol 2 (Discussion) (C H Beck, München, 1994).

[6] For some of the objections of one of the main critics see *Altmeppen*, DB 2001, 1131; DB 2001, 1399; replies by *Canaris* DB 2001, 1815 and *Lorenz* JZ 2001, 742.

[7] Directive 1999/44/EC of the European Parliament and of the Council of 25 May 1999 on certain aspects of the sale of consumer goods and associated guarantees, Official Journal L 171, 0012–0016.

[8] See previous note.

[9] For the advantages of the 'comprehensive solution' compared with the 'small solution' see then Federal Minister of Justice *Däubler-Gmelin*, NJW 2001, 2281.

[10] *Altmeppen* DB 2001, 1131; *Knütel* NJW 2001, 2519. *Heldrich* NJW 2001, 2521 describes the tense atmosphere at several conferences on the subject.

[11] For a brief evaluation of the work of this commission, of which Andreas Heldrich was a member see *Geiger* JZ 2001, 473. *Canaris* JZ 2001, 499 outlines many of the results reached by it.

II THE THRUST OF THE REFORM

1 The Principal Changes

The reform touches a number of central subsets of the law of obligations:

- The rules on statutes of limitation, which German law, contrary to many Common Law systems, qualifies as substantial rather than procedural law. The regular default period of limitation was cut from thirty to three years.[12] The change is, however, less radical than it seems at first glance because the statute of limitation now only commences to run when the creditor learns of the essential circumstances of his claim or ignores them due to gross negligence.[13] Independent of such subjective element, the claim is finally barred after 10 years.
- The consolidation into the Civil Code of a number of consumer protection statutes[14] and the Statute on General Conditions that proliferated outside the Code and threatened to destroy a Civil Law Code's very idea:[15] to systematise and unite the essential rules applicable to private law relationships in one statute.
- The codification of case law. The German Civil Code now contains legal rules for and definitions of a number of concepts originally developed by the judiciary. This aspect of the reform highlights one point of our subject today because to some degree it shows the similarities of the Civil Law and the Common Law in the law-making process. Contrary to a widely held prejudice, the legislation in Civil Law countries is by no means the only framer of the law: Similar to their Common Law counterparts, courts in Civil Law countries play a decisive role in devising new legal rules and concepts,[16] which — as we can see in this case the legislation sometimes merely adopts and codifies without changing them substantially. The Code now expressly recognises
  i incidental duties arising from the contractual or pre-contractual relationship of the parties beyond the law of torts,[17]

[12] § 195 German Civil Code (hereinafter: BGB).
[13] § 199 BGB.
[14] Among them the statutes on consumer credit, on distance contracts, on contracts negotiated away from business premises and on contracts relating to the purchase of the right to use immovable properties on a timeshare basis.
[15] K Zweigert and H Kötz *An Introduction to Comparative Law* 3rd edn (Clarendon Press, Oxford, 1998) § 10 III discuss the general concept of codification.
[16] Professor Markesinis has rightly pointed out that the practical difference in the lawmaking power of courts in Common Law and Civil Law systems is often overstated, see B Markesinis, *Foreign Law and Comparative Methodology* (Hart Publishing, Oxford, 1997) 194 *et seq*, 220 *et seq*, 362 *et seq*.
[17] §§ 241(2), 311(2) BGB.

ii a cause of action for violation of *pre*-contractual duties; the so called *culpa in contrahendo*,[18]

iii a cause of action for violation of incidental *contractual* duties; the judicial concept formerly called positive violation of a contractual duty,[19]

iv the general right to cancel long-term contracts for an important cause,[20]

v the private law version of *clausula rebus sic stantibus* (*Wegfall der Geschäftsgrundlage*).[21]

— In particular, the codification of the concept of positive violation of contractual duties paved the way to the undoubtedly paramount change of the law of obligations, that touches the concept and consequences of non-performance, or as we would now formulate properly: the violation of a duty as a fundamental and universal prerequisite of a claim for damages.[22]

2 The Pre-reform Problems

The need for reform will be recognised after a brief description of the pre-reform rules. German law governing the conditions of and remedies for non-performance was a perfectly versatile instrument of torture in the hands of law professors, but hardly a convincing legal approach. It goes without saying that it was largely out of step with the international trend.

We should mention only a few oddities. Sales law until now distinguished between factual and legal vices of the goods sold and stipulated different remedies and periods of limitation for the two categories of vices. Whereas the claim for a factual vice of an immovable had to be raised within one year, the statute allowed thirty years in the case of a legal vice. The buyer of goods with a legal vice — among others — had a right to

[18] §§ 280 (1), 311(2), 241 (2) BGB. Numerous court decisions have shaped and extended much further this concept, initially developed by *Jhering* JherJb 4 (1861) 1 for a much smaller area of application. It has also received wide attention in the German legal literature. For pre-reform overviews see eg B Markesinis, W Lorenz and G Dannemann, *The German Law of Obligations*, Vol I (Clarendon, Oxford, 1997) 65 *et seq.*; Münchener Kommentar/*Emmerich* 3rd edn (C H Beck, München, 1994) Vor § 275 n 48 *et seq*.

[19] §§ 280 (1), 241 (2) BGB. Positive violations of a contractual duty (*positive Vertragsverletzungen*) were 'discovered' by *Hermann Staub*, Die positiven Vertragsverletzungen und ihre Rechtsfolgen, Festschrift für den XXVI. Deutschen Juristentag (Guttentag, Berlin, 1902) 29. For an explanation of this concept see B Markesinis, W Lorenz and G Dannemann, above n 18, 418 *et seq*; Münchener Kommentar/*Emmerich* above n 18, Vor § 275 n 218 *et seq* (also for a critical evaluation of the gap in the BGB claimed by Staub).

[20] § 314 BGB.

[21] § 313 BGB. For an overview over this concept see B Markesinis, W Lorenz and G Dannemann, above n 18, 516 et seq; Münchener Kommentar/*Roth* 3rd edn (CH Beck, München, 1994) Vor § 242 n. 496 et seq. The earliest proponent of this concept under the German Civil Code is probably *Oertmann*, Die Geschäftsgrundlage (Deichert, Leipzig, 1921).

[22] § 280 (1) BGB.

damages,[23] whereas the buyer of goods with a factual vice had such remedy only where the seller had guaranteed a characteristic of the goods or had fraudulently concealed the vice.[24] This distinction between legal and factual vices might have been acceptable if it had been based upon convincing criteria mandating such treatment. But what difference does it really make if a person buys a piece of land with the purpose of building a family home only to find out that the plan fails because the municipality does not allow building family homes there or the plan fails because a neighbour has a servitude on the land preventing the erection of family homes? The municipal restriction was considered to be a factual vice[25] that generally would not allow a claim for damages and would have to be raised within one year, while the neighbour's servitude would have been a legal vice[26] that allows a claim for damages that can still be pursued after twenty nine years.

Further complicating matters, German courts came up with a distinction between a claim for damages arising from the diminished quality of the good sold (so called damages for vice) and a claim for damages caused to the body or property of the buyer (so called damages for consequences of the vice).[27] In sales law the courts applied the six-months period of limitation for movable goods to both claims.[28] However, this distinction does not seem to have been subtle enough in the law of manufacturing contracts, where apart from the statutory stipulation of different remedies than in sales law, the Federal Supreme Court additionally distinguished between damages for close consequences of the vice and damages for distant consequences of the vice.[29]

To be honest, we have never quite grasped the difference between close and distant consequences of the vice in manufacturing contracts.[30] But the difference must have been an important one because the claim for close consequences of the vice had to be raised within six months, while that for distant consequences had to be raised within thirty years. An illustration will demonstrate the issue. Suppose that a home owner enters into a contract with a carpenter under which the carpenter agrees to manufacture bookshelves. If one of the bookshelves turned out to be defective that would be a factual vice and the homeowner would have a claim for damages against the negligent carpenter to which the six-months period

[23] Former §§ 440, 434, 437, 325 BGB.
[24] Former §§ 463, 480 BGB.
[25] According to Bundesgerichtshof/Federal Supreme Court (hereinafter: BGH) 7.2.1992 BGHZ 117, 159 public law restrictions on land are usually factual vices.
[26] BGH 19.11.1999 NJW 2000, 803 is a typical example of classifying private law servitudes as legal vices.
[27] BGH 29.5.1968 BGHZ 50, 200; BGH 2.6.1980 BGHZ 77, 215.
[28] BGH 2.6.1980 BGHZ 77, 215.
[29] BGH 20.1.1972 BGHZ 58, 85.
[30] The former Federal Minister of Justice denounced this distinction as not being justifiable according to any rational criteria. See Däubler-Gmelin, above n 9, 2283.

of limitation would apply. Similarly, if the bookshelf collapsed and damaged the homeowner's edition of the Encyclopedia Britannica, the Federal Supreme Court would probably have considered this damage a *close* consequence of the vice so that the homeowner would also have to raise the claim within six months. But if the homeowner were unfortunate enough to happen to sit next to the bookshelf when it collapsed, the same judges would allow the homeowner thirty years to pursue his contractual cause of action for personal injury.

Given such intricacies, the tribulations of German law students can easily be visualised, as can the tomes written on the proper distinction between factual and legal vices, close and distant consequences of the vice and how desperately the courts strove to avoid drastic inconsistencies in the law. Given this situation, the neutral observer should have expected everyone fervently to support improving this sad state of the law. What is good for the students should be good for the country. We have a hunch, however, that many of the numerous law professors who fumed about the reform of the law of obligations that was meant to eliminate some of these inconsistencies, were less motivated by their declared sense of responsibility for the German law of obligations, but rather by their fear of having to rewrite their class material and to invent new problems for exams. Be that as it may: the statute now establishes a largely unitary approach to non-performance. Why is that a symptom of convergence between Civil and Common Law? We will analyse this in the following section.

III THE UNITARY APPROACH TO NON-PERFORMANCE AS A SYMPTOM OF HARMONISATION BETWEEN CIVIL LAW AND COMMON LAW

1 The Elements of the Unitary Approach

As a central element of the reform, the legislator has all but completely discarded the double-track approach to non-performance with respect to conditions and types of remedies. Before the reform, the German Civil Code provided a general system of remedies for impossibility and delay (among them damages or, strictly alternatively, the right to withdraw from the contract) and special remedies for vices in sales law, landlord and tenant law and the law of manufacturing contracts, the areas of the law with the greatest practical relevance. As we mentioned before, to make matters more complicated, the two tracks partially crossed each other. The remedies and thus also the periods of limitation for different types of vices were not identical, the vendor being liable for legal vices under the general regime of the law of obligations but for factual vices only under the specific system of sales law.

The post-reform German Civil Code establishes the principle that the non-performing party — no matter whether performance has become impossible, the goods to be delivered have a legal or a factual vice or he has violated an incidental duty — is liable for damages.[31] In sales law and the law of manufacturing contracts, however, the vendor or manufacturer receives a 'second chance' for performance before being liable for damages if the non-performance can be remedied. For example, the buyer of defective goods can claim damages or withdraw from the contract only after the vendor has failed to remedy the defect within a reasonable time period stipulated by the buyer.[32] The debtor's right to 'remedial performance', that is intended to give priority to the contract's performance instead of withdrawing from it or claiming damages for non-performance, had previously not been provided for statutorily in sales law, but only in the law of manufacturing contracts.[33] Vendors, however, often reserved this right, a practice that had in principle received the legislative stamp of approval by the statutory stipulation of the vendor's duty to bear the cost of remedial performance.[34] Here the reform brings the law more into line with common contractual practice. The specific remedy of '*Wandelung*' in sales law, a remedy similar to withdrawal from the contract, but the root of numerous fruitless debates,[35] has been bid farewell into legal history. The concept of impossibility, for the original legislator of the Civil Code the paradigm of its rules on liability for non-performance, has been greatly reduced in importance and now serves almost exclusively as an objection for the debtor. If performance is impossible for the debtor, his relevant duty is extinguished.[36] This extinction, however, does not preempt a possible liability for non-performance.[37]

The unitary approach to non-performance is not only visible with respect to the consequences of non-performance, but also with respect to the prerequisites of the remedies. As we mentioned, the legislator has ended the unequal treatment of factual and legal vices and the vendor now has an affirmative duty to deliver the goods sold without any vices.[38] Every vice of the goods therefore gives rise to a claim for damages unless the vendor acted without fault. The unitary approach also largely disposes of the distinction between close and distant consequences of the vice.[39] In

[31] § 280 (1)1 BGB. Furthermore, withdrawal from the contract does not any more exclude claims for damages, § 325 BGB.

[32] §§ 437, 634 BGB in its interplay with §§ 281 (2), 323 (2) BGB which provide for the expiry of a time period for remedial performance or its impossibility as a prerequisite for claiming damages or a right to withdrawal, respectively.

[33] Former § 633 (2)1 BGB.

[34] See the former provision of § 476a BGB.

[35] See eg Larenz, Schuldrecht II 1 13th edn (C H Beck, München, 1986) 53 for a discussion of the much-debated legal nature of the remedy.

[36] § 275 BGB.

[37] § 283 (1) BGB.

[38] § 433 (1)2 BGB.

[39] It does remain, however, important for questions of the proper basis of a claim (§ 280 or § 281 BGB) and thus the question whether the buyer can only claim damages after unsuccessfully asking for remedial performance, Palandt/Heinrichs, *Gesetz zur Modernisierung des Schuldrechts, Ergänzungsband zu Palandt*, BGB, 61st edn, (CH Beck, München, 2002) § 280 n 18.

sum, the new approach integrates the liabilities for vices, non-performance, impossibility, delay or violation of incidental duties under the headline of 'violation of duty'.

In our opinion, the reform will considerably ease the problems which arose from having to deal with all these cases of non-performance, though, as is the case with every reform, it will always create new problems.

2 Aspects of Harmonisation and why the Harmony is not Perfect

Not only has the statute been considerably improved, but the legislator unmistakably took a step towards a Common Law approach to non-performance. An obvious degree of harmonisation between the Civil Law and Common Law countries, which are member states of the European Union, is, of course, mandated by the requirements of the EU directive on the sale of consumer goods and associated guarantees.

a) Harmonisation

The German legislation has taken several steps in the direction of typical Common Law rules. Instead of the double-track system of specific remedies for certain types of contracts (particularly sales) and the general remedies in the case of impossibility or delay, that was already characteristic of classical Roman law,[40] the German law of obligations' approach now rests on one important concept: the violation of duty. The violation of duty is the general condition for any remedy in any contract, and in every case of non-performance (with the aforementioned exception of remedial performance) the creditor is entitled to claim damages or withdraw from the contract. Choosing such a general rule is obviously more similar to a Common Law system of non-performance than to a Civil Law system. The authors of the reform, by the way, are not shy to acknowledge the Common Law's influence, particularly their inspiration from the United Nations Convention on Contracts on the International Sale of Goods (CISG),[41] which to a large degree in itself is a compromise between Common Law and Civil Law concepts.[42] The priority given to remedial performance in sales and manufacturing contracts clearly borrows from Articles 45–51 of CISG. The reformers also kept an eye on international law harmonisation projects such as the drafting of the 'Principles of European Contract Law'[43] and of the UNIDROIT 'Principles of

[40] For a brief description of the historical background see Staudinger/*Honsell*, BGB 13th edn. (Sellier/de Gruyter, Berlin, 1995) Vorbem zu §§ 459 ff, note 5 *et seq.*
[41] *Däubler-Gmelin* above n 9, 2283.
[42] K Zweigert and H Kötz above n 15 § 36 V give a brief account of the CISG's background.
[43] O Lando and H Beale (eds) *Principles of European Contract Law* (Kluwer, The Hague, 2000).

International Commercial Contracts'[44] that are both characterised by the attempt to combine Common and Civil Law approaches to contract law.

b) *Aspects of Non-harmonisation*

The harmony between Common Law and Civil Law in the new German law of obligations is, however, not perfect. We did not fully adopt the Common Law concepts of non-performance. A clear and striking difference remains with respect to a requirement of the debtor's subjective responsibility where the claim brought against the debtor is a claim for damages. Common Law systems usually impose a duty to pay damages for non-performance without requiring any kind of fault by the debtor.[45] By operation of the law, the debtor has to guarantee his or her (proper) performance. German law, in contrast, continues to grant a damages claim only on the condition that the debtor acted with fault, which usually means that he acted at least negligently, unless he has given a guarantee.[46] The *culpa* principle, the requirement of fault as a condition of a damages cause of action, thus remains one of the main pillars of the German law of obligations.[47] This theoretical difference between the Common Law and German law may in practice, however, influence the outcome of the case less frequently than it seems because German law presumes the existence of fault[48] and the debtor will usually have great difficulty in proving his complete innocence. The fault requirement is thus considerably attenuated by the presumption of fault against the non-performing party.

Another conceptual difference remains as a result of introducing the concept of remedial performance, which is foreign to Common Law systems, into German sales law. Even though the UK and Ireland have had to devise similar rules for consumer sales, and the CISG has a similar system, this is certainly a Civil Law rather than a Common Law concept and Germany has even exceeded the requirement of the EU directive on sales of consumer goods by applying it to every category of sale, not only the sale of consumer goods as required by the directive.

The reform did not exactly copy Common Law systems either by codifying the concept of incidental duties in § 241 (2) of the Civil Code that, for example, encompass duties of protection with respect to the body and property of the other party to the contract. Even though Common Law countries do not anymore fully reject a general good faith principle,[49] on

[44] UNIDROIT (ed) *Principles of International Commercial Contracts* (UNIDROIT Rome 1994).
[45] For English law see G Treitel, *The Law of Contract* 11th edn (Sweet & Maxwell, London, 2003) 840 *et seq*.
[46] § 276 BGB.
[47] *Däubler-Gmelin* above n 9, 2287 *et seq*.
[48] Because of the negative formulation of § 280(1)(2) BGB.
[49] See eg § 1-203 UCC.

which such duties ultimately rest, they are generally much more reserved towards deriving duties from the pre-contractual or contractual relationship which the parties did not expressly provide for. The recognition of these incidental duties in the reformed German statute thus seems to be a step away from the consensus with Common Law countries. One should not forget, however, that the Common Law systems in practice will often reach similar results by deriving comparable rules from tort law.

A further important systematic difference is the concept of a Code. Whereas Codes in Common Law countries, if they exist at all, often are mere compilations of statutes, the German legislator expressly intended to avoid the further proliferation of private law statutes outside the Code and to preserve the Code's systematic and logical unity for which it has been famed.[50]

IV A NOT STRICTLY LEGAL ASPECT OF HARMONISATION

Finally we will touch on an aspect of convergence between Civil Law and Common Law in the reform that are not of a legal nature in the strict sense. The reform's goal was not only to improve the law as such, but also to strengthen German law on an international scale. Although German law, particularly its Civil Code, undoubtedly has influenced a great many foreign legal systems,[51] German lawyers are usually reluctant to admit this influence or even deliberately to try to obtain it. In particular, US lawyers are usually less inhibited in this respect. It was a certain surprise, therefore, that the Minister of Justice responsible for the reform has openly emphasised that an important goal of the reform of the law of obligations was to re-enter the competition of legal systems with a renewed and understandable law of contracts.[52] Particularly the codification of so far purely judicial concepts, such as *culpa in contrahendo*, was expressly meant to achieve greater transparency of German law for outsiders (and for students of law, which says a thing or two about the opacity of German law[53])[54] and to render German law at the same time a more attractive alternative for choice-of-law clauses in international transactions. This open-mindedness to the demands and requirements of international trade so far seemed to belong to the domain of the more pragmatic Common Law countries.

[50] See F Wieacker, *Privatrechtsgeschichte der Neuzeit* 2nd edn (Vandenhoeck & Rupprecht, Göttingen, 1967) 477.
[51] K Zweigert and H Kötz above n 15, § 10 IV.
[52] Däubler-Gmelin, above n 9, 2283.
[53] B Markesinis, above n 16, 136, 361 with some justification criticises the complex style of German court decisions, rendering them almost inaccessible to foreigners.
[54] Canaris above n 11, 519.

V CONCLUSION

Looking at the reform as a whole, it might not be perfect. It is, however, decidedly a marked improvement compared with the rules previously applicable to non-performance which we have briefly described. The reform also proves the value of the international legal dialogue that has greatly contributed to finding appropriate solutions in Germany. Drawing on other countries' experience, and in this case that of many Common Law countries, has proven most fruitful for the prudent evolution of German law. The convergence of Civil and Common Law approaches to contracts law seems to indicate that we are internationally on a track towards common convincing solutions in contract law.

7

The New Approach to Breach of Contract in German Law

DAGMAR COESTER-WALTJEN*

I INTRODUCTION**

ON 1 JANUARY 2002 the new German law of obligations entered into force.[1] As has already been stated,[2] the new law should replace the extremely complicated and partly unsatisfactory statutory and judge-made rules[3] with a modern unified approach to all kinds of breach of contract following — at least in many though not in all aspects — international trends and models. In particular, the United Nations Convention on the International Sale of Goods (CISG), of which Germany is a member state, has had considerable influence.[4] In addition, the Principles of European Contract Law (PECL) and the new German law do not differ much with regard to the solutions provided for breach of contract.

* University of Munich.

** Abbreviations used in the text and footnotes have the following meaning: PECL = Principles of European Contract Law; BGB = German Civil Code; HGB = German Commercial Code; Unidroit = Unidroit Principles on International Commercial Contracts; CISG = UN Convention on Contracts for the International Sale of Goods; a.F. = alte Fassung, old version; BGH = Federal Supreme Court; RGZ/BGHZ = Reports of the decisions of the Federal Supreme Court in civil cases (volume, page); legal periodicals and reports are cited in the usual way (see *Kirchner*, Abkürzungsverzeichnis); the translation of the new provisions of the BGB cited here are by Prof. Dr. Dr.h.c. mult. Werner Lorenz, Munich.

[1] As to the background of the reform see H Schulte-Nölke *The New German Law of Obligations: an Introduction* (www.iuscomp.ag 2002); P Schlechtriem 'The German Act to Modernize the Law of Obligations in the Context of Common Principles and Structures of the Law of Obligations in Europe' (2002) *Oxford University Comparative Law Forum* 2; T Möllers 'European Directives on Civil Law — Shaping a New German Civil Code' (2003) 18 *Tulane European & Civil Law Forum* 1.

[2] AH Heldrich and GM Rehm 'Modernisation on the German Law of Obligations: Harmonisation of Civil Law and Common Law in the Recent Reform of the German Civil Code' (chapter 6 of this collection).

[3] See in detail Schlechtriem above n 1.

[4] The German Act to modernise the Law of Obligations is also closely linked to the implementation of three European directives, among them the most important directive 1999/44/EC on consumer sales which on its part is widely modelled on the CISG, for this see Schlechtriem (above n 1) II.4.1.

In this chapter I would like to concentrate on two remedies for breach of contract, namely termination of contract and damages.

II THE NOTION OF 'VIOLATION OF AN OBLIGATION'

It has to be recalled that the German terminology does not speak of breach of contract but of 'violation of an obligation'[5] because the rules cover impediments not only to contractual but also to statutory obligations.[6] Thus, these provisions apply in all cases in which there is a legal relationship between two or more persons[7] obliging at least one party to perform a certain obligation towards the other party, giving (at least) one party the entitlement to certain benefits or the right to recovery. The provisions apply irrespective of whether only one party is the obligor (as for example the tortfeasor or a party to a unilaterally obliging contract[8]) or whether both parties owe each other a certain performance *vice versa* (as will be the case in most business transactions and in many day-to-day contracts). But there are some provisions which take account of the special situation of reciprocal contracts.[9]

Because of the broad field of application, the rules have a relatively high level of abstraction. In this respect they differ considerably from the Principles of European Contract Law which are less abstract and therefore easier to understand. In addition, the German legislator did not follow the modern tendency[10] to speak of non-performance, but of a violation though he wanted to include also cases where performance is not possible at all.[11] The violation of an obligation in the meaning of the new law includes all kinds of non-performance. Therefore, what we are talking about here may consist in a defective performance, in a failure to perform at the time performance is due (either too early or too late),

[5] H Schulte-Nölke speaks of 'breach of duty' or 'breach of (an) obligation'.

[6] During the legislative process there was a vivid discussion about the adequate terminology for §280 BGB, whereby the notion of 'non-performance' was considered as the only possible alternative, cf *Medicus*, JuS 2003, 521, 527; *Palandt/Heinrichs*,BGB, 63 edn, (Munich, CH Beck, 2004) §280 BGB, Rdn 3.

[7] Such a relationship is — for example — also contained in the rights and duties assigned by §§742ff BGB, see OLG Brandenburg, FPR 2002, 133, and in the relationship between the administrator in insolvency and the parties involved in insolvency proceedings, see LG Erfurt, *Neue Juristische Wochenschrift–Rechtsprechungs Report Zivilrecht* (2003) 49.

[8] In German law for example all kinds of gratuitous contracts like contracts of donation (§§516 ff BGB), mandate (§§662 ff BGB) are only unilaterally-obliging.

[9] §§ 320 ff BGB.

[10] Art 8.101 PECL; Art 7.1.1 Unidroit.

[11] Though it can be disputed whether there is a violation of an obligation when performance is not possible and the law even says that the debtor is freed from his (primary) obligation when performance is impossible (§ 275 BGB), the non-performance in such a case is nevertheless treated as violation of the obligation (§ 280 BGB), thus the different terminology does not lead to a different treatment of the cases so far, even though this is not so obvious.

non-performance at all and violation of an accessory duty (for example a duty not to infringe the goods of the other party or not to disclose that party's trade secrets). In all these cases there may be a violation of an obligation, whether or not the violation is excused or not excused.

The remedies available may include the right to withhold one's own performance[12] or the automatic discharge thereof,[13] the right to reduce the price[14] or to terminate the contract[15] as well as the right to damages as the case may be. However, it has to be stressed that independent of these

[12] §320 BGB; cf Art 9.201 PECL, Art 7.1.3. Unidroit.

[13] §326 BGB (Release from counter-performance and termination in case of lapse of obligation to perform):

(1) If the debtor is released from performing under §275(1) to (3), the claim to counter-performance is lost; in case of part performance §441(3) shall apply mutatis mutandis. Sent. 1 does not apply in case of non-conforming performance if the debtor need not remedy to perform according to §275(1) to (3).
(2) If the creditor is solely or by far more responsible for the circumstance by reason of which the debtor is released from performing under §275(1) to (3), or if the circumstance for which the debtor is not responsible arises at a time when the creditor is in default of acceptance, the debtor retains his claim for counter-performance. He must, however, deduct what he saves in consequence of release from the performance, or what he acquires or wilfully omits to acquire by a different use of his labour.
(3) If the creditor demands delivery under §285 of the substitute received for the object owed, or assignment of the claim for compensation, he remains obliged to make the counter-performance. This is diminished, however, in accordance with §441(3) insofar as the value of the substitute or of the claim for compensation is less than the value of the performance due.
(4) Insofar as counter-performance has been made which according to this provision was not due, it may be demanded back under §§346 to 348.
(5) If the debtor is released from performance under §275(1) to (3) the creditor may terminate the contract; §323 shall apply mutatis mutandis to such termination, no period of grace being necessary.

[14] §§437 Nr 2, 441; §§634 Nr 2, 638; §536 BGB; cf Art 9.401 PECL, Art 50 CISG.

[15] §323 BGB (Termination of contract in case of non-performance or non-conforming performance):

(1) If a debtor under a mutual contract does not perform when performance has fallen due or does not perform conforming to the contract, the creditor may terminate the contract, provided he has, without success, granted the debtor a reasonable period within which to perform or to remedy to perform.
(2) The period of grace is unnecessary, if
    1. the debtor seriously and definitively refuses to perform,
    2. the debtor does not perform at the time fixed or within a period of time fixed by the contract and the creditor's interest in the performance is dependent upon timely performance, or
    3. there are special circumstances which, upon a balance of interests of both parties, justify an immediate termination.
(3) If the neglect of duty is of such nature that a period of grace is inappropriate, a warning will take its place.
(4) The creditor may terminate the contract even before the performance has become due if it is obvious that the conditions for termination will materialize.
(5) If the debtor has performed in part, the creditor may terminate the entire contract only if he is not interested in part performance. If the debtor has not

remedies the creditor retains the right to performance as long as such performance is possible, be it a monetary or a non-monetary obligation. Unlike most common law jurisdictions the right to specific performance is the first and primary remedy of the creditor — at least in theory. This traditional approach of German law has been sustained and even strengthened by the reform: the creditor may insist on performance and may even enforce this right (except for personal services, §888 II ZPO).[16] In practice enforcement is sought less often for non-pecuniary obligations. The debtor on the other hand in many instances has a right to a second chance to perform. Thus most of the remedies are only available to the creditor after he has given notice of an additional period for performance.[17] This approach adheres closely to the idea of *pacta sunt servanda* which is mirrored also in the Principles of European Contract Law,[18] though (only) the latter but not German law provide exceptions when substitute transactions seem reasonable.[19] In contrast, German law is very rigid with regard to the right to performance and even sets incentives for performance insofar as the creditor can claim the substitute which the debtor would receive through the act making his performance impossible.[20] If, for example, the seller bound by contract to give certain goods to A, sells these goods at a better price to B, and thereby makes impossible the performance of his contract with A, he would have to pay A — on A's request — the money he has got from B (or to assign to A his claim against B for that money). Thus, traditionally in German law, even the so-called efficient breach has been made unattractive.[21]

performed in conformity with the contract, the creditor may not terminate the contract if the neglect of duty is insignificant.

(6) Termination is excluded if the creditor is either solely or by far more responsible for the circumstance which would entitle him to termination, or if the circumstance for which the debtor is not responsible occurs at a time when the creditor is in default of acceptance.

§376 HGB varies the right to termination in commercial contracts when time is of essence.

[16] §§281 I, 323, 437 Nr. 1, 638 Nr. 1 BGB; cf Art. 9.101, 9.102 PECL; Art. 7.1.4, 7.2.1, 7.2.2, 7.2.3 Unidroit.

[17] *Ibid.*

[18] Arts 8.104, 8.106, 9.101(1), 9.102(1).

[19] Arts 9.101(2)(a), 9.102(2)(d) PECL; similarly Art 7.2.2 Unidroit; see also the compromise in Art 28 CISG — enforceability sustained.

[20] §285 BGB: (Delivery of a substitute)

(1) If the debtor, in consequence of the circumstance which according to § 275 (1) to (3) releases him from the obligation to perform, acquires a substitute or a claim for compensation for the object owed, the creditor may demand delivery of the substitute received or assignment of the claim for compensation.

(2) If the debtor may claim compensation instead of performance, the compensation is diminished if he exercises the right specified in (1) by the value of the substitute received or of the claim for compensation.

[21] Promoters of the economic analysis of law claim that it would be reasonable from an economic point of view to allow the vendor for example to sell the goods to third parties who are willing to pay more, if the interest of the buyer in the goods does not exceed this price.

III THE ROLE OF IMPOSSIBILITY

From the principle of specific performance it also follows that it is crucial whether performance is impossible or not.[22] As long as the debtor (for example the seller) could provide the goods or services promised — even though he might have to undertake special (financial or other) efforts — the performance has not become impossible and a claim for specific performance would be successful (and enforceable).[23]

If performance has become impossible — either to everybody or only to the debtor — the debtor's duty to perform is terminated, but not the contract as such.[24] Thus, in case of impossibility the relationship between debtor and creditor subsists, but there is a violation of an obligation (ie the non-performance) and this might give rise to secondary remedies.

As long as performance is possible (even if it might be more burdensome than the debtor expected), the creditor may ask for specific performance and the non-performance will not be regarded as a case of impossibility.[25]

Only under very extraordinary circumstances may the debtor claim that the expenses in order to perform are extraordinarily disproportionate to the benefit which the creditor will obtain from performance[26] or — in

[22] §275 BGB (Termination of the obligation to perform):

(1) The claim to performance is terminated insofar as performance is impossible for the debtor or for every one.
(2) The debtor may refuse to perform insofar as this would require an effort which, having regard to the substance of the obligation and the requirements of good faith, would be grossly disproportionate to the creditor's interest in such performance. In determining the effort reasonably to be expected from the debtor it must also be considered whether the debtor is responsible for the failure to perform.
(3) Furthermore, the debtor may refuse to perform if he has to perform personally and such performance cannot reasonably be expected from him when weighing the impediment preventing him from performing against the creditor's interest in the performance.
(4) The rights of the creditor are determined according to §§280, 283 to 285, 311a and 326.

[23] Impossibility of performance had played a central role under the former rules, however it had proved not to be relevant in practice. Besides the old law provided a rather complicated system with the distinction between initial and subsequent, imputable and non-imputable, subjective and objective impossibility. Nevertheless the new law carries on this category of dysfunction, however with a few changes, see below and n 60. Schlechtriem characterises the adoption of impossibility in §275 I BGB as 'a step back' towards traditional conceptions which conflicts with the new concept of §311 a I BGB, see Schlechtriem, above n 1, III.2.a.
[24] §§275 I, 311 a I BGB; *ibid*.
[25] The case of temporary impediments to performance produces special problems, the solution of which the legislator has left to the courts; for the old approach comp. RGZ 158, 331; BGH LM Nr. 4 zu § 275 BGB; for the new law P Schlechtriem (above n 1, III.2.a), with reference to § 308 BGB a.F.
[26] §275 II BGB; so called practical impossibility (example: the ring sold has fallen into the sea); see for details: *Canaris*, JZ 2001, 501; these cases have to be distinguished from a change of circumstances which has led to a considerable disturbance of the balance between the (objective) values of performance and counterperformance (cases of frustration, *Störung der Geschäftsgrundlage*, §313 BGB).

the case of a contract for personal services — where it is outrageous to ask for performance.[27] In these situations the law treats the debtor as if it was impossible for him to perform his contractual obligations; thus he does not have to perform. Instead the creditor may take advantage of the remedies in case of impossibility. The crucial point under the new rules is to distinguish between the different dogmatic principles governing §275 I and §275 II, III BGB.[28] Whereas in the case of §275 I BGB the contractual obligation to perform is determined automatically (ie by statutory rule), §275 II, III BGB only lead to the obligor's right of refusal which does not produce any effects until raised. On the other hand the obligor is not forced to invoke this defence, in fact he can decide to perform despite the practical or moral impediment.[29]

Though specific performance is the first and primary remedy in case of non-performance (as long as performance is possible), in practice most creditors seek the so called secondary remedies whether or not performance is possible.[30] Secondary remedies invoked are mainly termination of the contract and damages. Both remedies may (now) be cumulated when the prerequisites of both have been met.[31]

IV THE RIGHT TO TERMINATE

The right to terminate the contract is a remedy at the choice of the creditor. This remedy makes sense only where mutual obligations exist and it is limited to these cases (§§320 *seq* BGB). There is no automatic termination of the contract[32], nor is any judicial pronouncement necessary, nor is any special form required. It suffices that the aggrieved party tells the other that it terminates the relationship, provided it has good cause to do so. Good cause may result from different situations and has several prerequisites.

[27] Moral impossibility, §275 III BGB (for example: the clown does not want to appear on stage because his wife is lying on death-bed; or: the employee has to go to his home country for military service, otherwise he will have to fear severe criminal sanctions), cf BAG, DB 1983, 396.

[28] The text of which is set out at n 22 above.

[29] So-called *'überobligationsmäßige Leistung'*, see *Reischl*, JuS 2003, 250, 256; Huber/Faust, *Schuldrechtsmodernisierung* (Munich, CH Beck, 2002) Kap 2, Rdn 12.

[30] Though the remedies may differ with regard to their prerequisites depending on impossibility, delay or infringement of rights and may partly depend on the question whether or not the violation is excused, see below.

[31] §325 BGB: (Compensation and termination) In a mutual contract termination does not preclude the right to demand compensation. Cf Art 9.103 PECL, Art 45 CISG.

[32] It has to be noted, however, that the law provides for the automatic discharge of the creditor's obligation in cases where the debtor's performance is impossible (caveat: §326 I 1 BGB, above n 13), and this impossibility is neither due to a fact or circumstance within the creditor's responsibility nor happened during *mora creditoris*, § 326 I 1, II BGB; this has pretty much the same effect as a termination of the contract, cf §326 IV BGB.

1 Kinds of Violations

The first prerequisite is that there has been a violation of an obligation (whatsoever) which need not be a fundamental breach. In this respect, German law differs from many other legal systems which allow termination only in cases of fundamental breach.[33] The German law has the advantage of avoiding the problematic definition of what constitutes a fundamental breach.[34] Thus, the violation may consist of delay, delivery of defective goods, delivery of the wrong quantity, of a breach of an accessory duty, or total non-performance.

However, there are some safeguards which serve similar goals as the restriction to fundamental violations or fundamental breach. For example, in cases of part-performance the creditor may terminate the complete contract only if the performed part is of no interest to him.[35] If, for instance, the seller has sold six antique chairs but can deliver only four of them because the other two antique chairs have been destroyed, the buyer may terminate the contract with regard to the two chairs and fulfil the contract on his part with regard to the four chairs. If, however, he can show that four chairs are of no interest to him, then he may terminate the complete contract. If the performance has been defective, termination depends on the weight of the defect; minor defects do not give rise to the right of termination.[36] In such cases the aggrieved party is principally bound by the contract but may reduce its own performance according to the lesser value of the goods or services received.

If the breach consists of a violation of an accessory duty the contract may be terminated only if the subsistence of the relationship would be unacceptable.[37] This applies mainly in situations in which reliance and trustworthiness have been destroyed. If this is not the case the contractual relationship remains unchanged, both parties have to perform, but the aggrieved party may in addition claim damages for the detriments caused by the violation of the accessory duty under §280 BGB.

It seems that these rules provide a fair weighing of the conflicting interests of the aggrieved and the defaulting party, without causing too many problems and too much uncertainty. They make sure that minor violations may not be used as an excuse for terminating the contractual relationship.

[33] See also Art 9.301 PECL, Art 49 CISG; Art 7.3.1 Unidroit; as to this cf P Schlechtriem, above n 1, III.2.b.
[34] Cf Art 8.103 PECL.
[35] §323 V 1 BGB (above n 15).
[36] §323 V 2 BGB (above n 15), cf Art 9.306 PECL, Art 49 CISG.
[37] §324 BGB (Termination in case of neglect of duty under §241 II):

> If the debtor of a mutual contract neglects a duty under §241(2), the creditor may terminate the contract if he cannot reasonably be expected to abide by the contract any longer.

2 Additional Period of Time

Secondly, the law requires, in principle, that the aggrieved party must by notice to the other party allow an additional period of time for performance[38] to avoid hardship and surprise. But there is no need to serve a notice on the non-performing party in order to put the latter into breach (*Mahnung, mise en demeure*).[39] The non-performance as such is the violation of an obligation and suffices for the remedy. The additional period for good performance must be such that the debtor has a fair chance to perform. The duration depends on the circumstances of the case.

Of course, there are situations in which an additional period of time does not make sense — as for example when performance is impossible anyway,[40] or has been refused definitely by the debtor,[41] where the damage has been done already,[42] or where further delay seems unacceptable.[43] In all these cases the law dispenses with this prerequisite.

3 The Role of Fault

The right to terminate is not limited to non-excused impediments of performance.[44] Even if the non-performance was caused by *force majeure* the aggrieved party may terminate. The only further prerequisite is that the impediment is not caused by the creditor himself or happened after the creditor's wrongful prevention of performance (*mora creditoris*).[45] Thus, the buyer may terminate the contract if the seller does not deliver the goods in time, even if time is not of the essence and even if the delay is due to circumstances outside the control of the seller.

The right to terminate ends when the aggrieved party has received the delayed performance or accepted the defective service or goods as

[38] This is not only an option for the creditor as provided in Art. 8.106 PECL but a prerequisite to the right to terminate. According to the PECL the additional period is a prerequisite also if the delay does not constitute a fundamental breach, Arts 9.301, 8.106(3) PECL; similarly Art 7.1.5 Unidroit.
[39] Under the former rules the right to terminate because of delayed performance depended on the *mora* of the debtor and where no exact time for performance had been agreed upon a notice (*Mahnung*) was necessary, §§326, 284 BGB aF. Under the new law notice is still necessary if the creditor wants to avail himself of the consequences (damages for delay, strict liability — §§ 286, 287, 288 BGB) of *mora* (*Verzug*, late performance).
[40] §326 V BGB (see above n 13).
[41] §323 II No 1 BGB (see above n 15).
[42] §324 BGB (see above n 36).
[43] §§323 II No 2, 3, 324 BGB (see above nn 15 and 37).
[44] Under the old law termination was only possible in case of 'Verzug' (*mora*) of the debtor which meant an unexcused delay (but fault of the debtor was presumed, §285 BGB), §§326, 284, 285 BGB aF.
[45] §323 VI BGB (see above n 15).

performance (possibly by reducing the price[46]). There is no deadline for the exercise of the right to terminate except the general rule of good faith, neither is there any deadline for the insistence on performance (where performance is still possible[47]) outside the statute of limitations except for just-in-time contracts between merchants.[48]

The idea behind this set of rules is the following: The parties consented to the terms of the contract because of the mutual promises to perform. If one side cannot perform in exactly the way promised, then the other party should not be bound to abide by the contract, because the equilibrium of the promises is destroyed. Hence, the aggrieved party should have the choice to decide whether it wants to affirm the contract or whether it wants to terminate the relationship. Insofar, each party bears the risk of its own ability to perform.

4 Consequences of Termination

At termination both parties are released from their obligations. Both parties have the right to recover money paid, property supplied and other means of performance or counter-performance.[49]

If performance cannot be returned — for example in the case of services or when the goods delivered have been consumed or destroyed[50] — the value of these benefits may be recovered[51] again with some exceptions.[52] A decrease in the value of the goods just because the goods have been used for the intended purpose need not be compensated. Neither is there a duty to compensate for the value of the non-restorable or damaged goods if the cause of the termination only became noticeable during the processing or conversion of these goods[53] or if the party entitled to restoration has caused the damage or distortion of the goods itself.[54] The same applies if the goods have been destroyed at that party's place[55] or if this happened without gross negligence or intent of the party who has the right to terminate the contract.[56] The latter two provisions shift the risk of

[46] §§441, 638 BGB.
[47] *Ibid.*
[48] §376 I 2 HGB — the merchant has to indicate immediately after the time of performance has lapsed that he insists on performance.
[49] §346 I BGB, cf Arts 9.307, 9.308, 9.309 PECL, Arts 7.3.5, 7.3.6 Unidroit.
[50] Inability to restore does not hinder the termination of the contract (any more). For the old law see the problematic rules in §§350–2, 327 BGB a.F.
[51] §346 II BGB, cf Art 9.309 PECL.
[52] §346 III BGB.
[53] §346 III No 1 BGB.
[54] §346 III No 2 BGB.
[55] §346 III No 2 BGB.
[56] §§ 346 III No 3, 277 BGB.

accidental loss or damage, the first to a lesser extent than the last. The wisdom of this rule has been doubted because the risk of accidental loss of goods normally passes with delivery of these goods.

This short overview concerning the mechanism of termination already indicates, how complicated and detailed are the legal rules which deal with these questions. This is partly due to the special system of German codification which implies a high level of abstraction, because the rules — as for example those for termination of the contract — apply to all situations of termination, not only for breach of contract, but also if a right to termination has been reserved or results from another situation (like for example the right to revocation in consumer contracts).

V THE RIGHT TO DAMAGES

The aggrieved party may, instead or in addition, ask for damages under the new law. Like the right to terminate the contract, the right to damages may also arise from all kinds of violations (non-performance). But despite the unitary concept of violations of obligations the legal rules on damages differ slightly depending on the kind of non-performance and the kind of damage that has been suffered.[57] This is not the place to go into too many details; only a general line should be drawn.

1 Different Conceptions

With regard to all kinds of impediments for all kinds of damages the general principle applies that the non-performance must be imputable to the obligor.[58] The obligor is imputable when he has committed fault[59] or has entrusted performance to another person who acted with fault.[60] Furthermore impediments are imputable to the obligor where he had guaranteed his performance or undertaken special risks.[61] With regard to

[57] §§ 280, 281, 282, 283, 284, 311 a II BGB.

[58] See also Art 9.501 PECL; Art 7.4.1 Unidroit.

[59] §276 I BGB (below n 73).

[60] §278 BGB (below n 74); cf Art 8.107 PECL.

[61] §276 BGB (below n 73); in case of initial impossibility (see §311 a II BGB, which constitutes an independent basis for a claim) the imputable fact is the knowledge or negligent ignorance of the impossibility to perform and only insofar the debtor is liable to damages. It is here that the former concepts of initial or subsequent impossibility remain important because of the different view on the obligor's liability. Until the conclusion of the contract the obligor is subject to duties to supply information, whereas after this crucial point his duty of correct performance is concerned, compare Reischl, JuS 2003, 250, 255. Contrary to the old rule (§306 BGB aF) the contract is valid despite the initial impossibility.

§311 a I BGB (Failure to perform due to an impediment existing at the time of conclusion of the contract):

these two latter cases there will be imputability without fault; there is strict liability of the obligor as far as he has accepted responsibility. Thus, non-fault impediments are not always excused impediments. We shall come back to this later. For the moment it suffices to state that the prerequisites of the right to terminate and the right to damages differ especially with regard to the question of excuse or non-excuse for non-performance. The right to terminate exists even where the non-performance is excused, the right to damages does not. Thus, contrary to some other legal systems termination is the device which is more easily accessible, for damages the creditor has to overcome additional hurdles.

In other respects the prerequisites are very similar. Thus, in principle, the right to damages does not depend on a fundamental breach.

2 Different Kinds of Damage Claims

If we speak of damages, three different categories of monetary compensation have to be considered.

The most important category concerns damages for non-performance (or damages instead of performance). Here the claim for damages substitutes or supplements the performance.[62] Thus, after receiving the

(1) A contract remains effective even though the debtor is released from performance according to §275(1) to (3), and the impediment existed already at the time of contracting.
(2) The creditor may choose between compensation instead of performance and reimbursement of his outlays as laid down in § 284. This does not apply if the debtor did not know of the impediment and is not responsible for his lack of knowledge. §281(1) sent 2 and 3 and subsection (5) shall apply *mutatis mutandis*.

See also Art 4.102 PECL.

[62] §281 BGB (Damages instead of performance in case of non-performance or non-conforming performance):

(1) Insofar as the debtor does not perform or does not perform in conformity with the obligation after it has become due, the creditor may demand compensation instead of performance according to §280(1), if he has, unsuccessfully, granted the debtor a reasonable period within which to perform or to remedy to perform. If the debtor has fulfilled his obligation in part, the creditor may only demand compensation instead of full performance if he is not interested in part performance. If the debtor does not perform in conformity with the obligation, the creditor may not claim compensation instead of full performance if the neglect of duty is insignificant.
(2) The period of grace may be dispensed with, if the debtor seriously and definitively refuses to perform, or if there are special circumstances which, upon a balance of interests of both parties, justify the immediate enforcement of the claim for compensation.
(3) If the neglect of duty is of such nature that the granting of a period of grace is not feasible a warning will take its place.
(4) The claim to performance is excluded as soon as the creditor demands compensation instead of performance.

damages the aggrieved party should be in the same financial position as it would have been had the contract been performed exactly in the way promised. Therefore, profits, for example, which the buyer lost, because he did not get the goods promised or because the goods which were delivered were defective or were of a smaller quantity than that for which he contracted, but which he would have gained in case of a perfect performance, will be included. Also included may be the value of the price or counter-performance already paid or made by the aggrieved party (*großer Schadensersatz*[63]). But it does not necessarily mean that the aggrieved party may not keep the defective goods delivered (provided the aggrieved party did not terminate the contract at the same time) and just claim the balance between good and defective performance (*kleiner Schadensersatz*). It is, in principle, for the aggrieved party, when seeking damages for non-performance, to decide whether it wants damages for complete non-performance (thereby returning goods already delivered) or simply asks for the balance between good and defective performance. In case of lost profits the burden of proof is with the claimant; he need not, however, show that he could in fact have sold the goods for a certain price, but only that according to normal circumstances the market value for retail would have been a certain sum (so called abstract computation of damages).[64] Yet, according to the prevailing view[65] this applies only to merchants and the adversary may produce evidence that in the given case the loss has been not so high or that there was no loss at all.

The second category of damages is less complicated: the aggrieved party may ask for simple damages, ie that loss which it suffered from the violation of the other party's obligation — independent of the performance as such.[66] In this case the claim for damages does not substitute the original

(5) If the creditor demands compensation instead of full performance, the debtor is entitled to reclaim his performance according to §§346 to 348. §282 BGB (below n 88);

§283 BGB (Damages instead of performance in case of termination of the obligation to perform):

If the debtor is released from the obligation to perform according to §275 (1) to (3) the creditor, observing the requirements of §280(1), may demand compensation instead of performance. §280(1) sentence 2 and subsection (5) shall apply *mutatis mutandis*.

[63] See OLG Karlsruhe, IBR 2002, 314: damages concerning a building contract.
[64] §252 BGB (lost profit):

The compensation shall also include lost profits. Profit is deemed to have been lost if it could probably have been expected to be earned in the ordinary course of events, or according to the special circumstances, especially in the light of the preparations and arrangements made.

[65] BGH, NJW 1980, 1742, 1743.
[66] §280 I BGB (damages for neglect of duty):

claim for performance, but exists beside the latter.[67] If for example one party violated an accessory duty (damaged some goods of the other on delivery), the loss caused must be compensated. The same applies — in principle, though under some additional prerequisites — for the loss caused by late performance, §§280 II, 286 BGB.[68] (provided the contract has been or will be performed). In the latter case the claim for (simple) damages is subject to a notice of default (*Mahnung*)[69] and dependent on the debtor's responsibility for the delay.[70]

Finally there is a third kind of damages in the widest sense: Instead of damages for complete non-performance the aggrieved party may claim frustrated expenses incurred in the expectation of performance.[71] Strictly

(1) If the debtor fails to comply with a duty incumbent upon him under the obligations entered into, the creditor may demand compensation for the damage done. This does not apply if the debtor is not responsible for the failure to comply with the duty.
(2) The creditor may only claim damages for delayed performance in accordance with the additional requirements laid down in §286.
(3) The creditor may only claim damages instead of performance in accordance with the additional requirements laid down in §§281, 282 or 283.

[67] For the demarcation see *Hirsch, Jura* 2003, 289ff; *Medicus,* JuS 2003, 521, 523.
[68] §286 BGB (default by the debtor):

(1) If the debtor does not perform after a warning issued after the debt has become due, he is in default because of the warning. Bringing an action for performance as well as service of a judicial order for payment are equivalent to a warning.
(2) No warning is required, if

1. a time for performance is fixed by the calendar,
2. the performance must be preceeded by an event and an adequate time for the performance has been fixed in such a way that after the occurrence of this event it may be reckoned by the calendar,
3. the debtor seriously and definitively refuses to perform,
4. upon a balance of interests of both parties special reasons justify an immediate default.

(3) The debtor of a counter-performance will, at the latest, be in default unless he performs within 30 days after the obligation became due and a bill or a comparable listing of payments was received; in case of a debtor who is a consumer this holds good only if the bill or the listing of payments has drawn special attention to these consequences. If the time of receipt of the bill or the listing of payments is uncertain, a debtor who is not a consumer will, at the latest, be in default 30 days after the debt has fallen due and the counter-performance has been received.
(4) The debtor is not in default so long as the performance does not take place because of a circumstance for which he is not responsible.

[69] There are again some exceptions under which such notice is not necessary, for example if the time for performance is set at a certain date; see §286 II, III BGB.
[70] §286 IV BGB (see n 68); here again there is a presumption of fault, see below n 78.
[71] §284 BGB (reimbursement of futile outlays):

speaking, this is not a claim for damages for non-performance because logically those expenses would have been incurred even if the contract had been performed properly.[72] This kind of claim is an interesting alternative in cases in which the performance is of non-commercial value (non-profit) to the creditor. If, for example, party A has rented a congress room for non-profit purposes and has invested a lot of money in invitations and in preparations for the event, these (frustrated) investments may be claimed instead of damages for non-performance (which might be insignificant because A would have gained no economic advantage had the landlord performed the lease), if the landlord will not let the room at the agreed date.

3 The Role of Fault

As already stated above damages will be awarded only if the violation of a duty is imputable to the obligor.[73] In general, German law does not impose strict liability; each party is held responsible (only) for his own intentional and negligent acts. In some relationships only gross negligence will count. In addition to his own acts the obligor is responsible for the negligent acts of those persons who had been acting on his behalf or for his benefit in the process of performance.[74] However, there are also situations of strict liability. A debtor who has to pay money is always under strict liability.[75] The same applies, if by statutory rules or by

> Instead of claiming damages in lieu of performance the creditor may demand reimbursement of any outlay justifiably made in reliance of receiving performance, unless such outlay would have been useless even if the debtor had not breached the duty.

[72] Such a claim gains special importance in and is thought for situations where the performance would not have redempt those additional costs (because other values would have been at stake) and therefore the loss by the non-performance does hardly exceed the price.

[73] §276 BGB (responsibility of the debtor):

> (1) The debtor is responsible for wilful conduct and negligence unless a more severe or a more lenient responsibility has either been laid down or may otherwise be derived from the substance of the obligation, especially from undertaking a guarantee or a risk of procuring performance. The provisions of §§ 827, 828 shall apply *mutatis mutandis*.
> (2) A person who does not exercise ordinary care acts negligently.
> (3) A debtor may not be released beforehand from responsibility for wilful conduct.

[74] §278 BGB (responsibility for persons employed in performing obligation):

> A debtor is responsible for the fault of his legal representative and of persons whom he employs in performing his obligation to the same extent as for his own fault. The provision of §276(3) does not apply.

[75] BGHZ 107, 92, 102.

contract the obligor has to bear the respective risk. For example, the law provides that the obligor during a delay, which is imputable to him, is under strict liability;[76] in case of non-acceptance of the creditor, on the other hand, the risk of the obligor is limited to intent and gross negligence.[77] Strict liability also applies if the obligor has guaranteed his performance or guaranteed a certain quality of the goods or the services. The courts apply high standards for such a guarantee because of the severe consequences that can flow from a failure to meet the standard set out in the guarantee. On the other hand a party promising to get certain goods is held to have undertaken the risk for all impediments of the market (but for example not for disturbances by war, death etc.). This principle comes close to, but is not identical with the rule in Art 79(1) CISG, because in the case of a guarantee a party may be liable even if the failure was due to an impediment beyond his control and he could not reasonably have been expected to take this impediment into account.

Though German law applies the principle of fault in general and strict liability only under special circumstances, the difference between the German solution and those legal systems which adhere to the strict liability concept is not as big as it might appear at first sight, because there is a presumption of fault in German law. The debtor has to prove that the failure or defect in performance was not imputable to him. He bears the full burden of proof.[78] If he cannot discharge this burden he will be held liable. For discharge he has to prove his non-imputability in such a way that the court is fully convinced. In case of a *non liquet* he will not be discharged.

If the debtor is liable according to these rules, his liability may be reduced by the contributory negligence of the other party.[79] The opponent

[76] §287 BGB (liability during default):

> A debtor is responsible for any negligence during his default. He is also responsible for the performance in case of accident, unless the damage would have arisen even if he had performed in due time.

[77] §300 I BGB (effects of creditor's default; limiting of liability; passage of risk):

> (1) During the default of the creditor the debtor is responsible only for wilful conduct and gross negligence.
> (2) If a thing described by class (ie unascertained goods) is owed, the risk passes to the creditor from the moment at which he is first in default by not accepting the thing offered.

[78] §280 I 2 BGB (above n 65); an exception to this general concept is stated in §619 a BGB, see for example Lorenz/Riehm *Lehrbuch zum neuen Schuldrecht* (Munich, CH Beck, 2002) Rdn 184.

[79] §254 BGB (contributory fault):

> (1) If any fault of the injured party has contributed to causing the damage, the obligation to compensate the injured party and the extent of the compensation to be

might have contributed (by a negligent act) to the causation of the violation of a duty or might have failed in mitigating the loss resulting from this violation. As by now in most legal systems, contributory negligence in either form does not impair the claim altogether but simply causes a reduction in the damages payable.

4 Special Prerequisites for Damages Instead of Performance

When damages instead of performance are sought, this remedy (as the right to termination) depends on the lapse of an additional period of time for performance[80] except where this would be without sense or unacceptable.[81] The debtor should have another chance to perform correctly, even though his first performance was late or defective. The situation is exactly the same as in case of the right to terminate. The second chance — before the performance may be substituted by a secondary right (the claim to damages) — is very characteristic of German law. This right of the debtor corresponds with the creditor's right to specific performance and stresses the principle of *pacta sunt servanda*. Detriments caused to the creditor until performance finally takes place might be compensated by a claim to (simple) damages for delay.

There are again situations in which the additional period of time does not make any sense and therefore this rule either does not apply or can be dispensed with. This is the case when the performance has become impossible[82] or — because of the debtor's violation of accessory duties — unreasonable.[83] The time allowance is dispensable if the debtor has denied performance definitively and seriously.[84] With regard to defective services or goods the details of 'remedial performance' to be allowed to the seller/undertaker are set out in the respective chapters of the law.[85]

made depends upon the circumstances, especially upon how far the injury has been caused predominantly by the one or the other party.

(2) This applies even if the fault of the injured party consisted only in an omission to call the attention of the debtor to the danger of unusually high damage which the debtor neither knew nor should have known, or in an omission to avert or mitigate the damage. The provision of §278 applies *mutatis mutandis.*

See also Art 77 CISG.

[80] §281 BGB (above n 62).
[81] §§281 II, 282, 283 BGB (above n 62, below n 88).
[82] §283 BGB (above n 62).
[83] §282 BGB, (below n 88); for an example see *Medicus*, JuS 2003, 521 *seq*.
[84] § 281 II BGB (above n 62).
[85] §§437 No 1, 439; 634 No 1, 635 BGB; the separation of those rules which apply only to certain kinds of contracts and those which apply to all debtor/creditor relations (§§275ff BGB) becomes visible here. Though this is systematically consequent, it does not make orientation easy for 'outsiders'.

As in case of termination, damages instead of full performance can only be asked for if in the case of part-performance the performed part is not of interest to the aggrieved party,[86] in the case of defective performance the defect is not only a minor one[87] and in the case of violation of an accessory duty where it seems to be unacceptable to the aggrieved party to receive performance.[88] Thus, though the violation need not be a fundamental one, not every minor violation results in the creditor's right to demand damages instead of the full performance; in these cases the claim to damages only supplements (but does not substitute) the performance.

If the aggrieved party has asked for damages instead of full performance (and can do so) any (part or defective) performance already delivered has to be returned or compensated for according to the above-mentioned rules for the termination of the contract.[89]

5 Damages in Case of Delay

Delay in performance is a violation of an obligation as already pointed out above. In consequence, the rules on termination[90] as well as the rules on damages[91] may apply (even if time is not of the essence). With regard to damages the distinction between (simple) damages and damages instead of performance have to be observed, because they serve different goals and have different prerequisites.

In case of delay 'damages instead of performance' mean that — after the additional period of time for performance has lapsed and the debtor has lost his right to perform — the creditor may ask for compensation of the loss he suffered because he did not get performance at all. 'Simple damages' according to §§280 II, 286 BGB concern (only) compensation for the loss the creditor suffered because he did get the performance at a later stage (*Verzögerungsschaden*). For both kinds of claims the debtor has to prove that the delay is not imputable to him if he is not to be liable in damages. The delay must be imputable to the debtor according to the principles of §§276, 278 BGB.[92] For simple damages — subject to some

[86] §281 I 2 BGB (above n 62).
[87] §281 I 3 BGB (above n 62).
[88] §282 BGB (damages instead of performance in case of neglect of a duty under §241(2)):

> If the debtor neglects a duty under §241(2) the creditor, observing the requirements of §280(1), may demand compensation instead of performance if he cannot reasonably be expected to accept performance from the debtor.

[89] §281 V BGB, see above Section IV.4.
[90] §323 BGB (above n 15).
[91] §§280ff BGB.
[92] For damages instead of performance: §§281 I, 280 I 2; for simple damages: §280 II, 286 IV.

exceptions — a notice to perform (*Mahnung*) must have been issued whereas damages instead of performance can be asked for after an additional time for performance has been given. Though in many instances in practice the act of the creditor may meet both requirements, there is a slight difference between them, because a notice to perform does not necessarily give an additional period of time and the additional time allowance does not necessarily meet the standards of a notice to perform. This is unfortunate because it complicates the law unnecessarily and it may mislead the persons concerned. On the other hand the new law has the advantage for the creditor that he can liquidate the contractual relationship according to §281 BGB without having to prove the formal prerequisites of §286 BGB, especially the fact that performance is still possible.[93]

6 Scope of Damages

Instead of going into detail about the scope of damages two points should be stressed which seem characteristic to German law on recovery of damages after the reform as well as before. First, unlike many legal systems and contrary to an international trend[94] damages are not limited to losses which the non-performing party had or could have reasonably foreseen, and secondly non-pecuniary loss is recoverable only in certain cases.

To the first issue: In principle, every pecuniary loss caused by non-performance may be recovered. Instead of foreseeability the principle of adequate causation applies and every kind of loss which — from the standpoint of an objective experienced observer at the time of the imputable act — could occur not only in extraordinary accidental circumstances will be regarded as adequately caused.[95] To limit the concept of causation there is an additional controlling device: The harm suffered must be within the protective purpose of the rule violated (*Schutzzweck der Norm*[96]), ie that the loss is not outside the mischief the undertaken duty was designed to prevent. Though this rule does not limit the area of responsibility to the same extent as the foreseeability test, it is

[93] In this sense *Reischl*, JuS 2003, 250.
[94] See Art 9.503 PECL, Art 7.4.4 Unidroit, Art 74 CISG.
[95] See Traeger *Der Kausalbegriff im Zivil- und Strafrecht* (Marburg 1904) 159. There is adequate causation if an event had in a general and appreciable way enhanced the objective possibility of a certain consequence — taking into account all the circumstances of an 'optimal' observer at the time the event occurred and additional circumstances known to the debtor.
[96] This rule was elaborated by Rabel *Das Recht des Warenkaufs* (Berlin, de Gruyter, 1936) 495ff.

relatively easy to handle, produces foreseeable and fair results and has not led to an enormous increase in the damages awarded.

Now to the second issue: Non-pecuniary loss has been recoverable in German law only where the statute said so expressly.[97] Up to recently this has been — outside tort law — the case only for wasted holidays where a supplier of travel facilities violated his contractual duties[98] and for discrimination in labour law[99] — both provisions induced by EU Directives.[100] In tort law moral damages could be awarded in case of injuries to health, body, liberty and sexual self-determination by negligent acts,[101] in addition serious infringements of the right to privacy could produce the right to moral damages.[102] But now a new law entered into force on 1 August 2002. According to the new rule, compensation will be granted for non-pecuniary loss in case of injury to the body, health, sexual self-determination, and in the case of deprivation of liberty. This applies within statutory relationships (like tort) as well as in contractual relationships.[103] Outside such injuries (which are at least not typical consequences of non-performance), the infringement of privacy and the two special provisions mentioned above, non-pecuniary loss cannot be awarded. However, already under the old law a device has been developed to convert non-pecuniary loss into pecuniary loss by taking into account the expenditures involved for the enjoyment of the goods in question.[104] The deprivation of enjoyment of a good of general and central importance for living — such as a car — has been regarded as economic loss with regard to frustrated expenditure.[105]

VI COMBINATION OF THE DIFFERENT REMEDIES

A party may insist on specific performance and in addition may ask for compensation for the loss it suffered until the performance was correct. For example, the creditor of a delayed performance may claim damages

97 §253 I BGB; see the more general approach in Art 9.502 PECL, Art 7.4.2 Unidroit.
98 §651 II f BGB.
99 §611 a II, III BGB.
100 For §611 a BGB see Council Directive (EEC) 76/207 [1976] OJ L39/40; for §651 of BGB see Council Directive (EEC) 90/314 [1990] OJ L158/59.
101 §847 BGB as in force until 31 July 2002.
102 This has been (and will be still in future) judge-made law (BVerfG NJW 2000, 2187) focusing on Arts 1, 2 German Constitution; B Markesinis and H Unberath *The German Law of Torts* 4th edn (Hart Publishing, Oxford, 2002) 924; D Coester-Waltjen 'Der Ersatz immaterieller Schäden im Deliktsrecht' 2001, *Jura* 133.
103 §253 II BGB.
104 BGHZ 71, 234; BGHZ 98, 212.
105 BGH, NJW 1986, 2037 (holiday cottage); this commercialisation has not been accepted in case of deprivation of enjoyment of fur-coats, motorboats, trailers.

in respect of losses which have been suffered by reason of the delay until the late performance takes place. The violator of an accessory duty may have to compensate that violation and still perform the contract. Thus, specific performance and simple damages are combinable. If the aggrieved party wants specific performance it cannot at the same time exercise its right to terminate the contract. However, as long as performance has not been completed the creditor may switch to termination (if the prerequisites for the right to termination are fulfilled).

The request for specific performance is not possible any more if the aggrieved party has asked for damages instead of performance[106] or has declared the termination of the contract, §349 BGB.

In principle, termination of the contract and all kinds of damages[107] are compatible, §325 BGB.[108] The fact of termination will, however, influence the computation of the damages. In most cases termination of the contract will not be asked for by the creditor when he can claim damages instead of performance because the latter remedy will give him full compensation. However, if the contract had been already partly or fully performed from his side — for example by the transfer of a certain good — and he wants not only the value of his performance back, but the delivered good itself, then he should be advised to terminate the contract and ask for his goods back and at the same time he may claim damages instead of performance, for example the profits lost because of non-performance.

Termination of contract and simple damages can be combined, but this is less likely to happen, because if the debtor has been imputable for the violation (which is the prerequisite for all damages), and if the prerequisites for termination are fulfilled then the aggrieved party will normally ask for damages instead of performance. At the time, however, it is not completely clear whether the damages instead of performance may include damages caused to other goods of the aggrieved party by the defective performance of the other (so called *Mangelfolgeschaden*). If one excludes these damages, then the combination of termination of contract and simple damages makes sense. Simple damages and damages instead of performance may also be combined, but the claim to frustrated expenditures takes the lieu of damages instead of performance.

[106] §281 IV BGB (above n 61).

[107] The only exception: If A asks only for the difference between the value of the fully correct performance and the part or defective performance (*kleiner Schadensersatz*) termination at the same time would make no sense.

[108] Under the old law, termination of contract and the claim for damages were incompatible, §§325, 326 BGB aF. As the claim for damages was — in the majority of cases — more beneficial for the creditor, the courts were often faced with the problem how to interpret a declaration of 'termination', cf 'Derleder' *Neue Juristiche Wochenschrift* 2003, 998ff.

VII CONCLUSION

This roughly drawn picture of German law for breach of contract may suffice for the moment. There are other interesting problems — such as the duties arising from precontractual relationships,[109] frustration of contract (*clausula rebus sic stantibus*)[110] — which deserve detailed analysis. Nevertheless the new law has achieved a considerable improvement in

[109] See §§241, 311 BGB.

§241 BGB (duties inherent in an obligation):

(1) The effect of an obligation is that the creditor is entitled to claim performance from the debtor. The performance may consist of refraining from acting.
(2) An obligation may oblige each party, having regard to its substance, to take into consideration the rights, legally protected interests and (other) interests of the opposite party.

§311 BGB (obligations arising from legal transactions and from obligations similar to legal transactions):

(1) For the creation of an obligation by legal transaction and for any modification of the substance of an obligation, a contract between the parties is necessary, unless otherwise provided by law.
(2) An obligation with duties under §241(2) will also arise from

1. the beginning of contract negotiations,
2. initiating the conclusion of a contract whereby one of the parties, having regard to a possible contractual relationship, either grants the other party the possibility of affecting his rights, legally protected interests and other interests, or entrust the other party with them, or
3. similar business contacts.

(3) An obligation with duties under §241(2) may also arise in relation to persons who are not meant to become contracting parties. Such an obligation will come about especially where the third party takes special advantage of confidence, thus exercising considerable influence on the contract negotiations or the conclusion of the contract.

[110] See §313 BGB (collapse of the basis of the transaction and absence of the basis of the transaction):

(1) If circumstances which have become the basis of the contract have changed fundamentally after the contract was concluded, and the parties, had they foreseen this change, would not have made this contract or would have made a different contract, adaptation of the contract may be demanded insofar as one of the parties, considering all circumstances of the particular case and having regard especially to the contractual or statutory distribution of risk, cannot reasonably be expected to abide by the unchanged contract.
(2) It is equivalent to a change of circumstances if essential assumptions which have become the basis of the contract turned out to be wrong.
(3) If adaptation of the contract is not possible or would be too hard on one of the parties, the aggrieved party may terminate the contract. In continuing contracts termination is replaced by giving notice.

the legal rules: it is not too complicated but at the same time it does not impose uniform solutions but makes distinctions between different situations and, finally, it achieves a fair balance of the interests of debtors and creditors. But the law is far from being perfect; it could be drawn up in a less complicated fashion, with fewer exceptions and clearer principles. But there is always the hope for improvement — perhaps next time by a European legislator.

8

Remedies for Breach through the Lens of the Third Party Beneficiary

NILI COHEN

I CONTRACT FOR THE BENEFIT OF A THIRD PARTY: THEORETICAL AND PRACTICAL JUSTIFICATIONS

A CONTRACT FOR the benefit of a third party expands the boundaries of contract. It has both theoretical and practical justifications. From the point of view of the contracting parties such a contract is a manifestation of the principle of freedom of contract. Contracts increase the economic welfare of the parties. A contract enables the parties to plan ahead and to rely on it. If the parties wish to confer upon a third party a benefit under their contract, there is no reason why not to implement their wish as long as it does not jeopardise the free will of that other party.

From the point of view of the beneficiary a contract for the benefit of a third party — if duly limited with regard to its coercive power on the third party — expresses the legitimate expectations of the beneficiary and protects her interest. Since such a contract operates for the benefit of the third party, the presumption is that the third party would be willing to accept its benefit. Yet she will not be coerced to accept it. As the contract may be concluded even without the knowledge of the beneficiary, she is, as a matter of Israeli law, given the right to repudiate the benefit.[1]

The third party is not an active participant in the contract, and she might not even know about it at all. But her autonomy of will is sustained retrospectively after the creation of the contract. She can either approve of the benefit or reject it. She is not required actively to approve it. It suffices that she does not reject the contract. Silence is regarded as an approval.

[1] Section 35 of the Contracts (General Part) Law 1973 (27 LSI 117) provides: 'The beneficiary's right to demand fulfillment of the obligation becomes void retroactively if within a reasonable time after one of the parties to the contract informs him of the right he informs one of them of his repudiation thereof'.

This is the rule whenever a benefit is conferred upon a party, either by a gift[2] or by a contract based on a gratuitous offer.[3]

The contract for the benefit of a third party has practical reasons as well. Parents may wish to confer a benefit on an unborn child; or in a divorce settlement the parents may seek to guarantee the rights of their infants. The contract for the benefit of an unborn child or an infant is an efficient and a convenient way to guarantee the children's rights. Both the unborn and the infant are incapable of participating in the contracting process. A contract for their benefit exempts them from this impossible task. They do not have to take any part in the creation of the contract, and yet they can still benefit from it.[4]

Similarly where there is a wish to confer a benefit upon a person who dwells in an enemy state[5] a contract for his benefit is an efficient and useful device for that purpose. Such is also the case when there is a wish to confer a benefit upon an indeterminate group of people that could be ascertained only at a later stage after the conclusion of the contract. The benefit will be conferred where the party could be ascertained, but the contract can be made effective at an earlier stage. For example, a contract between a hospital and a blood transfusion centre was regarded by a French court[6] as a contract for the benefit of each of the patients that might need a blood transfusion in the future. As soon as it is created such

[2] Section 3 of the Gift Law 1968 (22 LSI 113) provides for a presumption that the recipient of a gift accepts the gift, unless he notifies the donor that he objects to it within a reasonable time after he is notified about it.

[3] Section 7 of the Contracts (General Part) Law states that an offer which is exclusively for the benefit of the offeree is presumed to have been accepted by him unless he objects to it within a reasonable time after it comes to his knowledge.

[4] In English law the institution of trust could have been employed to achieve the same purpose in this case and the following ones: GH Treitel *The Law of Contract* 11th edn (Sweet & Maxwell, London, 2003) 646–51. This was crucial since this contract was recognised there only in 1999: below n 17.

[5] CA 8109/98 *Abu Chatum v Abu Chatum* 55(2) PD 267 (Hebrew) where a contract was made with two brothers and their mother, whereby the mother bought one third of their property, and they took upon themselves an obligation to transfer it to their brother who lived in Jordan (then an enemy State of Israel). The court did not eventually decide that the contract was for the benefit of the brother in Jordan, because on a factual basis it concluded that he became a direct party to it.

[6] CA Aix-en-Provence, 12 Juillet 1993, D 1994, 13 note Vidal. In that case the centre was liable to a patient to whom the blood transfused was contaminated with syphilis. Cf the English case *A v National Blood Authority* [2001] 3 All ER 289 where the blood transfused was infected with Hepatitis C and the plaintiffs' claims were dealt within the rules of product liability. Indeed French law used the third party beneficiary device in order to impose contractual liability, where liability in tort was difficult to establish: H Kötz 'Rights of Third Parties' in A von Mehren (ed) *Contracts in General* (vol 7 of *International Encyclopedia of Comparative Law*) (Tübingen, The Hague, 1990) 20–1 esp n 99. A similar development occurred in German law where a category of 'contracts having a protective effect for third parties' has been created by case law, mainly to overcome the rigid requirement of tort law and of the intention test in the regular contract for third party beneficiary: H Kötz, *ibid*, 22–4; P Gottwald *Münchener Kommentar zum Buergerliches Gesetzbuch* 4th edn (Beck, München, 2003) band 2a comments 96–171 to BGB §328, 2097–123.

a contract imposes on the blood transfusion centre an obligation to supply non-defective blood, thus giving an immediate protection to each and every future patient in need.[7]

Another example taken from an Israeli case[8] is the following: when a new bus central station was about to be erected in Tel-Aviv, an agreement was entered into between the contractor of the station and the municipality of Tel-Aviv for the benefit of the people who lived around the space of the future station. The difficulty in ascertaining who exactly lived there and the wish to save transaction costs with each of the inhabitants prompted an agreement with the municipality for the benefit of the people in that community.[9]

In commercial contexts a contract for the benefit of a third party might serve — similarly to assignment — as a short-cut device of paying off debts. This occurs when one of the parties is a debtor of the beneficiary. Under the contract for the benefit of a third party, the other party pays off a sum of money to the beneficiary thereby discharging the first party's debt to the beneficiary.

There is a striking resemblance between assignment and a contract for the benefit of a third party. Both are designed to transfer a benefit — in many cases a sum of money as a discharge of a debt — from one person (assignor, creditor) to another (assignee, beneficiary) through a mediator (debtor). In both there is an assumption that the debt is not discharged unless it was actually paid off to the assignee or beneficiary.[10] The difference obviously is that in assignment the assignee replaces the original creditor, whereas in a contract for the benefit of a third party, the third party joins the contractual scene alongside the original creditor.

Another frequent example of a contract for the benefit of a third party is an insurance contract, in particular, where the benefit inures upon the death of a person, mainly life insurance and pension funds. This is a

[7] Would the liability of the centre extend to a person who was contaminated by the person to whom the blood was transfused? This depends on whether there was an intention by the centre and the hospital to benefit not only the blood donees but also those who might come in contact with them.

[8] CA (TA) 1412/95 *Bezalel v The New Bus Central Station*, Dinim District Court 32(7) PD 627 (Hebrew).

[9] The fact that the third parties' identity is not necessarily known at the time of the contract has served in American law as a tool in constitutional interpretation. A contract for the benefit of a third party might overcome the inter-temporal gap stemming from the difference in time between the enactment of the Constitution and its current application to present beneficiaries. Hence, the constitutional rights emanate from a contract between the federal government and the States as legal entities for the benefit of the citizens (present and future): E Parnes 'They the People: A Third Party Beneficiary Approach to Constitutional Interpretation' (2003) 43 *Santa Clara Law Review* 495.

[10] Section 48 of the Contracts Law: 'Where for the purpose of fulfilling an obligation the debtor assumes another obligation towards the creditor or transfers to him a right in respect of a third party, it is presumed that it is not intended to terminate such first-mentioned obligation unless the other obligation has been fulfilled or the right realised'.

common way of providing welfare by dividing property among preferred heirs not within the limits of the laws of succession.[11]

II THE ISRAELI LEGISLATION AND SOME COMPARATIVE REMARKS

A contract for the benefit of a third party was introduced into Israeli law through the Contracts (General Part) Law 1973.[12] Before this legislation, Israeli contract law was to a large extent governed by the common law, which did not recognise the right of a third party beneficiary to sue under the contract. Prior to the enactment of the Contracts Law, Israeli case law was uncertain whether to follow the common law in that respect: there were conflicting views with regard to the question whether a third party had an independent right to sue under a contract to which he was not a party.[13] This conflict has not been resolved to this date.[14] But currently, following the express recognition of a third party's right, this question is of almost no importance.

Israeli legislation adopted an institution well-recognised by legislation in most Continental systems and also by American law which had not followed the footsteps of English Common Law and early in 1859 recognised the independent right of action of a third party beneficiary.[15]

Though there were recurrent attempts by English case law and through the legislator[16] to introduce the contract for the benefit of a third party into English law, this was not fully recognised until the Contracts (Rights of Third Parties) Act 1999.[17] Twenty-six years after the Israeli legislation, no doubt partly due to the integration with Continental Europe, English law has finally recognised the right of a third party to sue under a contract to which he was not a party.

This chapter focuses on Israeli law, but as the Israeli law offers no novelties, and follows the basic model of this contract as reflected in

[11] Section 147 of the Succession Law 1965 (19 LSI 58) states that the 'amounts payable in consequence of person's death under insurance contracts, because of his membership in a pension fund or benefit fund ... are not part of the estate ...'

[12] Hereinafter, the Contracts Law.

[13] G Shalev 'Third Party Beneficiary: A Comparative Analysis' (1976) 11 *Israel Law Review* 315, 336–7.

[14] In CA 8109/98 *Abu Chatum v Abu Chatum* 55 PD(2) 267 the court decided not to decide: above n 5.

[15] *Lawrence v Fox* 20 NY 268 (1859). For an interesting historical analysis, see A Waters 'A Property in a Promise: A Study of the Third Party Beneficiary Rule' (1985) 98 *Harvard Law Review* 1148.

[16] For a historical survey see VV Palmer *The Path to Privity: The History of Third Party Beneficiary at English Law* (Austin Winfield, San Francisco, 1992).

[17] On this legislation and the issue of privity of contract in general see R Merkin (ed) *Privity of Contract: The impact of the Contracts (Rights of Third Parties) Act 1999* (LLP, London, 2000).

German law[18] and also American law, the solutions suggested here might be relevant to other legal systems.[19] Chapter four of the Israeli Contracts Law deals with the subject of contracts for the benefit of a third party in five short sections, the most important of which is section 34 which deals with the conferment of the right. It provides as follows:

> An obligation assumed by a person by contract in favor of a person who is not a party to the contract (such person hereinafter referred to as 'the beneficiary') confers on the beneficiary the right to demand fulfillment of the obligation if the intention to confer this right on him is apparent from the contract.

The other sections deal with the repudiation of the right by the beneficiary (section 35);[20] the termination of the right by the parties (section 36); the defences available to the debtor (section 37); and the independent right of the creditor as against the debtor to demand performance in favour of the beneficiary (section 38).

All these sections deal with the substantive aspects of the contract, focusing naturally on the beneficiary's rights, while trying to strike a balance between the beneficiary and the other parties to the contract. None of them deal with any remedies available to the beneficiary for the protection of his right.

One might have assumed that the remedial elements of the beneficiary's right are dealt with in the Contract (Remedies for Breach of Contract) Law 1970[21] which had been enacted about three years before the enactment of the Contracts (General Part) Law. A quick glance at the Remedies Law shows that this law does not address at all the problems concerning the particular situation of a contract for the benefit of a third party

[18] Sections 328–35 of the German Civil Code (BGB) served also as a model for European contract law: O Lando and H Beale *The Principles of European Contract Law* (Kluwer Hague, 2000). For a detailed survey on German law: P Gottwald *Münchener Kommentar zum Buergerliches Gesetzbuch* 4th edn (Beck, München, 2003) band 2a 2069–159.

In France the subject has developed mainly by case law on the basis of section 1121 of the Civil Code which states (in English translation) that '[O]ne may … stipulate for the benefit of a third party, when such is the condition of a stipulation which one makes for oneself or of a gift which one makes to another. He who has made such a stipulation cannot revoke it if the third party has declared his wish to take advantage of it'.

For a general survey see F Terré, P Simler and Y Lequette *Droit Civil: Les Obligations* (Dalloz, Paris, 1999) sec 486–411, 470–88; Levroument and Mondoloni 'Stipulation Pour L'Autrui' in *Répertoire de Droit Civil* (vol 10 of *Encyclopédie juridique*), (Dalloz, Paris, 1998).

[19] For a comparative survey see H Kötz 'Rights of Third Parties' in A von Mehren (ed) *International Encyclopedia of Comparative Law* (Tübingen, The Hague, 1990) vol 7, 4–51; also Appendix B to Law Commission for England & Wales, Consultation Paper No 121 'Privity of Contracts: Contracts for the Benefit of Third Parties' in R Merkin (ed) *Privity of Contract: The impact of the Contracts (Rights of Third Parties) Act 1999* (LLP, London, 2000) 309–19.

[20] Above n 1.

[21] 25 LSI (1970/1) 11, hereinafter, the Remedies Law.

presumably for the simple reason that, when it was enacted, it was not clear whether this contract was recognised in Israeli law.

English legislation took a different and a more satisfying approach: section 1(5) of the Contracts (Rights of Third Parties) Act states that:

> [F]or the purpose of exercising his rights to enforce a term of the contract, there shall be available to the third party any remedy that would have been available to him in an action for breach of contract if he had been a party to the contract (and the rules relating to damages, injunctions, specific performance and other relief shall apply accordingly).

Hence, the English act addresses specifically the question of remedies, though obviously such a brief section cannot fully examine all the issues concerning the subject.

Absent any specific provision in Israeli law, we might conclude that in determining the range of remedies under Israeli law in the case of a contract for the benefit of a third party one should focus on the basic concepts underlying this contract and those underlying the remedies for breach of contract in Israel. Hence the problem of third party beneficiary's rights enables us to examine from a specific angle the basic concepts of Israeli remedies for breach of contract.

In the following section I shall shortly introduce the basic categories of the contract for the benefit of a third party. They will serve as a clue for the application of the remedies for breach to this context.

III CATEGORIES AND DISTINCTIONS

As indicated by its title a contract for the benefit of a third party directly confers a benefit on the third party and an independent cause of action to claim the benefit. On the face of it, it bears a resemblance to a contract of gift. As in the case of a contract of gift,[22] the benefit is conferred once the beneficiary knows about the benefit and does not reject it.[23] In other words and as mentioned above, similarly to a contract of a gift, in order to confer the benefit upon the beneficiary, it suffices that the beneficiary remains silent. But though there is an apparent resemblance between

[22] Gift Law 1968, section 3, above n 2. The difference is that a contract for the benefit of a third party is binding even though the beneficiary is not aware of his right whereas an undertaking to make a gift is binding only when the donee knows about his right.

[23] The Contracts Law, section 35, above n 1. It follows that if the beneficiary does not repudiate after being informed by one of the parties of his right, he is entitled to the performance, and would be under a duty to accept it: P Gottwald *Münchener Kommentar zum Buergerliches Gesetzbuch* 4th edn (Beck, München, 2003) band 2a comment 30 to §328 of the BGB, 2081; comments 7–10 to §334 of the BGB, 2152–3.

the contract for the benefit of a third party and a contract of gift, the background behind the creation of a contract for the benefit of third party is not limited to gifts and in many cases it involves a purely commercial transaction.

The Israeli Contracts Law refers to the parties of the contract by the titles of debtor and creditor:[24] the debtor is the party who has to render the performance to the beneficiary; the creditor is the party to whom the promise to perform for the benefit of the third party is given. I shall follow this terminology, though — as we shall shortly see — it does not always fit the various categories under consideration.

The wording of Israeli law describes the typical case where a party — the creditor — wishes to confer the benefit on a third party — the beneficiary — and he does it through the debtor. This indicates that behind the coverage of the contract there are hidden relations between the creditor and the beneficiary which stimulate the transaction, and serve as the real, practical reason for the transaction.[25] This will be reflected in the following categories.

First category: the contract is predicated on a pre-existing obligation of the creditor towards the beneficiary. To give a simple example: the creditor and the beneficiary are involved in commercial relations under which the creditor owes the sum of 100 to the beneficiary. The current contract between the debtor and the creditor is a sale agreement where the creditor is a seller, and the debtor is a buyer who has to pay the price (100) not to the seller but rather to the beneficiary. This payment is designed to discharge the creditor's (seller's) pre-existing debt to the beneficiary.

Second category: the contract is predicated on the intention of the creditor to give a gift to the beneficiary. For example: an insurer (debtor) is under an obligation to pay the beneficiary a sum of money upon the death of the insured (the creditor), which the insured intends as a gift *mortis causa* to the beneficiary; a mother (a creditor) would like to give to her daughter (a beneficiary) as a gift a book she is going to buy from a bookseller (a debtor); an uncle (a creditor) wishes to give a sum of money as a present to his nephew (a debtor) on condition that part of the money be given to a student in need (a beneficiary).[26]

The first two categories are the typical categories of the contract for the benefit of a third party. They indeed focus on the relations between the

[24] American and English law use the titles: promisor and promisee. So do French law (promettant (promisor) and stipulant (promisee)) and German law (Verschprechender (promisor) and Verschprechesempfanger (promisee)).

[25] In German law the relations between the creditor and the debtor are called cover-relations (Deckungsverhaeltnis) and the relations between the beneficiary and the creditor are called value-relations (valutaverhaeltnis): P Gottwald *Münchener Kommentar zum Buergerliches Gesetzbuch* 4th edn (Beck, München, 2003) band 2a comments 26–8 to §328 BGB, 2079–80.

[26] This is the *donatio sub modo* which §330 of the BGB presumes that the parties intend the contract to be for the benefit of the third party.

creditor and the beneficiary. They fit squarely into the terminology used by the Israeli legislator.

The third category is somewhat different: here the contract is predicated on either a pre-existing obligation or an intention to confer a gift by both the creditor and the debtor. Unlike the former categories both parties have a common interest regarding the beneficiary. For example, both the creditor and debtor owe a certain amount of money to the beneficiary, and they both agree that a payment by the debtor or by both will discharge their pre-existing debt. But they also can mutually agree to confer a gift on the beneficiary, a case prevalent in family contexts, for example in a divorce settlement where both parents mutually agree to confer benefits (money, apartment) upon their child.

In this category the terminology employed by the Contracts Law relating to a debtor and a creditor as parties to the contract does not fit, for the reason that the parties are both debtors of the beneficiary, and at the same time in the relations *inter se* they are both debtors and creditors. The simple contractual picture of a debtor and a creditor does not exist here. However, for the sake of simplicity and since the last category is less prevalent than the two former ones, I shall refer later on mainly to the first two categories.

These two categories which focus on the relations between the creditor and the beneficiary, reflect the well-known distinction between a commercial transaction and a gratuitous transaction,[27] which cuts through every legal system, including the Israeli one.[28] In the context of a third party beneficiary it gained enormous importance mainly in the Restatement (First) of Contracts which, in section 133, made the classical classification between a creditor-beneficiary and a donee-beneficiary.[29] The creditor-beneficiary is the one to whom the creditor in the present contract owes a debt (the first category); the donee-beneficiary is the one to whom the creditor in the present contract confers a gift (the second category).

Several implications stem from the classification between a commercial beneficiary and a gratuitous beneficiary, the most important of which relates

[27] Regarding the relations between the debtor and creditor the classification might be different; see below text to n 62.

[28] L Fuller 'Consideration and Form' (1941) 41 *Columbia Law Review* 799; A von Mehren 'Civil Law Analogues to Consideration' (1959) 72 *Harvard Law Review* 1009; MA Eisenberg 'The Principles of Consideration' (1982) 67 *Cornell Law Review* 640; MA Eisenberg 'Donative Promises', (1979) 47 *University Chicago Law Review* 1, 5; RA Posner 'Gratuitous Promises in Economics and Law' (1977) 6 *Journal Legal Studies* 411, 412; J Gordley 'Enforcing Promises' (1995) 83 *California Law Review* 547; A Farnsworth *Changing Your Mind: the law of regretted decisions* (Yale University Press, New Haven, 1998) chapters 7 and 8; D Friedmann and N Cohen *Contracts* vol 1 (Aviram, Tel-Aviv, 1991) 470–510 (Hebrew).

[29] Section 302, Restatement (Second) of Contracts has shifted the focus to the test of the intention of the parties, but it still retains to some extent the distinction between the two types of beneficiaries, though in a more implicit and relaxed manner. Section 302(1)(a) relates to a

to the revocability of the beneficiary's right. The common understanding is that the right of a commercial beneficiary ought to be more immune than that of a gratuitous beneficiary. Therefore, the power of revocation in the case of a gratuitous beneficiary ought to be broader than the parallel right in the case of a commercial beneficiary.[30]

It is interesting to note that the Israeli Law itself does not explicitly refer to these categories and their ramifications, though we are given a hint as to their existence in section 36 which deals with the revocability of the beneficiary's right.

Section 36(a) states that as long as the parties (or one of them) have not notified the beneficiary about the right, they are free to terminate it. It follows that the right is irrevocable once the beneficiary gets notice about it through one of the parties. Then section 36(b) provides for a special rule regarding an obligation to be fulfilled in consequence of a person's death. In such a case, as in life insurance, or membership of a pension fund, the right becomes irrevocable only upon the person's death. Till that event the creditor has the right to change the beneficiary or replace him with another one, even though the beneficiary knows about the right.[31]

Section 36 attempts to echo the distinction between creditor-beneficiary and donee-beneficiary in the following way: it seems that section 36(a) deals with commercial cases. Hence, the power to terminate the beneficiary's right is shorter than that which is specified in section 36(b), which apparently deals with gratuitous cases.

But the classifying factor which the legislature employed to distinguish one category from the other — a contract with an obligation to be fulfilled in consequence of a person's death — is not precise: not all life insurance or pension funds cases involve gratuitous transactions, and not all other contracts under 36(a) involve commercial transactions.[32]

beneficiary the performance to whom satisfies a debt owed by the promisee; section 302(1)(b) relates to a beneficiary to whom the promisee intends to give the benefit of the promised performance. For a survey see M Eisenberg 'Third Party Beneficiaries' (1992) 92 *Columbia Law Review* 1358, 1376ff; JF Powers 'Expanded Liability and the Intent Requirement in Third Party Beneficiary Contracts' [1993] *Utah Law Review* 67.

[30] Yet paradoxically enough the rule in the Restatement First was diametrically opposed: the right of a donee-beneficiary was more immune than that of a creditor-beneficiary: under section 142 of the Restatement (First) of Contracts the very creation of the contract made the donee-beneficiary's right irrevocable, while under section 143 the creditor-beneficiary's right became irrevocable upon a change of position. American courts did not follow these rules, and this is currently reflected in section 311(3) of Restatement (Second) of Contracts whereby the beneficiary's right (and this applies to all types of beneficiaries) is irrevocable only upon the beneficiary's material change of position in reliance on the contract, or if he brings suit under the contract, or if he manifests assent to the promise at the request of either the promisor or the promisee. See generally *Farnsworth on Contracts* 3rd edn (Aspen New York, 2003) 694–7.

[31] All this is subject to a contrary intention by the parties.

[32] Indeed what emerges of section 36(b) of the Contracts Law is that other insurance contracts are subject to the rule of section 36(a). But section 11(c) of the Insurance Contract Law

Therefore the more plausible solution would be the following one: whenever a transaction governed by section 36(a) is gratuitous (from the point of view of the beneficiary) and absent any specific provision, the principles of the Gift Law, which might be regarded as the default rules of gratuitous transactions under Israeli law, shall apply. Under the Gift Law the donee's right becomes irrevocable once he had detrimentally changed his position. The fact that he knows about his right does not suffice.[33]

In our case: if the beneficiary learns about her right from one of the parties, her right shall still be revocable if this is a gift by the creditor. The right shall become irrevocable once the beneficiary detrimentally changed her position. Section 36(a) of the Contracts Law would thus be subject to the general principles of the Gift Law.[34]

We indicated that the major implication of the distinctions presented above relates primarily to the revocability of the beneficiary's right. It should be emphasised though that, unless otherwise indicated, our assumption throughout the discussion of remedies will be that the beneficiary's right is irrevocable and cannot be altered or annulled by the parties (or by the creditor). But the implications of the above distinctions are not limited to the issue of revocability; they play a role also in the sphere of remedies and they will cut through our following discussion of remedies.

IV THE BENEFICIARY AND THE CREDITOR AS SEVERAL CREDITORS

A contract for the benefit of a third party confers 'on the beneficiary the right to demand fulfillment of the obligation if the intention to confer this right on him is apparent from the contract' (section 34 of the Contracts Law). The section, in particular the word 'confers', uses 'proprietary' form. It indicates that the beneficiary is the 'owner' of the direct and independent right under the contract.

The fact that the beneficiary is the owner of his right is also reflected in section 38, which provides that '[T]he beneficiary's right shall not derogate from the creditor's right to demand from the debtor the fulfillment of the obligation in favor of the beneficiary'.[35]

1981 (35 LSI 91) states that the insured can change the beneficiary till the occurrence of the event of the insurance. It follows that all insurance contracts are subject to the rule of section 36(b) *mutatis mutandis*, and not to the rule of section 36(a).

33 Section 5(b) of the Gift Law states that as long as the recipient of the gift did not change his position relying on the undertaking the donor is allowed to revoke his undertaking, unless he waived in writing his right to do so.

34 This is the solution adopted in the tentative draft of the Israeli Civil Code: section 236(b) applies the grounds of revocation of gift specified in section 236(a) to a third party beneficiary who is a donee.

35 Following section 335 of the BGB. Cf section 305(1) of the Restatement (Second) of Contracts which states: 'A promise in a contract creates a duty in the promisor to the promisee to perform the promise even though he also has a similar duty to an intended beneficiary'.

Section 38 is designed to preserve the right of the creditor. But even more so it is aimed at protecting the beneficiary's right: the right of the creditor is to secure the performance towards the beneficiary, following the original intention of the parties. The creditor cannot claim the performance for himself.

Both the beneficiary and the creditor have rights under the contract emanating from the same obligation. Hence they might be regarded as several (common) creditors by virtue of the contract. This, however, is a very peculiar situation of 'several creditors' which deviates from the standard model of such creditors described in section 59(a) of the Contracts Law. Under this section:

> [W]here one obligation exists vis-à-vis two persons, it is presumed that each of them may demand its fulfillment, but they shall not recover from the debtor more than is due from him. The debtor may at his choice fulfill the obligation towards one of his creditors so long as judgment has not been given in favor of the other.[36]

The presumptions of the section might definitely apply where the contract specifies several beneficiaries. But they are fully rebutted in the simple case where the claimants are the beneficiary and the creditor: that which provides that each of the creditors is entitled to demand the performance for himself, and that which provides that the debtor has an option to fulfil the obligation to the creditor he chooses.

The rules in our case are altogether different and are the following: the creditor can require performance only for the benefit of the beneficiary, without any choice; the debtor is required to give performance only to the beneficiary without any choice.

Furthermore, if the debtor gave the performance to the creditor and not to the beneficiary, he would be regarded as not performing at all. It might well be that the debtor could claim restitution from the creditor, and then transfer the benefit to the beneficiary as the performance due. Also the beneficiary is likely to have a direct claim against the creditor who might be regarded as holding the performance in trust for the benefit of the beneficiary.[37] But this will not discharge the debtor from his duty to give the performance to the beneficiary. The debt of the debtor will remain

For a general survey on the position in Continental systems which all in all recognise the right of action of the creditor: H Kötz 'Rights of Third Parties' in A von Mehren (ed) *International Encyclopedia of Comparative Law* (Tübingen,The Hague, 1990) vol 7, chapter 13 50.

[36] For a general survey see M Deutch 'Several Creditors' in D Friedmann (ed) *The Law of Obligations — General Part* (Aviram, Tel-Aviv, 1994) 331–428 (Hebrew).

[37] Cf section 126 of the Restatement of Restitution. On the difficulty in English law regarding that point see R Goff & G Jones *The Law of Restitution* 6th edn (Sweet & Maxwell, London, 2002) 28–001–28–003.

outstanding as long as the beneficiary does not get the performance he is entitled to.

This has a crucial outcome where the creditor is insolvent. The debtor in this case would have to fully perform twice: first, to the creditor who was not finally entitled to the performance but from whom no recovery can be had; and second, to the beneficiary, who is the party entitled to the performance.[38]

This result stems from the different status each party — the creditor and the beneficiary — holds as against the debtor with regard to the benefit. The creditor is a secondary creditor. He himself is not entitled to the benefit. Whereas the beneficiary is the principal creditor, because he is the only one entitled to the contractual benefit.[39]

This situation reflects a contrasting analogy to the surety-principal debtor relations. The principal debtor and the surety are two debtors who are both under a duty to the creditor to pay the same debt. The creditor can sue both (though he should first approach the principal debtor). But there is a hierarchy between them: the final burden to discharge the debt is on the principal debtor. The surety is only a secondary debtor, who having discharged the debt, is entitled to be fully indemnified by the debtor.[40]

A similar — though not entirely symmetric — contrasting hierarchy is reflected in our context. The debtor is obliged to perform both to the creditor and the beneficiary. But unlike the surety-principal debtor relations where both are obliged to perform vis-à-vis the creditor, here the duty of the debtor is asymmetric: the beneficiary is the only one who is entitled to the contractual performance, while the contractual creditor is a secondary creditor, who is not entitled to performance at all. His only entitlement is to demand performance for the beneficiary, and if the entitlement is conferred upon him, he is under a duty to restore it to the beneficiary.

The special status of the creditor as a secondary creditor and the beneficiary as a principal creditor will be reflected in the law of remedies to which I shall now refer.

[38] Cf CA 393/73 *Association of Journalists v ISL* 28(1) PD 470 (Hebrew), in the context of assignment: where the debtor paid the debt, by mistake, to the original creditor, and afterwards the latter became insolvent, the debtor was bound to pay again to the assignee.

[39] Indeed in German law the creditor and beneficiary are considered 'several creditors of a special kind'. The right of the creditor is considered 'an accessory right': P Gottwald *Münchener Kommentar zum Buergerliches Gesetzbuch* 4th edn (Beck, München, 2003) band 2a comment 1 to §335 BGB, 2155. But though they are both considered creditors under the contract, they are not considered 'several creditors' under French law: Levroument & Mondoloni, 'Stipulation Pour L'Autrui' in *Répertoire de Droit Civil* (vol 10 of *Encyclopédie juridique*), (Dalloz, Paris, 1998) section 85, 16.

[40] If the debtor is insolvent, the final burden would be imposed on the surety. For the different types of several creditors: D Friedmann and N Cohen 'Adjustment Among Multiple Debtors' in A von Mehren (ed) *International Encyclopedia of Comparative Law* (Tübingen, The Hague, 1990) vol 10 chapter 11.

V CONTRACTUAL REMEDIES: GENERAL

Section 1(a) of the Remedies Law defines 'the injured party' as 'one who is entitled to the performance of the broken contract'. The beneficiary who is entitled to performance squarely responds to the definition of 'the injured party', but also the creditor is within that definition: he also is entitled to claim performance, even though the performance will not inure to his benefit.

In the context of a contract for the benefit of a third party we have two injured parties: the creditor and the beneficiary. From the point of view of the debtor, he is exposed to two separate claims and to enforced double liability, but several procedural safeguards might protect him against this risk. If he is sued by one of the injured parties, he might demand joinder of the other party.[41] Also, in order not to run the risk of payment to the wrong creditor, he might employ the procedure of inter-pleader.[42]

And what are the remedies of the injured party? Section 2 of the *Remedies Law* states that if a contact is broken 'the injured party is entitled to enforcement or to its termination, and is entitled also to damages, in addition to the above remedies or in their stead ... '. This section confers upon the injured party the full range of contractual remedies, while emphasising that the choice among the remedies is that of the injured party and not the party in breach.

The remedies available to the injured party under Israeli law are enforcement, termination and damages. Enforcement and termination are alternate remedies. Damages can follow enforcement or termination and could be granted independently. Following termination both parties are entitled to restitution.[43]

In principle, and as explicitly stated in section 2 of the Remedies Law, it is the injured party who has the choice which remedy to pursue.[44] In our context where we have two injured parties — the creditor and the beneficiary — the main problem relates to the question who has the ultimate choice and what degree of co-operation between them is required, a problem characteristic to each and every case of several creditors.

In the following sections I shall discuss the various remedies for breach under Israeli law and consider their application to the context of contracts for the benefit of a third party.

[41] So that a final decree should await joinder of the creditor: Restatement (Second) of Contracts section 307 comment (a).

[42] Regulations 24 and 224 of Civil Procedure Regulations 1984 (Hebrew).

[43] Section 9 of the Remedies Law.

[44] Retrospectively when enforcement is not granted, the contract is terminated. In that case the choice of the injured party is rejected, and it is the choice of the party-in-breach that prevails: D Friedmann 'On the Relations between Termination and Enforcement' in S Shetreet (ed) *Collection of Lectures For Judges* (Hebrew University, Jerusalem, 1976) 87 (Hebrew).

VI ENFORCEMENT

Enforcement is the primary remedy under Israeli law. The Israeli legislator deviated from the deep-rooted-common law tradition and posited enforcement — which is the equivalent of specific performance — as the principal remedy for breach of contract. Israeli law does not take the position that damages is the rule and performance is the exception (in cases where damages are an inadequate remedy). Rather, the starting point is that the injured party is entitled to enforcement or specific performance, and it is upon the party in breach to show why this should not be granted.[45]

Enforcement might be regarded as the natural remedy to which the beneficiary is entitled. More than any other remedy it incarnates the performance interest of the beneficiary, which is mentioned in section 34 of the Contracts Law, providing that the contract 'confers on the beneficiary the right to demand fulfillment of the obligation'.

The role of the creditor in enforcement is rather limited: as provided in section 38 of the Contracts Law he cannot claim the performance for himself, but rather for the beneficiary, whose right, we assume, is irrevocable. If the creditor files a claim, he might be regarded either as claiming for the beneficiary or as a trustee for the beneficiary.[46] The beneficiary is not under a duty to join the creditor as party to the claim against the debtor, but the creditor might be considered a proper party to the action.[47]

The remedy of enforcement is subject in Israeli law to four major exceptions: it will not be granted where enforcement is impossible;[48] where the contract is for personal services;[49] where performance would require undue supervision by the court;[50] and where it would be unjust to grant it.[51] The claim of the beneficiary for enforcement is subject to all these exceptions.

Section 37 of the Contracts Law also provides: 'Any plea available to the debtor against the creditor in connection with the obligation is also available to him against the beneficiary'.[52] Therefore, in the claim of the beneficiary for the enforcement of the contract, the debtor may raise as

[45] Section 3 of the Remedies Law starts by stating: 'The injured party is entitled to the enforcement of his contract ... ' and then enumerates the exceptions in which enforcement would be denied, below text to notes 48–51.

[46] Compare comment (b) to section 307of the Restatement (Second) Contracts.

[47] So that a final decree should await joinder of the creditor: above n 41.

[48] Section 3(1) of the Remedies Law.

[49] Section 3(2) of the Remedies Law.

[50] Section 3(3) of the Remedies Law.

[51] Section 3(4) of the Remedies Law.

[52] This section raises the question what rights and remedies are available to the debtor against the creditor and whether the interest of the beneficiary should be taken into account in exercising these rights and remedies. Also it raises the question of the debtor's right of set-off against the beneficiary. It seems that if the right of set-off arises from the same contract, it can be employed against the beneficiary, but not if it originated from other relations

against the beneficiary any defences he might have against the creditor. In addition to that he might also raise independent defences stemming from the conduct of the beneficiary himself or from a contract with him. Thus, waiver by the beneficiary might well serve as a defence against enforcement making it unjust against the debtor.[53]

Enforcement also includes an injunction.[54] If the debtor is under a duty to transfer an asset to the beneficiary, both the beneficiary and the creditor are entitled to an injunction against her, if she intends to transfer the asset to someone else.

Is there any importance in this context of the distinction between the two main categories of beneficiaries mentioned above, that is between a donee and a commercial beneficiary? Let us examine the following example: a debtor undertakes to transfer an asset to the beneficiary. The value of the asset is 100. The undertaking is actually designed as a gift by the creditor to the beneficiary. The creditor changes her mind, but meanwhile the beneficiary has changed her position and has suffered a loss of 10. Is the beneficiary entitled to the performance value (100) or the reliance value (10)?

In a purely two-parties-gift, an Israeli court would presumably have a discretion either to enforce the contract and confer the asset or its value on the beneficiary, or merely grant her the reliance value.[55] Since the context of our situation is the same, it seems that the gift principle should apply here as well, irrespective of the fact that the formal cover of the transaction is not a gift but rather a contract for the benefit of a third party.[56] Therefore, the court should either order the debtor to transfer the asset (or its value (100)) or to compensate the beneficiary for the reliance loss (10).

between the debtor and the creditor. This is the approach of English law: *Contracts (Rights of Third Parties) Act 1999* (UK) section 3; also of German law: P Gottwald *Münchener Kommentar zum Buergerliches Gesetzbuch* 4th edn (Beck München, 2003) band 2a comment 15 to §335 BGB, 2158. For a general discussion of the rights available to the debtor see N Cohen 'Contract for the Benefit of a Third Party' in D Friedmann and N Cohen (eds) *Contracts* (Aviram, Tel-Aviv, 2003) vol 3 [24.82]–[24.93] (Hebrew).

[53] Within section 3(4) of the *Remedies Law*. But a waiver by the creditor regarding the remedy of enforcement (after the beneficiary's right has become irrevocable) would not be available against the beneficiary. Once the beneficiary's right is irrevocable he gains control also over the remedies available to him in enforcing his right. Therefore a waiver by the creditor on enforcement would be invalid without the approval of the beneficiary. The creditor's waiver on enforcement should be interpreted as a waiver by the creditor on his right to claim enforcement against the debtor.

[54] Section 1(a) of the Remedies Law.

[55] D Friedmann and N Cohen *Contracts* (Aviram, Tel-Aviv, 1991) vol 1 [489] (Hebrew). This follows the position under section 90 of Restatement (Second) of Contracts.

[56] Restatement (Second) of Contracts, section 90 covers also the case where C, not a party to the promise, detrimentally relies on it. See the illustrations *ibid*, 244. See also N Cohen 'Good faith in Bargaining and Principles of Contract law' (1989) 9 *Tel-Aviv University Studies in Law* 249, 301–8.

When the beneficiary is also a creditor of the creditor, the claim of the beneficiary against the debtor is designed to discharge the creditor's debt. But if the parties did not otherwise agree, as long as the debt of the creditor has not been satisfied,[57] it remains outstanding. Therefore the beneficiary will be entitled to sue both the debtor and the creditor: the former as a principal debtor by virtue of the contract for the benefit of the third party; the latter as a secondary debtor by virtue of the original debt.

It follows that if the creditor owes 100 to the beneficiary, and under the contract the debtor undertook to transfer an asset to the beneficiary (designed as a full discharge of the debt), the beneficiary would be entitled to claim the 100 from the creditor and the asset from the debtor, but she could be satisfied only once.[58] If the debtor delivered the asset to the beneficiary, the debt would be discharged, and no further action could be brought by the beneficiary (against the creditor) or by the creditor (against the debtor). If, however, it transpired that the creditor paid the 100, the beneficiary would have no claim against the debtor,[59] but the creditor would then be subrogated to the rights of the beneficiary against the debtor, and she would stand in the shoes of the beneficiary with regard to any claim against the debtor, including any security that the beneficiary would have held against the debtor.[60]

VII DAMAGES

1 The Beneficiary's Claim

Damages is a monetary remedy which serves as a substitute for enforcement and occasionally as a supplement to it, when enforcement does not fully address the loss sustained as a result of the breach. Damages may be also granted independently of enforcement, where the contract is terminated. The same rules applicable to any injured party apply also to the

[57] An agreement that the contract for the benefit of a third party extinguishes the original debt, is actually a novation, which requires the approval of all the parties involved. In our case: with the approval of the creditor (the beneficiary) a new debtor (the debtor) agrees to take upon himself the liability of the former debtor (the creditor) towards the creditor (the beneficiary). Novation or assignment of debt is discussed in section 6 of *Transfer of Obligations Law 1968* (23 LSI 277).

[58] It is not clear whether the beneficiary has first to sue the debtor (as the primary debtor). The rules regarding sureties which might apply by analogy would impose on the beneficiary a duty first to approach the debtor, and then the creditor (who is regarded as surety) unless either of the following obtains: there is an agreement to the contrary; the debtor is insolvent; the debtor is dead or is not in Israel; or the action against him is coupled with hardship (section 8 of *Guarantee Law 1967* (21 LSI 41).

[59] If he was partly satisfied, the debt would be reduced to that extent, and the beneficiary would still be entitled to sue both the debtor and creditor for the remaining amount.

[60] Restatement (Second) of Contracts section 310.

beneficiary's action (whose right is irrevocable). Therefore, the right of the beneficiary to claim damages will be limited by the rules of foreseeability (or remoteness) and mitigation.[61]

In addition to that, in the particular case where the beneficiary's right stems from a gift, it might be limited by section 12 of the *Remedies Law* which provides that, if the injured party did not give any consideration for the promised performance, or if the consideration for it was not reasonable, the court might limit his rights with regard to the consequential loss that was caused as a result of the breach.

Hence if the debtor and the creditor have undertaken to give a gift to the beneficiary, his right to consequential damages — for example, loss of earnings from the asset that was promised to him — might be limited.

Things would be different if the transaction between the debtor and creditor was commercial in nature. For example, a mother buys an apartment for her daughter which she intends to give her as a gift and the daughter has an independent direct action against the seller. This is a contract for the benefit of a third party where the seller is the debtor, the mother is the creditor, and the daughter is the beneficiary.

The relation between the mother and the daughter is indeed gratuitous. But the relation between the buyer (the mother) and the seller of the apartment is purely commercial. If the seller was in breach, he could not limit the claim for damages on the basis of section 12. Since we have two injured parties each of them plays a different role. It is true that the main injured party — the daughter — did not give any consideration, but the other injured party — the mother — did give consideration, and the seller cannot be regarded as a party to a gift contract. Therefore, the daughter is entitled to the apartment from the date of delivery, and if the seller breaks the contract and does not deliver on time, the daughter could claim for loss of rent. Section 12 will not apply to this case.[62]

2 The Creditor's Claim

I mentioned earlier that the creditor is not entitled to claim enforcement for himself. Enforcement can be claimed only in favour of the beneficiary. With regard to damages matters are more complex.

Following a breach by the debtor both the creditor and the beneficiary might suffer damage. What are the guidelines with regard to the creditor's claim for damages? Would the creditor be entitled to claim damages

[61] Section 10 (foreseeability) and 14 (mitigation) of the Remedies Law.

[62] Since between the mother and daughter the transaction is gratuitous this would enable the mother to revoke even after her daughter knows about the gift. The power of revocation will cease with the reliance of the daughter on the gift, by analogy to section 5(b) of the Gift Law: above n 33.

reflecting the beneficiary's loss, even though he himself did not suffer any loss?

First to the question of the loss the creditor himself might suffer. Here again a distinction ought to be drawn between the two categories of contract for the benefit of a third party, namely, a gratuitous transaction and a commercial transaction.

Where the beneficiary is a donee, usually the creditor does not have an economic interest in the transaction. Hence, if the debtor breaches his obligation towards the beneficiary, the creditor's loss is symbolic, and he would be entitled merely to nominal damages.

Things are altogether different where the transaction is commercial, as in the case where the debtor undertakes to pay the creditor's debt. In this case the loss suffered by the creditor might be substantial, and he can recover from the debtor so long as there is no conflict with the right of the beneficiary.[63] Thus, if the debtor did not perform and the creditor himself, after the breach by the debtor, satisfied the beneficiary's debt, the creditor could now recover in full the amount of the debt and any consequential loss that was caused to him as a result of the breach by the debtor.

And now to the question whether the creditor could claim also the loss caused to the beneficiary as a result of the breach in addition to the loss caused to himself. Let us consider the following case: a tourist agency undertook to supply tourist services to a buyer and her husband. The husband is a beneficiary in a contract made between the agency and his wife. Clearly the wife could claim damages in respect of the loss she suffered as a result of the breach by the agency. But presumably she will also be able to sue for the loss sustained by her husband.[64] Thus, in this case the same rule as to enforcement applies also to damages: as the creditor can claim enforcement for the benefit of the beneficiary, she could similarly claim damages, which are a substitute for enforcement. But it is clear that as the creditor cannot hold for herself the performance, similarly she cannot hold the damages for herself. The amount of damages reflecting the beneficiary's interest will be held by the creditor in trust for the beneficiary.[65]

[63] Restatement (Second) of Contracts section 305 comment (a).

[64] But the husband would not be able to claim damages for the wife, because the creditor can act on behalf of the beneficiary but not vice versa.

[65] Such was the case in *Jackson v Horizon Holidays Ltd* [1975] 3 All ER 92, where the head of the family claimed damages caused to himself and his family as a result of the breach of contract by the debtor, a tourist agency. It was held that the father was a trustee for the amount of damages received for his family.

For other contexts where under the common law a claim for the damages of a third party is allowed: *The Winkfield* [1902] P 42, where a bailee sued for the damage caused to the owner, and was regarded as holding in trust the damages received on behalf of the owner.

English law allows for claiming third party's damages only in limited circumstances, in particular where the third party does not have an independent claim: *Alfred McAlpine Construction v Panatown* [2001] 1 AC 518 (HL) reversing the decision of the Court of Appeal which unanimously recognised the right of the creditor to sue for third party's losses: (1998)

From the point of view of the debtor, the tourist agency, it is exposed to the risk of enforced double-liability: it could be sued by the wife who claims also on behalf of her husband, and also by the husband, who will independently sue for himself. The tourist agency *could* join the husband to the proceedings.[66] But to the extent that the tourist agency is bound to pay the creditor also for the loss sustained by the beneficiary, this amount will be deducted from the beneficiary's claim.

The creditor and the debtor could agree on liquidated damages. If this amount reflects the performance value of the beneficiary, the latter will be entitled to claim it for himself. The creditor will not be entitled to this amount, and will be regarded as the beneficiary's trustee if he claims it. This holds true in cases where the transaction is intended as a gift to the beneficiary. But, in a case where the debtor is due to discharge the creditor's debt to the beneficiary, breach by the debtor might cause substantial loss to the creditor. He will be entitled to the liquidated damages as long as he does not compete with the beneficiary's claim.

VIII TERMINATION

Section 2 of the Israeli Remedies Law confers upon the injured party the option whether to claim enforcement or termination.[67] The injured party can immediately terminate the contract if the breach is fundamental.[68]

Construction Law Review 46. For different views regarding the rule of third party losses and its limits following the decision of the Court of Appeal: GH Treitel 'Damages in Respect of a Third Party's Loss' (1998) 114 *Law Quarterly Review* 527 (claiming there is no support to a rule that does not recognise the claim for third party's loss, and supporting such a claim where the third party does not have a right of action); D Wallace 'Third party Damage: No Legal Black Hole?' (1999) 115 *Law Quarterly Review* 394 (supporting a claim by the creditor for third party loss with no reservation, justifying it in the performance interest of the creditor); H Unberath, 'Third Party Losses and Black Holes: Another View' (1999) 115 *Law Quarterly Review* 535 (supporting such a claim in the cases where the loss of the creditor is transferred to the third party). For a comparative survey, mainly between English and German law, see H Unberath *Transferred Loss* (Hart Publishing, Oxford, 2003).

This rule has not been changed by the enactment of the *Contracts (Rights of Third Parties) Act*: the creditor's rights are governed by the common law. It follows that under current English law the creditor could not claim the beneficiary's substantial damages, as the latter has by virtue of the Act an independent claim.

66 Regulation 24 of Civil Procedure Regulations 1984.

67 A terminological note: the word 'termination' is used in several contexts. In section 36 of the Contracts Law it is used to express the power of the creditor and the debtor (s 36(a)) or the creditor only (s 36(b)) to cancel or alter the right of the beneficiary. In our remedial context we refer to the power of the injured party to cancel unilaterally the agreement following a breach by the other party.

68 Section 6 of the Remedies Law. Under the same section a breach is fundamental if a reasonable party had he known about it at the time of the creation of the contract, would not have entered the contract; or if the parties agreed that the breach shall be regarded as such. Under section 8 the termination requires a notification to the party in breach within a reasonable time after the breach.

Even if the breach is not fundamental the injured party can terminate a contract on condition that he give an additional period of time for performance and the party in breach does not perform.[69]

Is the beneficiary a proper party for claiming termination? The beneficiary falls within the definition of an 'injured party'. But is it appropriate to confer the power of termination on one who is not a party to the contract?

The response of the English legislation as reflected in section 1(5) of the Contracts (Rights of Third Parties) Act is negative. It states that the third party is entitled to 'any remedy that would have been available to him in an action for breach of contract if he had been a party to the contract ...'.

The remedies that are available to the beneficiary are those that would have been given to him in an action for breach. Since the remedy of termination is in English law a self-help remedy, which does not require recourse to the court, it is not a remedy available in an action, and therefore is not available to the beneficiary.[70]

From the point of view of Israeli law the problem will be discussed in the following order: first, I shall examine whether there is any limitation on the right of the creditor to terminate the contract following a breach by the debtor; second, I shall explore the course of action open to the beneficiary following a breach by the debtor, and examine whether this might be regarded as a termination. I should emphasise again that the discussion is based on the assumption that the beneficiary's right is irrevocable.

1 The Creditor's Option

The right of the beneficiary to performance is subject to any defences the debtor might raise against the creditor (section 37 of the Contracts Law). But also the creditor may assert some claims against the debtor. For example, suppose that the creditor assumes an obligation to manufacture a product, the material for which the debtor undertakes to supply. The debtor is under a duty to pay the price to the beneficiary. If the debtor

[69] Section 7 of the Remedies Law. But the court has under this section a discretionary power to intervene in the case of termination for non-fundamental breach if the party in breach objected to the termination and the court deems the termination to be unjust.

[70] Law Commission for England and Wales, Report No 242 'Privity of Contract: Contract for the Benefit of Third Parties' section 3.33; R Merkin (ed) *Privity of Contract* (LLP, London, 2000) 110 [5.49].

This is also the position of French law (though the termination there is not a self-help remedy): F Terré, P Simler and Y Lequette *Droit Civil: Les Obligations* (Dalloz, Paris, 1999) [501] 481, and it is the prevailing view in German law: Palandt *Bürgerliches Gesetzbuch* 60th edn (Beck, Munchen, 2001) [328–6] clarifying that the power to terminate is the creditor's unless the contract empowers the beneficiary to terminate or this power is assigned to him by the creditor. But see P Gottwald *Münchener Kommentar zum Bürgerliches Gesetzbuch* 4th edn (Beck, München, 2003) band 2a comment 19 to §335 BGB, 2159 (third party might be allowed to terminate also for the creditor).

does not supply the material, she is in breach of contract, and the creditor could terminate the contract for the breach. This termination would result in the annulment of the beneficiary's right, whose right is irrevocable. Hence, the question is whether there should be a limitation on the creditor's right to terminate , due to its possible negative impact on the beneficiary's seemingly immune right. If such limitations do exist, then the contract will not be terminated, and that might lead eventually to the enforcement of the beneficiary's right.

The question whether the creditor's rights are limited by the presence of a beneficiary arises also in the sphere of rescission due to consensual defects. When the creditor wishes to rescind the contract for mistake, misrepresentation, compulsion or extortion, does he need the approval of the beneficiary? The answer seems to be in the negative. A defect in the creditor's will eradicates the contract. Rescinding the contract in these circumstances is evidence that the creditor never agreed to the contract, and was never willing to be bound by it.[71] It is the will of the party to the contract that counts. Therefore, in exercising his power of rescission due to consensual defects, the creditor is autonomous and not dependent on the beneficiary who is not a contractual party and whose will did not constitute the contract.

The parallel question with regard to termination following a breach by the debtor is, however, more complex. It bears an analogy to the situation where two several creditors to the same contract have conflicting positions with regard to the remedy each of them would like to pursue following their debtor's breach: one opts for termination of the contract; the other wishes to enforce it.

When the several creditors stand on the same footing and have a similar status, it seems that the remedy of enforcement — where this remedy is actually available — should get preference. The reason for this is that giving preference to termination will thwart the possibility of later granting enforcement; whereas ordering enforcement first still enables termination to take place at a later stage, if enforcement turns out futile.

This ought to apply *a fortiori* to the competition between the creditor and the beneficiary, whose right is irrevocable: it is the beneficiary — not the creditor — who is entitled to the performance of the contract. Furthermore, in many cases the creditor is under a duty to obtain the promised performance for the benefit of the third party.[72] This gives a clear preference to the choice of the beneficiary in enforcing the contract.

[71] Things might be different where the defect is a result of a mistake the other party did not know about. According to section 14(b) of the Contracts Law the court has a discretion whether to rescind the contact. In exercising its discretion the court might take into consideration the interests of the beneficiary. In other cases of rescission the party whose will was defected has the power to unilaterally rescind the contract without any interference by the court.

[72] This would be naturally the case where there are pre-existing relations between the creditor and the beneficiary: text following n 25 above.

In short, a situation where one creditor is secondary (the creditor) and the other one is principal (the beneficiary) imposes upon the secondary party a duty to co-operate with the principal in order to accomplish the performance of the right.

Therefore, though the creditor has an immediate power to terminate the contract if the breach of the debtor is fundamental, this power, as is the case with any other powers and rights in Israeli civil law, is subject to the principle of good faith.[73] Hence, if the breach can be cured, the debtor is interested and is willing to perform, the beneficiary is interested, and the performance will not unduly overburden the creditor, there is no justification to allow the creditor terminate the contract. In other words, absent any other agreement to the contrary, a pre-condition for the termination of the contract in these circumstances would be its approval by the beneficiary.[74]

This should apply *a fortiori* to a non-fundamental breach. Under the Remedies Law the injured party can terminate a contract following a non-fundamental breach, on condition that he gives an additional period of time for performance to the party in breach. Even then, termination of the contract could be invalidated if the court deemed it unjust. But a condition for the invalidation of the termination is that the debtor objected to the termination.[75]

It appears that in our context, even absent the debtor's objection, the fact that the beneficiary objects to the termination might suffice for the intervention of the court. It is even more so if both the debtor and the beneficiary object to the termination. It follows that, similarly to the case of fundamental breach, also where the breach is non-fundamental the creditor should first seek the approval of the beneficiary to the termination of the contract.

In conclusion, the need to obtain the approval of the beneficiary in both fundamental and non-fundamental breach would be subject to the following reservations.

[73] CA 2106/91 *Mazor v Hidi* 47 PD(5) 788, 795–6 (Hebrew); CA 158/80 *Shalom v Mota* 36 PD(4) 793, 811 (Hebrew).

[74] This is the approach of German law: P Gottwald *Münchener Kommentar zum Bürgerliches Gesetzbuch* 4th edn (Beck, München, 2003) band 2a comments 10, 18 to §335 BGB, 2157, 2159. Obviously, under German law the creditor would be able to unilaterally terminate if the beneficiary's right is revocable: *Ibid*. In French law (which also limits the right of the creditor to terminate and where termination is made by court) there is a view that a termination without the beneficiary's approval is effective as between the creditor and the debtor, but it leaves the contract intact as against the beneficiary, unless he is joined to the proceedings in which the termination was made. The debtor will be bound to perform to the beneficiary, but he will have a restitutionary claim against the creditor: Levroument & Mondoloni, 'Stipulation Pour L'Autrui' in *Répertoire de Droit Civil* (vol 10 of *Encyclopédie juridique*), (Dalloz, Paris, 1998) [79]–[80] 15.

[75] Above n 69.

First, where it is impossible to perform the contract, there is no need to get the beneficiary's approval. For example, when the property, which was the subject-matter of the contract was sold to a good faith purchaser, there is no possibility to perform the contract.[76] Such is also the case where a musician undertook to play at the beneficiary's wedding, and the day of the wedding had passed. Actually, the primary contractual duty to perform in such cases has in effect been 'self-terminated', even without termination by the creditor. This 'automatic' termination saves the need for an active termination by the creditor, and hence saves also the need for approval of such termination by the beneficiary.

Second, if it is clear that the debtor is not willing to perform and that the court will not enforce the contract, there is no need to get the approval of the beneficiary. For example, if the debtor is unwilling to perform a contract for personal services which will not be enforced,[77] the primary contractual duty to perform will be practically terminated. Therefore there is neither a need for a notice of termination by the creditor, nor a need to get the beneficiary's approval.

Third, where the debtor has already rendered performance to the beneficiary, but later on breaks the contract and does not render performance to the creditor, there is no need to get the approval of the beneficiary for the termination of the contract. For example, suppose that the debtor is required to pay the price of property sold to him by the creditor in three installments, one installment being payable to the beneficiary and the other two installments to the creditor. The property is delivered to the debtor. The debtor pays the first installment to the beneficiary, but defaults on the other two to the creditor. When the creditor seeks to terminate the contract for the breach she need not seek the approval of the beneficiary. The reason is that the beneficiary will not be jeopardised by the termination of the contract: she has already received the performance due to her, and she will not be subject to any duty of restitution after the termination of the contract, because the performance to her was made before the breach.[78]

2 The Beneficiary's Option

As mentioned earlier it is doubtful whether the remedy of termination is available to the beneficiary who is not after all a party to the contract.[79] But it is clear that, if the debtor does not duly perform, the beneficiary

[76] The assumption is that the property is irreplaceable. But the beneficiary might be entitled to claim the price from the debtor under section 52 of the Contracts Law: below n 81 and accompanying text.
[77] Under the exception specified in section 3(2) of the *Remedies Law*.
[78] See below text to notes nn 87–9.
[79] See above n 70.

should not be bound to accept a defective performance, and it seems natural that he might reject such a performance.

Such a rejection gives the debtor a chance to cure the defective performance, unless the performance is either impossible or it turns out to be useless to the beneficiary. In other words, mere rejection of the performance by the beneficiary is not tantamount to the termination of the contract. The power of termination is in the hands of the creditor.[80]

Obviously following the rejection by the beneficiary (or in any case where the performance was not rendered with no excuse) the beneficiary could claim damages from the debtor. In such a case the primary duty to perform will be self-terminated, otherwise the debtor might be subject to double liability: first, through the beneficiary's claim for damages; and second, through the creditor's claim for enforcement.

If performance is impossible, but the debtor has a right of indemnity or compensation against a third party (eg an insurer), the beneficiary is entitled to claim that sum from the debtor or the third party.[81] In that case the contract will continue to exist, and the creditor will be liable to perform her counter-obligation to the debtor. For example, suppose that the debtor is under a duty to deliver a book to the beneficiary, and the creditor is to give a painting to the debtor in exchange for the book. The book was insured by the debtor against loss. The book is lost, and the debtor is unable to perform but, if the beneficiary so chooses, she is entitled to the insurance money.[82] Her choice means that the contract is still subsisting, the only difference is that the book she is entitled to is substituted for the insurance money. Therefore, the creditor is liable to perform and deliver the painting to the debtor.

IX RESTITUTION

Section 9(a) of the Remedies Law, which deals with restitution following termination for breach, states that

> Where a contract is terminated the party in breach shall restore to the other party what he received under the contract, or pay him the value of what he has received if restitution is impossible or unreasonable or the injured party

[80] But to situations where the contract is likely to be regarded as self-terminated: above text to nn 76–7.

[81] Section 52 of the Contracts Law states that '[W]here the fulfillment of an obligation has become impossible, and the debtor has accordingly a right to compensation or indemnification against a third party, the debtor shall transfer the right or what he has received thereunder to the creditor to the extent of the value of the obligation'.

The application of the section to our context means that the beneficiary (and not the creditor) is the party entitled to the substituted performance.

[82] This is the position of German law from which (§281, BGB) section 52 of the Israeli law was derived: P Gottwald *Münchener Kommentar zum Bürgerliches Gesetzbuch* 4th edn (Beck, München, 2003) band 2a comment 14 to §335 BGB, 2158.

> has thus elected; and the injured party shall restore to the party in breach what he received under the contract, or pay him the value of what he has received if restitution is impossible or unreasonable or the injured party has thus elected.

The section does not relate to the special situation where the benefit was transferred or given by the debtor to a third party.[83] For example, following a contract of sale the buyer sells the asset she had previously bought to a third person. Now the original owner (the original seller) terminates the contract as a result of the buyer's breach. Could the original owner claim restitution from the third party (not a third party beneficiary)?

Israeli case law and literature developed a theoretical basis for the applicable rules to the subject.[84] In principle, if the benefit was transferred to the third party by virtue of a void contract (eg for absence of a written constitutive document) or by a contract that was not in fact entered into (eg for incompatibility between offer and acceptance), the third party was bound to make restitution, unless he acquired the property in market overt. Where the contract is valid, but the benefit was transferred before the breach, he is not subject to restitution. The reason is that the acquisition of the third party was not tainted. Therefore his title was complete, and the original owner could claim restitution only from his buyer.

Matters are different if the transfer occurs after the breach. In that case the third party acquires tainted property. He will be subject to a duty to make restitution unless he can purify his acquisition, namely if he was a purchaser in good faith and for value. These basic principles seem appropriate to apply also where the third party is a third party beneficiary. In the following sections I shall examine specifically the application of these principles to our context.

1 The Debtor's Claim against the Beneficiary[85]

Under an agreement between a debtor and a creditor the debtor transferred an asset to the beneficiary. Later on it transpired that the contract

[83] The same applies to rescission for a defect in the making of the contract. Section 21 of the *Contracts Law* states that 'Where a contract is rescinded, each party shall restore to the other party what he received under the contract, or if restitution is impossible or unreasonable pay him the value of what he has received'.

[84] D Friedmann 'Remarks regarding the Rights of the Original Owner against Third Parties following the New Israeli Legislation' (1975) 4 *Tel-Aviv Universtiy Law Review* 245 (Hebrew); N Cohen 'Rescission of a Contract and its effect on Unregistered Transaction in Land' (1983) 35 *Hapraklit* 215 (Hebrew); D Friedmann *The Law of Unjust Enrichment* 2nd edn (Aviram, Tel-Aviv, 1998) [28.12]–[28.24] (Hebrew); M Mautner 'The Eternal Triangles of the Law: Towards a Theory of Priorities in Conflicts involving Remote Parties' (1991) 90 *Michigan Law Review* 95.

[85] Under the contract the beneficiary is not likely to be liable to the debtor, otherwise the contract is not for his benefit. But the beneficiary is subject to the duty of cooperation and to the principle of good faith in the performance of contract (section 39 of the Contracts Law).

was void (because of lack of a written document). The beneficiary (and also the creditor[86]) is subject to a duty to make restitution.

When the contract is not void, but rather voidable, the beneficiary is subject to a duty to make restitution, unless he is a good faith purchaser for value. Take the case where a creditor is in default, but the debtor transfers an asset to the beneficiary. The debtor then terminates the contract after the transfer of the asset to the beneficiary. The beneficiary acquires the asset by virtue of a voidable contract. He (and the creditor) would be subject to a duty to make restitution by the debtor[87] unless he acquired the property for value in good faith. But if the property is transferred to the beneficiary before the breach by the creditor, and the debtor terminated the contract only after the breach, the debtor would be entitled to claim restitution from the creditor and not from the beneficiary. The reason is that the transfer of the property to the beneficiary occurred before the breach. The beneficiary has fully acquired the right to the asset and there is no cloud over the acquisition. He will be protected even though he did not give any value for the asset. In these circumstances it is the creditor who will be bound to restore to the debtor the value of the asset.

The English case of *Pan Ocean Shipping v Creditcorp Ltd (The Trident Beauty)*, could serve as an illustration even though it dealt with assignment.[88] We pointed out earlier the striking similarities between assignment and a contract for the benefit of a third party.[89] In both cases the creditor transfers the contractual benefit to a third party: in assignment the transfer is made after the creation of the original contract between the debtor and the creditor, without considering the wish of the debtor; in a contract for a third party beneficiary the transfer to the beneficiaryis agreed upon between the debtor and the creditor and is part of the original contract.

Therefore, eg if the beneficiary agreed to accept a benefit, and later on retreats with no legal cause, she would be liable to the debtor for any loss he suffers from that breach; P Gottwald *Münchener Kommentar zum Bürgerliches Gesetzbuch* 4th edn (Beck, München, 2003) band 2a comment 30 to §328 BGB, 2081; comments 7–10 to §334 BGB, 2152–3.

[86] In German law there is a view that the beneficiary is subject to restitution when the contract is void. But according to another view the debtor could not claim restitution from the beneficiary if the contract between the beneficiary and the creditor is valid. Only the creditor would be subject under this view to restitution. Hence, according to the latter view, where the beneficiary is the creditor of the creditor under a valid contract, and the debtor paid the beneficiary a sum of money as a discharge under a void contract, the payment to the beneficiary will not be recoverable by the debtor, who will have a right of recovery only against the creditor: For a detailed survey see P Gottwald *Münchener Kommentar zum Bürgerliches Gesetzbuch* 4th edn (Beck, München, 2003) band 2a comments 11–18 to §334 BGB, 2153–5.

[87] Unless the transfer of the property to the beneficiary after the breach by the creditor can be regarded as a waiver of the debtor's claim against the beneficiary.

[88] [1994] 1 WLR 161; A Burrows 'Restitution from Assignee' [1994] *Restitution Law Review* 52; D Friedmann 'Restitution from an Assignee' (1994) 110 *Law Quarterly Review* 521.

[89] Above text to n 10.

In *Pan Ocean Shipping* the creditor assigned his right to the assignee. The debtor paid the assignee. After a while the creditor broke the contract with the debtor. The debtor terminated the contract, and claimed restitution from the assignee. The court denied his right to restitution from the assignee.

This result is well grounded. It reflects the proper rule that should apply also to a third party beneficiary: the debtor who has transferred the benefit to the third party before the breach by the creditor, can claim restitution only from the creditor.

2 The Debtor's Claim against the Creditor

Why should the creditor be subject to a claim for restitution if the benefit was rendered to the beneficiary and not to him?

The Israeli case of *Car Rental Agencies Ltd v Tarablus*[90] will serve as an illustration. In this case a contract had been entered into between a company and its director, on the one hand, and a group of investors, on the other hand. The investors undertook to invest some money in the company, and they were to receive certain rights in the company in return. The company and the director broke their obligations towards the investors. The investors terminated the contract for the breach, and claimed restitution of the sum they had invested both from the company and the director.

This was not a case of a contract for a third party beneficiary, but rather a multi-party contract. But the situation nevertheless resembles that of the third party beneficiary contract: in both cases the benefit is channelled by the debtor (the investors) only to one of the creditors (the company). The other creditor (the director) can sue the investors only for the benefit of the company. In other words, similarly to the third party beneficiary contract, the company is a principal creditor (it is entitled to the benefit) whereas the director is a secondary creditor (he is only entitled to sue the debtor in order to compel him to perform towards the company).

In arguing that he should be exempt from restitution, the director claimed that since it was the company, and not him, who had received the benefit, only the company should be liable to restore it. The court rejected the director's argument. It ruled that not only the company but also the director was subject to the duty to make restitution. But the justices were divided as to their reasoning. Justice Cahan explained that, since the contractual obligations were joint and several, and since the duty of restitution was also contractual, the latter duty should apply jointly and severally to the director and the company.

Justice Barak regarded the duty of restitution as extra-contractual, and as governed by the principles of restitution. He applied to the case the

[90] CA 186/77, 33 PD(1) 197 (Hebrew).

analogy of a third party beneficiary, and ruled that the director, though he had not physically received the benefit, nevertheless received it normatively. Giving the benefit to the company was what he had bargained for. Therefore, with the termination of the contract both the director and the company became subject to the duty to make restitution.

Justice Asher tried to reconcile the two approaches with regard to the nature of the duty to make restitution, by ruling that, though the duty to make restitution is not contractual but a legal duty, it is implicitly included in the contract, and as such is subject to the rules of joint and several obligations.

Similarly to the opinion of Justice Barak but on a somewhat different basis, I regard the duty to make restitution as a reflection of the duty of performance. Therefore the nature of the duty to make restitution should be examined from the point of view of the right to performance. From that point of view the director in our case was a secondary creditor and the company was a principal creditor. With the termination of the contract, and with the resulting duty of restitution, the creditors become debtors: the one who was principal as to the benefit — the company — ought to become principal as to the obligation to make restitution; and the one who was secondary as to the benefit — the director — ought to become the secondary debtor as to the duty to restore. It follows that as both were entitled to claim the benefit, they are both now subject to the duty to restore it.

Hence, a distinction ought to be drawn between the relations towards the party claiming restitution (the investors) and the interrelations of the parties who are subject to the duty to make restitution (the company and the director). Towards the investors both parties are liable. Regarding the relations *inter se* the final burden is on the company. The result would be that, if the director was liable to restore the benefit to the investors, he would have a right to be fully indemnified by the company. But if he cannot be indemnified, for example because the company is insolvent, the final burden is on him and not upon the investors.

In general terms we might say that when the creditor and the beneficiary are jointly and severally liable, the beneficiary would be a principal debtor and the creditor — a secondary one. Both are exposed to an action by the debtor, but the final burden should lie on the beneficiary.

3 The Beneficiary's Claim against the Debtor

The duty of restitution is mutual. It is imposed on both parties to the contract. Could there be any circumstances whereby the debtor would be liable in restitution to the beneficiary? At first glance the question seems peculiar: why should the beneficiary who is not supposed to transfer any benefit to the debtor, be entitled to restitution from the debtor?

The problem will be examined by the following illustration: suppose that the creditor has undertaken to pay the price of a property that the debtor ought to transfer to the beneficiary. The creditor paid part of the price and then defaulted. The debtor terminates the contract[91] and is under the duty to restore the sums of money she had received from the creditor.

On the face of it, it is the creditor, who paid the money to the debtor, who would be entitled to receive back the money after the termination of the contract. But in many cases where the beneficiary's right is irrevocable the creditor is liable to the beneficiary to obtain the performance due by the debtor. This is most likely to be the case where the beneficiary is a creditor (of the creditor). If the creditor by her own default brought about the termination of the contract, she would be liable for the loss incurred by the beneficiary. The sum that was given to the debtor to acquire the beneficiary's right might be regarded as a (partial) substitute of the property.[92] Indeed, due to the default of the creditor the beneficiary could not get the promised property, but at least she should be entitled to its substitute. It follows that in these circumstances the debtor should be bound to restore this sum to the beneficiary and not to the creditor.[93]

X CONCLUSION

I have introduced the range of remedies for breach of contract in Israeli law through the special lens of the third party beneficiary's right. A breach by the debtor of his obligation in a contract for the benefit of a third party gives rise to two claims by two injured parties: the beneficiary, the primary victim, who is not a party to the contract, and the creditor, who is a party to the contract, but is a secondary victim. The beneficiary and the creditor are hence several creditors and the exercise of remedies by each is limited due to the presence of the other. Furthermore, the creditor, as a

[91] But it seems that following the principle of good faith, the debtor might be required to give the beneficiary the option of performance (instead of the creditor), in particular when the breach is non-fundamental or in any case where after the breach the debtor gave the creditor an extended time to perform. A specific provision in the Insurance Contracts Law 1981 follows this line: section 45 states that where the contract of insurance is terminated by the insured, the insurer has to notify the beneficiary (whose right is irrevocable), and the latter has an option within 45 days to adopt the contract and to step into the shoes of the insured.

[92] D Friedmann *The Law of Unjust Enrichment* 2nd edn (Aviram, Tel-Aviv, 1998) [23.54]–[23.55] (Hebrew). Insofar as the sum received by the debtor does not cover the beneficiary's loss, she might recover the rest from the creditor.

[93] In this respect the position of the Law Commission that the beneficiary does not have any restitutionary claim against the debtor might seem too broad: Law Commission for England and Wales, Report No 42 'Privity of Contract: Contract for the Benefit of Third Parties' [3.33(2)].

secondary creditor, will occasionally be subject to the will of the beneficiary. But due to the special position of the beneficiary as a creditor outside the contract, he may not exercise the whole range of contractual remedies.

From the point of view of the debtor the major concern is to limit the risk of enforced double liability on him. Another concern is to confine the debtor's liability to the contractual boundaries, which means that the defences available to him derive not only from his relationship with the beneficiary, but also from his relationship with the creditor.

The remedy of enforcement — the primary remedy under Israeli law — is the natural remedy available to the beneficiary. In a conflict between the beneficiary who seeks enforcement and the creditor who seeks termination, preference ought to be given to the beneficiary. He is the primary creditor; enforcement is likely to protect his right most effectively; also termination can follow enforcement, but enforcement cannot be available, after the contract has been terminated.

The remedy of enforcement is subject to the exceptions specified in the law. For example, enforcement will be denied where performance is impossible. But if the debtor has in this case a right of indemnity or compensation against the third party, the beneficiary will be entitled to claim it from the debtor or the third party as a substituted performance.

Enforcement will be denied where it is deemed unjust. Hence, any defence stemming from the relationship between the creditor and the debtor and also the relationship between the debtor and beneficiary will be available to the debtor against the beneficiary.

When the creditor exercises a right of termination, he should obtain the approval of the beneficiary, unless the contract cannot be performed or the court would not enforce it. The beneficiary, not being a party to the contract, cannot terminate the contract, though he is not bound to accept defective performance.

In such a case, if the beneficiary seeks damages from the debtor, the contract with the creditor will be self-terminated otherwise the debtor might be subject to double liability. But if the beneficiary is not interested in claiming damages from the debtor, the creditor has an option whether to keep the contract with the debtor or to terminate it.

The scope of damages the beneficiary might claim from the debtor is likely to be limited by the nature of the transaction: for example, if the beneficiary received the benefit as a gift by both the creditor and the debtor he might not be entitled to recover consequential losses. The beneficiary could also recover liquidated damages which reflect his performance interest.

The creditor could claim damages for his own loss, including liquidated damages so long as his claim does not compete with that of the beneficiary. The creditor could also claim damages — as trustee or on behalf of the beneficiary — for losses inflicted upon the beneficiary.

Termination by the creditor results in a mutual duty of restitution. The debtor and the creditor are the parties to the contract who are apparently subject to the duty to make restitution. Even though the creditor is not the recipient, the debtor is entitled to recovery from him. A recovery from the beneficiary might be available only if the contract is void or the transfer to him took place after the breach and if he could not be regarded as a good faith purchaser.

In exceptional circumstances the beneficiary might claim recovery from the debtor, though the latter has not received a benefit from the beneficiary. This might happen when the debtor terminated the contract as a result of the creditor's breach and the creditor is under a pre-existing duty to the beneficiary. In that case the beneficiary — and not the creditor — might be entitled to recover the value of the benefit received by the debtor from the creditor. This is deemed a substitute for the benefit that — due to the fault of the creditor — was withheld from the beneficiary.

9

Between Contract and Tort: Pure Economic Loss in Europe

MAURO BUSSANI & VERNON VALENTINE PALMER

I INTRODUCTION

THIS CHAPTER AIMS to provide a theoretical matrix that situates the remedies available to the victims of pure economic loss in a comparative perspective. To this purpose we will rely on the results of a seven year long collective inquiry we conducted within the framework of 'The Common Core of European Private Law' project.[1] The research covers thirteen European jurisdictions (Austria, Belgium, England, Finland, France, Germany, Greece, Italy, The Netherlands, Portugal, Scotland, Spain and Sweden) and has been carried out on the basis of a factual approach through the use of a questionnaire. Each hypothetical case was formulated with the view of taking account of any relevant circumstance occurring in any of the legal systems under consideration, so that these circumstances would be considered in — and therefore become comparable with — the analysis of every other system.

After placing on the table the relevant questions that surround the issue (Section II), in the following pages we will first discuss the notion of pure economic loss (Section III), then we will try to single out a factual taxonomy of the principal ways in which this damage may arise (Sections IV–V). Dwelling on the general characteristics of the liability regimes in the jurisdictions we covered (Sections VI–VII) will enable us, in the final part of the essay (Section XIff), to focus on the operative rules of some of the above legal systems. Their features seem to us paradigmatic in showing how 'pure' and 'not pure' economic loss are not different in kind, but distinguishable only by the circumstances in which the loss originates and

[1] M Bussani and VV Palmer *Pure Economic Loss in Europe* (Cambridge University Press, Cambridge, 2003).

the technical limits imposed on the set of remedies available for their recovery.

II QUESTIONS TO BE ANSWERED

Pure economic loss is one of the most discussed topics of comparative law scholarship. Fascination with the subject (which may at first glance appear dry and technical) has developed into a wealth of literature about this frontier notion.[2] It stands at the cutting edge of some crucial questions such as: How far can tort liability expand without imposing excessive burdens upon individual activity (or, as some may wish, to what extent should tort rules be compatible with the market orientation of the legal system?[3]) and — of particular concern in this volume — as a matter of policy, should the recovery of pure economic loss be principally the domain of the law of contract?

The truth is there has never been a universally accepted definition of 'pure economic loss'. Perhaps the simplest reason is that a number of legal systems neither recognise the legal category nor distinguish it as an autonomous form of damage. Nevertheless where the concept is recognised, as in Germany and common law systems, it is apparently

[2] The literature is overwhelmingly weighted to those countries where the concept is well-recognised by practitioners, judges and scholars. See S Banakas *Civil Liability for Pure Economic Loss* (Kluwer, Hague, 1996); JM Barendrecht 'Pure Economic Loss in the Netherlands' in EH Hondius (ed) *Netherlands Reports to the Fifteenth International Congress of Comparative Law Bristol 1998* (Intersentia Rechtswetenschappen, Antwerpen, 1998) 115–35; R Bernstein *Economic Loss* 2nd edn (Sweet and Maxwell, London, 1998); B Feldthusen *Economic Negligence: The Recovery of Pure Economic Loss* (Carswell, Toronto, 1989); J Kleineman *Ren förmögenhetsskada* (Juridisk Tidskrift, Stockholms, 1987); C Lapoyade Deschamps 'La reparation du prejudice pur en droit francais' in S Banakas *Civil Liability for Pure Economic Loss* (Kluwer, Hague, 1996) 89–101; W Posch and B Schilcher 'Civil Liability for Pure Economic Loss: An Austrian Perspective' in S Banakas *Civil Liability for Pure Economic Loss* (Kluwer, Hague, 1996) 149–76; J Spier (ed) *The Limits of Liability: Keeping the Floodgates Shut* (Kluwer, Hague, 1996) (discussion of eight 'Tilburg Hypotheticals' — four of which concern pure economic loss); Ch von Bar 'Liability for Information and Opinions Causing Pure Economic Loss to Third Parties: A Comparison of English and German Case Law' in B Markesinis (ed) *The Gradual Convergence* (OUP, Oxford, 1994) 99ff; B Markesinis *The German Law of Obligations* 3rd edn (OUP, Oxford, 1997) Vol II (The Law of Torts); JM Thomson 'Delictual Liability for Pure Economic Loss: Recent Developments' 1995 *Scots Law Times* 139; Herbots 'Le Duty of Care et le dommage purement financier en droit comparé' (1985) 62 *Rev Droit International et Droit Comparé* 7–33; L Khoury 'The Liability of Auditors Beyond Their Clients: A Comparative Study' (2001) 46 *McGill Law Journal* 413; WH Van Boom, H Koziol and CGA Witting *Pure Economic Loss* (Springer, Wien, 2003).

[3] P Benson 'The Basis for Excluding Liability for Economic Loss in Tort Law' in DG Owen (ed) *The Philosophical Foundations of Tort Law* (OUP, Oxford, 1995) 427, 431. The same author, articulating a well known tòpos among tort lawyers (see eg G Viney *Introduction à la responsabilité* (LGDJ, Paris, 1995) 21ff; PG Monateri *La responsabilità civile* (Utet, Torino, 1998) 8ff).

associated with a rule of no liability and there a definition is likely to be found.[4] The contrasting approaches here obviously do not follow the familiar common law/civil law divide, for the civil law is itself divided to some extent over this question.

The approach we followed in the study on which this chapter is grounded was to make no supposition in advance about the nature or definition of this notion. We hoped it might be possible to let a neutral, fact-based questionnaire flush out the rules and responses of each national system. Therefore in framing the questionnaire we did not hesitate to mix into the facts instances of what can be seen as damage arising from a contract, property damage, personal injury and other infringements that particular traditions may regard as absolute rights (ie rights opposable to the world at large — *erga omnes*). In this way we were attempting to clarify the gray zones that exist between recoverable and non-recoverable loss. The questionnaire alleges facts and avoids the use of what could be classified as legal artifacts such as the expression 'pure economic loss' itself. Because there is no recognition of the term in some systems, and in any event less than complete consensus about its meanings in others, we rigorously excluded all use of the term in the hypotheticals. This enabled us to let the remedial dimension flow out of the reports without superimposing on it any theoretical template.

III PURE VS CONSEQUENTIAL ECONOMIC LOSS

The outcome of the research, about the underlying notion of 'pure economic loss', can be shortly stated as follows. What is made clear by the national reports is twofold: the negative cast and the patrimonial character of that loss. In countries where the term is well recognised its meaning is essentially explained in a negative way. It is loss without antecedent harm to the plaintiff's person or property. Here the word 'pure' plays a central role, for if there is economic loss that is connected to the slightest damage to person or property of the plaintiff (provided that all other conditions of liability are met) then the latter is called *consequential* economic loss and the whole set of damages may be recovered without question.[5] *Consequential* economic loss (sometimes also termed parasitic loss[6]) is

[4] G Schwartz refers to 'the general economic loss no liability doctrine' in his essay 'The Economic Loss Doctrine in American Tort Law: Assessing the Recent Experience' in Banakas (ed), above n 2, 103–30.

[5] Perhaps another way to describe pure economic loss is to say it does not arise as a consequence of some earlier physical loss, and it is not a court's substituted value for physical loss.

[6] For this usage, see *Prosser and Keeton on Torts* 5th edn (West Publishing Co, St Paul, Minnesota, 1984) §43, 291.

recoverable because it presupposes the existence of physical injuries, whereas pure economic loss strikes the victim's wallet and nothing else. In Sweden, where the legislator says that only victims of crimes may recover for pure economic loss, the Tort Law Act, §2 defines the notion exactly in these terms: 'In the present act, "pure economic loss" (*ren formögenhat-sskanda*) means such economic loss as arises without connection to personal injury or property damage to anyone'.[7] A similar definition seems to prevail in England and Germany.[8]

The reader will discern from these preliminary remarks that the distinction under discussion is highly technical, perhaps even artificial. This impression is based upon two technical features of the exclusionary rule. The first feature is that 'consequential' economic loss only describes a relationship of cause and effect *within the same patrimony* (the plaintiff's). All relation of cause and effect running *between patrimonies* is technically excluded. Put another way, when pecuniary loss is described as 'pure' (rather than 'consequential') it is apparent that each patrimony is viewed as an interruption of causation. For instance an injury to B (say the bread-winner of the family) may have an immediate and foreseeable economic consequence upon A (his dependent child). Yet this causal impact is disregarded by the way our subject is defined. The child's loss of support will not be called 'consequential' economic loss, though clearly it did arise as a 'consequence' of physical injury to a parent. It is clear, then, that those legal systems which employ these labels conceive of economic loss as an isolated phenomenon, as if the plaintiff's patrimony were a separate world, cut off from all others. It is also apparent that this logic defies economic and social reality. In the real world 'a practically unlimited range of interests are intertwined in an almost unlimited variety of ways'.[9] The affairs of economic actors are highly interdependent, connected to one another by a web of rights and duties that bind together contractual, proprietary and any other sort of legal interests. In these circumstances it is reasonably foreseeable that damage to any one interest may affect other interests. Indeed it has been rightly said that 'no reverberation from the initial damage, so long as it arises through this interdependence of interests, can intelligibly be distinguished as extraordinary or unforeseeable'.[10] Yet the inevitable effect (of what we might call the exclusionary rule's 'atomistic' approach to causation) is that the scope of 'consequential' loss

[7] W van Gerven et al (eds) *Tort Law — Scope of Protection* (Hart Publishing, Oxford, 1998) 44.
[8] See Lord Denning's statement that '... it is better to disallow economic loss altogether at any rate when it stands alone, independent of any physical damage' in *Spartan Steel & Alloys Ltd v Martin & Co Ltd* [1973] QB 27. Regarding *reiner vermögensschaden*, van Gerven, above n 7, 43, speaks of a 'worsening of one's overall economic position (loss of profit, diminution in the value of property, etc) that is not directly consequential upon injury to the person or damage to a particular piece of property'.
[9] P Benson, above n 2, 431.
[10] *Ibid*. See also G Brüggermeier *Common Principles of Tort Law* (BIICL, London, 2004) 93 ff.

is artificially narrow, and accordingly the incidence of 'pure' economic loss is greatly multiplied.

A second technical aspect is that, although all countries following the exclusionary rule may be in 'acoustical' agreement on the proposition that 'consequential loss' is recoverable, they actually do not agree in concrete instances how it will be applied. Since consequential loss is a causal construct influenced (in its ultimate results) by policy considerations, it is perhaps unsurprising to find divergent interpretation at the national level. Some national courts have developed rules that require a more stringent connection between antecedent physical loss and the economic harm that results. Under such rules the court may conclude that the plaintiff's loss was 'pure' (hence unrecoverable) because there was insufficient relation to prior physical harm sustained by the plaintiff. Yet judges in other systems, employing less exigent notions, may deem the same loss 'consequential' and thereby permit its recovery.[11]

Despite the foregoing caveats about the artificial and technical aspects of this concept, we must not lose sight of the fact that consequential economic loss (and for the purpose of this generalisation we apply this term of art even to systems which do not actually use it) is in principle recoverable in every European system within our study — whether the source of the loss is intentional or negligent conduct, or an activity subject to strict liability. Ignoring for the moment, then, the divergent European views toward the recoverability of 'pure' economic loss, here at least is an area of common ground that is worth noting.

Furthermore the recoverability of economic loss, even when 'pure', is not regarded as doubtful when such loss stems from the infringement of statutorily protected interests, such as those we met in our case studies,[12] and those protected by antitrust, copyright and patent laws.[13]

Taken in the aggregate, the above considerations lead us to say that consequential loss and 'pure' economic loss are not different in kind or in principle, but distinguishable only by the circumstances in which they

[11] For further details, see Editors' Comparative Comments under cases 1 ('Cable I — The Blackout') and 9 ('Fire in the Projection Booth') in M Bussani and VV Palmer, above n 1. Cf J Stapleton 'Comparative Economic Loss: Lessons from Case-Law Focused "Middle Theory"' (2002) 50 *UCLA Law Review* 531 ff; J Stapleton 'Cause-in-Fact and the Scope of Liability for Consequences' (2003) 119 *Law Quarterly Review* 388 ff, and Ch von Bar *The Common European Law of Torts* (OUP, Oxford, 2000) vol II 30–5, 487–9.

[12] See especially the answers to Case 4 ('Convalescing Employee') in M Bussani and VV Palmer, above n 1. Cf Ch von Bar, above n 11, 54–6.

[13] The same could be said as to some other fields, particularly the field of 'business torts'. Although legal systems such as France, the Netherlands, the UK and Portugal handle these problems with the help of the general law of obligations (the 6th book of the Dutch civil code devotes an entire chapter to unfair advertising), these subjects are not dealt with here. Since the rules in these areas largely depend on policy factors which are only partially common to our field and would deserve detailed investigation, reasons of space compelled the editors to place limits on the research. For a general survey, Ch von Bar, above n 11, 4–200, 245–9 and, more closely related to our issue, 52–6; W van Gerven, J Lever and P Larouche (eds) *Tort Law* (Hart Publishing, Oxford, 2000) 208–8, 358–94.

originate[14] and the technical limits which have been imposed on their recoverability.[15]

IV THE STANDARD CASES: A TAXONOMY

Broadly speaking, pure economic loss arises out of the interdependence of relationships and interests in the modern world. These relationships are sometimes two-dimensional and other times three-dimensional. In the

[14] It is of interest to note that breach of European Community law may entail liability for pure economic loss. The liability of the Community institutions and its servants in the performance of their duties finds its source in art 288(2) EC Treaty. The liability of a member State has its origins in the case law of the European Court of Justice, particularly the preliminary rulings pursuant to art 234 EC Treaty. It is true that under these provisions plaintiffs can recover only when s/he falls into a group of persons which the infringed provision was designed to protect, but no 'in principle' restriction is made regarding the interests that are protected. Indeed, since Community law is primarily concerned with economic matters, breaches of Community law will typically result in economic or purely economic losses. The compensability of these losses when caused by Community institutions has been clearly set forth in Cases C–104/89 and C–37/90 *Mulder v Council of the European Communities* [1992] ECR I–3061. With regard to the member States, their liability has been clearly endorsed in Cases C–46/93 and C–48/93 *Brasserie du Pêcheur v Germany; R v Secretary of State for Transport; Ex parte Factortame* [1996] ECR I–1029, wherein the ECJ explicitly rejects the use of German and English national rules which would have prevented individuals from benefiting from the use of Community law to impose liability on member States. The rejection was particularly important in the case of the English rule requiring proof akin to abuse of power to establish the tort of misfeasance in public office, and in the case of the German hierarchy of protected interests under BGB 823. For a comparative survey, see W van Gerven, J Lever and P Larouche (eds), above n 13, 889ff; see T Heukels and A McDonnell (eds) *The Action for Damages in Community Law* (Kluwer, Hague, 1997); P Craig 'Once More Unto the Breach: The Community, the State and Damages Liability' (1997) 113 *Law Quarterly Review* 67ff. See also B Markesinis, above n 2, 902ff.

It is a different, and still open issue, whether individuals are entitled to compensation under national law when other individuals infringe Community law and thereby cause economic loss. Under the laws of the Member States a right to recovery is generally acknowledged in cases of breach of a Community law provision which imposes direct obligations upon individuals — such as arts 81 and 82 EC Treaty, or other provisions having the so called 'horizontal' direct effect: see W van Gerven 'Bridging the Unbridgeable: Community and National Tort Laws after Francovich and Brasserie' (1996) 45 *International Comparative Law Quarterly* 507ff and, recently, upholding 'horizontal' direct effect of arts 81 and 82 EC Treaty, Case C–453/99 *Courage Ltd v Bernard Crehan* [2001] ECR I–6297.

[15] One should note that the exclusionary rule is associated with economic loss caused by negligent behavior, not intentional wrongdoing. European systems do not begin to diverge until the question becomes one of liability for negligence. All systems agree that intentionally inflicted pure economic loss is recoverable in circumstances where the conduct in question is regarded as culpable, immoral or contrary to public policy. The significance of this point is of more practical importance than it may appear at first sight. Its range of application may be somewhat greater than the narrow, infrequent form of liability which the words 'intentionally inflicted' harm suggest. In some systems a broad, flexible meaning is given to the 'intention' element (see eg Ch von Bar in B Markesinis (ed) *Gradual Convergence* above n 2, 104). Furthermore, though harder to prove than negligence, the incidence of financial fraud is not a rare occurrence. A consistent rule across Europe is therefore an important protection. Secondly, we think it is interesting to observe from the comparative point of view

following pages we attempt to draw up a taxonomy of the principal ways in which it arises within such relationships. Our list will not exhaust all the conceivable ways in which such damage may arise. Our only interest lies in tracing the most recurrent and typical patterns which we refer to as the 'standard cases'. Although we have sometimes borrowed and other times given new names to these standard situations, we have not attempted to explain or employ all of the descriptive labels and tags that writers and judges have used. These diverse and contradictory ideas are not always compatible with the results of our own study and would serve no purpose here. With these provisos in mind, we venture to set forth four categories that seem to be functionally and relationally distinct.[16]

1 'Ricochet Loss'

Ricochet loss classically arises when physical damage is done to the property or person of one party and that loss in turn causes the impairment of a plaintiff's right. This situation is three dimensional and certain authors call it 'relational economic loss'.[17] A direct victim sustains physical damage of some kind, while the plaintiff is a secondary victim who incurs only economic harm. To illustrate, A has a contract to tow B's ship. C's negligent act of sinking the ship makes it impossible for A to perform his contract and thus deprives him of expected profits. A's financial loss is the ricochet effect of C's negligence toward B. The loss is purely economic

that the shift to higher degrees of culpability tends to broaden the scope of recovery in all systems. This at least suggests that the exclusionary rule should not be conceived as a simple rule based solely on the nature of plaintiff's damage. The material nature of the loss, in our view, is no more than one element in a complex balancing which decides where and when limits will be imposed in tort. To tailor reasonable limits scholars, judges and legislators must consider other important factors as well, including the actor's state of mind. The existence of a balancing process is not so apparent in systems such as the French which appear to make little use of the distinction between intentional and careless fault, but the complex interaction of scienter with other factors clearly surfaces in the English and German systems. In those systems, where harm is intentionally inflicted, restrictions on the recoverability of the type of harm are dropped, and in addition, concepts of remoteness of causation are relaxed. As David Howarth correctly notes, the overall result is that intentionality removes restrictions on liability that do not exist in the first place in other jurisdictions. 'The General Conditions of Unlawfulness' in A Hartkamp et al (eds) *Towards a European Civil Code* 2nd edn (Kluwer, Hague, 1998) 411.

[16] For a longer taxonomic list consisting of eight categories (in which we think there is considerable overlap), see W Bishop and J Sutton 'Efficiency and Justice in Tort Damages: The Shortcomings of the Pecuniary Loss Rule' (1986) 15 *Journal Legal Studies* 347, 360–1. Benson's taxonomy consists of five situations, two of which he calls 'exclusionary situations'. His three other situations are called 'non-exclusionary': P Benson, above n 3, 427–30.

[17] See this terminology and analysis in R Bernstein *Economic Loss* 2nd edn (Sweet & Maxwell, London, 1998) 163ff and B Feldthusen *Economic Negligence* (Carswell, Toronto, 1989) 199ff.

since no property interest of A's has been impaired.[18] A ricochet loss can also arise from the impairment of an employment contract. For instance, B is a key employee in A's business or sporting team. C's negligent driving leads to B's death or incapacity, thus causing A's team or business to lose profits and revenues. Here B's injury is physical, but A's loss is purely financial.

2 'Transferred Loss' (Via Contract or by Operation of Law)

Here C causes physical damage to B's property or person, but a contract between A and B (or the law itself) transfers a loss that would ordinarily be B's onto A. Thus a loss *ordinarily falling on the primary victim* is passed on to a secondary victim. The transfer of the loss from its 'natural' to an 'accidental' bearer differentiates this from a case of ricochet loss where the damage in question is not transferred but is a distinct damage to the interests of the secondary victim.[19] These transfers frequently result from leases, sales, insurance agreements and other contracts that separate property rights from rights of use or specifically reallocate risk bearing. To illustrate, A is a time-charterer of a ship owned by B. The day before the time charter is to go into effect and while the ship is in B's possession, C negligently damages the ship's propeller, thus necessitating repairs and a two week delay, which causes A to lose all use of the ship. Here B suffers property damage and ordinarily B as owner would recover for the consequential loss of the ship's use, but the right of use had been transferred to A by the time charter. So A's loss is purely pecuniary because he has no antecedent property loss.[20] A similar effect can result under a sales contract which reserves title in B (seller) while the goods are in shipment but places the risk of loss in transit upon the buyer A. If the goods (still technically owned by B)[21] are damaged in transit by the carrier's negligence, then a loss normally incurred by the owner has been transferred to A. A's loss is purely financial since he has no property interest in the goods.[22]

A similar result is reached when the transfer occurs by operation of law. For instance B, A's employee, may be injured by the negligent driving of C and thus find himself unable to work for three months.

[18] The example closely follows *La Société Anonyme de Remorquage à Helice v Bennets* [1911] 1 KB 243.

[19] This category receives extensive consideration in Ch von Bar *The Common European Law of Torts* (OUP, Oxford, 1998) vol I, 507–12.

[20] The illustration is based upon *Robins Dry Dock v Flint* 13 F 2d 3 (2d Cir 1926), 275 US 303 (1927) as well as Case 8 ('The Canceled Cruise') in M Bussani and VV Palmer, above n 1.

[21] As is well known, who should be called the 'owner' of goods in shipment depends on the law applicable to the transfer of ownership, and above all on the validity and extent of the principle of transfer of possession. See Ch von Bar, above n 19, 509 (n 499 therein).

[22] This illustration is based upon *The Aliakmon* [1986] AC 785.

Nevertheless a statute requires A to continue to pay B's salary, even though no work is received in return. Thus what ordinarily would have been B's loss is statutorily transferred to A as a combined result of C's negligence and the effects of the pay continuation statute.[23]

Transferred loss cases are liability neutral from the perspective of the tortfeasor and should avoid fears of indeterminate liability. An additional argument in favour of an award of compensation is that the tortfeasor who is clearly liable to the primary victim should not benefit from the accidental operation of rules which by pure chance exclude him from liability.[24]

3 Closures of Public Markets, Transportation Corridors and Public Infrastructures

Here economic loss arises without a previous injury to anyone's property or person. There may be physical damage, but it is to 'unowned resources' that lie in the public domain.[25] A single negligent act may necessitate the closure of markets, highways and shipping lanes which no person owns, yet the closure inflicts economic loss directly on individuals whose livelihoods closely depend upon the use of these facilities. This category raises the greatest concern about liability to an indeterminate class in an indeterminate amount. Financial ripple effect is then at its maximum. To illustrate, C negligently spills chemicals into the river, and all traffic on the waterway is suspended for two weeks during a cleanup effort. As a result shippers must take more expensive overland routes, and marinas, boat suppliers, hotel operators, and commercial fishermen in the area suffer severe economic loss.[26] A similar chain of loss may arise when C negligently allows infected cattle to escape from his premises, and the government must order all cattle and meat markets to close. As a result broad classes of plaintiffs will suffer pure economic loss, including cattle raisers who are unable to sell their stock and butchers who are unable to obtain supplies.[27]

[23] The example is taken from Case 4 ('Convalescing Employee') in M Bussani and VV Palmer, above n 1.

[24] According to von Bar, the concept of transferred loss is intended 'to prevent someone appealing to rules whose purpose is not to protect that person, but to protect others': *The Common European Law of Torts*, vol I, above n 19, 510–11.

[25] V Goldberg 'Recovery For Economic Loss Following the Exxon Valdez Oil Spill' (1994) 23 *Journal Legal Studies* 1, 37.

[26] This illustration resembles the facts of Case 15 ('A Closed Motorway — The Value of Time') in M Bussani and VV Palmer, above n 1, as well as *Louisiana ex rel Guste v M/V Testbank (The Testbank)* 752 F 2d 1019 (1985).

[27] See the facts in Case 6 ('The Infected Cow') in M Bussani and VV Palmer, above n 1 and the case of *Weller v Foot & Mouth Disease Research Institute* [1966] 1 QB 569.

4 Reliance upon Flawed Data, Advice or Professional Services

Those who furnish advice, prepare data or render services concerning financial matters often understand that the information will be furnished to a client and then relied upon by third persons with whom they have no contractual relation. If the advice, data or services are carelessly compiled or executed, this may not necessarily breach the provider's contract with his/her client (even if there is breach, the damage will usually be strictly financial) but the relying third party will sustain pure pecuniary loss. For instance, C an accountant carelessly conducts an audit of B, a publicly traded company, and vastly overstates the company's net financial worth. Relying upon the accuracy of the audit, investor A buys shares in B at twice their actual value.[28] Here A's loss arises not in consequence of physical damage to B, but on the basis of misplaced reliance.[29] Similarly, erroneous information about a client's solvency may lead to financial losses. Thus A, before extending credit to B, takes the precaution of asking C (the merchant bank where B kept its account) for an assessment of B's creditworthiness. C carelessly replies that B is 'good for its ordinary engagements' (when in fact B would soon go into liquidation) and thereby influences A to advance credit and to lose a large sum.[30] Here A's loss is purely financial, not because it ricochets off or is transferred from someone else's physical damage, but because it arises directly from A's reliance.

Professional services for a client may cause pecuniary loss to a non-client. B, an elderly man, asks C, his lawyer, to prepare a will in which he will leave $100,000 to A. C takes no action for six months, whereupon B dies intestate and A thereby receives nothing.[31] A's loss is purely economic.

[28] See Case 17 ('Auditor's Liability') in M Bussani and VV Palmer, above n 1.

[29] According to Honoré, losses attributed to plaintiff's 'reliance' pose a causation issue which is different in kind than causation in the context of physical damage. His discussion seems pertinent to the concern of some that this category of pure economic loss opens the floodgates of liability. When a person is said to 'rely' on another's statement, he or she often has two or more (typically many more) reasons or motives for reaching a decision and acting on it. The question whether A's statement 'caused' B's response is highly indeterminate. A potential investor in Eldorado Mines, for instance, may be influenced by a false statement in a prospectus as well as by advice from his stockbroker, by his own review of the company books, and so forth. How are we to say that from among all these reasons that the false statement in the prospectus 'caused' his financial loss? T Honoré 'Necessary and Sufficient Conditions in Tort Law' in DG Owen (ed) *Philosophical Foundations of Tort Law* (Clarendon Press, Oxford, 1995) 382–3.

[30] These facts are taken from the well-known case of *Hedley Byrne & Co v Heller & Partners Ltd* [1964] AC 465 (HL). For other instances of pecuniary harm from incorrect information, see Case 18 ('Wrongful Job Reference') and Case 20 ('An Anonymous Telephone Call') in M Bussani and VV Palmer, above n 1. See also HB Schafer 'Liability of Experts and the Boundary between Tort and Contract' (2003) 3 *Theoretical Inquiries* 453 ff.

[31] See *White v Jones* [1995] 2 AC 207 (HL); *Lucas v Hamm* 11 Cal Rptr 727 (1967); *Ross v Caunters* [1980] Ch 297; and Case 14 ('Poor Legal Services') in M Bussani and VV Palmer, above n 1.

V PRESENT VS FUTURE LOSS

Examples given in the preceding paragraph would suggest that patrimonial injury may take two distinguishable forms. It may relate to the existing as opposed to the anticipated wealth of the victim. In the first sense, the plaintiff's present wealth may be simply depleted by poor financial advice, or by wasting time and petrol circumnavigating a motorway that was closed due to an accident. In the second sense, the plaintiff may instead lose that which he or she expected to acquire, such as the profits from productive machinery suddenly shut down, or a testamentary legacy lost because of a defectively drawn instrument, or a sport club's reduced gate receipts due to the accidental death of the club's star player. Sometimes, when an expectation is destroyed *in utero* and proof that it would have materialised is difficult, it is called the loss of a chance.[32]

As between these types of wealth, it is the loss of expected wealth — unrealised profits, cancelled legacies — which presents the sharpest question for tort systems to deal with. The difficulty is not simply that the demand for proof is more exigent — by definition expectancies explore a future that only might have occurred — but also the appropriateness of affording protection in tort. For when an economic expectation receives legal protection in tort, as in principle it does under French law, a plaintiff can be compensated to the same extent *as if* he or she were protected by a contract with the tortfeasor.[33] In countries where an exclusionary rule of tort law exists, we may find a tendency to say that wealth expectancies should be protected in contract.[34] For instance German courts are generally unable to approach the question through tort, but at the same time

[32] For instance: a commission unlawfully rejects a candidate's application for a job or a fellowship. See eg Conseil d'Etat, 12.11.1965, in Rec. Lebon, 1965, 613 ('le réquérant, évincé d'un concours auquel il se serait présenté avec des chances sérieuses de succès en raison de ses titres et travaux, a subi un préjudice'. As to the debate, see G Viney and P Jourdain 'Les effets de la responsabilité' in J Ghestin (ed) Traité Droit Civil 2nd edn (LGDJ, Paris, 1998) 71ff; N Jansen 'The Idea of a Lost Chance' in (1999) 19 *Oxford Journal Legal Studies* 271ff (discussing the German and English experience); PG Monateri, above n 3, 283 ff, 583ff.

[33] See G Viney and P Jourdain, above n 32, 71ff, 195ff; G Viney, above n 3, 360ff. See also our comparative Comments to Case 18 ('Wrongful Job Reference') in M Bussani and VV Palmer, above n 1 regarding the distinction to be made between cases in which the lost chance is to be understood as a distinct loss in itself (an autonomous loss), as distinguished from the case where the concept is invoked as an equitable means of proving a loss.

[34] Note for example the tense unease in the following statement from a British judge: 'I do not consider that damages for loss of an expectation are excluded in cases of negligence arising under the principle in *Hedley Byrne*, simply because the cause of action is classified as tortious. Such damages may in principle be recoverable in cases of contractual negligence; and I cannot see that, for present purposes, any relevant distinction can be drawn between the two forms of action…' per Lord Goff of Chieveley in *White v Jones* [1995] AC 207. On this subject see also J Stapleton 'The Normal Expectancies Measure in Tort Damages' (1997) 113 *Law Quarterly Review* 257; H Reece 'Loss of Chances in the Law' (1996) 59 *Modern Law Review* 188.

they willingly stretch contractual concepts that make the defendant liable to the plaintiff, though there is no actual contract between the parties[35].

In these circumstances it becomes difficult to tell where tort ends and contract begins. We seem to be at the frontier where functions meet and merge, for though it has been theorised that contract creates wealth whereas tort only protects that which we already have,[36] the notion of pure economic loss presents, at a European level, a challenge to traditional views about the relationship between contract and tort law. A distinguished Austrian scholar has pointed out that we must not lose our way in the conceptual shadows of this borderland.

> Liability based on tort and liability based on breach of contract usually are taken as clearly separated contrasts. But I think they are the two ends of liability based on fault and that between them there is a connecting chain of intermediate stages. This understanding is important because one has not to sort liability in one of these two categories and, therefore, is able to avoid abruptly different treatment of rather similar cases.[37]

VI LIABILITY REGIMES IN EUROPE

Whether the recovery of pure economic loss is tackled by legal systems through tort or contractual remedies is a question which depends on both the factual elements of the case on the table and the domain respectively assigned to the two remedial fields. Thus the goal of the following pages is to provide a general framework that situates the issue of pure economic loss within each liability regime and at the same time arranges these systems and rules in some functional and explanatory way.

Putting the initial focus of the survey on tort law rules is nothing but a tribute paid to reality. All legal systems under review officially start with conceiving of (or simply debating) compensation for pure economic loss within the domain of tort. We will try to make clear, however, how far contract law, in some systems, is able to penetrate in the tort citadel whenever the latter is unfit to meet the needs at stake.

VII FROM FAÇADES TO OPERATIVE RULES

In situating the problem of pure economic loss within a comparative perspective we will cast a glance upon the liability regimes of Europe,

[35] See below nn 12–14.
[36] JA Weir 'Complex Liabilities' in *XI International Encyclopedia of Comparative Law* (Martinus Nijhoff, Amsterdam, 1976) 5, n 6 therein: 'Contract is productive, tort law protective'.
[37] H Koziol (ed) *Unification of Tort: Wrongfulness* (Kluwer, Hague, 1998) 25. See also P Giliker 'A Role for Tort in Pre-contractual Negotiations? An Examination of English, French and Canadian Law' (2003) 52 *International Comparative Law Quarterly* 969 ff.

comparing the exterior architecture to the interior working of the system. It is well known that in modern legal systems we may at first sight observe two alternatives. There may be liability whenever a person causes damage to another; there may be liability only in certain typical situations. The former, known as the principle of *neminem laedere*, is the solution of the French *Code Civil*. The latter, enacted in the German BGB, was the solution traditionally associated with Roman law and traditional common law. Every tort system in our study may be seen as a variant of these two alternatives, and each individual tort structure is at least the beginning point for the analysis of the recoverability of pure economic loss. These imposing structures, however, are not necessarily the most reliable means of viewing liability rules or of predicting outcomes: if we were to depend upon them as the exclusive criteria of classification, this would not present the systems in a helpful way. As we explain below, a functional and explanatory analysis must distinguish appearances from reality. It must take into account a wide variety of factors, traits and formants in order to arrive at the essential differences and similarities between the systems.

In this perspective we are often called upon to distinguish between the system's façade and its interior, ie operational rules that lie behind or within it. What we mean by 'the façade' is simply the exterior wrapper, the outer appearance, or even better, the initial and dominant perception received by the observer regarding the recoverability of pure economic loss. In a codified system this perception is usually conveyed by the blackletter words the legislator has used; in an uncodified system it may be the words of judges hardened into precedents or the writings of old institutional writers. In either case the façade will be the objective set of public signals which *apparently* controls our issue. At first glance a given system may seem committed to a wide principle of recovery; another system may seem committed to a general rule of no recovery though a series of exceptions may be made. Or another system may seem resolutely opposed to all recovery because pure financial loss is regarded as an unprotected interest. These initial perceptions, we repeat, are due to the system's façade.

In resorting to the façade metaphor, we do not wish to imply that initial perceptions are always false and misleading. Obviously that would simply overstate the case. Nor can we say that all façades are mere camouflage for hidden forms of lawmaking. To the contrary, we have found that in a few systems the first impression given by the legislator or judge as lawgiver is also the lasting impression left by the jurisprudence and the doctrine. Even here we think the word façade is appropriate and useful to indicate a genuine or authentic impression that in fact withstands further scrutiny. Nevertheless, it is also clear that for certain systems the deeper one delves into the doctrine, the cases and the operational rules, the more one is surprised by the contradictions and contrasts between outer appearance and inner reality. What began as a general clause may be administered as a scheme of protection focused upon absolute rights — ie what German jurists refer to as rights to life, body, health, freedom, property enforceable against the world at large: *erga omnes*.[38] That, however, may not be the end of the story. For what appears to be a scheme of absolute rights may be a decoy for an expansion of contractual actions which function much like tort remedies. It is for this reason that accepting façades at face value can be hazardous; they are very rarely a sufficient basis for a functional classification of these systems.

Conscious, therefore, that façades are sometimes *trompe l'œil* and that interior solutions are the principal interest of our study, we have attempted to organise the material into three functional and explanatory groupings which we call the liberal, pragmatic and conservative regimes of tort. It is important to understand, however, that these may be subject-specific characteristics that have limited relevance outside of the context of pure economic loss. We emphasise this caveat for an obvious reason. Our purpose is not to describe the *general* characteristics of any of these systems: that would be worth a treatise unto itself in each case, and would have nothing to do with the precise issue we have selected. We must therefore confine our 'characteristics' to the subject at hand, without any pretension that they may be applied widely to other subjects not studied here.

VIII LIBERAL, PRAGMATIC AND CONSERVATIVE REGIMES

Keeping in mind the jurisdictions covered by our study,[39] within the *liberal regimes* we group together five countries: France, Belgium, Italy, Greece and Spain. A leading characteristic of a liberal regime is the presence of a unitary general clause in the codified law which does not, a priori, screen out pure economic loss. Lacking a *numerus clausus* of protected interests imposed by the legislator, these regimes have no in-principle objection to allowing compensation for stand-alone economic harm. The unlawfulness of causing such a loss is not an antecedent abstract question but only an outcome dependent upon whether the normal elements of fault liability are satisfied. These systems are not simply liberal in appearance and approach but in their results as well. As compared to other regimes, they yielded the greatest number of successful actions in our hypothetical cases.

[38] Discussed in J Gordley 'The Rule Against Recovery in Negligence for Pure Economic Loss: An Historical Accident' in M Bussani and VV Palmer, above n 1.
[39] Austria, Belgium, England, Finland, France, Germany, Greece, Italy, The Netherlands, Portugal, Scotland, Spain and Sweden.

A second characteristic is that liberal regimes reach solutions to questions of purely pecuniary loss almost exclusively on the basis of extra-contractual liability and not by crossing over to contract principles. The liberal regimes deal with pure economic loss autonomously in tort, unlike many conservative regimes where recourse to contractual and statutory solutions is a standard means of tempering the rigidity of the law of tort.

A final characteristic of this regime, but one difficult to discern and substantiate, is the possible use of surreptitious techniques to keep this liability issue under control. To the extent that judges in liberal regimes have any policy restraining recovery for pure economic loss, as some observers suspect they do,[40] they do not admit or deal with it openly. It would of course be possible to carry out such a policy covertly through subtle manipulation of the ordinary requirements of the general clause (particularly the causation requirement)[41] but judicial tendencies of this kind would be unavowed, uncertain and difficult to detect, concealed even from a fact-based method such as ours. The term pure economic loss and the debatable issues surrounding it therefore would remain generally unrecognised in the literature and jurisprudence of these countries.

The *pragmatic regimes* embrace England, Scotland and the Netherlands. Our choice of the term *pragmatic* relates to a shared approach to the problem and has little to do with how often a plaintiff succeeds. The judges in the Netherlands appear to be considerably more receptive to this form of loss than the judges in the United Kingdom, but it is the similarity in their reasoning, their technique and their candour which prompts us to group them with their English and Scottish counterparts.

These systems are characterised by a cautious case-by-case approach which carefully studies the concrete socio-economic implications of granting recovery for pure economic loss.[42] Results are not driven by the dictates of wide tort principle, nor by a checklist of absolute rights. The principal method of screening recoveries is through the 'duty of care' concept. The duty of care question is a matter of judicial policymaking that is overtly carried out by the judges. Each new situation requires an ad hoc

[40] See eg L Khoury 'The Liability of Auditors Beyond Their Clients: A Comparative Study' (2001) 46 *McGill Law Journal* 413; B Markesinis 'La politique jurisprudentielle et la réparation du préjudice économique en Angleterre: Une approche comparative' (1983) *Review International Droit Civil* 31, 44.
[41] In French law, for instance, the requirements of causation are applied strictly insofar as the liability of a company accountant (*commissaire aux comptes*) toward the public is concerned. Consequently compensation for pure economic loss is granted only rarely. See the French response, under Case 17 ('Auditor's Liability'), in M Bussani and VV Palmer, above n 1.
[42] It is important to note that the cases proceed on the basis of the *judge's* perception of the socio-economic consequences: there is no *evidence* of the economic effects of a finding of liability.

determination that a 'duty' to guard against this harm should exist at all. Unless this issue is decided affirmatively, there is no reason to proceed further and consider whether the normal elements of tortious liability have been satisfied.

Thus there is an abstract prior question to be answered, but unlike the approach in the conservative regimes, the question has not been pre-judged by a legislator, nor in our view, by a rigid conception of absolute rights. The judges themselves are expected to make a policy choice, and they exercise this function openly and discursively. And there seems to be no flight into contract law as relief against their own decisions which refuse liability in tort.[43] The tort scheme dominates the field.

Among the *conservative regimes* we have placed Germany, Austria, Portugal, Sweden and Finland. A striking characteristic of this regime is that pure economic loss does not figure among the so-called 'absolute rights' which receive protection under their tort law. Its exclusion from BGB §823.1's enumeration is well known and clear, but even in conservative systems where no enacted list is to be found, the same result has been achieved by other means. As developments in Austria and Portugal amply show, the judiciary's and/or the doctrine's readiness to import German doctrinal influence may result in a philosophy of absolute rights that is superimposed upon the general clause. The second characteristic is that the recoverability of pure economic loss is therefore an exception and any remedy must be found elsewhere in the system, either on the basis of more specific tort provisions or by an expansive application of contract principles. If we focus, however, upon recoveries permitted by the tort law system and make that the point of comparison, the system is quite conservative in its results. Answers to our questionnaire basically yielded far fewer successful actions than in the other regimes. This gives rise to a third characteristic: the recovery of pure economic loss in these systems often receives extensive lateral support from the law of contracts and/or certain statutory mechanisms, and when that lateral contribution is added to the overall picture, results in these systems are considerably liberalised. To the extent that these contractual actions have been stretched to function as tort remedies, the tort façade progressively becomes a misleading indicator.

Having considered these general characteristics rather abstractly, we turn to discuss some country's approach in greater detail. The choice falls upon the legal systems (France, England, Germany and Austria, in the order we will deal with them) whose features appear to be paradigmatic of each of the three façades we singled out.

[43] Of course, English contract law, which insists upon the requirement of consideration and rather restrictive notions of privity, makes recourse to contractual solutions theoretically very difficult.

IX FRANCE: AN ENIGMATIC LIBERALISM

The general formula *neminem laedere*, 'injure no one', is the basis of Article 1382 of the *Code Napoléon*, which reads 'any act whatever of a man which causes damage to another (*tout fait quelconque de l'homme qui cause à autrui un dommage)* obliges him by whose fault it occurred to make reparation'.[44] Because of its encompassing reach as well as its indeterminate potential, this unitary principle does not screen out recovery for pure economic loss. It does not set forth a *numerus clausus* of protected interests: the legislator imposes no *a priori* check upon the judge's free sense of what constitutes recoverable harm.[45] Therefore the question whether causing pure economic loss is a source of tortious liability becomes a judicial question, a matter of jurisprudence and the advice of doctrine. Put another way, the protection of pure economic loss in France must be viewed as an oracular outcome, for there is no external, pre-existing concept of unlawfulness concerning this loss to determine or to exclude liability.

Articles 1382 and 1383 have consistently been found not to contain any *a priori* limitations on the scope or nature of protected rights and interests, nor to contain an *a priori* class of protected persons. Thus there has been no difficulty in admitting the economic loss of victims by ricochet, whether it be the expenses of a father forced to make repeated voyages to the bedside of his son who was injured in Greece through the defendant's negligence,[46] or the expenses of an unmarried cohabiting partner of the injured victim.[47] The French general clause is considered hostile to the theory called Aquilian relativity (*relativité aquilienne*) which explores the 'purpose' of legal rules to find the ambit of a defendant's liability to the plaintiff, thus de-emphasising the role of causation. But in French law there is no relational 'duty' requirement as in English law and the role of causation is not de-emphasised.[48] In this optic, the concept of unlawfulness nearly becomes invisible: one could say it has been globally reassigned to the subsidiary determinations of fault, causation and damage.

While the unlawfulness question may have disappeared from view, it may possibly be operating at a different level, the level of judicial policy working tacitly within rather capacious notions. Obviously, the French judge retains at least some rough concept of unlawfulness, for there are

[44] Art 1383 adds that 'Each one is liable for the damage he causes not only by his own act but also by his negligence or imprudence'.

[45] Of all the European codes, writes Ch von Bar, above n 19, 22, 'the French Code Civil gives the courts the least guidance'.

[46] Cass 1st Ch 20 Dec 1960, D 1961.141, note Esmein.

[47] See W van Gerven et al, above n 7, 144–6; Y Chartier 'La Réparation du Préjudice' (Dalloz, Paris, 1983) nn 184–98.

[48] G Viney, above n 3, 566; Ead 'Pour ou contre un principe général de responsabilité pour faute?' (2002) 49 *Osaka University Law Review* 31, 44; W van Gerven *et al*, above n 7, 32.

still areas where a person is free to cause harm, including pure economic harm, without incurring liability under the *Code Civil*.[49] An entrepreneur may deliberately set up business next door to a business competitor and through fair competition drive him into bankruptcy.[50] These instances, however, are exceptions that have been carved away from the general presumption in favor of actionability. They emerge from an inductive search of the case law. By developing justifications for non-liability based on the existence of particular factors, it has become possible to absolve a person who causes harm without abandoning the general principle that a person should make reparation for all harm he or she causes. The exercise of policy is more difficult to detect, however, at the discrete level where the judge creates no exception but simply attributes a negative result in the particular case to a tenuous causal link or perhaps to the indeterminateness of the plaintiff's loss. Here unlawfulness is not a severable hurdle but simply the result of applying subsidiary elements of act, fault, causation and damage. Judgments denying relief at that level are not unknown in the jurisprudence. For example, a partnership could not recover for deals that failed to be concluded when the company president who was negotiating them was negligently injured.[51] A creditor whose borrower was negligently killed could not recover from the tortfeasor the sums which the deceased could not repay.[52] The reasoning in these cases seems unexceptional: the harm was not considered a 'certain' or 'direct' consequence of the negligent act. Obviously a latent concern with

[49] For instance, a doctor who negligently fails to terminate a woman's pregnancy incurs no liability to the parents for the extra expenditures of supporting a healthy but unwanted child. Civ. 1re, 25 juin 1991, D. 1991. 566, note Ph. Le Tourneau. It has been held, however, by the Cour de Cassation en Assemblée Plénière (17.11.2000, JCP, 2000, n 50, II.10438, pp 2293 ff), that an infant could claim damages resulting from being born with a handicap in circumstances where the negligence of his mother's doctor prevented her from exercising her choice to avoid giving birth to a handicapped child.

[50] See G Viney, above n 3, 375.

[51] Cass 2nd Civ Ch, 12 June 1987, JCP 1987.IV.286.

[52] Cass 2nd Civ Ch, 21 Feb 1979, JCP 1979.IV.145. On similar facts, see Cass 2nd Civ Ch. 25 June 1975, Bull Civ, II, no 195. But see also, in the reverse perspective, Cass, 1st Civ Ch, 13 Feb 2001, JCP 2002.II.10099, note C. Lisanti-Kalczynsky. B Markesinis, above n 40, 45–6, argues that the latter affords an excellent example of a concealed policy to place limits upon the recovery of pure economic loss via the manipulation of causal requirements. The plaintiff's debtor was killed in a car accident and the debtor's heirs refused to accept his succession. Accordingly the succession could not pay the debts of the deceased, including the debt owed to the plaintiff, so the plaintiff sought redress from the tortfeasor responsible for the car accident. The Court of Appeal ruled, however, that the plaintiff's loss should not be viewed as the 'certain' result of the defendant's act and it was thus unrecoverable. In view of the length of time for repayment and the risks that the debtor might discontinue his work, the anticipated repayment was aleatory. The Cour de Cassation, however, quashed this decision, ruling that repayment of a loan of money is never aleatory in a juridical sense, and returned the case to another Court of Appeal. The Court of *renvoi* in turn ruled that while the loss was certain, it was not 'direct', since the refusal of the heirs to accept the debtor's succession broke the chain of causation with a *nova causa interveniens*. Bordeaux, 17 mai 1977, D, 1978 (observ. Larroumet), and this decision was confirmed by the Cour de Cassation. Cass Civ 2e, 21 fév 1979, JCP 1979, IV, 145.

saddling excessive liability upon the tortfeasor may have influenced these pronouncements, but no one can be sure.[53]

X THE ACTUAL IMPACT OF THE REFUSAL OF CONCURRENCE OF ACTIONS

A particularity of French law is the *non-cumul* of tort and contract actions. Unique in all of Europe,[54] this rule, in our view, probably propels French tort law in the direction of allowing reparation for pure economic loss. Like Molière's *Gentilhomme* who spoke prose or poetry and nothing in between, the French plaintiff discovers that he or she must sue in contract, if he or she has one with the defendant; if there is no contract, he or she must sue the defendant in delict.[55] If the plaintiff is refused relief in contract for pure economic loss, he or she cannot then sue in tort, for there is generally no concurrence of actions. The rule has been praised for bringing certainty of application to a system which, since its general delictual clause incorporates pure economic loss within its reach, would otherwise lack the theoretical means to prevent unrestrained concurrence or to exclude from its compass *dommage purement contractuel*.[56] We would argue that it has another important effect as well. This forced choice has, in our view, encouraged the attitude that contract and tort should be broadly equivalent conduits for the recovery of pure economic loss. This is not to claim that the two actions operate in an identical manner. They do not. For instance, the prescriptive period is usually shorter for most actions in contract,[57] and clauses limiting liability do not operate in delict.[58] Rather,

[53] There might be a relative lack of emotive appeal in pure economic loss as compared to the flesh and blood of physical damages. If cases of pure economic loss are intuitively less esteemed by French judges, as L Deschamps suggests ('La réparation du prejudice pur in droit français', in S Banakas, above n 2, 89–101) then perhaps one might expect cold detachment in the causal analysis that discourages recoveries.

[54] See G Viney *La Responsabilité: Conditions* (LGDJ, Paris, 1982) nn 216–31; Ch von Bar, above n 19, 449ff; T Weir, above n 36, n 52; S Banakas 'Liability for Incorrect financial Information: Theory and Practice in a General Clause System and in a Protected Interests System' (1999) 7 *European Review Private Law* 261, 268.

[55] There are a few recognised exceptions to the rule (for details, see P Malaurie and L Aynès *Droit Civil: Les Obligations* 1st edn (Cujas, Paris, 1985) nn 526–8, 370–3; G Viney, above n 3, 403, 411ff) but these are not germane to the discussion in the text.

[56] von Bar, above n 19, 452ff; P Schlechtriem 'The Borderland of Tort and Contract — Opening a New Frontier?' (1988) 21 *Cornell International Law Journal* 467ff.

[57] Contractual periods vary from one, two, five or ten years, depending on the type of contract, and contractual prescription begins to run from a relatively fixed date. See Code Civil Arts 2270, 2272–7. Prescription in delict, however, is generally ten years after *manifestation* of the damage and thus the life of an action is liable to be much greater than in contract. Code Civil Art 2270–1 (Loi 5 July 1985). Note, however, that tort actions based on defective products will prescribe in three years from the date of the victim's knowledge of his own damage and the wrongdoer's identity (CC 1386–17) but in no event after the product has been in circulation ten years (CC 1386–16).

[58] For further differentiations, see Malaurie et Aynès, above n 55, 360–2 nn 517–20 therein.

our point is attitudinal. Having left the litigant without an option, French law can ill afford to discriminate on the sheer nature of the damage (as some 'conservative' systems do) against tort plaintiffs presenting pure economic loss cases. That would be so unfair to one class of litigants that we think the rule, in the French context, serves to ease objections to this form of loss and to foster the expectation that tort law will achieve results in parallel with the law of contract.

To sum up, France presents an appearance of maximum permissiveness toward pure economic loss as well as an appearance of maximum indifference to the strong policy arguments usually made elsewhere against its recovery. Rudden draws attention to the paradox that 'the French seem to ignore almost all of Cardozo's warnings without suffering ill effects'.[59] Against all predictions that the sky will fall, the French judge is serene. To those who argue that the floodgates of liability must be firmly closed, the French experience must seem counterintuitive, an empirical enigma awaiting an answer.

XI THE PRAGMATIC REGIME OF ENGLAND

Among pragmatist regimes — which, as we said, show no recourse to contract law as relief against tort law rules which refuse compensation — one that can be studied to usefully serve the limited purposes of this chapter is England.

As is well known, the English façade tends to make a continental lawyer think more of the criminal law (where all crimes are typically nominate) than the law of tort.[60] Most of these torts arose in defence of protecting a plaintiff's life, limb and property and are far removed from affording relief for pure economic loss. There are, to be sure, a series of intentional economic torts, notably actions for deceit, interference with trade, inducing breach of contract, passing off, misfeasance in public office,[61] intimidation and conspiracy, and if the defendant has intentionally caused such loss, the claim for pure economic loss may fit into one of these pigeonholes. If the loss was occasioned by negligence, however, these actions are unavailable. The plaintiff's chief recourse must therefore be to the tort of negligence.

[59] B Rudden 'Torticles' (1991–92) 6/7 *Tulane Civil Law Forum* 105, 107.
[60] C von Bar, above n 19, 281 n 254. The language of the common law has always made a connection between civil and penal redress. 'We "commit" a tort as we "commit" an offense. We can be "guilty" of either or both; and all our crimes are nominate'. B Rudden, above n 59, 126.
[61] Cf S Arrowsmith *Civil Liability and Public Authorities* (Earlsgate Press, Winteringham, 1992). See *David v Abdul Cader* [1963] 1 WLR 834 (PC); and, obiter in *X (some minors) v Bedfordshire County Council* [1995] 2 AC 633 (HL); *Three Rivers District Council v Governor and Company of the Bank of England* [2003] 2 AC 1 (HL).

The generic tort of negligence would appear, at first glance, to hold great promise for the recovery of pure economic loss. Animated by the 'neighbour principle' which *Donoghue v Stevenson* established in 1932, this tort has been compared to a general clause covering all forms of negligent behavior. This is generally true within the realm of protection from physical harm (bodily injury or damage to property).[62] But according to a leading authority, *Murphy v Brentwood District Council*,[63] negligence is not primarily applicable to the compensation of pure economic loss. This means that the nature of the plaintiff's damage controls the existence of a duty to avoid causing it. Indeed, the common law as a matter of policy begins with the proposition that there is, as a rule, no duty of care to avoid causing pure economic loss. The occasions upon which such a duty is recognised are exceptional and must be kept exceptional. This deep misgiving is based upon an instinctive fear of wide liability, customarily expressed by recourse to the floodgates metaphor or the 'nightmare scenario', but more fundamentally by a cautious case by case approach which studies the economic and social implications of each extension. The judges are willing to impose a 'duty of care' only when satisfied on utilitarian grounds that — in the particular case brought before them — it is socially and economically convenient to do so.

These exceptional cases are highly fact-sensitive and cover narrow fact situations. The exceptions began with *Hedley Byrne & Co Ltd v Heller & Partners*[64] and then multiplied. The general principle of no liability for pure economic loss survives, but with a number of exceptions that may be increased in the future if the courts find it 'fair, just and reasonable' to do so.[65] Thus far the exceptions are limited to negligent misstatements made and relied upon (in a context of 'virtual' contract),[66] negligent

[62] Even here the principle has been overridden in certain exceptional situations where, for reasons of policy, it was though inadvisable to impose a duty of care, though harm to plaintiff's property was the foreseeable result of defendant's negligence. See eg *The Nicholas H* [1996] AC 211.

[63] [1991] 1 AC 398.

[64] [1964] AC 465.

[65] On the meaning of this phrase, which reserves judicial options for future development (in marked contrast to the more principled methodology announced in *Anns v Merton London Borough Council* [1978] AC 728 (HL)), see eg *Caparo Industries plc v Dickman* [1990] 2 AC 605 (HL).

[66] *Hedley Byrne*, above n 30. One should be aware, however, that if, after a misrepresentation, the parties actually enter into a contract with each other, it is doubtful whether there is any practical need to resort to the rule of *Hedley Byrne*, since liability may end up being based on contract under s 2(1) of the *Misrepresentation Act 1967* (UK).The text provides that 'Where a person has entered into a contract after a misrepresentation has been made to it by another party thereto and as a result thereof he has suffered loss, then, if the person making the misrepresentation would be liable to damages in respect thereof had the misrepresentation been made fraudulently, that person shall be so liable notwithstanding that the misrepresentation was not made fraudulently, unless he proves that he had reasonable ground to believe and did believe up to the time the contract was made that the facts represented were true'. Through this rule 'the tort of negligence became otiose' in this context: Ch von Bar, above n 19, 449.

interference with the performance of a contract,[67] negligent defamation in the writing of a reference for a former employee,[68] professional negligence in the drawing up of a will,[69] and breach of statutory duty.[70] What appears characteristic and consistent in these exceptions is the limited quantitative exposure of the defendant to a defined number of plaintiffs, or even better, a single plaintiff. The danger of unbounded financial repercussion is avoided. The total liability can be calculated in advance as not exceeding the value of a lost legacy, a lost job or a lost investment. The plaintiff is a particular individual — the potential legatee of a will or a former employee — whose interests are very distinctly contemplated by the defendant at close range. But the presence of other factors which demonstrate a closer degree of proximity between the parties than mere foreseeability of economic harm may be insisted upon, such as the defendant's 'assumption of responsibility' for the plaintiff's economic well being coupled with the plaintiff's reliance upon it.[71] The class of claimants is thereby limited, as if an invisible privity paradigm structured the resulting bond in tort.[72]

It may be noted that although actions may be brought concurrently, a contract action cannot be used in these circumstances for there is no 'consideration' and therefore no contract between plaintiff and defendant. Given its insistence on consideration, England's rigid contract law cannot protect legal strangers against such losses. It was therefore faced with the choice either to expand its tort law opportunistically or to deny these actions altogether.[73]

XII THE CONSERVATIVE REGIMES OF GERMANY AND AUSTRIA

In a volume devoted such as this one to the remedies which lay astride contract and tort law, it is doubtless that what we called 'conservative'

[67] *Junior Books v Veitchi* [1983] 1 AC 520 (HL). This Scottish case, however, has been disapproved in almost every later English case. See also J Stapleton 'Duty of Care Factors: A Selection from the Judicial Menus' in P Cane and J Stapleton (eds) *Essays in Honour of J Fleming* (OUP, Oxford, 1998) esp nn 82–3; JM Thomson 'A Prophet Not Rejected in His Own Land' (1994) 110 *Law Quarterly Review* 361.
[68] *Spring v Guardian Assurance plc* [1995] 2 AC 296 (HL).
[69] *White v Jones* [1993] 3 WLR 7301(CA); [1995] 2 AC 207 (HL).
[70] For relevant references, see Ch von Bar, above n 19, 328ff.
[71] The phrase 'assumption of responsibility' originates in *Hedley Byrne,* above n 30, 528 (Lord Devlin). It seems to make recourse to an underlying contract model to earmark occasions when it is appropriate to impose a duty of care: the assumption of responsibility and reliance upon it must be voluntary. See Lord Goff's speech in *Henderson v Merrett Syndicate Ltd* [1995] 2 AC 145 (HL), discussing the role played by voluntariness. See also JM Thomson *Delictual Liability* (Butterworths, London, 1994) 59.
[72] The opposite view is maintained in Germany. See below nn 12–14.
[73] B Markesinis 'An Expanding Tort Law — The Price of a Rigid Contract Law' (1987) 103 *Law Quarterly Review* 354.

regimes deserve the highest degree of interest. This is why we think it useful to dwell on two jurisdictions of this group. Indeed, both Germany and Austria offer, though from different starting points, a good example of how the operative rules of a legal system can be stretched in order to meet the needs of the victims of pure economic loss.

XIII GERMANY: NARROW IN TORT BUT WIDE IN CONTRACT

As we have seen, in spite of their conspicuous theoretical and actual differences liberal and pragmatic regimes sometimes end up screening and refining the pure economic loss issue through the inner technicalities of tort law. To the contrary, the German legal system seems to deny even preliminary access to this kind of damages. Indeed, this prophylactic role is vested in a text that envisions liability only for injuries to certain enumerated rights. According to § 823(1) of the BGB, individuals are liable if they wilfully or negligently injure 'the life, body, health, freedom, property or other right' of the victim. Deliberately excluded in this list of so-called 'absolute rights' is any reference to injuries of a purely financial kind. It is therefore undisputed that, as a basic rule, pure economic loss is not recoverable in tort. Compensation may be obtained in tort in some exceptional situations, but the plaintiff must find a cause of action in some provision other than § 823(1) BGB.[74]

On the surface, German tort law rules have changed little since their enactment more than a century ago. The real change has been accomplished through case law. While this is certainly not a phenomenon peculiar to German law,[75] nevertheless it is worth stressing if we are to understand a system that attempted a rigid legislative solution.

[74] For instance, under §824 BGB, which provides that a person who declares or publishes, contrary to the truth, a statement which is likely to endanger the credit earnings or prosperity of another is liable for 'any damage' arising therefrom, even if he does not know of its untruth but should know of it. Here the protection against pure economic loss is the crux of the rule, but its scope is narrowed by the privilege granted in §824(2) (on this subject, and for further references see, in English, B Markesimis and H Umberath *The German Law* of *Torts* 4th edn (Hart Publishing, Oxford, 2002) 892f; W van Gerven, J Lever and P Larouche, above n 13, 65ff, 189. This provision has some relevance to the resolution of Cases 18 ('Wrongful Job Reference') and 20 ('An Anonymous Telephone Call') in M Bussani and VV Palmer, above n 1.

[75] Towards the end of the last century, French courts developed a case law imposing liability for making a void contract, for seduction, for misleading information, for unfair competition, and so forth — all pursuant to a code that left open the meaning of 'dommage' and the interests to be protected. The courts in Germany, at the same time, felt the need to impose liability in the same types of cases, so that the legislator, in drafting the code, was able to enumerate the cases in which liability would be imposed: R Sacco 'Legal Formants: A Dynamic Approach to Comparative Law' (1991) 39 *American Journal Comparative Law* inst II. See also J Gordley, above n 38.

For instance, the German Civil code requires the violation of a right (an 'absolute' one) but new rights have been added to the traditional set through interpretation. In this way German law developed the so-called 'right of the established and ongoing commercial enterprise'. Something similar happened to § 823(2) BGB, where wording about the infringement of 'a statute intended for the protection of others' became a vehicle to compensate pure financial losses arising out of such infringement, provided that the type of loss can be included within the sphere of the statutory aim.[76]

But this is not all. §826 BGB provides that a person is liable if she intentionally causes harm to another in a manner contrary to public policy. To understand the subjective requirements of this provision, it is not deemed necessary that 'the defendant actually intended to cause harm'; it will be enough 'if he was conscious of the possibility that harm might occur and acquiesced in its doing so'.[77] The role this rule plays with regard to our issue can be appreciated if one looks at the factual situations to which it has mainly been applied. These are, for example, participating as a third person in a breach of contract committed by a contracting party, delaying someone's bankruptcy in order to obtain personal benefit at the expense of other creditors, giving false information or omitting to give information in circumstances where there is a duty to give it.[78]

XIV THE FLIGHT TO CONTRACT

In solving questions of pure economic loss, contract remedies are more widely employed in Germany than in other countries. The reason for contract's enlarged role is probably twofold : on the one hand, apart from rules permitting the concurrence of tort and contract actions, tort law is considered too weak and narrow to safeguard all financial interests that merit legal protection. On the other hand, contract claims may seem to be the relatively safer path to those who dread unleashing the floodgates of tort, since there is certainly less danger of boundless damages occurring in a breach of contract situation. For whatever reason, courts and scholars certainly expanded the sphere of contractual liability beyond the limits marked by the BGB. This was accomplished through the exploitation of various devices, including the much longer prescriptive period in

[76] Ch von Bar, above n 19, 45ff, 49.

[77] K Zweigert and H Kötz *Introduction to Comparative Law* 3rd edn (Weir translation Clarendon, Oxford, 1998) 463; B Markesinis, above n 2, 895.

[78] K Larenz and Canaris *Lehrbuch* 13th edn (Besonderer Teil, München, 1994) 276. See other references in Ch von Bar 'Liability for Information and Opinions Causing Pure Economic Loss to Third Parties: A Comparison of English and German Case Law' in B Markesinis (ed) *The Gradual Convergence* above n 2, 104ff; and M Coester and B Markesimis 'Liability of Financial Experts in German and American Law' (2003) 51 *American Journal of Comparative Law* 275 ff.

contract (thirty years as opposed to three[79]), the greater ease of establishing breach of contract rather than fault, (§282 BGB) and the stronger regime of vicarious liability in contract (§278 BGB). The range of contractual duties was stretched to include 'implied' duties of care, so that liability might arise not only from the violation of the parties' express obligations but also the breach of a host of judicially-imposed duties of care. German interpreters likewise extended these duties over time so that in some cases they precede the conclusion (*culpa in contrahendo*)[80] and survive the termination or the performance of the contract itself.

The most important innovation of all, however, was that courts and commentators lowered the privity barrier in contract and applied these duties in favor of those who were not parties to any contract. The principal instrument in this regard is the 'contract with protective effects for third parties' (*Verträge mit Schutzwirkung für Dritter*) which brings strangers to a contract under its umbrella and permits them to sue a promisor for breach of one of the contract's secondary obligations, notably (for our subject) some breach causing purely financial harm to the plaintiff. The function of the contract with protective effects is arguably tort-like in that the protected third party need not stand in a close personal relationship to the promisor nor be specifically identified in advance. At the same time it is operationally free of the 'absolute rights' requirement of German tort law and permits recovery of purely financial harm.[81] Other kinds of economic losses may also be handled by contract law. This will include the multi-purpose device of pre-contractual liability (*culpa in contrahendo*) and the extended application of the joint and several liability rules to redress the loss incurred by the contractor.

All these rules are firmly established today and, as a result, many cases that an English or French lawyer would consider solely a matter of tort law are actionable in Germany in contract.

[79] On this point however, the 'Gesetz zur Modernisierung des Schuldrechts' — in BGBl, 29 November 2001, I, Nr 61, p 3138 ff, in force as from 1 January 2002 — has totally changed the legal landscape, establishing different terms for the prescription of tort (up to 30 years) and contract (up to 10 years) actions. See H-P Mansel 'Die Neuregelung des Verjährungsrecht' in *Neue Juristische Wochenschrift*, 2000, 89 ff; W Däubler, 'Neues Schuldrecht — ein erster Überblick', in 2001, *Neue Juristische Wochenschrift*, 3729 ff; M. Schwab, 'Das neue Schuldrecht im Überblick', in *JuS*, 1, 2002, 1 ff. See also Heidrich and Rehm Chapter 3 above.

[80] See its application to Case 19 ('Breach of Promise') in M Bussani and VV Palmer, above n 1. Under this doctrine contractual duties may arise as soon as the parties set up a pre-contractual 'contact', thus well before any contract is concluded and even when none is ever in fact concluded. See B Markesinis, above n 2, 688ff.

[81] It is not the only possibility under German law. Another institution of possible application in this field (but not relevant to our cases) is the *Drittschadensliquidation* which B Markesinis — in *The German Law of Torts* (OUP, Oxford, 1990) 47–9 — describes as a quasi-contractual judge-made doctrine that allows a creditor to a contract to claim in contract for loss resulting from its breach, even though the loss falls not upon him but upon a third party.

XV AUSTRIA: A MASSIVE INTERIOR TRANSPLANT

Austrian code provisions on delict bear the same natural law imprint which inspired French codistic rules. The scope of protection is seemingly not limited by the typecast actions of German law. Article 1295 ABGB provides:

> A person is entitled to demand indemnification for the damage from a person causing an injury by his fault; the damage may have been caused either by the violation of a contractual duty or without regard to a contract.

Yet paradoxically, as far as operative rules and outcomes are concerned, Austrian law follows the intellectual lead of German thought[82] and must be classified among the conservative tort regimes of Europe. Thus, as a general rule, pure economic loss is not recoverable in tort. There are a few tort provisions which permit compensation but on an exceptional basis. As in Germany, therefore, this has prompted an expansion of contractual actions somewhat to redress the deficit in tort. We will look first at available tort actions and then turn to contract.

XVI THE TRANSFORMED GENERAL CLAUSE

Rather than a change of façade, Austrian courts and scholars have redecorated the interior of this provision. They have restricted the class of persons entitled to damages: 'a person', as mentioned in art 1295 ABGB, is not any person. Likewise 'a damage' is not any kind of damage, but is limited to the *direct* infringement of life, body, health and property. In this manner Austrian judges and scholars crafted an approach to pure economic loss along German lines despite an utterly different legislative prescription.

Thus, the subject of pure economic loss (*reiner Vermögensschaden*) did not attract much juristic interest in Austria until thirty years ago when the concept itself was taken from German law together with its policy justifications.

The interior of the Austrian general clause was apparently transformed on the basis of three general arguments: a) a policy rationale rooted in the perceived need to control the risk of a 'boundless inflation of claims for liability for damage';[83] b) heavy reliance upon the use of simple causal labels to close the floodgates; Austrian judges and scholars systematically control recovery by characterising the causal connection to pure economic

[82] For a short and useful historical survey of cultural factors which led Austrian jurists, from the second half of the 19th century, to fall back on German legal thought, see K Zweigert and H Kötz, above n 77, 160ff.

[83] W Posch and Schilcher 'Introduction' to Austrian Report, on file with the authors.

loss as indirect, as opposed to direct;[84] c) recourse to the same unlawfulness criteria found in German law, with the result that purely financial loss does not qualify as infringement of an absolute right. To be sure this kind of reasoning was or is actually shared by other legal models,[85] but the stark contrast between the code's French façade and its German interior is more remarkable than elsewhere[86] and once again illustrates the need to consider all legal formants and meta-legal factors in describing and articulating liability rules.

Turning our attention from the general clause, we find other code provisions which are more favourable to the recovery of pure economic loss, but these cover somewhat exceptional situations. One is Art 1295(2) which states: 'A person who intentionally injures another in a manner in violation of public morals is liable therefor . . .'. This provision protects against purely financial damage, but only when the tortfeasor commits a 'truly grave, abominable wrong'.[87]

Another exceptional basis in tort relates to the infringement of a statute which is intended for the protection of others. Again, damages for pure economic loss can be obtained, whether the protective statutory rule was broken negligently or intentionally: however, it must be clear that the statute was intended to protect against this type of loss.[88]

XVII THE RESORT TO CONTRACTUAL ACTIONS

Having veered widely from the danger of 'boundless' claims in tort, the Austrian interpreters called upon the contractual actions to bring greater

[84] Thus in cable cases, Meroni-like cases and others, it seems that the Austrian courts dogmatically label the financial loss as 'indirect', as a matter of policy in order to limit liability, not because of a careful application of the principles of causation. See the reasoning in the answers to Cases 1 ('Cable I — The Blackout'), 2 ('Cable II — Factory Shutdown'), 3 ('Cable III — The Day to Day Workers') and 5 ('Requiem for an Italian All Star'), in M Bussani and VV Palmer, above n 1.

[85] Leaving aside the role vested in causation throughout all tort law systems, it suffices to advert to the historical prominence of the notion of *illicéité* within French tort law debate, or of the overt reference to policy factors in scholarly and judicial opinions within the common law systems — reference which seems to have a more cryptic, but no less incisive role in German law.

[86] This disparity has not been immune to criticism. See RR Reischauer in P Rummel *Kommentar zum ABGB*, II, 2nd edn (Abteilung für Allgemeine Zivilrechtsdogmatik Linz 1992) §1294 n 16, observing that the 'continuous squinting at the German BGB has obscured the view'.

[87] W Posch and Schilcher, above n 83.

[88] See Art 1330. Another ground for recovery arises for negligent advice or statements given by experts and others with specialised knowledge: Arts 1299, 1300. This last provision states:

> An expert is liable when he gives, for a consideration, negligently bad advice in matters of his art or science. In other cases, a person giving advice is liable only for damage which he has knowingly caused to another by giving the advice.

balance into the system. In the 1960s courts and scholars accepted from Germany the notion of contractual liability for the breach of pre-contractual duties (the theory of *culpa in contrahendo*)[89] and they also readily imported the concept of 'contracts with protective effects' for third parties.[90] The doctrine of 'positive violation of contract' is another import from Germany that permits wider contractual liability. A positive violation is assumed in the case of the breach of an implied duty of care and protection, and such constructive duties may include the duty to respect a contracting party's financial interests. As a consequence, these contractual actions were expanded well beyond their original limits. Nevertheless, it would appear that the Austrian Supreme Court is somewhat more hesitant than German courts to accept recoverability of pure economic loss whenever a pre-contractual duty or a duty *vis-à-vis* a third party who is within the protective effect of a contract is broken.[91]

XVIII CONCLUSION

In the above pages we have attempted to set forth a coherent way of describing the various approaches of the legal systems to the issue of pure economic loss.

The ways of approaching the problem are multifarious. We find the issue absorbed within the mainstream of the general clause in the liberal regimes and, in some others, we find it driven by the fear of 'liability in an indeterminate amount for an indeterminate time to an indeterminate class'.[92] This fear is, of course, managed through technical devices. These are, basically, the duty of care element in the pragmatic regimes and the unlawfulness requirement in the conservative systems — though some of these conservative regimes seek intense 'lateral' support to the recoverability of pure economic loss through contract law rules.

Comparative analysis of European regimes, however, makes clear a further point. Our classification of the systems into liberal, pragmatic and conservative regimes is designed to provide a framework that the reader may use to understand how jurists of a particular country reason their way to solutions. These however are only façades, starting points, and

[89] See Frotz 'Die rechtsdogmatische Einordnung der Haftung für culpa in contrahendo' in *Privatrechtliche Beitraege: Gedächtnisschrift fuer Franz Gschnitzer* (Veroeffentlichungen der Universitaet, Innsbruck, 1969); W Posch 'Austria' in EH Hondius (ed) *Precontractual Liability:Reports to the Xiiith Congress, International Academy of Comparative Law, Montreal, Canada, 18–24 August 1990* (Kluwer, Hague, 1990).
[90] W Posch and Schilcher, above n 83. Cf Bydlinski 'Vertragliche Sorgfaltspflichten zugunsten Dritter' (1960) *Juristische Blattes Law*, 359.
[91] W Posch and Schilcher, above n 83.
[92] *Ultramares Corp v Touche* 255 NY 170, 179 per Cardozo CJ (1931).

not the end of the journey. Here our cautionary distinction between exterior appearances and operational interiors plays a capital role. We have seen that the façades are sometimes deceptive edifices that conceal a complex theoretical substructure. Indeed, the usual way of approaching legal systems' notions and rules is strongly affected by what we can call the 'façade effect', that is to say, by a (covert or explicit)[93] set of assumptions which sometimes drive the observer far away from the actual rules and rationales one finds at work in the given legal system.

Therefore, without an in-depth factual analysis many of the actual questions raised by the pure economic loss issue are bound to receive either no answer or only a misleading one. This is why we embarked on the research we mentioned at the beginning of this chapter.

[93] R Sacco 'Legal Formants: A Dynamic Approach to Comparative Law' (1991) 39 *American Journal Comparative Law* 1ff, 21–7.

Part Three

Specific Performance and Damages

10

Understanding Specific Performance

LIONEL SMITH[1]

I INTRODUCTION

IF WE WANT to know when specific performance should be available, we are immediately driven to ask, what is it for? Or, to put the same question differently, what are we trying to accomplish when we grant it? This is the question that this paper tries to answer. If we can understand what it is for, we should be on a clearer path towards understanding when specific performance is most appropriately granted.[2]

If we ask the same question about compensatory damages, we have a pretty clear answer: we are trying to put the plaintiff in the same patrimonial position as if the contract had been performed. Similarly, if we ask the same question about disgorgement of gains, we can say that the function is to put the defendant in the same patrimonial position as if the contract had been performed.

It is not so clear what we are trying to accomplish when we grant specific performance. It is notorious that specific performance is, in some cases, overcompensatory, because it seems to override the plaintiff's duty to mitigate her loss during the period between breach and judicial order.[3] And even apart from mitigation, specific performance more generally leads us to ignore facts which have occurred after the breach but before the trial, even if the effect of those facts would be to reduce the measure of compensatory damages.[4]

[1] James McGill Professor of Law, Faculty of Law and Institute of Comparative Law, McGill University, Montreal.

[2] The chapter does not attempt to provide a complete answer as to when specific performance should be granted. One further issue is that there are a number of reasons to *resist* the granting of specific performance, which work against the reasons *for* granting it discussed herein. Examples include the difficulty of curial supervision and the well-known issue of a reluctance to order specific performance of personal services.

[3] *Domowicz v Orsa Investments Ltd* (1993) 15 OR (3d) 661 (Ont Gen Div).

[4] This is clearly illustrated by *Semelhago v Paramadevan* [1996] 2 SCR 415; 136 DLR (4th) 1 (SCC), which will be discussed in detail below.

II THE FAILURE OF ECONOMIC ANALYSIS

In broad terms, prescriptive economic analysts of law assume that the best legal rule is the one that will generate the most efficient result. Efficiency in this context means maximising utility, subject to the constraint that interpersonal utility comparisons are not feasible.[5] In other words, goods should be placed with those who value them most highly, and the measure of how highly one values a good is how much one is willing to pay for it.[6] This mode of analysis has frequently been applied to specific performance. It is certainly true that it is one way to answer the question, 'what is specific performance for?' The answer here is 'it exists to maximise utility'. And the hope of the economic analyst is that an efficiency analysis will generate some principles that will say when specific performance should be available and when not.

One of the most famous aphorisms in the common law is the statement of Oliver Wendell Holmes: 'The duty to keep a contract at common law means a prediction that you must pay damages if you do not keep it — and nothing else.'[7] There are two ways to understand this statement: as a claim about the law of contract, and as a claim about the nature of law. It seems plain that Holmes meant it as a claim about the nature of law. It is nothing but a statement, as it applies to contract law, of his famous Bad Man view of the law, set out in more detail earlier in the same article:

> Take the fundamental question, What constitutes the law? You will find some text writers telling you that it is something different from what is decided by the courts of Massachusetts or England, that it is a system of reason, which may or may not coincide with the decisions. But if we take the view of our friend the bad man we shall find that he does not care two straws for the axioms or deductions, but that he does want to know what the Massachusetts or English courts are likely to do in fact. I am much of his mind. The prophecies of what the courts will do in fact, and nothing more pretentious, are what I mean by the law.[8]

This was the foundation of American legal realism, although it bears saying that the foundation was and is a rather shaky one. Holmes himself thought that this was the best way to learn and understand the law as it is; he did not intend that it should say anything about how the law had developed, or more importantly how it should develop. Here is what he said still earlier:

> I wish, if I can, to lay down some first principles for the study of this body of dogma or systematized prediction which we call the law …

[5] RA Posner *Economic Analysis of Law* 5th edn (Aspen Law & Business, New York, 1998) 13.
[6] *Ibid*, 16.
[7] Justice OW Holmes 'The Path of the Law' (1897) 10 *Harvard Law Review* 457, 462; reprinted (1998) 78 *Boston University Law Review* 699, 702.
[8] *Ibid*, 460–1; 701–2.

> I take it for granted that no hearer of mine will misinterpret what I have to say as the language of cynicism. The law is the witness and external deposit of our moral life. Its history is the history of the moral development of the race. The practice of it, in spite of popular jests, tends to make good citizens and good men. When I emphasize the difference between law and morals I do so with reference to a single end, that of learning and understanding the law. For that purpose you must definitely master its specific marks, and it is for that that I ask you for the moment to imagine yourselves indifferent to other and greater things.[9]

Karl Llewellyn is another figure associated with legal realism, but he also only meant to say something about the best way of learning the law. He repeated the phrase about 'what courts will do' in a slightly modified form, and long regretted it.[10] Llewellyn made it clear that, in his view, legal realism was not a philosophy of law.[11]

Many have understood Holmes to have made a claim about the law of contract. Reading the word 'damages' as confined to compensation for loss, they have taken Holmes' aphorism as the unquestioned basis of the idea that, while a plaintiff is entitled to be compensated in money for his loss of bargain, any other legal response (including specific performance) is extraordinary and requires careful justification. It seems absolutely clear, when one reads the whole article, that this interpretation is indefensible. Quite apart from the earlier material extracted above, we should notice that Holmes was too good a lawyer to ignore specific performance.

> I have spoken only of the common law, because there are some cases in which a logical justification can be found for speaking of civil liabilities as imposing duties in an intelligible sense. These are the relatively few in which equity will grant an injunction, and will enforce it by putting the defendant in prison or otherwise punishing him unless he complies with the order of the court. But I hardly think it advisable to shape general theory from the exception, and I think it would be better to cease troubling ourselves about primary rights and sanctions altogether, than to describe our prophecies concerning the liabilities commonly imposed by the law in those inappropriate terms.[12]

So while Holmes took a narrow view of the availability of specific performance, he thought that, where it is available, there was indeed a duty to perform. Of course, a bad man would still have a choice when

[9] *Ibid*, 458–9; 700.

[10] He repeated it in the first edition of his great book on legal education, *The Bramble Bush*, and bemoaned the results in the foreword of the second edition: *The Bramble Bush* 2nd edn (Dobbs Ferry, Oceana, 1951) 8–10.

[11] K Llewellyn *Deciding Appeals: The Common Law Tradition* (Little, Brown & Co, Boston and Toronto, 1960; reprinted Hein & Co, Buffalo, 1996) 508–12.

[12] Holmes, above n 7, 462–3, 703.

ordered to perform a contract; in this case, a choice between performance or jail. And it would follow that in the case of a contractual promise to pay a fixed sum of money, even at common law there is a duty to perform the contract: here the common law (in the narrow sense that excludes equity) enforces the contractual promise specifically, rather than requiring the plaintiff to be content with a claim for damage suffered.[13] It seems therefore that Holmes thought that it became sensible to talk about a 'duty' if but only if the consequence of non-performance was the activation of state-sponsored enforcement, rather than the creation of another civil obligation to make compensation for loss suffered.

Let us return to the aphorism: 'The duty to keep a contract at common law means a prediction that you must pay damages if you do not keep it — and nothing else'. It seems absolutely clear that 'and nothing else' means, 'and no other (moralistic, theological, or other) import should be attached to the idea of a *duty* in this context (which is an artificially restricted context, confined to a discussion of the best way to learn and understand the positive law, ignoring equity)'. It is a claim about the meaning of 'duty'.

But many have taken the aphorism as a claim about the law of contract. They take the words 'and nothing else' as meaning 'and no other remedial responses follow upon a breach of contract'. In fact some authors have only grudgingly accepted even the right to claim for loss of bargain; most famously, Fuller and Perdue, who argued in favour of damages measured by the plaintiff's reliance.[14] Friedmann has convincingly shown, not only that their argument has never been accepted by the courts, but that it contains an internal inconsistency.[15] The main impact of their argument has been terminological, in that many authors and courts use the phrase 'expectation interest' to refer to the plaintiff's legal entitlement to the value of performance of the contract. Following Friedmann, I will instead use the phrase 'performance interest'.

For whatever reason, economic analysts are the ones who most clearly follow this interpretation of Holmes. That is, while they are willing to accept compensation for the performance interest, their axiomatic assumption is that any other response must be justified.[16] The literature

[13] *White & Carter (Councils) Ltd v McGregor* [1962] AC 413 (HL Scot), discussed further below.

[14] LL Fuller and WR Perdue 'The Reliance Interest in Contract Damages' (1936) 46 *Yale Law Journal* 52, 373.

[15] D Friedmann 'The Performance Interest in Contract Damages' (1995) 111 *Law Quarterly Review* 628.

[16] This approach is evident in one of the seminal articles, G Calabresi and DA Melamed 'Property Rules, Liability Rules and Inalienability: One View of the Cathedral' (1972) 85 *Harvard Law Review* 1089. This article assumes that compensation ('liability rule') is an automatic entitlement, but anything else requires justification. Specific enforcement, labeled 'property rule', requires justification, as does 'inalienability'. Like most economic analysis of law, it fails completely to notice the possibility of a response measured by the defendant's

on the economic analysis of the availability of specific performance is voluminous, but it is pretty inconclusive.[17] In the absence of detailed empirical evidence about transaction costs, it is not possible to draw conclusions about whether the availability or the non-availability of specific performance would be more efficient.[18]

In simple terms, then, prescriptive economic analysis has a clear answer to the question, 'what is specific performance for?' At the same time, however, it has failed to generate clear answers as to when it should be available. And it is certainly true that the answers that it does give are not those that the courts are using.

There is one other objection to this mode of analysis, which extends beyond the confines of this chapter. The aims of prescriptive economic analysis could be explained in this way. Given a set of entitlements, what legal rules protect them most efficiently?[19] In other words, efficiency analysis is not generally deployed as a justification for any particular distribution of goods in society.[20] It takes some distribution for granted, and then asks what is the best (most efficient) set of legal rules to protect peoples' entitlements under that distribution. There is a problem with this methodology. It assumes that a 'right' can be meaningfully distinguished from the 'remedy' which protects that right. The right is taken as generated by some other normative framework. For example, the plaintiff has an interest in land. Then it is assumed that there is a live issue as to how it should be protected: by damages only, or by injunction or other coercive order. One might, however, believe that 'right' is not distinguishable from 'remedy.'[21] On this view, whatever normative framework told you that the plaintiff owned the land would also tell you how that ownership

wrongful gain. For an attempt to redress this, see S Levmore 'Unifying Remedies: Property Rules, Liability Rules, and Startling Rules' (1997) 106 *Yale Law Journal* 2149.

[17] AT Kronman 'Specific Performance' (1978) 45 *Universtiy Chicago Law Review* 351; A Schwartz 'The Case for Specific Performance' (1979) 89 *Yale Law Journal* 271; P Linzer 'On the Amorality of Contract Remedies — Efficiency, Equity and the Second Restatement' (1981) 81 *Columbia Law Review* 111; TJ Muris 'The Costs of Freely Granting Specific Performance' (1982) *Duke Law Journal* 1053; E Yorio 'In Defense of Money Damages for Breach of Contract' (1982) 82 *Columbia Law Review* 1365; TS Ulen 'The Efficiency of Specific Performance: Toward a Unified Theory of Contract Remedies' (1984) 83 *Michigan Law Review* 341. Although it deals only briefly (at 834–9) with remedies, a recent addition is EA Posner 'Economic Analysis of Contract Law after Three Decades: Success or Failure?' (2003) 112 *Yale Law Journal* 829. Posner observes (at 830) that 'economic analysis has failed to produce an "economic theory" of contract law, and does not seem likely to be able to do so.'

[18] IR Macneil 'Efficient Breach of Contract: Circles in the Sky' (1982) 68 *Virginia Law Review* 947.

[19] Posner, above n 5, 15; although he observes (at 36–9) that the existence of *some* protected distribution is more efficient than a Hobbesian state of nature; but the analysis is indifferent to who owns what.

[20] See however Posner, *ibid*, chapter 16.

[21] PBH Birks 'Rights, Wrongs and Remedies' (2000) 20 *Oxford Journal Legal Studies* 1. See also JL Coleman and J Kraus 'Rethinking the Theory of Legal Rights' (1986) 95 *Yale Law Journal* 1335. See further D Friedmann, chapter 1 in this volume.

could be enforced. If this were true, then there would no longer be any room for economic analysis, of the prescriptive mode that takes some distribution for granted and then tries to work out the most efficient way to protect it. The distribution, taken for granted, would come along with a bundle of protective sanctions. There would be no question for economic analysis to answer.

It may well be that a fully developed theory of contract law, which bases the enforcement of promises on fundamental principles of justice, would also dictate whether or not specific performance should be available. That is the argument in the next section of this paper.

III TAKING CONTRACTS SERIOUSLY

If we understand the right to performance of a contract as a patrimonial entitlement, we immediately have a perspective that corresponds much more closely to the reality of the law. Such an understanding can be developed out of fundamental philosophical conceptions. One of the most sophisticated theories is that of Benson.[22] When contract is understood in this way, the right to compensatory damages for the performance interest follows inevitably, as a matter of corrective justice.[23] The right to performance is something that belongs to the plaintiff, and the defendant is not at liberty to take that away, regardless of considerations of efficiency.[24] So too does the right, in at least some cases, to disgorgement of the defendant's gains earned in breach of contract. If the defendant's performance belongs to the plaintiff, then so too do any profits.[25] This approach also helps us to understand the law of penalties and forfeiture, which otherwise is notoriously difficult to square with the principle of freedom of contract.[26]

If we understand a contractual promise as a patrimonial entitlement of the promisee, specific performance seems to make sense. It should be the natural remedy in contractual matters, as indeed it is in many civil law jurisdictions. But there is still a difficulty that can be expressed by asking 'what is specific performance for?' Compensatory damages protect the

[22] P Benson 'The Idea of a Public Justification for Contract' (1995) *33 Osgoode Hall Law Journal* 273; P Benson 'The Unity of Contract Law' in P Benson (ed) *The Theory of Contract Law: New Essays* (Cambridge University Press, Cambridge, 2001) 118.
[23] EJ Weinrib *The Idea of Private Law* (Harvard University Press, Cambridge, Massachusetts, 1995) 136–40.
[24] See eg *Angullia (Ahmed) bin Hadjee Mohamed Salleh Angullia v Estate and Trust Agencies (1927) Ltd* [1938] AC 624, 634–5 (PC Singapore); *White & Carter (Councils) Ltd v McGregor* [1962] AC 413 (HL Scot).
[25] *Adras Ltd v Harlow GmbH* (1988) 42(1) PD 221 (SC Israel), noted D Friedmann (1988) 104 *Law Quarterly Review* 383; *Attorney-General v Blake* [2001] 1 AC 268, 283 (HL).
[26] LD Smith 'Relief Against Forfeiture: A Restatement' (2001) 60 *Cambridge Law Journal* 178.

performance interest by putting the plaintiff in the position she would have been in if the contract had been performed. Disgorgement of profits also, in a way, protects the performance interest, by putting the defendant in the position he would have been in if he had performed. What is specific performance for? What does it do? The answer that I will arrive at could be expressed in this way: it prevents a defendant from expropriating a plaintiff's patrimonial entitlement to performance.

At one level, specific performance is the best way to protect the performance interest, because it gives the plaintiff the actual performance which was promised, not just some money as compensation. And yet, it is notorious that specific performance is, in some cases, over-compensatory. The plaintiff gets more than she would get in compensatory damages. The main reason is that the need to mitigate seems to drop out of the picture.[27] If the plaintiff is insisting on the conveyance to her of a particular estate in land, and if she knows that this conveyance will be specifically ordered, it does not really make sense to require her to watch out for a chance to purchase another one by way of mitigation. That would be inconsistent with our granting of specific performance. On the other hand, if we are not going to grant specific performance, then we can reasonably say to a non-mitigating plaintiff that the extra loss was caused by her own conduct in failing to mitigate.

But let us look a little more closely at what happens when specific performance is available, and the plaintiff does not mitigate. We overcompensate. How do we make sense of this? One view would be that specific performance, far from being the best way to protect the performance interest, is actually a kind of cack-handed way of protecting it. It gives a kind of compensation with one eye closed, because it ignores the more sophisticated compensatory detail added by the doctrine of mitigation. In that it is inaccurate, it is defective, and we would have to justify the defect with some corresponding virtue.

Another view would be that it is actually a good thing that specific performance overcompensates. This would require us to identify and justify some value, other than compensation for the performance interest, which is protected by specific performance but not by compensatory damages (which include the rules on mitigation).

One way to illustrate the difficulty is by considering the turning of specific performance into a money award — 'damages in lieu of specific performance', or, 'damages under Lord Cairns' Act', referring to the statute of 1858 which created the jurisdiction. If specific performance and compensatory damages were both about protecting the same performance interest, then compensatory damages would be equal to damages in lieu of specific performance. It seems that this was the goal of those who

[27] *Domowicz v Orsa Investments Ltd* (1993) 15 OR (3d) 661 (Ont Gen Div).

drafted the relevant statute; damages in lieu of specific performance, or of an injunction, would be the same as common law damages. The Act was intended to widen dramatically the ability of the Court of Chancery to award damages. But it must be remembered that it was one of the steps on the way to the Judicature Acts. The granting of this new jurisdiction was one way to bring the two court systems closer together. The intention was not to create a wholly new measure of damages.[28]

There was a surprise in *Wroth v Tyler*,[29] when it was suggested that damages in lieu of specific performance could be higher than common law damages. The case arose at a time of unprecedented increases in the value of land, and the value of the estate in question had risen dramatically between breach and trial. Megarry J held that common law damages had to be measured at the time of breach, so excluding this pre-trial increase. He did not want to grant specific performance, but he took the view that in granting damages in lieu, the measure would include the pre-trial increase. So here the difference in measures turned, in effect, on the view that it was the common law that measured compensatory damages in a rather inflexible way. Subsequent cases doubted this strongly. In *Johnson v Agnew*,[30] it was said by Lord Diplock that there was no reason to calculate damages differently under the Act than at common law; and of course the common law could develop and grow in such matters as the time for assessment of damages. The common law could look at what had happened between breach and trial. It could therefore capture a pre-trial rise, subject to the rules on mitigation.

But a more recent case adds another twist. *Semelhago v Paramadevan*[31] was a typical case of a breach of a contract to convey an estate in land. It was agreed that specific performance was available, although the case is important as casting doubt on whether every contract for the transfer of an interest in land should be automatically specifically enforceable.[32] But the plaintiff was to get damages in lieu of specific performance, the estate having been conveyed by the defendant to a third party. The value of the estate had risen between breach and trial. The plaintiff, not surprisingly, had kept his own house during that time. The trial judge awarded $120,000, basically applying *Wroth*. The Ontario Court of Appeal accepted the argument that in calculating damages in lieu, certain items should be deducted: namely, the interest which the plaintiff had avoided paying on the mortgage he needed to buy the estate; the interest he had earned on

[28] PM McDermott *Equitable Damages* (Butterworths, Sydney, 1994) 28–34; LD Smith 'Review' (1996) 75 *Canadian Bar Review* 388, 391.
[29] [1974] Ch 30.
[30] [1980] AC 367, 400 (HL). See also *306793 Ontario Ltd v Rimes* (1979) 25 OR (2d) 79, 100 DLR (3d) 350 (Ont CA).
[31] [1996] 2 SCR 415; 136 DLR (4th) 1 (SCC).
[32] [20]–[22].

the money he would have used for the down payment; and the legal fees associated with the conveyance. The award was reduced to $81,000. The defendant appealed and presented an even more ambitious version of the damage assessment. He observed that the value of the plaintiff's old house had also risen, in basically the same amount as the house that was the subject of the dispute. So he argued that the damages must take account of the fact that, had the defendant performed, the plaintiff would have acquired the gain in the sold estate, but he would not have acquired the gain in his old house, because he would have sold it. Thus the damages should have been $5,000. The Supreme Court of Canada rejected this argument and dismissed the appeal:

> The difference between the contract price and the value 'given close to trial' as found by the trial judge is $120,000. I would not deduct from this amount the increase in value of the respondent's residence which he retained when the deal did not close. If the respondent had received a decree of specific performance, he would have had the property contracted for and retained the amount of the rise in value of his own property. Damages are to be substituted for the decree of specific performance. I see no basis for deductions that are not related to the value of the property which was the subject of the contract. To make such deductions would depart from the principle that damages are to be a true equivalent of specific performance.[33]

In other words, damages in lieu of specific performance should put you in the position as if you had got specific performance.

This holding, so far from finding the over-compensatory effect of specific performance to be problematic, seems to say that it should be celebrated and protected, even when specific performance is converted into damages. Damages in such a case do not aim to put the plaintiff in the position she would have been in if the contract had been performed. Rather, they aim to put the plaintiff in the position she would have been in if she had got an order for specific performance and it had been obeyed. *Semelhago* shows that this is not the performance interest as it is commonly understood. Let us call it instead the 'specific performance interest'.

The effect in *Semelhago* is to take away the defendant's gain and give it to the plaintiff, in excess of the plaintiff's loss. It is a kind of disgorgement of the profit of a breach of contract, which of course is being more widely recognised all the time.[34] The Law Commission for England and Wales once said that disgorgement of the profit of a breach of contract was like 'monetised specific performance'.[35] Another way of looking at it would be that specific performance, when it is granted as such or in money,

[33] [19].
[34] See the cases in n 25 above.
[35] Consultation Paper no 132 *Aggravated, Exemplary and Restitutionary Damages* (1993), 196. See now Report no 247 (1997).

ensures that the defendant does not profit from the breach of contract. It puts the defendant in the position as if he had performed the contract. But in a case of this kind, it may do that even while putting the plaintiff in a better position than if the defendant had performed.

But disgorgement of the profit of a breach of contract is not well described as 'monetised specific performance'. The reason is that often, specific performance costs a defendant more than his gain. This is the reverse of the phenomenon that specific performance sometimes overcompensates; sometimes it 'over-disgorges' as well. If in a case like *Semelhago*, the defendant had sold the property to a third party, but for less than it was worth at the time of trial, then the order would be for an amount that exceeded the defendant's gain.

How can we describe the specific performance interest, in a way that covers the case in which specific performance is turned into money? It is not quite right to say that it puts the plaintiff in the position he would have been in if the contract had been performed, as *Semelhago* shows. In this it is not like compensation for the performance interest. Nor is it quite right to say that it puts the defendant in the position he would have been in if he had performed the contract, as the variation in the preceding paragraph shows. In this it is not like disgorgement of profits.

Maybe the specific performance interest is irreducible. It cannot be translated into 'put the plaintiff/defendant in the position as if ...'. Rather, specific performance itself is 'compel execution, even though this will overcompensate the plaintiff'. And a translation into money of the specific performance interest therefore does the same. This is a problem if the goal of specific performance is to compensate for the loss of the performance interest. Otherwise, it is not. In fact, it represents a wholehearted endorsement of the plaintiff's entitlement to performance (as distinct from compensation for the performance interest), and of the defendant's inability to take that entitlement away.

A developed theory of contract shows that the plaintiff's right to performance is a patrimonial entitlement, just like owning an estate in land. If that is so, the 'law of remedies' should not undercut it by giving the defendant an option to expropriate the plaintiff's patrimonial entitlement. Any loss of the right to performance must be carefully justified, preferably by reference to the plaintiff's own consent. One illustration of this is *White & Carter (Councils) Ltd v McGregor*.[36] The contract was for the plaintiff to put up advertisements on behalf of the defendant. The defendant immediately repudiated the contract. The plaintiff performed anyway and claimed, not compensatory damages, but the agreed price. The majority holding was that the claim should be allowed. The

[36] [1962] AC 413 (HL Scot).

defendant's breach gave the plaintiff an option to terminate the contract. But the option belonged to the plaintiff. It was not taken up. The contract was not terminated, leaving the plaintiff free to perform. And performance generated the obligation to pay the price.[37] Lord Reid said:

> It might be, but it never has been, the law that a person is only entitled to enforce his contractual rights in a reasonable way and that a court will not support an attempt to enforce them in an unreasonable way. One reason why that is not the law is no doubt because it was thought that it would create too much uncertainty to require the court to decide whether it is reasonable or equitable to allow a party to enforce his full rights under a contract.[38]

The decision has a narrow field of operation because in very few cases is it possible for the plaintiff to perform entirely, without any co-operation from the defendant. Usually therefore the defendant can keep the plaintiff from perfecting the right to claim the agreed price. Generally, even if the plaintiff wants to maintain the contract, the defendant can frustrate this choice. But an order for specific performance prevents him from doing so, and so prevents him from expropriating the plaintiff's right to performance.

Another illustration of the same principle is the widening recognition of a right to claim disgorgement of the profits of a breach of contract.[39] That type of claim can be justified on the basis that, since performance belongs to the plaintiff, so too do the profits that come from performance.[40] The defendant may not appropriate the incidents of this asset of the plaintiff, no more than he can appropriate the incidents of a tangible thing that belongs to the plaintiff.

Where specific performance is granted, the court is effectively applying the same principle that governed in *White & Carter*, except that the court supplies the co-operation of the defendant. The justification for the overcompensation that arises in a case like *Semelhago* is therefore exactly the same as that which justifies the result in *White & Carter.* The defendant wants to abandon the contract; the plaintiff wants to keep it on foot and get it performed. When specific performance is granted, the court is denying that the defendant has the ability to choose, unilaterally, to put an end to the contract and pay damages. Performance (not a right to be compensated for loss of the performance interest) belongs to the plaintiff. Anything else is making the best of a bad situation.

[37] An obligation to pay an agreed price is of course inconsistent with Holmes' aphorism (above, text at n 7), even in the narrow reading that excludes his later comment on equity, and even in the common reading which excludes all of the context set out above.

[38] [1962] AC 413, 430. Taken widely, the second sentence would suggest a routine availability of specific performance.

[39] See the cases above n 25.

[40] Of course there needs to be an inquiry as to how closely the profit is linked to the breach.

All three of those examples reflect a view of contract that implies that the plaintiff's right to performance is a patrimonial entitlement. This arguably is part of a lengthy process in which the remedial incidents of contract rights are being assimilated to those of real rights in tangible things. This process can be understood to have begun with the general recognition of tort liability for inducing breach of contract.[41] This trend could be seen to be reaching further perfection with the recognition of disgorgement for breach of contract. The same development is illustrated by the recognition that specific performance, while formally a supplementary remedy in the common law tradition, is becoming more widely available, even to the point where it might be seen to be the default remedy for breach of contract, as it is in the civil law tradition.[42]

It is fair to say that there is more than one side to this story. *White & Carter* was decided by a 3–2 majority; some courts have moved away from it, and some commentators doubt it.[43] Disgorgement remains rare. And while specific performance in general seems more readily available, the traditional rule that it was available as a matter of course for contracts to create or transfer an interest in land has recently come under increasing pressure.[44] There is no doubt that common law judges are practical people, and have frequently been concerned about whether a result made economic sense.[45] It is no accident that economic analysis of law is a product of the common law world. It bears remembering, however, even if we are measuring for efficiency, that certainty as to the remedial outcome is far more important than what exactly the remedial outcome is. In fact, bearing in mind the Coase Theorem, only with detailed information about transaction costs could we even choose, on efficiency grounds, between a rule of automatic specific performance and a rule of damages only.[46] The evidence is unclear, and so far as we know, there is nothing to choose between those rules on the criterion of efficiency.

[41] *Lumley v Gye* (1853) 2 E&B 216, 118 ER 749 (KB); D Friedmann 'Restitution of Benefits Obtained Through the Appropriation of Property or the Commission of a Wrong' (1980) 80 *Columbia Law Review* 504, 513–29. The process is arguably much older in that it underlies the institution of the use, forerunner of the trust. See LD Smith 'Property Transferred in Breach' in P Birks and A Pretto (eds) *Breach of Trust* (Hart Publishing, Oxford, 2002) 111.
[42] AS Burrows *Remedies for Torts and Breach of Contract* 2nd edn (Butterworths, London, 1994) 380–1.
[43] *Ibid*, 317–22.
[44] *Chan v Cresdon Pty Ltd* (1989) 168 CLR 242 (HC Aus) para 25; *Semelhago v Paramadevan* above n 31, paras 20–2. Of course one way to assimilate the treatment of land and other contracts would be to make specific performance more generally available, rather than making it less frequently available in land contracts.
[45] See eg the dissenting speech of Lord Keith in *White & Carter (Councils) Ltd v McGregor* [1962] AC 413 (HL Scot) 442.
[46] See the articles cited above nn 17–18.

IV CONCLUSION

But my own preference is to dispense with that inquiry. What is specific performance for? It prevents a defendant from expropriating a plaintiff's patrimonial entitlement to performance. The widening availability of specific performance, and the manner of its translation into money awards, show that the common law is beginning to take contractual obligations more seriously, and this is reinforced by the strong protection of the plaintiff's right to an agreed price, and the growing recognition of the plaintiff's ability to get disgorgement of the defendant's profit from a breach of contract.

A full answer to the question when specific performance should be granted would require an examination of the factors that militate against it.[47] This would involve some examination of the traditional bars to specific performance. Some of them (like the concern about curial supervision) seem to have some substance; others (like the requirement that damages be inadequate) are seemingly incoherent; still others (like the requirement of valuable consideration) may be relics of history. The argument herein is intended to applaud and encourage the apparent movement in the common law world toward a wider availability of specific performance. Not only does this give contractual obligations the weight they deserve, but it also presages a *rapprochement* between common law and civilian approaches.

[47] Two of these were mentioned above n 2.

11

The Deterrent Factor of Damages where Pricing is Affected

DAVID GILO*

I INTRODUCTION

CURRENT LITERATURE ON the economic analysis of contract remedies focuses on bilateral relationships between promisors and promisees. The prevalent expectation damages default rule is acknowledged in most analyses as socially efficient, as it makes the promisor bear the full harm caused by the promisor's breach and therefore encourages performance of the contract if and only if performance is socially desirable.[1] What current literature fails to identify, however, is that many promisors are firms selling their products or services in the marketplace, and, moreover, that expected damages for breach are often partly passed on to the promisor's customers, in the form of higher prices. In such settings, expectation damages may not suffice to make the promisor bear the full harm caused by breach, since some of the damages are ultimately borne by customers. A damages measure higher than expectation damages would then be desirable, in order to make the promisor bear the entire harm caused by breach and induce the promisor to take optimal precautions.

II THE CURRENT ECONOMIC ANALYSIS LITERATURE ON DAMAGES FOR BREACH

The quite well known results of the economic analysis literature generally justify the prevailing expectation damages default rule, according to

*Lecturer, The Buchman Faculty of Law, Tel-Aviv University. I wish to thank Omri Ben-Shahar, Ariel Porat, Yossi Spiegel and Omri Yadlin for valuable discussions.

[1] A few exceptions, nuances and critiques of expectation damages as the superior default rule are presented below in section II.

which the promisor pays the promisee damages so as to compensate the promisee for its reasonably expected[2] damages flowing from breach. As the literature shows, the virtue of expectation damages is that they make the promisor internalise the harm caused by breach, thereby inducing performance if and only if performance is socially efficient.[3] The expectation damages rule also has been shown to have the virtue of inducing the promisor to make efficient investments ('reliance investments') where such investments can improve the value of the contract to the promisor or lower the promisor's costs of performance.[4]

On the other hand, it has been shown that expectation damages have the drawback of inducing excessive reliance investments on the part of the promisee.[5] A related drawback of expectation damages is that, to the extent that the promisee can take actions to prevent breach or cooperate with the promisor, the promisee's incentives to do so are harmed under expectation damages, due to the fact the promisee is made whole regardless of whether the contract had been performed.[6] Furthermore, where reliance investments benefit not only the party making the investment, but also the other party (as in the case of a supplier's investment to improve the quality of the asset supplied, or when a buyer of a part adjusts his product line to better suit the supplier's parts) it has been shown that reliance damages may perform better, from a social perspective, than expectation damages.[7]

III THE MAIN POINT: A SIMPLE EXAMPLE

As mentioned, many promisors are firms operating in the marketplace. With such promisors, it is often the case that damages paid by them

[2] I Ayres and R Gertner 'Filling Gaps in Incomplete Contracts: An Economic Theory of Default Rules' (1989) 99 *Yale Law Journal* 87 show how the famous *Hadley v Baxendale* (1854) 9 Ex 341; 156 ER 145 rule, constraining expectation damages by what the promisor has reasonably foreseen at the time the contract is made, is a potentially desirable default rule. It induces promisees to inform the promisor of relevant details regarding the promisee's consequential damages from breach, thereby reducing information asymmetries in the contract.

[3] S Shavell 'Damages Measures for Breach of Contract' (1980) 11 *Bell Journal Economics* 466; WP Rogerson 'Efficient Reliance and Damages Measures for Breach of Contract' (1984) 15 *Rand Journal Economics* 39; T-Y Chung 'Incomplete Contracts, Specific Investments and Risk Sharing' (1991) 58 *Review Economic Studies* 1031; AS Edlin 'Cadillac Contracts and Up-Front Payments: Efficient Investment Under Expectation Damages' (1996) 12 *Journal Law Economics & Organization* 98. But see D Friedmann, 'The Efficient Breach Fallacy' (1989) 18 *Journal Legal Studies* 1, claiming that the notion according to which 'efficient breach' should be encouraged is often flawed.

[4] See eg Shavell, *ibid*; AS Edlin and S Reichelstein 'Holdups, Standard Breach Remedies and Optimal Investment' (1996) 86 *American Economic Review* 478, 490.

[5] Shavell, above n 3; Rogerson, above n 3; Edlin and Reichelstein, above n 3.

[6] R Cooter 'Unity in Tort, Contract, and Property: The Model of Precaution' (1985) 73 *California Law Review* 1, 3–4; R Cooter and A Porat 'Antiinsurance' (2002) 31 *Journal Legal Studies* 203.

[7] Y-C Che and T-Y Chung 'Contract Damages and Cooperative Investments' (1999) 30 *Rand Journal Economics* 84, 96–7, 102.

constitute a 'variable cost' from the promisors' perspective. That is, it is often the case that the level of damages the promisor expects to pay is an increasing function of the level of the promisor's operations (eg the quantity it supplies, the number of units it manufactures, the level of services it provides). Since variable costs generally affect the promisor's marginal costs,[8] and marginal costs affect the price that the promisor charges its customers, at least part of the damages the promisor expects to pay for breach of contract are transferred to the promisor's customers, and consequently not borne by the promisor. Accordingly, if we wish the promisor to bear the entire reasonably expected damages caused by breach, in cases where a portion of the damages is borne by the promisor's customers, rather than the promisor, damages need to be set at a higher level than the promisee's expectation interest.[9]

This chapter's main point can be illustrated through the famous often-cited case of *Hadley v Baxendale*.[10] In this case a miller contracted with a carrier to have a broken crankshaft transported to another town. The shipment was delayed and the miller sued the carrier for consequential damages of the profits lost while the mill was inactive. The court held that only foreseeable consequential damages should be awarded. The court set out its famous rule as to remoteness of damages, whereby the defendant is liable, firstly, for such loss as may fairly and reasonably be considered as arising naturally from the breach, and secondly, for such loss as may reasonably be supposed to have been in the contemplation of the parties at the time of the contract, as the probable result of its breach.

I wish to focus here not on the foreseeability of consequential damages, which was at the centre of the dispute in *Hadley*, but rather on the measure of damages, assuming they are reasonably foreseeable. Suppose the carrier's operations are such that the more shipments the carrier takes upon itself, the higher the probability of breach due to delay. Even for a fixed probability of delay for any particular shipment, this assumption is quite reasonable, since an increase in the number of shipments would raise the number of potential delays. Under such an assumption, the higher the level of the carrier's activity, the higher the probability of breach, and the higher the probability that damages will be awarded. Accordingly, from the carrier's point of view, expected damages for breach of contract are a variable cost, as the expected level of damages rises with the level of the carrier's activity. In such a case, at least some of the cost of expected damages will be passed-on to the carrier's customers, in the form of higher prices.[11]

[8] The marginal cost is the cost of supplying the marginal (or last) unit.

[9] The adjustment of the level of damages is expected to further raise the promisor's prices. This will be further discussed below in section IV.

[10] (1854) 9 Ex 341; 156 ER 145. See further A Kramer, chapter 12 in this volume.

[11] Interestingly, the price increase may also affect customers who wish to waive the carrier's liability for breach. Although the carrier may be willing to give a new customer, for example, a discount on account of such a waiver, granting services to this additional customer

In other words, the carrier is concerned not merely with its *costs* (reflected in possible damages it would have to pay in the case of delayed shipment) but rather its *profits*. The carrier's profits consist of its revenue minus its costs. While an increase in expected costs, caused by an expected imposition of damages for breach of contract, tends to reduce the carrier's profits, if this cost increase makes the carrier's price rise, and enough customers are nevertheless willing to purchase the carrier's services for this increased price, the carrier's revenue might rise as well. Accordingly, although the carrier's profits are generally harmed by the expected damages it would have to pay in the case of breach, these profits are not necessarily reduced by the total amount of damages. Some of these damages are passed on to the carrier's customers, due to the higher prices they need to pay.

Suppose the (reasonably foreseeable) damages of a shipper are 100. That is, the shipper's expectation interest is equal to 100. Assume further that the cost of precautions that could prevent breach (eg the cost of maintaining a sufficient number of vehicles) are a fixed cost, which does not depend on the number of shipments performed (we shall maintain this assumption from now on, and discuss its relaxation in Part V below.) We would like the carrier to bear this 100 for it to have optimal incentives to take actions or precautions to prevent breach. In the scenario portrayed above, however, a portion of these damages (eg 20) will be passed on to all of the promisor's customers, in the form of higher prices. Accordingly, the carrier bears only 80 of this 100. In order to restore the carrier's optimal incentives to prevent breach, damages need to exceed 100, so that, after taking account of the portion borne by customers, the carrier's profits would be reduced by 100. Under the assumption that a fifth of damages is borne by customers, damages would have to equal 125, instead of 100. A fifth of 125, which is 25, would then be borne by customers, while the rest, 100, would be borne by the promisor, providing it with adequate incentives.

One may ask whether it is efficient and just that the carrier's customers, in the above-mentioned example, have to bear a portion of damages equal to 25, on account of breach causing a particular promisee damages of only 100. Note, however, that in conjunction with the price rise resulting in customers bearing an additional price burden of 25, all

nevertheless may raise the probability that the carrier will fail to meet other deadlines. This would be the case if, due to a limited workforce and a limited number of vehicles, the probability of delay for any particular shipment is larger the more shipments the carrier has to handle. This normally affects the price the carrier charges this marginal customer, notwithstanding the waiver. Still, to simplify the analysis, let us assume that liability is not waived, eg because transaction costs of doing so are too high, or because liability is more efficient, as it better induces the carrier to take precautions, and it is therefore preferred by both parties. Transaction costs of granting waivers would be particularly prohibitive in the case of a promisor facing numerous small customers.

customers benefit from both elevated damages of 125, in the case of breach, and the promisor's improved incentives to prevent breach in the first place.[12] Therefore we infer that customers would not lose due to the somewhat higher prices that elevation of damages to 125 would cause.[13]

As will be illustrated below, the question of what portion of damages is passed on to customers depends on a few parameters, including the carrier's production characteristics, to what extent is the occurrence of breach dependent on the level of operation, the carrier's cost structure, the nature of competition between the carrier and its competitors in the market, and the structure of demand for the carrier's services. However difficult it may be to calculate exactly how much of the expectation damages of 100 is passed on to the carrier's customers, it is clear that in this example the carrier bears less than the expectation interest of 100 and will therefore have sub-optimal incentives to take precautions and prevent breach under the conventional expectation damages rule. While courts may not be able to seek the exact required level of damages, they are able to identify cases in which the problem focused upon here is particularly acute, as illustrated in section V below. In such cases, our analysis provides a justification for raising damages somewhat above the promisee's expectation interest.

IV WHEN ARE DAMAGES FOR BREACH A VARIABLE COST AFFECTING PRICES?

In my view the cases in which expected damages for breach affect the promisee's variable costs are quite common and relatively easy for courts to detect. The case in which increased level of operation raises the probability of breach (say, due to delay, as illustrated above via the *Hadley* case) serves as an important example. For another set of cases, imagine a firm with a product line that faces a probability of making defective products. Here too it would be plausible, in many cases, that the higher the level of the firm's operations, the higher the probability of a defective product, and the higher the expected level of damages for breach that the

[12] In case victims of breach are not really compensated in full, due to litigation costs, delay, miscalculation of damages or unforeseeable consequential damages, it is valuable to promisees that damages elevated to 125 improve the promisor's incentives to reduce the probability of breach.

[13] Exact assessment of whether customers are harmed requires a formal economic model, which is outside the scope of this article. In particular, such a model should ask whether customers who waived the promisor's liability would be harmed. Since in many cases any additional customer served by the promisor raises the probability that the promisor will breach other sales contracts, it is not necessarily the case that if such a customer waives the supplier's liability, it would enjoy a discount fully compensating her for the price increase caused by elevated damages. Still, such a customer continues to enjoy the benefit from elevated damages inherent in the promisor's improved incentives.

firm would have to bear vis-à-vis disappointed customers. Here too damages for breach constitute a variable cost, which is partly passed on to customers in the form of higher prices.

Where it is not the case that damages constitute a variable cost from the promisor's point of view, expectation damages continue to be a sensible measure of damages. In such case, the level of expected damages for breach is not affected by the carrier's level of activity and damages constitute a fixed, rather than variable, cost.

Fixed costs are costs that do not change as the firm's level of operation changes. A rational firm does not pass on any portion of its fixed costs to customers, via the price customers pay, since once fixed costs are borne by the firm, the firm's pricing decisions are determined only by the firm's costs of producing a marginal unit, and its revenue from supplying this marginal unit. The firm will continue supplying additional units (thereby normally reducing the price it charges in order to attract additional customers,) as long as the revenue from supplying a marginal unit is greater than the cost of producing this marginal unit. This process is done regardless of the firm's fixed costs.

Many cases of damages for breach of contract are of the 'fixed cost' type. For example, a buyer's failure to pay the supplier or failure to buy from the supplier as promised generally generate damages that constitute a fixed cost for the buyer, since the probability of breach is not affected by the buyer's level of operation. Here too, under our assumption that the costs of precautions are also fixed, the expectation damages benchmark is adequate. Furthermore, when the promisor is not a firm, but rather a public entity, or an individual, not conducting business or selling products or services, damages are absorbed in full by the promisor, and the expectation damages benchmark regains its attractiveness.

1 The Case of Intentional Breach

It might appear at first that my concerns arise particularly in the case of non-intentional breach, as in the above-mentioned *Hadley* example. Indeed, intentional breach is normally thought of as an opportunistic decision, which is not influenced by the promisor's level of operations. However, this need not be the case. The probability of the promisor committing intentional breach may rise as the promisor's level of operation rises. The carrier in the *Hadley* example may have a greater probability of *intentional* breach the more shippers he serves. For example, the more shippers the carrier serves, the more likely the carrier might find himself without an in-house vehicle to perform a given contract. The carrier may be able to lease outside vehicles on time in order to perform the contract, but he faces the choice of whether to do so. In such case, although breach is intentional, the probability of its occurrence is a rising function of the carrier's level of activity. Accordingly, a portion of damages for breach will be passed on to customers, and expectation damages alone would not suffice to induce the promisor to take optimal precautions to lower the probability of intentional breach.[14]

V FACTORS AFFECTING THE PORTION OF DAMAGES PASSED ON TO CUSTOMERS

1 The Effect of Demand for the Promisor's Product

One of the factors affecting the portion of expected damages passed on to the promisor's customers is the structure of demand for the promisor's product. The more inelastic is demand for the promisor's product (that is, the less likely are the promisor's customers to reduce their purchases in response to a price increase), the greater the portion of expected damages passed on to the promisor's customers. This implies that in markets where demand is relatively inelastic, such as basic commodities, gasoline, cigarettes, the distortions inherent in the conventional expectation damages rule are greater.

2 The Effect of the Promisor's Cost Structure

The portion of damages passed on to customers also depends on the promisor's cost structure. It is normally the case that a firm's marginal costs rise as it raises the quantity it produces. This stems from the fact that the marginal productivity of the firm decreases as the quantity produced rises. When a firm increases its level of operation, operation becomes less efficient, due to the workload, condensed workplace and limited machinery, etc. Still, this effect could be of different magnitudes for different firms. For some firms ('firms with relatively flat marginal cost functions') raising the level of activity reduces productivity only slightly and therefore only slightly raises the costs of producing marginal units. This could be the case for a firm with a large and efficient plant, plenty of machinery and extra workers, operating well below its full capacity of operation. For such firms, expanding the quantity produced may involve only a slight loss of productivity. For other firms ('firms with relatively steep marginal

[14] To be sure, under expectation damages, given the sub-optimal precautions the promisor took, his decision of whether to commit breach will be efficient. He will compare the cost of performance (including leasing an outside vehicle) with *total* damages for breach. However, as noted, expectation damages alone would make the promisor take insufficient precautions *ex ante* to prevent a situation where he lacks in-house vehicles in the first place.

cost functions') raising the level of activity significantly harms productivity and significantly raises marginal costs. This could be the case for a firm operating close to the peak of its capacity, with limited machinery and a limited number of workers, for which expanding the quantity produced substantially reduces productivity.

If the promisor is a firm of the former type — with a relatively flat marginal cost function — it passes on a greater portion of expected damages to customers than if the promisor were a firm of the latter type, with a relatively steep marginal cost function. The intuition for this result is that expected damages, which raise the promisor's marginal costs for each quantity produced, induce the promisor to raise prices and reduce the quantity produced relative to the case without damages. But reduction of the quantity produced, for promisors with a relatively steep marginal cost function (which suffer a substantial loss of productivity as their level of activity rises) considerably lowers the promisor's marginal costs. This counter-effect on marginal cost partly mitigates the effect of damages on price: charging more and producing less, due to imposition of damages and a rise in marginal costs for every quantity produced, helps the firm become more efficient, which, in turn, induces the firm not to raise prices as much.

Accordingly, it could be said that if the promisor is a firm with a relatively steep marginal cost function, its damages need to be inflated less than a firm with a relatively flat marginal cost function, in order to keep their optimal incentives to prevent breach intact. This conclusion assumes, however, that the effect of the level of operation on the probability of breach is the same for both kinds of firms. It would be reasonable to assume that, for a firm with a relatively steep marginal cost function (working close to the peak of its capacity, with few extra workers or machines, etc), raising the level of operations raises the probability of breach more than for a firm with a relatively flat marginal cost function. If the probability of breach rises due to congestion, increased probability of human error, or defective machinery, it would be plausible to assume that this effect is harsher for firms with a relatively steep marginal cost function.

In this sense, a firm with a relatively steep marginal cost function, in which raising the quantity produced raises considerably the probability of breach, possesses two characteristics that work in opposite directions when it comes to the effect of damages on price. On the one hand, a given level of expected damages has a smaller effect on price for such a firm because higher prices in this firm are accompanied by reduced quantity and regained efficiency. On the other hand, the link between such a firm's level of activity and its probability of breach and expected damages is stronger, making the effect of damages on prices stronger as well.

Therefore, when it comes to firms with a relatively steep marginal cost function, the two opposite considerations portrayed above tend to offset each other. Both considerations should then receive relatively little weight when deciding on the appropriate increase in damages above expectation damages.

When the Costs of Precautions are Variable Costs

We have assumed thus far that the promisor's costs of taking precautions or investing in the prevention of breach are fixed costs. This may be true in many cases. For example, in the *Hadley* example, the shipper may invest in additional in-house vehicles, hire additional scheduling co-ordinators or purchase more sophisticated software in order to prevent delays that cause him to breach contracts. Investment in an additional vehicle, as well as hiring additional staff at headquarters or purchasing new software all constitute fixed costs, as these costs, once made, remain unchanged when the shipper serves additional customers.

On the other hand, there may be cases in which the costs of the promisor's precautions to prevent breach are variable costs. For example, a factory may add features to each unit it produces that help ensure that the product is not defective. Such a precaution constitutes a variable cost, as it is expended for each additional unit produced. In such a case, not only are damages for breach a variable cost borne partly by consumers, but the costs of taking precautions too are a variable cost, borne partly by consumers. When the costs of taking precautions are partly passed on to consumers, promisors would tend to take more precautions than when precautions constitute a fixed cost, and are borne entirely by the promisor. As can be shown, this effect tends to offset the fact that damages too are partly passed on to consumers.

Accordingly, when both the costs of precautions and the costs of paying damages are purely variable costs, expectation damages would be adequate to provide the promisor with optimal incentives to prevent breach. Although a proportion of the damages are passed on to consumers, an identical proportion of the costs of precautions are passed on to consumers as well. The first distortion offsets the second, so as to reach an optimal result.

Another interesting implication of the current point relates to the case in which the costs of taking precautions are variable, but the costs of damages are fixed. This would be the case where, for example, reducing the probability of a defective product necessitates adding a component to each unit, but the probability of a defective product coming out of the plant remains constant, regardless of the number of units produced. Here damages are not even partly passed on to consumers, as they constitute a fixed cost, while the costs of taking precautions are partly passed on to consumers, as they constitute a variable cost. Interestingly, in such cases, a damage measure *lower* than expectation damages would provide the correct incentives, since otherwise the promisor in these cases tends to over-invest in taking precautions.

3 Competitive Interaction between the Promisor and its Competitors

Another factor affecting the question 'what portion of the promisor's expected damages is passed on to customers?' is the nature of competition between the promisor and its competitors. According to a wide variety of economic models, the more intensive is the competition between the promisor and competing firms, the more of the promisor's marginal costs are passed on to customers.

An important factor affecting the intensity of competition in a market is the degree of differentiation between competitors' products. Breakfast cereals, for example, are generally characterised by product differentiation. That is, some customers prefer one brand of breakfast cereal, and would purchase it even if a competing brand were somewhat cheaper, while other customers may rather purchase the competing brand, even if it is somewhat more expensive than others. In such markets, although the different brands are perceived as sufficiently interchangeable to be considered competitors, competition becomes less fierce as the differentiation between brands increases. Normally, then, a promisor in a market characterised by product differentiation is likely to bear more of the expected damages for breach[15] than in markets that lack differentiation.

Indeed, in markets without differentiation, such as bottled water, cement, sugar, detergents, gasoline, where competition is potentially fiercer, more of the damages paid by the promisor are ultimately passed-on to customers. This implies that in such markets the distortions inherent in the current expectation damages regime are particularly acute. It is in such markets that raising damages above expectation damages is even more important, in order to induce the promisor to take optimal precautions.

A similar parameter that affects the intensity of competition is competitors' capacity constraints. The more constrained are firms' capacities, either due to limited plant size or limited distribution channels or brand names, the less intense is competition. The reason is that when a firm with capacity constraints attempts to cut prices, it might find itself facing increased demand that it cannot fulfill. Accordingly, the more capacity-constrained are firms in the promisor's market, the more they are likely to bear the costs of damages for breach, and the less acute are the distortions inherent in the conventional expectation damages rule.

[15] I continue to assume here that expected damages constitute a variable cost. Eg I assume that the more units of cereal the promisor makes, the probability of a defective unit (or the number of defective units) rises.

Finally, if the promisor is a 'fringe firm', that is, a small competitor, which takes the industry price that the larger competitors in the industry set as given, and is too small to decide on its own price based on its marginal costs, none of the damages paid by the promisor would be passed on to customers. Such a fringe firm sets its price based on what is dictated by the whole industry, regardless of the expected damages for breach that the firm has to pay. In the case of such promisors, the conventional expectation damages rule would continue to be attractive.

VI PROPOSED DEFAULT RULE

As illustrated above, the current default rule, according to which the promisor pays merely expectation damages, will provide the promisor with insufficient incentives to prevent breach where damages are partly passed on to the promisor's customers. Conventional law and economics analysis assumes that, absent special considerations,[16] the most efficient legal rule should be chosen as the default rule. It is important to set an efficient default rule for it to govern cases where the parties' costs of contracting around an inefficient default rule prevent them from doing so. Accordingly, my analysis implies that in the cases focused upon here, the default rule should be changed to an increased level of damages.

Indeed, in those cases that I focus upon, where increasing damages is warranted, it would often be difficult to count on the parties to the contract to negotiate around the expectation damages default rule. For example, when a supplier of a product or service faces several customers which have insufficient information as to how much of the damages paid by the promisor are passed on to customers, or how this affects the promisor's incentives to lower the probability of breach, it would be naïve to assume that the promisor would voluntarily offer to pay elevated damages in case of breach, as the promisor's gains (eg in the form of increased demand or more appreciative customers) from doing so are expected to be low or nonexistent.

VII COURTS' INFORMATION ABOUT THE RELEVANT PARAMETERS

Obviously, in order to improve promisors' incentives by raising damages in appropriate cases, as proposed above, it is required that the courts have sufficient information about the relevant parameters. While under the conventional expectation damages rule all the court needs to know is

[16] See eg Ayres and Gertner, above note 2.

whether a breach occurred and what the promisee hoped to gain from performance, accurate implementation of my proposal requires the court to gain an understanding of the portion of damages that is passed on to the promisor's customers. As noted above, such accurate determination requires information about the promisor's market environment, including the intensity of competition between the promisor and its competitors, the structure of demand for the promisor's product, the promisor's cost structure, and the effect an increased level of operation has on the probability of breach.

Therefore, admittedly, accurate implementation of my proposal by the courts is a difficult task. Nevertheless, an attempt by courts to improve upon the conventional damages rule in the cases I focus upon is still worthwhile. In particular, as in a multitude of antitrust cases, courts take it upon themselves to analyse the structure of the market, and the structure of demand.[17] Furthermore, in various antitrust cases, when a transaction such as a merger or agreement is attacked under antitrust laws, it is often the case that an advantage or 'efficiency' inherent in the merger or agreement is claimed to justify it, notwithstanding the harm to competition. Courts are accustomed, in such cases, to asking whether a substantial portion of the alleged efficiency is expected to be passed on to customers, in the form of reduced prices.[18] Furthermore, courts often analyse the question whether certain costs or taxes borne by the firms would eventually be passed on, in part, to customers.[19] The inquiry that my analysis imposes is strikingly similar. In the case of breach of contract, the court should seek evidence regarding whether a substantial portion of the promisor's increase in marginal costs (reflected in the imposition of damages) are expected to be passed on to customers, in the form of higher prices.

VIII CONCLUSION

I have shown that the conventional damages measures, such as the prevailing expectation damages rule, provide the promisor with insufficient incentives to prevent breach in a wide variety of cases, in which damages for breach are partly passed on by the promisor to its customers. The law and economics literature failed to identify this distortion due to its concentration on bilateral relations between promisor and promisee.

[17] See eg *United States v E I Du Pont de Nemours & Co* 351 US 377, 394 (1956) (where the US Supreme Court investigated into both the definition of the relevant market, the market shares of the firms in it, and the elasticity of demand for the defendant's product.)
[18] See eg *Monsanto Co v McFarling* 302 F 3d 1291, 1306 (Fed Cir 2002); *Federal Trade Commission v University Health Inc* 938 F 2d 1206, 1211–23 (11th Cir 1991).
[19] See eg *National Electrical Manufacturers Assoc v Sorrell* 272 F 3d 104, 110 (2d Cir 2001).

Naturally, the literature's concentration on bilateral relations, although useful in many contexts, is extremely restrictive, and it abstracts from reality, as many promisors are firms acting in the market place. I have provided characteristics that could aid courts in identifying when part of the damages are expected to be passed on to customers and when the portion of damages passed on to customers is expected to be particularly significant. While these considerations are probably impossible to implement with precision, courts have proven in the past, particularly in antitrust cases, that they are able to explore issues that are no less complex than the one before us. Therefore, rather than ignoring the distortions I identify here, it would be justified, in appropriate cases, to adjust damages upward. This would improve the prospects of promisors bearing the entire harm caused by their breach, and accordingly taking optimal precautions to prevent the occurrence of breach.

12

An Agreement-Centred Approach to Remoteness and Contract Damages

ADAM KRAMER*

INTRODUCTION

THE FORESEEABILITY RULE that restricts contract damages awards, known by common lawyers as the 'rule of remoteness', is applied in both civil and common law jurisdictions.[1] Directly or indirectly, all these jurisdictions have taken the rule from Pothier, the eighteenth century French jurist,[2] who borrowed it from Molinaeus.[3] Both Molinaeus and Pothier employed the foreseeability rule on the grounds that the promisor has 'expressly or impliedly charged himself' with foreseeable losses and is 'presumed to have submitted to these only.'[4] In other words, the rule that only foreseeable losses may be recovered was originally adopted as a crude test of what losses the promisor had assumed responsibility for under the agreement. Thus the

*Written while Lecturer in Law, University of Durham; now a Pupil Barrister, 3 Verulam Buildings, London. I am grateful to Steve Smith, who supervised the writing of my LLM thesis at McGill University, of which this chapter is a latterday descendant. Thanks are also due to the editors of this volume for their helpful comments and suggestions.

[1] See, for example: the Appellate Division of the Supreme Court of South Africa's decision in *Victoria Falls & Transvaal Power C Ltd v Langlaagte Mines Ltd* 1915 AD 1, the French Civil Code article 1150, the Israeli Contracts (Remedies for Breach of Contract) Law 1970 section 10, the Louisiana Civil Code articles 1996, the Principles of European Contract Law article 9.503, the Quebec Civil Code article 1613, the Unidroit Principles for International Commercial Contracts article 7.4.4, the U.S. Restatement (Second) of Contracts §351 and Uniform Commercial Code § 2–715, the UN Vienna Convention on the International Sale of Goods article 74, and, in England and Wales, the famous case of *Hadley v Baxendale* (1854) 9 Ex 341. Cf the approach taken in the German Civil Code §252.

[2] RJ Pothier, *Traité des Obligations* (1761), part 1, chapter 2, article 3, para 160ff. For an English translation see RJ Pothier, *A Treatise on Obligations*, trans F Martin (Union, New Jersey, The LawBook Exchange Ltd, 1999).

[3] Carolus Molinaeus, also known as Charles Dumoulin, *Tractutus De Eo Quod Interest* (Venetiis, 1574), paras 51, 60–4. Pothier, *ibid*, cites Molinaeus at several points. See further GA Mulligan, 'Special Damages in South African Law' (1956) 73 *South African Law Journal* 27, 30–4, and R Zimmermann, *The Law of Obligations* (Oxford, OUP, 1996), 829.

[4] Pothier, n 2 above, at paras 162 and 160 respectively. See also Mulligan, *ibid*.

point of departure for this chapter: is the test as to recoverable losses based on the intentions of the parties? And if a promisor is presumed to have submitted to foreseeable losses, might not that presumption sometimes be capable of rebuttal?

In this chapter it will be argued that the allocation of responsibility for the consequences of breach is one of the matters that is determined by contractual agreement, even when it is not covered by the express terms of the agreement. According to this view, the central rule restricting awards of damages, the foreseeability requirement, is not a strict rule originating outside the contract for reasons of efficiency, fairness or proportionality, but is a rule of thumb that is justified when and to the extent that it indicates what the parties wanted. The foreseeability rule, and many of the other rules governing damages, should thus be understood as a framework for discovering what was agreed, not a default rule to operate when nothing was agreed.[5]

The common law reader may have already recognised that this argument is in essence the long-discredited tacit agreement/implied promise theory of remoteness, last supported in the latter half of the nineteenth century and having as its high-point the decision in *British Columbia and Vancouver's Island Spar, Lumber, and Saw-Mill Co v Nettleship*.[6] The discrediting that the theory suffered was, it is submitted, partial, clumsy and largely unconvincing. In addition, times have changed and we now have a much more sophisticated understanding of the interpretation of contracts. Under the modern approach, the English standard-bearer of which is the leading case of *Investors Compensation Scheme v West Bromwich Building Society*,[7] we are not afraid to find parts of the agreement outside the express words by looking to the factual matrix, the surrounding norms and the reasonable expectations. Indeed we are required to do so ubiquitously when we interpret express words and imply terms. Where once we balked at intention-based approaches to contract doctrines because of the objective principle of interpretation, we now realise that all communication is subject to such a principle, and necessarily so, and that for the parties to reach a single agreement between themselves the principle is necessary.[8]

[5] For default rule theories, see CJ Goetz and RE Scott, 'The Limits of Expanded Choice: An Analysis of the Interactions Between Express and Implied Contract Terms' (1985) 73 *California Law Review* 261 and I Ayres and R Gertner, 'Filling Gaps in Incomplete Contracts: An Economic Theory of Default Rules' (1989) 99 *Yale Law Journal* 87, and the (largely American) literature spawned by these articles, usefully summarised and discussed in CA Riley, 'Designing Default Rules in Contract Law: Consent, Conventionalism and Efficiency' (2000) 20 *Oxford Journal of Legal Studies* 367.

[6] (1868) LR 3 CP 499.

[7] [1998] 1 WLR 896 (HL).

[8] By the objective principle, even the meaning of an unambiguous express word is not part of the contract because it was intended but rather is part of the contract because it reasonably appeared to be intended. It seems that much of the criticism of agreement-centred approach comes from those who harbour a view of contractual intention that is inconsistent with the objective test, a test these same critics do not seek to replace.

The argument proposed will stand or fall on whether it convinces the reader that the agreement, objectively interpreted and rooted in implied norms as it is, can extend to the implicit allocation of risk and responsibility. The new orthodoxy is that parts of the agreement are tacit but are no less genuinely intended for that. It is submitted, perhaps impertinently, that it is for those who accept the new orthodoxy, but do not accept an agreement-centred approach to remoteness, to show that the implicit agreement covers details of primary terms (discovered in interpretation) and new primary terms (discovered through the implication of new terms) but does not cover the allocation of responsibility of the parties. If the agreement of the parties does stretch to the allocation of responsibility for consequences of breach, it would be hard to justify not giving effect to this allocation without seriously undermining the justifiability and coherence of the basic contractual aim of giving effect to what was agreed, since we would then be giving effect to some things that had been agreed but not others.[9] It should be noted that it is not being argued that the agreement includes an implied promise to pay damages, or that it necessarily even extends all the way to the consequences of breach, but rather that the allocation of risk and responsibility is implied and an imposed obligation to compensate gives effect to that allocation.[10]

Of course, it is difficult or impossible to prove this pudding except in the eating. The bulk of the argument contained herein is that the default rule theory is inadequate as an explanation of the law, and the implicit agreement theory is much to be preferred. Full of variables as it is, the foreseeability rule is simply too indeterminate usefully to serve as a default rule. As Fuller and Perdue observed, 'the test of foreseeability is less a definite test itself than a cover for a developing set of tests'.[11] The indeterminacy is not such a problem, however, when the rule is understood as a rough and ready rule of thumb for applying the parties' agreement, rather than a principle in its own right. Furthermore, the agreement-centred theory should have the first chance of explanation, since the default rule theory can only be convincing if the agreement-centred theory has failed. Default rules are externally imposed and should only be resorted to in default, ie when the agreement has

[9] Such selective application of the agreement would render the basic rule normatively arbitrary: E Weinrib, *The Idea of Private Law* (Cambridge, Mass, Harvard University Press, 1995), 39.
[10] One might conceptualise the approach proposed as closely analogous to the implication in fact of exclusion clauses.
[11] 'The Reliance Interest in Contract Damages' (1936) 46 *Yale Law Journal* 52, 85. M Tilbury, 'Remedies and the Classification of Obligations' in A Robertson (ed), *The Law of Obligations: Connections and Boundaries* (London, UCL Press, 2004) at 20, describes the test as 'weasel words'. Swinton even praises the remoteness test's role as a fig-leaf to keep the exercise of discretion on the basis of policy factors decent, K Swinton, 'Foreseeability: Where Should the Award of Contract Damages Cease?' in B Reiter & J Swan (eds), *Studies in Contract Law* (Toronto, Butterworths, 1980).

nothing to say on the matter in question.[12] It is argued herein that actually agreements have a lot to say about the allocation of responsibility, and that we shouldn't be fooled into thinking otherwise by what the agreement has to say not being explicit. Liquidated damages clauses and exclusion clauses are the explicit tip of the iceberg of the agreement.[13]

The implicit agreement theory, however, enables us to reconcile under one slightly improved doctrine of remoteness various doctrines that look to the allocation of responsibility. In England and Wales that would include the current rules of remoteness, the rules of mental distress damages and of loss of amenity, and the recently-emerged scope of duty test from *South Australia Asset Management Corp v York Montague*.[14] Such a change would be less a revolution than a recharacterisation. The proposed test will lead to largely the same results, still concentrating upon foreseeability, but will do so with more coherence and justification.

Such discussion is for later, however. First it is necessary to explore a little the relationship between contractual right and remedy, and what it might mean for the implicit agreement of the parties to stretch to the assumption of responsibility. Some examples of norms that may govern this area and give rise to reasonable expectations will be posited, and it

[12] A Morris, 'Practical Reasoning and Contract as Promise: Extending Contract-Based Criteria to Decide Excuse Cases' (1997) 56 *Cambrige Law Journal* 147, 162 and SJ Burton, 'Default Principles, Legitimacy and the Authority of Contract' (1994) 3 *South California Interdisciplinary Law Journal* 115, 116ff. Where default rules are based upon economic efficiency alone, the contrast with the theory proposed herein is obvious. The distinction between this theory and that by which default rules are based on conventionalism and the tacit expectations of the parties, see eg R Barnett, 'The Sound of Silence: Default Rules and Contractual Consent' (1992) 78 *Virginia Law Review* 821 and '… And Contractual Consent' (1994) 3 *South California Interdisciplinary Law Journal* 421, is less clear-cut. This is so because the process that operates in all interpretation is a type of 'default rule' process. Essentially, unless the parties say otherwise, the norms of society that one would reasonably expect to govern do govern. These norms apply in default, as in every communication, because it would be too costly to express everything in a contract. So there is a 'default rule' process, but the relevant norms are numerous and very specific and operate in the world of community practice (when I go into a coffee shop and ask for 'a cup' I am offering to pay for a cup of coffee, hot and not poisonous, and then to return the cup, unless I say otherwise). This process, unlike the process by which legal default rules govern, takes account of the specific variables of individuals by selecting between specific norms rather than applying a blunt blanket rule. Thus it is argued herein that rather than trying to make default rules that conform to the tacit understanding of the parties, we should first try to find out in individual cases what the tacit understanding of the parties were. Barnett says the same, and I don't know whether he would agree that the foreseeability rule of contract damages is a cover for an inquiry into the tacit understandings of the parties (as is argued herein), or whether he would be of the view that the tacit understandings have already run out (which is disputed herein).

[13] It is conceded that, at least in theory, there may be a limit to the community norms that are incorporated by means of tacit understandings and that eventually we may need to go outside the contract, but I agree with Randy Barnett that it is more a case of 'islands of imposed-by-law terms in a sea of consent-based obligation' than 'islands of consented-to terms amid a sea of state-imposed policy-driven obligations', '… And Contractual Consent' (1994) 3 *South California Interdisciplinary Law Journal* 421, 431.

[14] [1997] AC 191 [hereinafter *SAAMCO*], discussed below at 280.

will be demonstrated that our existing rules are best understood as an attempt to discover the implicit allocation of risk/responsibility. The community norms described herein are not supported by direct empirical evidence, rather they are inferred from the indirect evidence of current rules, the body of judicial decisions, and my own everyday dealings and communications with others. The detail of the norms is probably wrong; they are proposed only to demonstrate how one might go about discovering the implicit agreement of the parties.

The central thesis of this chapter is one that is relevant to all the jurisdictions that use the foreseeability test and some that don't. However, primarily by reason of the author's ignorance, the examples of detailed rules and their judicial application are drawn principally from English law.

OBLIGATION-CENTRED ACCOUNTS OF REMEDIES

The relationship between rights and remedies in the law of obligations is not easy to define.[15] Even if it is the case, and I do not concede that it is, that '[p]romise-keeping does not entail any preference of one remedy over another'[16] and breach of contract is a 'wrong' and so in principle gives a 'wide-open remedial potential' and a 'licence to mistreat the wrongdoer',[17] it is clear that our society and legal system has an established preference for compensation by way of damages awards as the primary remedy for torts and breach of contract. The question thus arises how this compensation is to be worked out in a particular case of commission of a tort or breach of a contract. Whilst of course it is correct that there are extrinsic policies and practical factors that affect the particular remedy awarded in a particular case, and these policies and factors should be identified, arguments that attempt to play down the importance of the right in determining the remedy[18] do no service to our understanding of the law, or at least the law of contract damages. More direct attempts to get to grips with the question at hand are made by Daniel Friedmann and Stephen Smith.[19] Friedmann argues that

[15] Discussion shall be confined to the law of torts and the law of contract.
[16] H Dagan, 'Restitutionary Damages for Breach of Contract: An Exercise in Private Law Theory' (2000) 1 *Theoretical Inquiries in Law* 115, 121.
[17] P Birks, 'Equity in the Modern Law: An Exercise in Taxonomy' (1996) 26 *University of Western Australia Law Review* 1, 12.
[18] See discussion in D Wright, 'Wrong and Remedy: A Sticky Relationship' [2001] *Singapore Journal of Legal Studies* 300 and Tilbury, n 11 above.
[19] D Friedmann, 'The Performance Interest in Contract Damages' (1995) 111 *Law Quarterly Review* 628 and 'Rights and Remedies' (1997) 113 *Law Quarterly Review* 424; SA Smith, 'Rights, Remedies, and Normal Expectancies in Tort and Contract' (1997) 113 *Law Quarterly Review* 426. See also S Smith, 'The Reliance Interest in Contract Damages and the Morality of Contract Law' (2001) *Issues in Legal Scholarship* (bepress.com), 36.

> the very recognition of a legal right entails some consequences regarding the remedy, one of which relates to the initial point of inquiry. This initial point relates to the value of legal right, at least where such value can be ascertained. The right of recovery may be qualified or subject to exceptions. The initial point is, however, clear.[20]

Friedmann goes on to argue that

> *the basic principle as to damages is identical in contract and in tort* ... This principle provides in essence that the purpose of damages is to put the plaintiff, in economic terms, in the position in which he would have been had the wrong (either a tort or breach of contract) not been committed. *The different results reached in tort and contract derive from the fact that they are usually called on to protect different rights*' [emphasis in original].[21]

Smith has added that 'The reason that different sums may be awarded depending on whether a cause of action is in tort or in contract is not because the measure of compensatory damages awarded is different, but because the nature of the breach of duty which the damages are meant to undo is different' and so apparent differences in the measure of damages awarded usually reflect differences in the 'underlying obligation'.[22]

However I would like to go a little further and investigate aspects of the relationship between rights and remedies that are hidden by the words Friedmann and Smith use. If damages awards in both contract and tort cases are determined by what Friedmann calls the value of the underlying right and Smith calls the nature of the underlying obligation, and it is respectfully submitted that they are, then the question arises as to what dimensions underlying obligations can and do take. The more detailed the underlying obligation (for example, if it governs the type of harm it is protecting from and the directness with which that harm must be caused to be wrongful) the more work the right does in determining the remedy and the less work there is left for external policies and rules.

Elsewhere I have investigated this question in the context of torts, particularly the tort of negligence.[23] I argued that, when tortious rules are interpreted against the background of societal norms of behaviour and responsibility from which they originate, one can derive the type of harm against which protection is provided and the proximity that the harm must have to the offending cause to give rise to recovery. In other words, rules of causation and proximity and the type of harm for which compensation

[20] Friedmann, 'The Performance Interest in Contract Damages', *ibid* 637.
[21] *Ibid* 639.
[22] S Smith, 'Rights, Remedies, and Normal Expectancies in Tort and Contract', n 19 above, 430–1.
[23] 'Proximity as Principles: Directness, community norms and the tort of negligence' (2003) 11 *Tort Law Review* 70.

is provided are to a great extent dictated by the underlying tortious obligation, as obligation-centred principles, rather than by independent policies originating outside the obligation. In this chapter I would like to investigate how this approach and these conclusions can be applied to contract law.

In one way, this project is easier to apply to contractual obligations. Tortious obligations derive from community standards and, as such, are the same for everyone and change little over time, thus their scope rarely needs to be addressed as the scope of most torts has been laid down after investigative interpretation over previous decades or longer.[24] Contractual obligations, however, stem from individual agreements made in individual contexts, and so just about every contract case requires the interpretive process to be engaged in anew. For this reason we are more familiar, and so comfortable, with the interpretive process in contractual cases. On the other hand, however, whereas it makes good sense to think of tortious obligations as being oriented towards particular types of harm caused in a particular way, at first sight it makes less sense to see contractual obligations as being similarly oriented. This is because tortious obligations are obligations not to cause harm, whereas contractual obligations are obligations to do or abstain.

Still, it does not require one to take Holmes' Bad Man's point of view, and to fully endorse the theory of efficient breach,[25] to see that contractual obligations might be oriented towards losses resulting from their non-performance. It is true that promises are treated by the parties as more than just obligations to pay damages (for example, promises are also significant in terms of morality, trust and cooperation),[26] but the legally-binding (and so coercive) nature of contracts at least partly undermines the moral and social force (the 'bond-creating function') of the promises those contracts contain.[27] In commercial cases in particular, the contract is often made with at least one eye on the remedies that would become available in the case of breach.[28] The common occurrence

[24] The proximity requirement in the tort of negligence, and the questions arising in *Hunter v Canary Wharf* [1997] AC 655, are important exceptions showing that there is still some interpretive work to be done.

[25] OW Holmes Jnr, *The Common Law* (1881), 301ff and OW Holmes Jnr, 'The Path of the Law' (1897) 10 *Harvard Law Review* 457. See further the correspondence between Holmes and Sir Frederick Pollock, in which the latter is very critical of Holmes' theory, M DeWolfe Howe, ed., *The Holmes-Pollock Letters* (Cambridge, Mass, Harvard University Press, 1941), volume 1, 79–80, 177 and volume II, 200–1, 233–5.

[26] J Finnis, *Natural Law and Natural Rights* (1980) 320 ff. See also S Smith, 'Performance, Punishment and the Nature of Contractual Obligation' (1997) 60 *Modern Law Review* 360.

[27] D Kimel, 'Neutrality, Autonomy, and Freedom of Contract' (2001) 21 *Oxford Journal of Legal Studies* 473; D Kimel, 'Remedial Rights and Substantive Rights in Contract Law' (2002) 8 *Legal Theory* 313; D Kimel, *From Contract to Promise: Towards a Liberal Theory of Contract* (Oxford, Hart Publishing, 2002).

[28] D Campbell, 'Chapter 1: Introduction' in D Harris, D Campbell and R Halson, *Remedies in Contract and Tort*, 2nd edn (London, Butterworths, 2002), 17–18; D Campbell and D Harris, 'In defence of breach' (2002) *Legal Studies* 208. See the statement of the arbitrators in *The Sine*

of exclusion and limitation clauses and liquidated damages clauses is merely the clearest manifestation of this fact. Even taking the internal, or good man's, point of view, and treating contracts as morally binding promissory commitments, one can see that promises entail an assumption of responsibility for the consequences of breach.[29] The existence of enforcement remedies such as specific performance and injunctions does not prevent the scope of responsibility for a breach being an important issue, both for the party that is deciding whether to perform and for the court that is deciding whether to compel performance.

AN OBLIGATION-CENTRED ACCOUNT OF CONTRACT LAW DAMAGES

As John Wightman has observed (commenting on the *SAAMCO* decision, to which we will later return):

> The tradition of seeing contract damages rules as imposed by law (subject to contrary express agreement) may have meant that the assessment of damages has not been sufficiently sensitive to the parties' reasonable expectations where these are not made express. The law on implied terms demonstrates the importance of primary obligations which have not been agreed by the parties. It would be surprising if there were not a similar need for secondary obligations to be shaped by factors which are not express but depend upon the expectations of the parties in their particular contracting community.[30]

To see the correctness of Wightman's comments does not require one to take the view that the obligation to pay damages is itself intended by the parties[31] (a view that not even Holmes held[32]), and besides, the question

Nomine that '[I]nternational commerce on a large scale is red in tooth and claw' and '[I]t is in the nature of things unlikely that the wrongdoer will make a greater profit than [the difference between the contract and market price]. And if he does, it is an adventitious benefit which he can keep', *AB Corp v CD Co: The Sine Nomine* [2002] 1 Lloyd's Rep 805, 806.

[29] See Diplock LJ in *The Heron II* [1966] 2 QB 695 (CA), 730.

[30] 'Negligent Valuations and a Drop in the Property Market: the Limits of the Expectation Loss Principle' (1998) 61 *Modern Law Review* 68, 76.

[31] See Diplock LJ in *The Heron II* [1966] 2 QB 695 (CA), 730–1, who says that entering the contract implies an undertaking of 'a secondary obligation to make monetary reparation for any loss sustained by the other party of a kind which the non-performer has reasonable grounds for assuming that he, the other party, knows is liable to result from the breach.' Later Lord Diplock seems to have preferred the more orthodox view that the obligation to pay damages is implied in law but may be varied by agreement (see *Photo Production Ltd v Securicor Transport Ltd* [1980] AC 827, 848–9). See also E Peden, *Good Faith in the Performance of Contracts* (Chatswood, NSW, Butterworths, 2003), 16, and the discussion in D Harris, D Campbell and R Halson, n 28 above, 90.

[32] See *The Common Law*, n 25 above, 302 and M DeWolfe Howe, n 25 above, volume II, 233–5.

is complicated by the wide-spread knowledge among contractors that the law will impose legal liability for breach. Rather than argue for an intended obligation to compensate, it is argued herein merely that obligations are *oriented* to particular consequences and that the risks of such consequences are allocated within the contract. As Cartwright observes,

> In contract the defendant consents to be bound to an agreement which contains within it a particular balance of risks and rewards: in consequence, the limit to the losses for which he is responsible is set by reference to what he can be taken to have accepted at the time of concluding the agreement.[33]

The final step to an award of damages is taken by the law itself in the well-known rule that 'where a party sustains a loss by reason of a breach of contract, he is, so far as money can do it, to be placed in the same situation with respect to damages, as if the contract had been performed'.[34] The crucial thing to recognise here is that the contract itself determines which of the infinite characteristics of the situation in which the non-breaching party was expecting to be, require compensation.[35] Wightman, above, put this in terms of 'shaping' the obligation to pay damages 'by factors which are not express but depend upon the expectations of the parties in their particular contracting community'. The emphasis on expectations, discussed below in terms of social norms, is valuable, but Leon Green puts it more precisely, in terms that German lawyers will recognise:[36]

> Parties, in making contracts, rarely contemplate *the losses* which would result from its breach. But they do count the advantages they will gain from its performance. *What interests does the contract promote or serve?* These are actually considered in the most part, and those which are shown to have been considered or reasonably falling within the terms in view of the language used and background of the transaction, mark its boundaries—the limits of protection under it. Did the parties intend (using intention in the sense indicated above) that the injured interest was to be protected? Did this

[33] J Cartwright, 'Remoteness of Damage in Contract and Tort: A Reconsideration' (1996) 53 *Cambridge Law Journal* 488, 505.

[34] Parke B in *Robinson v Harman* (1848) 1 Exch 850, 855.

[35] Lord Hoffmann makes the same point in a slightly different way. In arguing that the scope of responsibility is determined by the scope of the obligation, he says of *Robinson v Harman* 'I think that this was the wrong place to begin. Before one can consider the principle on which one should calculate the damages to which a claimant is entitled as compensation for loss, it is necessary to decide for what kind of loss he is entitled to compensation… For this purpose it is better to begin at the beginning and consider the lender's cause of action.' *SAAMCO* [1997] AC 191, 211.

[36] German law limits recovery by reference to the protective purposes of the contract that was breached, the 'Schutzzweck der Norm'. See H Beale, A Hartkamp, H Kötz and D Tallon, *Cases, Materials and Text on Contract Law* (Oxford, Hart Publishing, 2002), 824–7 and D Coester-Waltjen, chapter 4 in this volume.

> agreement fairly comprehend the advantage now claimed to have been lost? [emphasis in original][37]

It would be absurd to argue that a vendor, who has agreed to deliver on a particular date, is unaware of or uninterested in the importance of the delivery to the promisee. Such an uninterested vendor would be ambivalent between the following: the delivery may be important because the promisee wants the vendor to get out of the house more, it may be important because the promisee thinks the date specified is astrologically auspicious, it may be important because the promisee needs the goods on the specified date for use, or it may be important because the promisee estimates that the market will be up on that date so the goods will fetch a good resale price. If promises are to provide reasons for action, that does not mean that all promises must, in practice, provide equally good reasons for action. The significance of the consequences of breach varies with the circumstances of the contract and the parties to it.

If we recognise that the obligations are oriented towards consequences, purposes and interests, then we can see that the measure of damages, and maybe the answers to other remedial questions, are determined by the contractual agreement itself. For this reason, I think that when Friedmann concedes that the rules of remoteness are not self-evident even once the contractual or tortious right has been identified,[38] he concedes too much. It is argued herein that the scope of responsibility for breach of contract is implicitly determined by the contract itself. The orientation is a descriptive feature of each obligation that goes without saying and can be implied (in fact) through the ordinary process of interpretation, looking at the factual matrix and the apparent purposes through the lens of the objective test and the usual common sense principles.[39]

FLESHING OUT THE ACCOUNT: A LIST OF NORMS

A little will be said about how such an orientation should be identified, in other words how it is accessed through the pragmatic process of

[37] *Rationale of Proximate Cause* (Kansas City, Mo, Vernon Law Book Co, 1927), 51.
[38] D Friedmann, 'The Performance Interest in Contract Damages', n 19 above, 636–7. He also concedes that the difference between contract and tort rules of remoteness is probably historically grounded, at footnote 57. See also Daniel Friedmann's essay in chapter 1 of this volume.
[39] *Investors Compensation Scheme v West Bromwich Buildings Society* [1998] 1 WLR 896. To use the terminology of my earlier article on the implication of terms (A Kramer, 'The Implication of Contract Terms as an Instance of Interpretation' (204) 63 *Cambridge Law Journal*, 384), the orientation of an obligation is more secondary (descriptive of obligations) than primary (creating a new and independent obligation), and so the interpreter needn't be too sceptical as to the orientation of the obligation going without saying. There is a licence to infer the orientation because the parties clearly intended the obligations to have some significance but also clearly intended responsibility for the consequences of breach not to be of unlimited scope.

interpretation. As discussed elsewhere, in the absence of express disavowal, a promisor appears to intend, and so is by the objective test deemed to have intended, the principles and standards that it would be normal to intend in the circumstances.[40] The norms are important only when and to the extent that they reasonably appear by both parties to have been intended; they are what the parties would have reasonably expected to apply: this is why the reasonable expectations are part of the binding agreement. Thus in arms-length commercial transactions the norms will be inclined more towards the assumption that the parties are out to serve and protect themselves, whereas in less commercial arrangements such as employment the norms will factor in more of an assumption of cooperation. All depends upon the contracting culture.[41] The following, then, are some possible norms that one might expect to apply in the absence of disavowal, although it must be stressed again that these will only be expected to apply if and when it is normal for them to apply, and indeed on their face they could not all apply as some would sometimes conflict:

1 Every Obligation Has Some Orientation

It is elementary that if a contractual promise has been made it must have some orientation — some interests it seeks to further or protect or some consequences that were in mind — else why was it made/required? In other words, it is very unlikely that parties will have intended a contractual promise to be without orientation and so responsibility for consequences, as that would mean the promise would be 'illusory'[42] and could be breached with impunity. As Pollock has said, in the context of a discussion of the doctrine of consideration, whatever 'a man chooses to bargain for must be conclusively taken to be of some value to him'.[43] Thus whereas a promisor may well be able to argue that in a particular case a promisee did not suffer any relevant (contractually contemplated) loss in a particular case of a breach, it rarely makes any sense to argue, with regard to a particular term, that the promisee could never suffer any relevant loss as a result of breach.[44] If this does appear to obtain, then 'relevant loss'

[40] See A Kramer, 'Common sense principles of contract interpretation (and how we've been using them all along)', (2003) 23 *Oxford Journal of Legal Studies* 173.
[41] R Brownsword, 'After *Investors*: Interpretation, Expectation and the Implicit Dimension of the "New Contextualism"' in D Campbell, H Collins and J Wightman, *Implicit Dimensions of Contract* (Oxford, Hart Publishing, 2003), 123ff.
[42] Lord Mustill uses this word to make essentially the same point in *Ruxley Electronics and Construction Ltd v Forsyth* [1996] AC 344, 360.
[43] *Principles of Contract*, 10th edn (London, Stevens, 1936), 172.
[44] Although occasionally terms may be guidelines with little or no intended risk attached. See H Beale and T Dugdale, 'Contracts Between Businessmen: Planning and the Use of Contractual Remedies' (1975) 2 *British Journal of Law & Society* 45.

is almost certainly not being defined the way the parties appear to intend it to be defined. This is the problem with cases such as *Surrey CC and Mole DC v Bredero Homes Ltd*[45], and cases in which a promise is made for the benefit of a third party.[46] To say that specific relief may be available in such cases is no answer: the damages remedy, the primary remedy in our law of contract, should be made adequate by giving effect to the responsibility assumed in all cases in which this is possible.[47] Just because it is difficult to assess loss in cases where the obligation is oriented towards a non-financial interest does not mean that the court should not make an assessment anyway, as it does in personal injury cases all the time.[48] Where a promisor made a gain from the breach, that may even provide an evidentially presumed measure of promisee loss, but the focus should still be on compensating for the losses within the contract's orientation, not on restoring gain.[49]

2 It May be that the Promisor can *Prima Facie* be Assumed to be Taking Responsibility for all Consequences with Regard to which the Promisee Considered the Promise Significant

This reminds us only that a promisor knows what he is letting himself in for and *prima facie* assumes responsibility that extends as far as the losses for which he is a *sine qua non* cause, since cause in our society is often sufficient for blame. However many of the following norms greatly limit the scope of the apparently intended responsibility beyond this one.

3 The Promisor Enters the Contract Voluntarily

In this respect the promisor's situation is very different to that of a tortfeasor. The incurring of the obligation out of choice indicates that the

[45] [1993] 1 WLR 1361.
[46] Such as *Beswick v Beswick* [1968] AC 58.
[47] In those few cases where the very remedy of compensation is incapable of giving full effect to the responsibility assumed, as opposed to the inadequacy being merely of the current rules governing that remedy, specific relief will still be required. See the discussion below at text to note 160.
[48] As Lord Mustill observes in *Ruxley Electronics and Construction Ltd v Forsyth* [1996] AC 344, 361.
[49] See the interesting discussion in A Phang and P Lee, 'Restitutionary and Exemplary Damages Revisited' (2003) 19 *Journal of Contract Law* 1, 7ff. If such a rule were adopted the burden of proof would fall on the promisor to show that the promisee's loss was less than the promisor's gain. Even where the burden were not discharged, the damages would still not be awarded for disgorgement of gain/restitution of profit. As an aside, it is not unusual for an evidential shift in the burden of proof to cause confusion as to the substantive basis of damages measurements: arguably the whole idea of the reliance interest is merely a mis-

incurring of the obligation is in the nature of a gift or sale (depending upon whether it is in a deed or a contract with consideration) rather than in the nature of a compulsory transfer of rights forced by society and its rules. Because of this, the promisor is not obliged to assume any more responsibility than she wishes to, and, of course, it is apparent that a promisor (being at least partly self-interested) will want to assume as little responsibility as is necessary for her purposes or is required by the promisee who is buying the promise. In other words, the scope of responsibility will almost always be heavily circumscribed.

4 The Promisee Enters the Contract Voluntarily

The promisee is not like the potential victim of a tort because the promisee has not had the transaction and relationship imposed upon him but rather has entered into it voluntarily. Consequently, the allocation of responsibility is made by the parties in full knowledge of the possibility of breach, and with full opportunities for disclosure and negotiation, whereas in the case of most torts the allocation is made by society with no awareness, input or control on the (eventual) victim's part. As the rules are not those of society but those of the parties, and as the transaction has not been entered into involuntarily, there is no reason to be harsh to the promisor or to err on the side of the promisee.[50] In standard form and consumer cases this norm may well not apply.

5 As the Promisor is Rational, the Promise and Assumption of Responsibility will be Part of a Plan

The promisor will only usually accept responsibility for consequences for which he is able to plan, and in any case is unlikely voluntarily to

reading of an evidential presumption that the promisee would have at least broken even (recovered costs) if the contract had been performed, an evidential presumption which serves in cases in which it is hard to prove the profit but is rebutted when it can be shown that a loss would have been made.

[50] Note that these features of contracts also apply to the tortious responsibility arising under negligence and resulting from an 'assumption of responsibility' for the consequences of a statement not being (carefully checked to be) true or a service not being (carefully) performed. Such cases similarly involve a transaction voluntarily entered into by the victim in advance of any tort, by way of the victim's voluntarily relying upon the tortfeasor. There are good arguments for saying that the scope of responsibility in such cases should follow the contract model (the scope of responsibility assumed) rather than the tort model, particularly, but not only, when there is concurrent liability under a contract. See further A Burrows, 'Solving the Problem of Concurrent Liability' in *Understanding the Law of Obligations* (Oxford, Hart Publishing, 1998), A Burrows, 'Limitations on Compensation' in A Burrows and E Peel, *Commercial Remedies: Current Issues and Problems* (Oxford, OUP, 2003), 35–6; and J Cartwright, n 33 above, especially at 500ff.

take responsibility for all the consequences of breach: to do so would be to guarantee performance in all respects. Thus, firstly and most simply, the promisor will not usually assume responsibility for unforeseeable losses since he cannot take them into account in deciding whether to perform or in guarding against liability for non-performance.[51] Secondly and more importantly, it will be understood from the context of the promising that the promise is made (the performance is desired) for a particular reason or reasons: the promisee's reasons for wanting the promise, the promisor's reasons for wanting to give the promise.[52] It will be these desired results that the promisor can reasonably be expected to be guaranteeing, and usually no more (given the promisor's interest in assuming no less responsibility than that required to serve the purposes of making the promise).

6 Furthermore: The Promisor is Usually Looking to Make a Profit

At least in commercial cases, not only will the promisor not intend to assume unforeseeable losses (as discussed in the previous norm), but the promisor intends to make a profit and to run a business and to look out for herself. Thus the circumstances of the deal, particularly the magnitude of the price[53] and what insurance could have been available at what cost, are relevant in determining what responsibility the promisor reasonably appears to have intended to assume.[54]

[51] Where a promisee communicates knowledge to the promisor it is more reasonable to understand the promisor as having assumed responsibility for the losses disclosed by that knowledge because such knowledge is a precondition to the promisor planning and acting rationally. The opportunity to plan and the unlikelihood that one would assume responsibility for unforeseeable losses are why we require communication of special knowledge before liability is imposed, not because we want to increase economic efficiency by encouraging information disclosure (as economists have argued). Efficiency may be desirable, but except insofar as such norms inform the objective reasonable understanding of the assumption by the promisor (see norm 11 below) they have no place in our current discussion. For discussion of the mitigation rule, see below. For a recent questioning of the economic analysis see EA Posner, 'Economic Analysis of Contract Law After Three Decades: Success or Failure?' (2003) 112 *Yale Law Journal* 829, especially 837 and 853–4.

[52] Of course, the promisor's reasons may be direct (putting the promisee at ease about a certain thing) and indirect (earning a particular price paid by the promisee for the promise). In the latter case, the promisee's reasons are the same as promisor's reasons, because the promisor knows that the promisee is only paying on the condition that the promisor secures the promisee's desired results.

[53] See further footnote 91 and surrounding text.

[54] Cf the dependence on the price paid of the reasonableness of exclusion and limitation clauses under the Unfair Contract Terms Act 1977 and the fairness of clauses under the Unfair Terms in Consumer Contract Regulations 1999 (SI 1999, No 2083). See for example the discussion in *George Mitchell(Chesterhall) Ltd v Finney Lock Seeds Ltd* [1983] 2 AC 803, 817 and (CA) [1983] QB 284, 302.

7 Insurance and Prices are Often (in Business) Fixed Generally Rather than on a Contract-By-Contract Basis

When a price is fixed generally, rather than for a specific bespoke transaction, the price will be fixed on the basis of the average magnitude of losses not a specific loss caused in a specific way, and so the scope of the consequences ('type' of loss) for which risk has been assumed by the promisor will be wide and unspecific. However in cases in which it is reasonable to expect the promisor to insure his risk, it may only be reasonable to expect the type of loss for which risk has been assumed to be as wide as the insurance likely to be available. Thus where a specific loss that occurs is caused in a way that would take it outside the insurance that could be expected to have been taken out (and upon the basis of which the transaction was entered), responsibility for that loss will often not have been assumed.

8 It May be that a Promisee is Less Likely to Accept the Risk of Suffering Physical Harm than to Accept the Risk of Suffering Economic Loss[55]

If this is the normal attitude of promisees, then, in the absence of express words or conflicting norms, it would be more reasonable to interpret a promisor as accepting responsibility for physical harms than for economic harms. Consequently, in physical cases the type of loss for which liability was assumed can be drawn more widely and the likelihood for such loss to give rise to responsibility need be lower.[56]

9 A Promisee Usually Accepts the Risk of Suffering Idiosyncratic Non-economic Losses Due to Disappointment or Lack of Pleasure

These are things often taken to be subject to the vicissitudes of life and luck. Generally the risk of loss of enjoyment or amenity will not be assumed by the promisor, although where the promisee's purpose in entering the contract was clearly of this nature (as in some consumer cases) then this norm is displaced, particularly in cases where there is no other obvious orientation to an obligation (see norm (1) above). Norms such as these depend upon such apparently messy factors as how stoical a culture

[55] Perhaps because, in the case of physical harm, the promisee is less likely to be as neutral when faced with the choice between being harmed and compensated on the one hand, and not being harmed or compensated on the other.
[56] This might explain Lord Denning's approach in *Parsons v Uttley Ingham & Co Ltd* [1978] QB 791, CA.

expects its members to be, and can thus change (albeit slowly) as a culture becomes more or less blaming and litigious. This makes sense, since the culture is part of the background against which the parties are contracting.

10 It May be that a Promisor will not Normally Accept the Risk of Losses that are Exacerbated by the Promisee's Impecuniosity

At least in commercial cases.[57]

11 Often the Party that can most Easily or Cheaply Avert the Consequences can be Assumed to have taken Responsibility for them[58]

This is Posner's view of the remoteness rule,[59] although he would base it directly on efficiency, rather than taking the approach here by which it is assumed that sometimes the parties will intend the most efficient allocation of risk.[60] A norm of joint-cost minimisation may also explain the rule preventing recovery of avoidable losses, again on grounds of implicit understanding (ie intention) rather than external manipulation of the contract and remedies in the name of efficiency.[61]

12 A Party is Unlikely to take Responsibility for Losses Caused by the Fault of the other Party

First, then, the promisor is unlikely to assume responsibility for losses caused by the promisee's own fault. If the mitigation rule is to have an

[57] This norm may allow for a middle way between the old English rule banning all recovery attributable to impecuniosity (stemming from *Liesbosch Dredger (Owners of) v Owners of SS Edison ('The Liesbosch')* [1933] AC 449 and overruled recently in *Lagden v O'Connor* [2003] UKHL 64, [2003] 3 WLR 1571), and a stark approach allowing recovery whenever impecuniosity is reasonably foreseeable as not unlikely (which it will be in most cases).

[58] Waddams observes that it is generally more efficient for a property owner or other business claimant to insure against the risk of loss, which he can accurately estimate, than for the service-provider to take out liability insurance. See SM Waddams, *The Law of Contracts*, 4th edn (Toronto, Canada Law Book Inc, 1999), para 740, and *The Law of Damages*, 3rd edn (Toronto, Canada Law Book Inc, 1997), para 14.330. See also H Collins, *The Law of* Contract, 4th edn (London, Butterworths, 2003), 413. ASM Waddams observes, *The Law of Damages* at para 14.350, this norm is not applicable to personal injuries.

[59] Posner J, *Evra Corp v Swiss Bank Corp* 673 F.2d 951 (7th Cir 1982), 957, purporting to follow *Siegel v Western Union Telephone Co* 37 N.E.2d 868 (Ill. App 1941). See also R Posner, *Economic Analysis of the Law*, 5th edn (New York, Aspen, 1998), 140–1.

[60] This may be why in contracts of sale it is generally understood that the buyer is responsible for consequential losses she suffers resulting from late delivery by the seller. See Beale and Dugdale, n 44 above, 54.

[61] D Campbell and H Collins, 'Discovering the Implicit Dimensions of Contract' in D Campbell, H Collins and J Wightman, *Implicit Dimensions of Contract* (Oxford, Hart Publishing, 2003) 43.

agreement-centred foundation, the most likely foundation is this norm (supplemented by a more positive cooperative obligation to attempt to minimise losses for which the other party will ultimately be liable) and the preceding one (number 11). Second, when looking at the promisee's assumption of risk, this norm may have implications in cases of promisor fraud. It is an established norm of interpretation that it is presumed that a promisee would not agree to exclusions of liability for fraudulent or negligent actions of the promisor or promisor's agent (such a presumption rebuttable in most cases by a clearly worded exclusion clause).[62] Similarly, it may be that a promisee cannot be reasonably understood to agree that the usual implicit exclusion of promisor liability for unforeseeable losses extend to cases of fraudulent breach by the promisor. This is discussed further below.[63]

13 The Use of a Fixed Price will Often Imply the Corresponding Allocation of Risk of Market Changes[64]

14 There Will be Many More Norms that Result from Specific Business Practices that cannot Easily be Generalised, Especially where there is a Contracting Community in which Customs can Develop[65]

USING THIS ACCOUNT TO EXPLAIN THE LAW

At first sight, the account proposed herein is ill-fitted as a description of the present law. The current rule of remoteness is that loss is considered not to be too remote if it is of a type or kind[66] that, at the time of contracting,[67]

[62] See the discussion in *Canada Steamship Lines Ltd. v The King* [1952] AC 192, *Photo Production Ltd* v *Securicor Transport Ltd* [1980] AC 827 and *HIH Casualty & General Insurance Ltd v Chase Manhattan Bank* [2003] UKHL 6, [2003] 2 Lloyd's Rep 61. As the *HIH Casualty & General Insurance* case confirms, there is also a rule of public policy alongside the norm, which rule prevents the exclusion of liability for one's own fraud even in the face of a clearly worded exclusion (Lord Bingham [68], Lord Hoffmann [78] and Lord Scott [85]). In such a case the norm is not rebuttable and the intentions of the parties are overruled.
[63] See 'Fraudulent Breaches of Contract'.
[64] SM Waddams, *The Law of Contracts*, n 58 above, para 740.
[65] See further J Wightman, 'Beyond Custom: Contract, Contexts, and the Recognition of Implicit Understandings' in D Campbell, H Collins and J Wightman, *Implicit Dimensions of Contract* (Oxford, Hart Publishing, 2003). I agree with Roy Kreitner, see chapter 2 in this volume, that the type of contract (carriage, merger, insurance etc.) is important for the measure of damages, but I say it is important because the type of contract indicates the norms that the parties tacitly intended to apply, whereas he argues that the type of contract indicates the measure of damages that is suited to a particular situation for external reasons (such as fairness, social utility and administrative concerns).
[66] *Parsons v Uttley Ingham & Co Ltd* [1978] QB 791, *Brown v KMR Services Ltd* [1995] 4 All ER 598.
[67] *Hadley v Baxendale* (1854) 9 Ex 341.

was reasonably foreseeable as not unlikely[68] to result, in the light of the knowledge that can be reasonably imputed to the promisor and the knowledge that the promisor in fact had.[69] Losses that fall within this definition are said to be in the 'reasonable contemplation of the parties'. The orthodox view of the law seems to provide little room for doubting that that mere knowledge of the promisor, without some further assumption of responsibility, is sufficient to give rise to liability, and indeed this 'further assumption of responsibility' approach has been rejected by the House of Lords.[70] Judges do not discuss pricing, insurance and the other matters referred to in the norms mentioned above, and indeed mental distress and loss of enjoyment are usually understood as being based upon a separate test of recoverability to the ordinary remoteness test. First appearances can be deceptive, however, and it will be shown that something like the account proposed herein is the best explanation of the law not only for prescribing changes but also for the purposes of describing and justifying the law as it stands at present.

Are Damages Essentially about Foreseeability or the Scope of an Assumption of Responsibility?

In *Hadley v Baxendale,* Baron Alderson did not need to consider whether mere foreseeability of a loss was sufficient for promisor responsibility, as the loss in that case was held not to be foreseeable. Soon after the decision, however, John Mayne raised just this issue:

> But it may be asked with great deference, whether the mere fact of such consequences being communicated to the other party will be sufficient, without going on to show that he was told that he would be held answerable for them, and consented to undertake such a liability?[71]

Mayne's view is on the same lines as the view put forward here, namely that contractual obligations are oriented towards various purposes and consequences of breach on the basis of apparently intended assumption of risk. The rival view is that remoteness is merely a test of knowledge-informed foreseeability, and that liability does not depend upon express or even implied assent to the foreseen risk. The assumption of risk view was at its height in the late nineteenth and early twentieth centuries,

[68] *The Heron II* [1969] 1 AC 350.
[69] *Victoria Laundry (Windsor) v Newman Industries* [1949] 2 KB 528 reinterpreting *Hadley v Baxendale* (1854) 9 Ex 341.
[70] *The Heron II* [1969] 1 AC 350, 422.
[71] JD Mayne, *A Treatise on the Law of Damages* (London, Sweet, 1856), 8. This was the first edition of the book that in its twelfth edition became *McGregor on Damages*.

championed by Sir James Shaw Willes in England[72] and Oliver Wendell Holmes Jr in the US. Willes J put the view in the following terms:

> the mere fact of knowledge cannot increase the liability. The knowledge must be *brought home* to the party sought to be charged, under such circumstances that he must know that the person he contracts with reasonably believes that he accepts the contract with the special condition attached to it [emphasis added].[73]

Holmes observed in the seminal Federal US case on contract remoteness that: 'the extent of liability... should be worked out on terms which it fairly may be presumed [the defendant] would have assented to if they had been presented to his mind.'[74] Extra-judicially he has written that

> What consequences of the breach are assumed is more remotely, in like manner, a matter of construction, having regard to the circumstances under which the contract is made. Knowledge of what is dependant upon performance is one of these circumstances. It is not necessarily conclusive, but it may have the effect of enlarging the risk assumed ... The price paid in mercantile contracts generally excludes the construction that exceptional risks were intended to be assumed.[75]

By the mid-twentieth century the pendulum had swung away from the assumption of risk theory. Although Asquith LJ appeared to support the *Nettleship* view in the *Victoria Laundry* case,[76] a dictum of Lord Upjohn in *The Heron II* expressly stated that mere knowledge and foresight is enough, rejecting the view that liability must be made a term of the contract.[77] Although it was the stricter form of the assumption of risk theory (requiring that the assumption of responsibility be an actual term of the contract) that had been rejected, this dictum has been taken as laying to rest the *Nettleship* approach.[78] With the exception of South Africa, where the

[72] *British Columbia and Vancouver's Island Spar, Lumber, and Saw-Mill Co v Nettleship* (1868), LR 3 CP 499 *Horne v Midland Railway* (1872) LR 7 CP 583 (Court of Common Pleas). Willes was counsel for Mr Baxendale in *Hadley*: Danzig, 'Hadley *v* Baxendale' (1975) 4 *Journal of Legal Studies* 249, 257ff. For other English support see *Portman v Middleton* (1858) 4 CB (NS) 322; *Horne v Midland Railway* (1873) LR 8 CP 131 (Exchequer Court); *Elbinger Aktiengesellschaft v Armstrong* (1874) LR 9 QB 473, 478; *Patrick v Russo-British Grain Export Co*, [1927] 2 KB 535, 540, but see FE Smith, 'The Rule in Hadley *v* Baxendale' (1900) 16 *Law Quarterly Review* 275, 284ff. and Pollock in M DeWolfe Howe, n 25 above, volume 1, 120.
[73] *Nettleship, ibid* 509. See also Justice Willes' comments at 505.
[74] *Globe Refining Co v Landa Cotton Oil Co* (1903) 190 US 540, 543.
[75] *The Common Law*, n 25 above, 302–3. See also M DeWolfe Howe, n 25 above, volume 1, 119 and volume 2, 55.
[76] *Victoria Laundry (Windsor) v Newman Industries* [1949] 2 KB 528, 538–9.
[77] [1969] 1 AC 350, 422. Note that Lord Reid expressly reserved judgment on this point, at 387A, and Lord Hodson quoted a relevant passage from *Nettleship* without comment, at 398.
[78] In *GKN Centrax Gears Ltd v Matbro Ltd*, [1976] 2 Lloyd's Rep 555 (CA), Lord Denning MR expressly states that Lord Upjohn's comments have this effect at 574. See also Stephenson LJ

tacit agreement approach is good law even now,[79] modern judges and textbooks give little attention to the assumption of risk view, and base remoteness squarely on foreseeability and knowledge.[80]

However despite this, it is submitted that the implied assumption of risk approach is still good law and the basis for the current remoteness test. The paucity of explicit recognition that the test is based upon the implied assumption of risk is due to the rarity with which the tests lead to a different result, because foresight and reasonable knowledge will almost always be enough to give rise to an apparent assumption of risk. It will almost always be correct that '[o]nce the defendant has been given notice of unusual potential losses, he can act accordingly, whether by refusing to contract, or by raising the price, or by reducing the probability of breach, or by excluding liability'[81] and so by entering the contract the defendant, without more, impliedly assumes responsibility for foreseeable losses.[82] This is so providing the unusual potential losses are part of the mutual context in which the contract is made and in which it stands to be interpreted.[83] However foresight will not always be enough to infer an assumption of responsibility.[84]

at 577 and Bridge LJ at 580. See also Goff J's statement in *The Pegase: Satef-Huttenes Alberns SpA* v *Paloma Tercera Shipping Co SA* [1981] 1 Lloyd's Rep 175, 182 that '[t]he decided cases appear to support the opinion so expressed by Lord Upjohn.'

79 This approach was championed by Sir Wessel JA in the 1930's, see especially *Lavery & Co Ltd v Jungheinrich* 1931 AD 156, 176 and JW Wessel, *Wessel's Law of Contract in South Africa* (Johannesburg, Hortors Ltd, 1937), paras 3256 and 3266. The South African Supreme Court of Appeal has several times conducted interesting discussions of the issue, and although the discussions are critical of *Lavery*, the Court has so far passed up the opportunity to conclusively rule against the tacit agreement approach and has confirmed it subsists. See *Shatz Investments (Pty) Ltd v Kalovyrnas* 1976 (2) AD 545, 551 and *Thoroughbred Breeders' Association of South Africa v Price Waterhouse* (2001) (4) SA 551 (SCA), 582 and 597.

80 The Restatement (Second) of Contracts and the UCC expressly reject the 'tacit agreement' test for the recovery of consequential damages: Restatement (Second) Contracts, §351 cmt a (1980); UCC § 2-715 cmt 2 (1995). It seems that there is some American support for the test at the federal level, however, eg *Wells Fargo Bank v United States*, 33 Fed Cl 233, 242–4 n 8 (1995). The Scottish Law Commission considered proposing legislation to restate the rule of remoteness solely in terms of foreseeability (Scottish Law Commission Discussion Paper No 109, *Remedies for Breach of Contract* (1999), para 8.22 and proposition 24), although decided against it (Scottish Law Commission No 174, *Report on Remedies for Breach of Contract* (1999), para 7.31).

81 AS Burrows, *Remedies for Torts and Breach of Contract*, 2nd edn (London, Butterworths, 1994) 56.

82 Initially, Mayne thought that it undesirable to make such an inference as it would put the onus upon the promisor to refuse to contract or to renegotiate: JD Mayne, *A Treatise on the Law of Damages*, 1st edn (London, Sweet, 1856) 8. By the third edition, his views had changed: see below at n 84.

83 As Diplock LJ observes, *Robophone Facilities Ltd v Blank* [1966] 1 WLR 1428, 1448, special knowledge must be acquired from the promisee 'or at least ... he should know that the [promisee] knew that he was possessed of it.' For further discussion of the mutuality point see Kramer, above n 40, 178–9.

84 Mayne and Smith put it as follows: 'Where a person who has knowledge or notice of such special circumstances might refuse to enter into the contract at all, or might demand a higher remuneration for entering into it, the fact that he accepts the contract without requiring any higher rate will be evidence, though not conclusive evidence, from which it may be inferred that he has accepted the additional risk in case of breach.' JD Mayne and L Smith, *Mayne's Treatise on Damages*, 3rd edn (London, Stevens and Hayes, 1877) 33.

In short, the inference of assumption of responsibility from mere foreseeability is not justified in the following (overlapping) situations:[85]

i) Where the promisor has no choice but to enter the contract, entering the contract does not indicate a voluntary assumption of the risk of foreseeable losses as it was not voluntary. This may explain some of the common carrier cases.[86]
ii) Where the consequences of breach are severe, as compared to the benefits received by the promisor under the contract (the price), it will sometimes not be reasonable to infer that the promisor undertook the risk of such consequences merely from the promisor's apparent foresight of such consequences.[87] This point is made by Robert Goff J in *The Pegase*, who explains that where breach is not unlikely to result in 'particularly high profits ... or... particularly catastrophic results' such as the stoppage of a whole factory for want of machinery or raw materials (as occurred in both *Hadley v Baxendale* and *Nettleship*), more than mere foresight may be required to infer an assumption of risk.[88] As Halson explains, '[i]ndications of the implicit assumption of responsibility would come from D's adjustment of the proposed price, or from his adding some provision to the contract to deal with the risk, such as a clause restricting C's remedy or one which in specified circumstances excused D's non-performance'.[89] As the paradigmatic example shows, 'if I tell my taxi driver that I will miss the opportunity of making a profit of £1 million if I fail to reach an appointment on time, his acceptance of me as a passenger should not lead to the inference that he accepts the risk',[90] although things would be

[85] For example, even *Hadley v Baxendale* itself is probably not explicable on the basis of a foreseeability rule alone and is explicable on one or more of the bases that follow in the text. See further R Cooke, 'Remoteness of Damages and Judicial Discretion' (1978) 37 *Cambridge Law Journal* 288, 290.
[86] Haultain CJS makes this point well in *Rivers v George White and Sons Co Ltd* (1919) 46 DLR 145 (Sask CA), 147. Mayne introduces this point into the third edition of his text: Mayne and Smith, above n 84, 25, 28 and his second and third 'rules', 33. See also Diplock LJ at 728 in the CA in *The Heron II*. However in cases of extraordinary risk the common carrier may be able to refuse to contract or to demand extraordinary remuneration: Lush J in *Horne v Midland Railway Co* (1873) LR 8 CP 131,145.
[87] See JW Carter and DJ Harland, *Contract Law in Australia*, 3rd edn (Sydney, Butterworths, 1996), 783.
[88] N 79 above, 184. It is noteworthy that the American Restatement (Second) of Contracts takes the approach proposed in the text: under §351(3), courts are given a discretion to reduce damages for foreseeable loss if the loss is disproportionate to the price paid because in such circumstances the promisor may not be intended to bear the risk (see comment f and illustrations 17–19 to that section).
[89] D Harris, D Campbell and R Halson, n 28 above, 97.
[90] *Ibid*. In such a case the price charged does not reasonably appear to take account of the risk that would fall upon the driver if he were to be liable for the loss of the large profit, and so the driver does not reasonably appear to have taken the risk of the loss. For a brief discussion of

different if he upped the fare to £100,000.[91] In the absence of such indications of an assumption of responsibility, it is at least necessary that the loss was 'signalised' to the promisor as part of the 'purpose and intent' of the promisee in entering the contract such that 'he may fairly be held, in entering his contract, to have accepted the risk'.[92]

iii) Where the promisor has been communicated knowledge that renders losses foreseeable, it may not be reasonable to understand that promisor as implicitly accepting responsibility for the losses where the communication of the information was, albeit before the contract was entered into, too late to assist the promisor. If the promisor has already performed his promise to the relevant extent (for example where the goods have already been manufactured and boxed) and has already fixed the price (for example where, as is usual, the price is fixed generally) and has already taken out whatever insurance is to be taken out (for example where insurance is taken out generally) then the promisor cannot realistically make greater endeavours not to breach or secure an increased return or secure against the risk. In such circumstances it may well be too late reasonably to understand the promisor to have taken the risk, given that the usual justification for foreseeability giving rise to responsibility is that 'the parties might have specially provided for the breach of contract by special terms as to the damages in that case'.[93] Although the parties may still provide special terms, they are, as we all know, in practice unlikely to do so, and so the opportunity is more theoretical than real.

Since many transactions, particularly consumer ones, are standardised rather than negotiated individually, the situation discussed in the previous paragraph may be very common. As Atiyah observes of contracts of carriage, 'terms are likely to be fixed by the carrier on the basis of some general rate applicable to the weight or volume or quantity of the goods to be carried. It is normally impracticable to fix a separate rate for every contract.'[94] Because the price and the terms are fixed in advance,

this issue see PS Atiyah, *An Introduction to the Law of Contract*, 5th edn (Oxford, Clarendon Press, 1995), 467.

[91] See D Harris, D Campbell and R Halson, *ibid*, 92; see also SM Waddams, *The Law of Contracts*, para 740 and *The Law of Damages*, paras. 14.190–14.200, both n 58 above. As the taxi example shows, Burrows goes too far when he says that the 'fact that the claimant's losses are out of all proportion to what the defendant was to receive under the contract is irrelevant', A Burrows, 'Chapter 18: Judicial Remedies' in P Birks, ed., *English Private Law* (Oxford, OUP, 2000), 830.
[92] Per Lightman QC, *Seven Seas Properties Ltd v Al-Essa (No 2)* [1993] 1 WLR 1083, 1088 (Ch D).
[93] Alderson B in *Hadley v Baxendale* (1854) 9 Ex 341. See also, GH Treitel in *Remedies for Breach of Contract: A Comparative Account* (Oxford, Clarendon Press, 1988) 156.
[94] PS Atiyah, *The Rise and Fall of Freedom of Contract* (Oxford, OUP, 1979) 433.

as the consumer well knows, it will often not be reasonable to think that the promisor has accepted responsibility merely because the promisee has communicated a special circumstance to her. If a buyer mentions to a high street electronics salesman, before finalising the purchase of a television, that the television will be placed in a highly flammable room, then it is not reasonable to understand the salesman to be accepting the risk of the television malfunctioning, giving off sparks, and setting the house on fire. It is important to note that in this and many such cases, the risk in question may well be one that the vendor has already accepted, since it is reasonable in such cases to understand the promisor as fixing his risk broadly and in very general terms given that the pricing and insurance are done on that basis.[95] However the point being made here is that the particular communication of the special information makes no difference to the apparent scope of the assumed risk unless the promisor in some way 'signalises' an acceptance of the risk.[96]

iv) Where the promisor has been communicated knowledge that renders losses foreseeable, it may not be reasonable to understand that promisor as implicitly accepting responsibility for the losses where the communication of the information was casual;[97] fortuitous,[98] or from someone other than the claimant;[99] or to an employee who, albeit with authority to undertake responsibility, is unlikely to do so lightly and so impliedly and in commercial reality plays no part in negotiating the terms.[100] As with the case in the previous paragraph, the loss may still fall within the scope of the responsibility assumed, not because it is reasonable to think that responsibility was assumed in response to the communication of special knowledge, but rather because it is reasonable to think that the risk was fixed broadly with a general assessment of the possible losses.[101]

[95] Indeed, as Beale observes, 'the party in breach may have made the deliberate decision not to implement office procedures to deal with unusual risks because the costs would outweigh the benefits.' H Beale, *Remedies for Breach of Contract* (London, Sweet & Maxwell, 1980).

[96] N 92 above.

[97] Cf *Kemp v Intasun Holidays Ltd* [1987] 2 FTLR 234. See J Smith, *The Law of Contract*, 4th edn (London, Sweet & Maxwell, 2002), 222, J Beatson, *Anson's Law of Contract*, 28th edn (Oxford, OUP, 2002), 609.

[98] E McKendrick, *Contract Law: Text, Cases, and Materials* (Oxford, OUP, 2003), 1061.

[99] D Harris, 'Chapter 26: Damages' in HG Beale, ed., *Chitty on Contracts*, 29th edn (London, Sweet & Maxwell, 2004), H McGregor, *McGregor on Damages*, 17th edn (London, Sweet & Maxwell, 2003), para 6-176. But see H McGregor, *Contract Code drawn up on behalf of the English Law Commission* (Milan, Giuffre, 1993) at 120.

[100] Atiyah, n 94 above, 432–33. See also authorities cited above at note 91.

[101] See norm 7 above.

Despite this, in many, or perhaps the majority, of situations, foreseeability of the loss will be sufficient for the promisee to infer that the risk of loss was assumed by the promisor. This should not blind us, however, to the underlying principle according to which remoteness is dependant upon assumption of risk, with foresight important only insofar as it (along with the fact of subsequent entry into the contract) indicates an apparent assumption of risk.[102] As Halson puts it:

> This should be put in terms of the intention of the parties rather than in terms of reasonable contemplation or foreseeability. Although the categories of loss which are reasonably anticipated will often be those for which the parties intend D to be liable, their intention (express or implicit) should be the paramount test: it may sometimes be inferred from the express terms that there was an intention that D should not be liable for a particular loss even though it could have been reasonably anticipated.[103]

As McGregor observes, '[n]ot only must the parties contemplate that the damage resulting from the special circumstances may occur, but they must further contemplate that the defendant is taking the risk of being liable for such consequences should they occur.'[104] Recently, Waller LJ, *obiter*, approved McGregor's observation,[105] explicitly stating that 'simply drawing the attention of the [promisor] to special circumstances, does not necessarily impose a liability on the payer to be responsible for damages flowing from the special circumstances to which attention has been drawn' and stating that for the promisee to succeed at trial he would have to demonstrate that the promisee had 'accepted the risk' of the particular loss for which the claim was brought.[106] The formidable chorus of modern academic voices to this effect should be harkened,[107] and the test

[102] Bridge LJ is explicit about this *GKN Centrax Gears Ltd v Matbro Ltd* [1976] 2 Lloyd's Rep 555, CA 580. See also Diplock LJ in *The Heron* II, CA, 731 and 728; Salmon LJ in the *The Heron II* [1966] 2 QB 695, CA, 739; and the minority in *British Columbia and Vancouver's Island Spar, Lumber, and Saw-Mill Co v Nettleship* (1868) LR 3 CP 499.

[103] D Harris, D Campbell and R Halson, n 28 above, 90–1.

[104] *McGregor on Damages*, above n 99, para 6-177. This view is reflected in McGregor's *Contract Code*, above n 99, at article 437 and the accompanying discussion at page 121: in art 437, the requirement of foreseeability is supplemented by a requirement that, in addition, 'the party against whom the claim is made ... could reasonably be regarded as having contracted to be liable.'

[105] Referring to exactly this statement, although in the earlier 16th edition of *McGregor on Damages*. Waller LJ also approves Robert Goff J's statement in the *Pegase*, quoted later in this paragraph.

[106] *Mulvenna v Royal Bank of Scotland plc* [2003] EWCA Civ 1112 at paras [24]–[26].

[107] As well as those already quoted, see particularly D Campbell and H Collins, n 61 above, 45; H Collins, *The Law of* Contract, 4th edn (London, Butterworths, 2003), 413; F Dawson, 'Reflections on Certain Aspects of the Law of Damages for Breach of Contract' (1995) 9 *Journal Contract Law* 20; D Harris in *Chitty on Contracts*, n 100 above, paras 26-055, 26-056; D Harris, D Campbell and R Halson, n 28 above, 90–1; *McGregor on Damages*, above n 99, para 6–177; GH Treitel, *The Law of Contract*, 11th edn (London, Sweet & Maxwell, 2003), 970;

should be reformulated. We could do worse than adopt the formulation of Robert Goff J (as he then was):

> have the facts in question come to the defendant's knowledge in such circumstances that a reasonable person in the shoes of the defendant would, if he had considered the matter at the time of making the contract, have contemplated that, in the event of a breach by him, *such facts were to be taken into account when considering his responsibility for loss suffered by the plaintiff as a result of such breach*. The answer to that question may vary from case to case, taking in to consideration such matters as, for example, the nature of the facts in question and how far they are unusual, and the extent to which such facts are likely to make fulfilment of the contract by the due date more critical, or to render the plaintiff's loss heavier in the event of non-fulfilment [emphasis added].[108]

How Likely Must Occurrence of the Loss Be?

If, as is argued, foreseeability is important because of what it indicates about assumption of risk, then the level of likelihood of occurrence of the loss that must be foreseen is certain: a loss must be foreseeable as sufficiently likely that it can be inferred that the promisor assumed responsibility for it. This, in turn, is a question of fact requiring the application of a purposive test and norms of behaviour. If this is right, then ballpark figures/rules of thumb such as 'not unlikely' and 'serious danger', as put forward in the House of Lords in *The Heron II*, are helpful. As Dawson argues:

> The question in every case is the extent of the secondary obligation undertaken by the defaulting promisor at the time that he enters into the contract. The question is did the promisor implicitly or explicitly undertake responsibility for the loss which has occurred. Clearly if the particular damage that has occurred can be expected to arise in the usual course of things, a court is likely to find that the defendant assumed responsibility for that loss. Similarly, if a particular loss is highly unlikely to occur, it will be difficult (although not impossible) to say that the defendant has undertaken responsibility for that loss.[109]

If the proposed thesis is incorrect, however, then foreseeability is either an end in itself, or serves to indicate some other principle other than assumption of risk. If the former, then the test, made up of fuzzy words ('serious danger', 'not unlikely' etc), is inherently uncertain and so unhelpful

SM Waddams, *The Law of Contracts*, paras 740ff, and *The Law of Damages*, paras 14.200ff, both n 58 above. But see eg A Burrows, n 91 above, 830.

[108] *The Pegase*, n 78 above, 184.
[109] F Dawson, n 107 above, 33–4.

without a purposive principle behind it. If the latter, and there is some other principle behind the test, then what is that principle? For their Lordships in *The Heron II* to expend significant effort on pin-pointing a precise level of likelihood with which a loss must be foreseen, without explaining on what basis they were determining the level (except that it was stricter than tort), is to reduce proceedings to farce. As Cartwright observes, '[t]he question, 'how foreseeable?' cannot be separated from the question of why we use a test based on foreseeability: the content of a rule must fulfil the policy of the rule.'[110] Without a reasoned justification for the rule, we are left with 'abstract speculation on the literal meanings of words' which produces 'a pointless logomachy in the leading cases.'[111] However when we take an agreement-centred view, we can ask whether the risk was one the promisor 'when he was settling the balance of the bargain … could *realistically* have had in mind as the consequences of his failure to fulfil his obligations.'[112] This is a difficult test, but at least it has content.

Only the 'Type' or 'Kind' of Loss, and Not the Precise Loss, Must be Foreseeable as Not Unlikely

Probably the best explanation for why the courts haven't needed to accept that remoteness is about an assumption of risk, and haven't explicitly addressed the norms discussed above that decide whether or not there has been an assumption to be assessed, is that these norms are usually applied, where necessary, under the veil of the 'type or kind' test. It is common ground that it is not the precise loss that must be foreseen (as not unlikely), rather it is only the type or kind of loss, of which the actual loss is one manifestation.[113] To fix the level of probability by which a loss must be foreseeable (with hair-splitting precision in *The Heron II*) comes to nought if there is no precise way of fixing the level of generality with which a loss must be foreseeable. A general loss of profits may be foreseeable as 99 per cent likely to result from breach, but a particular loss of profits caused in a particular way through loss of a particular deal may be unforeseeable or foreseeable as 1 per cent likely.[114] Thus, as Harris

[110] N 33 above, 493. See also SM Waddams, *The Law of Contracts*, n 58 above, para 736.
[111] D Campbell and H Collins, n 61 above, 45.
[112] *Ibid*, 49.
[113] *Parsons v Uttley Ingham & Co Ltd* [1978] QB 791, *Brown v KMR Services Ltd* [1995] 4 All ER 598. In French law the extent of loss, and not only the type of loss, must be foreseeable: B Nicholas, *The French Law of Contract*, 2nd edn (Oxford, Clarendon Press, 1992). As the following discussion shows, common law manipulation of the concept of type means that similar results are reached in the common law and French systems.
[114] See *Victoria Laundry (Windsor) v Newman Industries* [1949] 2 KB 528 and *Brown v KMR Services Ltd* [1995] 4 All ER 598, which both fit this sort of pattern but were decided differently.

observes, '[t]he application of the test for remoteness to a particular set of facts therefore depends largely on the judicial discretion to categorise losses into broad categories.'[115]

The consequences of breach are the data that must be categorised into types on the basis of set criteria. Without agreed criteria, it is impossible to distinguish between type or extent, and the consequences of breach can be categorised into types in an infinite number of ways, none of them salient. Which features of losses render them different types and which features merely render them different extents of loss of the same type? With what level of specificity must a loss be foreseeable? This problem is often raised,[116] but no answers are ever provided because there is no accepted principle upon which such answers could be based.

It is submitted that the best way of making sense of the 'type/extent' distinction is to see it as part of the application of the basic test of assumption of risk. The degree of likelihood by which something must be foreseen and the characteristics by which the 'something' that must be foreseen is defined, the type, are both servants to the basic test of whether, and to what extent, it reasonably appears that risk was assumed for the consequences of a breach. The type/extent question is really an inquiry into whether the loss differs in significant ways from the sorts of losses envisaged at the time of making the contract. The key question, of course, is what count as 'significant ways'. The answer must be: 'whatever reasonably appears to have been significant to the promisor who was assuming the risk', the promisor who was setting the price, taking out insurance, and deciding how much effort to expend in seeking to perform.

When this is accepted, and norms of the sort suggested above[117] are brought into consideration, much of the mystery disappears. Sometimes, as Cartwright observes, 'unexpectedly high economic losses are indicative of a *different order of risk* undertaken by the defendant under the contract [emphasis added]',[118] but this will only be so where the magnitude of the economic loss indicates that it differs in a way that is significant, such that the promisor could not reasonably have been expected to have taken that loss into account when setting the price and taking out insurance. Where that is the case, the loss will sometimes still be similar in enough significant ways that the contemplated element of the loss (that

[115] N 99 above, para 26–050. See also SM Waddams, *The Law of Contracts*, para 737, and *The Law of Damages*, paras. 14.260–14.270, both n 58 above.
[116] A Burrows, n 91 above, §18.40 and n 81 above, 50; M Furmston, *Cheshire, Fifoot & Furmston's Law of Contract*, 14th edn (2001), 665 n 1; E McKendrick, n 98 above, 1071ff.
[117] See p 259 above.
[118] N 33 above, 506 footnote 65. See also *Brown v KMR Services Ltd* [1995] 4 All ER 598 (CA), per Stuart-Smith LJ at 620: 'But I do not see any difficulty in holding that loss of ordinary business profits is different in kind from that flowing from a particular contract which gives rise to very high profits, the existence of which is unknown to the other contracting party who *therefore does not accept the risk* of such loss occurring' [emphasis added].

which could have been taken account of when setting the price and taking out insurance) may still be recoverable.[119] In such cases, although the species of loss is not contemplated, providing the genus of the loss *is*, recovery may be made up to the value of an ordinary loss under the species that was contemplated but didn't in fact occur.[120]

Other 'type' issues can be explained once the agreement-centred, and so normatively focused, account of remoteness is adopted. For example, in *Parsons v Uttley Ingham & Co Ltd*,[121] a supplier of a defective food hopper was held liable for pig fatalities resulting in a then unforeseeable way from the pigs' consumption of mouldy nuts. It seems that the Court of Appeal in the *Parsons* case felt that risk reasonably appeared to have been assumed by the promisor for just about any physical damage to the pigs, that the promisor should have known that the hopper was intended to further the pigs' physical well-being, and that generally physical harm is likely to be less palatable to promisees than other harm and so the risk of it is less likely to be assumed by them.[122] In such cases neither the precise manner in which that damage is caused, nor the likelihood that it will be caused, make a significant difference to the promisor, and so they make no significant difference to the scope of risk that the promisor appears to have intended to assume. Indeed, the likelihood that a consequence will result is often barely relevant where its occurrence depends upon factors outside the control of the parties. Lord Pearce gives the following example in *The Heron II*:

> Suppose a contractor was employed to repair the ceiling of one of the Law Courts and did it so negligently that it collapsed on the heads of those in court. I should be inclined to think that any tribunal … would have found as a fact that the damage arose 'naturally, ie according to the usual course of things.' Yet if one takes into account the nights, weekends, and vacations, when the ceiling might have collapsed, the odds against it collapsing on top of anybody's head are nearly ten to one.[123]

As this demonstrates, if a consequence (such as the collapse of the ceiling) is the sort of consequence that is one of the things against which a contract is guarding, the relative improbability of its occurring will rarely

[119] As in *Victoria Laundry (Windsor) v Newman Industries* [1949] 2 KB 528.
[120] Pothier, above n 2, para 173, *Cory v Thames Ironworks Co* (1868) LR 3 QB 181. This will be fair where it reasonably appears to the promisee that price, but not insurance (which may not extend to the sub-species of loss actually suffered), is significant in determining the promisor's loss. In other words, it all depends whether or not the sub-species differ in a sufficiently significant way. This is a difficult aspect of the test, and deserves closer examination, but can only be an improvement over the present situation in which none of these issues are discussed.
[121] [1978] QB 791, CA.
[122] Norm 8 above.
[123] [1969] 1 AC 350, 417. See further F Dawson, n 107 above, 38.

render the losses resulting too remote because the improbability is, in such cases, not relevant to the promisor's apparent assumption of risk. In such cases the directness or indirectness of the loss may reasonably appear to be more significant to the assumption of risk (and sometimes the taking out of insurance against liability) than the likelihood of the loss.[124]

Indeed, the account proposed would bring within the sphere of remoteness and under one coherent principle several other doctrines of the law of responsibility for breach of contract that are not currently thought of as determined by the rules of remoteness, as follows.

Mental Distress, Loss of Amenity and Idiosyncratic Losses[125]

It is accepted that in awarding damages, courts seek to put the claimant in the position in which he would have been had the contract been performed. In recent decades the law's approach to the 'position in which he would have been' has become more sophisticated, recognising that it is not only financial goals (in terms of assets and profits) that motivate people to enter contracts, and that where the contract is understood to be one that is oriented towards other goals, the promisor will often reasonably appear to have assumed responsibility for the failure to achieve those goals. So far the courts have not allowed such losses to be recovered under the basic remoteness test, but rather have imposed a special rule, although the specialness of the rule is disappearing. It used to be thought that damages for mental distress were only available where 'the very object of a contract is to provide pleasure, relaxation, peace of mind or freedom from molestation',[126] but this has been broadened significantly in two House of Lords decisions. In *Ruxley Electronics and Construction Ltd v Forsyth*,[127] loss of amenity damages were awarded against a construction company when a swimming pool failed to provide the enjoyment that could reasonably be expected. This is a far cry from holiday[128] and wedding photograph[129] cases and in principle could extend to most consumer contracts.[130] More recently, in *Farley v Skinner*[131] the House of Lords tempered the special rule by holding that it is not necessary for peace of mind to be 'the very object' of the contract, and that 'it is sufficient if a major or important object of the contract is to give pleasure, relaxation or peace of mind.'[132]

[124] F Dawson, *ibid* 47.
[125] See further E McKendrick and K Worthington, chapter 13 in this volume.
[126] Bingham LJ in *Watts v Morrow* [1991] 1 WLR 1421, 1445.
[127] [1996] AC 344.
[128] *Jarvis v Swan's Tours* [1973] QB 233, *Jackson v Horizon Holidays* [1975] 1 WLR 1468.
[129] *Diesen v Samson* 1971 SLT (Sh Ct) 49.
[130] See especially the speech of Lord Mustill.
[131] [2001] UKHL 49, [2002] 2 AC 732.
[132] At [24].

It is argued that the reason for the current existence of a special rule is not any special feature of amenity or distress loss, but rather that the current doctrine of remoteness, with its over-concentration on foreseeability at the expense of the general principle of assumption of risk, is inadequate to account for these cases.

Bingham LJ has stated:

> A contract-breaker is not in general liable for any distress, frustration, anxiety, displeasure, vexation, tension or aggravation which his breach of contract may cause to the innocent party. This rule is not, I think, founded on the assumption that such reactions are not foreseeable, which they surely are or may be, but on considerations of policy.[133]

It is respectfully submitted that his Lordship is correct that mental distress and amenity cases cannot be explained on the grounds of foreseeability, as such losses may well be foreseeable in many more cases than recovery is, and should be, allowed.[134] However it is also respectfully submitted that the limitation on such recovery is not based on considerations of policy as his Lordship stated, but rather is based on the rarity with which responsibility for such losses will be assumed by the promisor. If the approach proposed herein is accepted then there would be no special rule for mental distress and loss of amenity damages, but rather such losses would be available whenever it reasonably appears that responsibility for them has been assumed. This determination would depend upon whether the contract is oriented towards pleasure or other non-financial consumer goals, given that all contractual obligations must be intended to have some contractually significant goals (see norm 1 above) but that generally (since such losses are hard to quantify, often ephemeral, and to be expected as vicissitudes of modern life[135]) such losses will not be within the scope of responsibility of the contract (see norm 9 above). As Green observed, the question to ask is: 'What interests does the contract promote or serve?'[136] The test as to whether pleasure was 'an important object' of the contract is merely to emphasise that for recovery such pleasure must be not merely foreseeable but also an understood orientation of the contract within the responsibility of the

[133] *Watts v Morrow* [1991] 1 WLR 1421, 1445.

[134] D Yates, 'Damages for Non-Pecuniary Loss' (1973) 36 *Modern Law Review* 535, 538; AS Burrows, 'Mental distress damages in contract — a decade of change' [1984] *Lloyds Maitime Commercial Law Quarterly* 119, 121. Contrast the approach of the Scottish Law Commission Report 174, *Report on Remedies for Breach of Contract* (1999), which recommended that non-patrimonial losses should be recoverable subject only to the ordinary remoteness rule (§3.8) and yet understood the ordinary remoteness rule solely in terms of foreseeability (§7.31).

[135] For example, contract-breaking itself is an 'incident of commercial life which players in the game are expected to meet with mental fortitude', per Lord Cooke in *Johnson v Gore Wood & Co (No 1)* [2002] 2 AC 1, 49.

[136] N 37, 51.

promisor, and that usually this will not be the case. Under this test, it seems that in the usual surveyor case there is no apparent assumption of responsibility for peace of mind as such contracts are contemplated as being solely financial in orientation, but that this can be displaced where there is a specific undertaking to investigate a matter that is important for the buyer's peace of mind.[137] With this understood, there is no need for a special rule to supplement the basic contemplation test (as reformulated herein).[138]

Cases of skimped performance, in which the promisor, in providing a service, has provided less than was required under the contract specifications,[139] and cases of promises for the benefit of a third party, can be brought within the same umbrella.[140] All are questions of whether the promise was oriented towards some valued purpose of the promisee, whether or not it had financial value. This is the same idea as the 'consumer surplus' idea that was raised in both *Ruxley* and *Farley*.[141]

SAAMCO

The most important recent decision on the scope of assumed responsibility for the consequences of breach is that of the House of Lords in *South*

[137] This is one explanation for the different results in *Farley v Skinner* [2001] UKHL 49, [2002] 2 AC 732 and *Watts v Morrow* [1991] 1 WLR 1421. However things are not so simple. If the special agreement to investigate noise levels is an extra obligation undertaken by the surveyor, then it introduces new liability and new losses. However if the surveyor is already obliged to investigate noise levels then the 'special agreement' amounts merely to a special communication as to losses resulting from breach, in other words an intimation by the promisee that if the promisor breaches the promisee will lose enjoyment. In this case much would depend upon whether the intimation was too late (discussed above at 270) or too casual (discussed above at 271). And is it not implicit that a house-buyer is seeking peace of mind and that an obligation to investigate noise levels is not only about financial value but also about enjoyment? For this latter point see E McKendrick and M Graham, 'The Sky's the Limit: Contractual Damages for Non-Pecuniary Loss' [2002] *Lloyds Maritime & Commercial Law Quarterly* 161, 163.

[138] See *McGregor on Damages*, above n 99, paras 3-021 and 3-030, and Lord Scott in *Farley v Skinner* [2001] UKHL 49, [2002] 2 AC 732 at [75].

[139] *City of New Orleans v Firemen's Charitable Association* 9 So 486 (1891), *Surrey County Council v Bredero Homes Ltd* [1993] 1 WLR 1361, *White Arrow Express Ltd v Lamey's Distribution Ltd.* (1996) 15 Trading LR 69, (1995) *The Times*, 21 July.

[140] See the discussion of Lord Griffiths in *Linden Gardens Ltd. v Lenesta Sludge Disposals Ltd.* [1994] 1 AC 85 and Lords Goff and Millett in *Alfred McAlpine Construction Ltd v Panatown Ltd* [2001] 1 AC 518.

[141] The idea is most clearly formulated in D Harris, A Ogus and J Philips, 'Contract Remedies and the Consumer Surplus' (1979) 95 *Law Quarterly Review* 581, cited in *Ruxley* by Lord Mustill at 360, and in *Farley* by Lord Steyn at [21] and Lord Hutton at [48]. Lord Scott's judgment in *Farley* is particularly important for its grounding of the remedy in that case within a broad intangible interests theory. See further B Coote, 'Contract damages, *Ruxley*, and the performance interest' [1997] *Cambridge Law Journal* 537, E McKendrick, 'Breach of contract and the meaning of loss' [1999] *Current Legal Problem* 37, J Cartwright, 'Compensatory Damages: Some Central Issues of Assessment' in A Burrows and E Peel, *Commercial Remedies: Current Issues and Problems* (Oxford, OUP, 2003).

Australia Asset Management Corp v York Montague,[142] although none of their Lordships used the word 'remote' or 'remoteness' anywhere in their judgments.[143] There is no space to investigate the complicated facts of the case, which are ably discussed elsewhere;[144] essentially, some property valuers negligently overvalued property and so the banks that had engaged the valuers lent money against the security of the property. The valuers were not held liable for all the banks' losses even though the banks would not have advanced the money had the valuations been careful (and so accurate), since the part of the loss that was due to the property market falling was held to be part of the banks' responsibility. This was so because the valuers had not undertaken to advise on whether and how much to lend against the properties, only to provide valuation information. Part of the responsibility, and so the risk, for acting upon that information must lie with the banks.

Lord Hoffmann, giving the only reasoned speech, explained that, as in tort, it is necessary before quantifying losses to determine the extent of liability under the obligation assumed, meaning 'the kind of loss in respect of which the duty was owed' which 'is defined by the term which the law implies' which requires 'construction of the agreement as a whole in its commercial setting' and in the light of its purpose.[145] This is exactly what is being proposed in this account: the orientation of the obligation was towards the provision of accurate information rather than advice, and so losses caused by the market drop are attributable to the acts of the banks in deciding to lend the money, and not to the breach by the promisor (even though but for the careless valuation the losses would not have occurred). The market losses are of a different type or kind with regard to this contractual obligation because of the nature of the service that was being provided.[146] Lord Hoffmann explicitly decides the assumption of responsibility issue on the basis of implied intention:

> The scope of the implied duty in the sense of the consequences for which the valuer is responsible, is that which the law regards as best giving effect to the express obligations assumed by the valuer: neither cutting them

[142] [1997] AC 191.

[143] In reference to a judge's discussion of a *SAAMCO* scope of duty point, Waller LJ observes in *Mulvenna v Royal Bank of Scotland plc* (2003), n 106 above at [24] 'I prefer to approach *what is in reality the same point* by reference to the cases on remoteness' [emphasis added].

[144] E Peel, '*SAAMCO* Revisited' in A Burrows and E Peel, *Commercial Remedies: Current Issues and Problems* (Oxford, OUP, 2003); T Dugdale, 'The impact of *SAAMCO*' (2000) 16 *Professional Negligence* 203.

[145] [1997] AC 191, 211.

[146] Similarly, an ordinary mountaineer's accident, although it would not have been suffered but for a doctor's breach (as the expedition wouldn't have gone ahead), is of a different type or kind of loss to injury resulting from failure of the mountaineer's knee (on the mountain or elsewhere), because of the nature of the service that is being provided. It must be noted that the words 'type or kind' are used as labels marking the conclusion as to what features of loss are significant to the scope of responsibility assumed, they are not fixed tests of themselves.

> down so that the lender obtains less than he was reasonably entitled to expect, nor extending them so as to impose on the valuer a liability greater than he could reasonably have thought he was undertaking.[147]

That this decision does not mention remoteness merely indicates that the current remoteness test is not yet sufficiently sophisticated to operate as one coherent principle encompassing all of the law of assumption of responsibility for consequences.[148]

Fraudulent Breaches of Contract

The agreement-centred account of contract damages put forward herein has been principally applied to explaining how one can have a theory of contract damages which gives a central place to foreseeability of loss, but still explains the many situations in which foreseeable losses are not (and should not be) recoverable. However there is one important situation in which this assumption of responsibility account might lead to recoverability even when loss is not foreseeable, in other words, a situation in which the account enlarges responsibility beyond the foreseeability test rather than reducing it.

The situation I have in mind is that of the fraudulent breach of contract. It was suggested in norm 12 in the list of norms above that a party is unlikely to take responsibility for losses caused by the fault of the other party. If, and when, this norm is strong enough, the clear unspoken refusal to accept losses deliberately or fraudulently caused by the promisor may outweigh other unspoken norms, such as 5, 6 and 7 above, by which it is usually concluded that a promisor will only accept responsibility for foreseeable losses. If this is the case, then it would be reasonable to infer that the parties had agreed that the promisor would be liable for all, or perhaps all direct, losses resulting from a deliberate or fraudulent breach. This result is found in French and related legal systems, as well as in the Principles of European Contract Law,[149] but not in Common

[147] [1997] AC 191, 212.

[148] See J Wightman, n 31 above, 75–6: 'The classical remoteness test is not therefore well suited to reflect the subtleties of how the risks of an occasioned harm should be distributed'; T Dugdale, n 144 above, 223–4; *McGregor on Damages*, above n 99, para 6–45. In addition, I have argued elsewhere that most questions of legal causation in the tort of negligence (as opposed to questions of factual quantification) can be better resolved by investigating the scope of the tortious duty in the light of social norms (see A Kramer, n 23 above). It may be that, as well as contractual remoteness issues, contractual questions of causation should be similarly governed by the scope of the contractual duty, in other words its orientation, and the *SAAMCO* decision and discussion certainly seem to indicate this. There is not space to elaborate this further here, but it is the author's view that legal questions of causation are essentially indistinguishable from the remoteness issues discussed herein. See further L Green, n 37 above, 54ff.

[149] French Civil Code articles 1150–1, Louisiana Civil Code articles 1996–97, Principles of European Contract Law article 9.503, Quebec Civil Code article 1613.

Law or Scottish or German legal systems.[150] It should be noted, however, that I would seek to explain such a result not on the basis of punishment or evidential burdens or delict, but rather on the basis that the parties impliedly agree to such a result.[151]

It should also be emphasised that this result, like most of those proposed in this chapter, depends for its applicability on the extent to which a particular norm is accepted as prevalent in the national or other community in which the parties contract. It may be that the common law world, in which the irrelevancy of fault to contract damages and the theory of efficient breach have long attracted discussion and some support, has evolved a culture in which the norm is not part of the reasonable expectations of the contractors, whereas other legal systems such as the French legal system do not have such a culture. It should also be noted that what amounts to 'fraud', and what limitation, if any, should take the place of the foreseeability test in fraud cases, have deliberately not been elaborated upon: they are matters, and very difficult matters, for elsewhere, and ultimately for the particular community norm.[152]

CONCLUSION

This chapter has sought to justify the account proposed herein by its consistency with our general approach to contractual obligations, which is to find their content in the apparent intention of the parties. However, the proposed account is to be preferred not only because it fits with the general agreement-centred approach to contractual obligations. It also provides a more coherent and sense-making description of the existing law. The apparently clear rule of 'foreseeability of the type of loss as not unlikely' has been shown to be unacceptably unclear by providing no guidance as to how to apply the vague concepts of 'type of loss' and 'not unlikely'. Moreover, even dishonest manipulation of this test cannot satisfactorily resolve cases such as the taxi-driver who is paid an ordinary

[150] For a summary, see the notes accompanying article 9.503 of the Principles of European Contract Law.

[151] Treitel briefly discusses the various explanations in 'Chapter 16: Remedies for Breach of Contract (Courses of Action Open to a Party Aggrieved)' in A von Mehren, chief ed., *International Encyclopedia of Comparative Law: Volume VII: Contracts In General* (Tübingen, Mohr Siebeck, 1976) at a para. 16–81.

[152] In the French and Quebec Civil Codes, fraud includes intention and gross negligence and in such cases all 'immediate and direct losses' are recoverable (French Civil Code articles 1150–1, Quebec Civil Code article 1613, and notes accompanying article 9.503 of the Principles of European Contract Law). In the Louisiana Civil Code, 'bad faith' breaches give rise to liability for all losses that are a 'direct consequence' of the breach (article 1997). The Principles of European Contract Law disapply the foreseeability requirement to cases of 'intentional and grossly negligent' breach, but make no mention of the test to apply in its stead, or to directness in general (article 9.503).

fare in the knowledge that tardiness will result in his passenger losing a huge financial gain. Furthermore, in situations in which the foreseeability test cannot cope even when applied in a contorted manner, the law has responded to this, as it must, by creating separate rules for mental distress, amenity and *SAAMCO*-type cases, essentially supplementing the inadequate foreseeability test with further tests that look at the implicit assumption of responsibility.

It is time that we take stock of the situation and treat the *SAAMCO* and mental distress tests as warnings as to the inadequacy of the foreseeability test, interim solutions to the problem, and indications of the way forward. The foreseeability test should be reconceived, along with the mental distress and *SAAMCO* tests, as being applications of one basic principle that looks to the scope of the implied assumption of responsibility (and the orientation of the obligation, if that metaphor is thought to be helpful). Foreseeability should be seen as a good but inconclusive indication of an assumption of responsibility, and the label remoteness may be applied to this new approach or discarded, according to taste. Problems of determining *how likely* a forseeable loss must be, and *how precisely* it must be foreseeable, will then fall away as mere indications of what responsibility reasonably appears to have been assumed. Waddams has observed that:

> The rule in *Hadley v Baxendale*, like all legal rules in a developing common law system, is an interim rule. It seemed sufficient in 1856. The fact that it has stood so long suggests that it answers a need with considerable success. But the subsequent decisions suggest that the rule is incomplete; it is now encrusted with exceptions and presumptions and will eventually yield to a revision.[153]

Now is the time for such a revision.

POSTSCRIPT: OTHER PARTS OF THE LAW OF CONTRACT THAT MAY BE EXPLICABLE ON THE SAME BASIS

There may be other aspects of the law of damages that can be explained, or at least partially explained, by the agreement-centred approach applied herein. One of these is the principle of avoidable harms, also known as the mitigation principle. Whereas that principle may be understandable on the basis of external, policy-based, principles of fairness or the avoidance of waste,[154] it may also be explicable on the basis

[153] SM Waddams, *The Law of Contracts*, above n 58, para 742.
[154] See the discussion by M Bridge, 'Mitigation of Damages in Contract and the Meaning of Avoidable Loss' (1989) 105 *Law Quarterly Review* 398.

of an implied community norm that parties will take reasonable steps to minimise their own loss.[155] This may seem remote from the assumed attitude of parties in individualistic transactions that are low on cooperation and high on adversarialism, but then in those cases the standard of reasonableness may be less onerous than in more cooperative cases. If we are to be accurate, we must recognise that the principle of avoidable harms, by its reference to 'reasonable' steps to mitigate, is in truth not one norm but a complicated set of norms that determines what is to be expected in a variety of situations. Furthermore, what counts as reasonable depends upon what the mitigating party is willing to accept in substitute for the performance promised to them (most obviously when the mitigation is through purchase of a replacement), and in such cases it should be the shared orientation of the contract that governs what features of the promised position the mitigating party is permitted to hold out for and which features they must sacrifice in the name of avoidance of loss.

Related to this last point, another aspect of damages that may be better understood by the proposed approach is that of the adequacy of damages, which is central to the exercise of a common law court's discretionary decision to award specific performance. One element in the assessment of whether a damages award is adequate compensation should be the disparity between the purposes and values that are protected in the award of damages and the purposes and values that fall under the orientation of the contract. When the court, in a case of contract for the sale of a unique good, awards specific performance, it should be when and because the uniqueness of the property was part of the orientation of the contractual obligation.[156] Even if the promisee values the property's uniqueness and the promisor is aware of this, unless the uniqueness is part of the orientation of the contract — the agreed stakes — then specific performance should not be awarded because damages in such a case are adequate. They are adequate because they fully compensate for all the values and purposes towards which the contract was oriented, which is all that the promisee is entitled to. To award specific performance in such a case is, in some ways, to order the promisor to make a gift, since it forces the promisor to compensate for the non-fulfilment of a goal for which the promisor had not assumed responsibility.[157]

[155] See norms 11 and 12 above.
[156] All property is unique, but the unique identity is not usually important to the purchaser.
[157] Kimel argues that, following the harm principle, specific performance is only justifiable when an award of damages (the less harmful remedy) is not as effective at redressing the harm: D Kimel, *From Promise to Contract*, n 27 above, 104. SA Smith, 'Performance, Punishment and the Nature of Contractual Obligation' (1997) 60 *Modern Law Review* 360, argues that specific performance should be available only when necessary, since whenever specific performance is potentially available it is possible that the performance of a promise was motivated by the threat of compulsion.

As the modern trend in awards of damages is towards recognition of purposes and values of a non-financial nature,[158] specific performance will less often be justified on the basis of a contractual value not being covered by the compensation award. One situation in which specific performance might still be needed is when it is difficult to estimate the amount of compensation for non-financial loss, and so there is a high risk of over-estimating and so punishing the promisor.[159] Specific performance might also be needed when no amount of money is equivalent to the contractually contemplated loss that has been suffered. When specific performance is impossible or undesirable in such cases, an award of punitive damages may be justifiable, since otherwise the promisor is able to avoid fulfilling the responsibility assumed under the contract (because paying compensatory damages are inadequate). In such cases the law may be justified in viewing the promisor as a tortfeasor, since the promisor is in effect reducing the promisee's patrimony without her consent. Note that this is not a simple case of efficient breach, in which the promisor can make a profit even after fully compensating the promisee for those things for which he was responsible under the contract. Our case is one in which it is impossible to compensate the promisee for those things for which the promisor assumed responsibility under the contract. If such cases do exist, which depends upon the view taken as to what money can compensate for, they will be rare: the old example of breach of a promise to marry springs to mind.[160]

Finally, there is the question of what goes to the root of the contract so as to bring about frustration or a repudiatory breach of an intermediate term. This is a similar question of allocation of risk to that discussed in this chapter, and is determined by reference to the information contemplated by the contract. For example in *Blackburn Bobbin Company Ltd v TW Allen & Sons Ltd*,[161] a contract for the sale of Finland birch timber was held not to be frustrated on the outbreak of war because the risk of the Finnish timber being unobtainable fell upon the promisor vendor, the promisee not having the necessary knowledge of the promisor's routes and not having assumed (shared) risk for a particular route. In the words of Pickford LJ, the continuance of the usual mode of shipping was not 'contemplated'[162] by both parties as necessary for the fulfilment of the contract. The magic remoteness word 'contemplated' is used twice,[163]

[158] Discussed above at 'Mental Distress, Loss of Amenity and Idiosyncratic Losses'.
[159] Smith, n 157 above, 374.
[160] More common is the situation in which the cost of cure is awarded because the simple valuation ('difference in value') of compensation is deemed to be inadequate when put against the values and purposes contemplated by the contract.
[161] [1918] 2 KB 467.
[162] At 469, 470.
[163] *Ibid*.

and it is submitted that this is no coincidence as the same issue arises here as in remoteness cases: the issue of assumption of risk, for which foreseeability is necessary but not sufficient. Of course, 'contemplation', like reasonable expectations, is used often in interpretation cases too, for example by all their Lordships who gave reasoned opinions as to the interpretation of a release in *BCCI v Ali*.[164] The word 'contemplation' signifies a family of inquiries into what the parties reasonably appear to have intended, and remoteness is an important member of this family.

[164] [2001] UKHL 8, [2002] 1 AC 251.

13

Damages for Non-Pecuniary Loss

EWAN McKENDRICK* AND KATHERINE WORTHINGTON**

THE QUESTION OF the extent to which damages can be recovered for non-pecuniary losses suffered as a result of a breach of contract has been debated at length both in the courts[1] and in the academic literature.[2] Yet it continues to trouble the courts. This uneasiness might be said to arise from an attachment to traditional understandings of loss in contract law in which loss is understood in purely financial terms.[3] Judges routinely make reference to the function of damages as set out by Parke B in *Robinson v Harman*:[4]

* Professor of English Private Law, University of Oxford and Fellow of Lady Margaret Hall.
** European University Institute, Florence.

1 See, for example, *Hobbs v London and South Western Railway Co* (1875) LR 10 QB 111; *Addis v Gramophone Co Ltd* [1909] AC 488; *Cook v Swinfen* [1967] 1 WLR 457; *Diesen v Samson* 1971 SLT (Sh Ct) 49; *Jarvis v Swan Tours Ltd* [1973] QB 233; *Jackson v Horizon Holidays Ltd* [1975] 1 WLR 1468; *Heywood v Wellers* [1976] QB 446; *Jackson v Chrysler Acceptances Ltd* [1978] RTR 474; *Perry v Sidney Phillips & Son* [1982] 1 WLR 1297; *Hayes v James and Charles Dodd* [1990] 2 All ER 815; *Watts v Morrow* [1991] 1 WLR 1421; *Knott v Bolton* (1995) 11 Const LJ 375; *Ruxley Electronics and Construction Ltd v Forsyth* [1996] AC 344; *Farley v Skinner* [2001] UKHL 49; [2002] 2 AC 732 and *Hamilton Jones v David & Snape (a firm)* [2003] EWHC 3147 (Ch); [2004] 1 All ER 657. The issue has also been a live one in the Commonwealth: see *Dillon v Baltic Shipping Co (The Mikhail Lermontov)* (1992) 176 CLR 344, *Brown v Waterloo Regional Board of Commissioners of Police* (1982) 136 DLR (3d) 49 (Canada), *Rowlands v Collow* [1992] 1 NZLR 178 and *Mouat v Clark Boyce* [1992] 2 NZLR 559 (both New Zealand).

2 See, for example, A Tettenborn 'Non-Pecuniary Loss: the Right Answer but Bad Reasoning' (2003) 2 *Journal of Obligations and Remedies* 94; C Mitchell 'Promise, Performance and Damages for Breach of Contract' (2003) 2 *Journal of Obligations and Remedies* 67; N Enonchong 'Breach of Contract and Damages for Mental Distress' (1996) 16 *Oxford Journal of Legal Studies* 617; E Macdonald, 'Contractual Damages for Mental Distress' (1994) 7 *Journal of Contract Law* 134; D Harris, A Ogus and J Phillips, 'Contract Remedies and the Consumer Surplus' (1979) 95 *Law Quarterly Review* 581; B Jackson 'Injured Feelings Resulting from Breach of Contract' (1977) 26 *International and Comparative Law Quarterly* 502; F.D. Rose (1977) 40 *Canadian Bar Review* 333; N Palmer and A Hudson, 'Damages for Distress and Loss of Enjoyment in Claims Involving Chattels', in N Palmer and E McKendrick (eds), *Interests in Goods* 2nd edn (London, LLP, 1998), 867.

3 On which see generally E McKendrick, 'Breach of Contract and the Meaning of Loss' [1999] *Current Legal Problems* 53.

4 (1848) 1 Exch 850, 855.

> the rule of the common law is, that where a party sustains loss by reason of a breach of contract, he is, so far as money can do it, to be placed in the same situation, with respect to damages, as if the contract had been performed.

Thus where specific performance is not available, the placing of an injured party 'in the same situation ... as if the contract had been performed' is traditionally achieved through compensating the lost economic interest in the contract.[5] Whilst this approach may be appropriate in many commercial contexts, it would be absurd to suggest that all contractual interests may be incorporated under this head. The value which a contracting party expects from completion frequently involves benefits above and beyond those seen strictly in financial terms. Indeed, a number of recent cases show that the courts have recognised and continue to recognise the need for a more expansive notion of loss that can translate and absorb non-pecuniary benefits/harms.

Contracting parties may suffer non-pecuniary loss in at least two senses. First, the injured party may actually *contract for* some non-pecuniary benefit (such as enjoyment, peace of mind, or freedom from distress or molestation[6]). In such a case, breach of the particular (often implied) term will involve the loss of some non-pecuniary benefit. This type of loss is referred to in this chapter as a 'positive loss'. Secondly, a breach of contract (in particular, a breach of a consumer contract) may *entail* some form of non-pecuniary loss. For example, a consumer may not have contracted for any particular non-pecuniary benefit but, as a result of the breach, may nevertheless have suffered some non-pecuniary loss which is not too remote a consequence of the breach. In such a case the claimant may be entitled to recover these 'consequential losses' from the party in breach. This type of loss is referred to in this chapter as 'consequential' loss. At the boundaries, especially in talking of implied contractual terms, there may well be overlap between these two types of loss. In any case, under either head it is clear that a more expansive notion of loss than a notion which encompasses purely financial loss will be required properly to compensate the injured party. It is equally clear that in both cases any expanded notion of loss will have to be limited by the normal principles applicable to contract (and, where relevant, tort) damages.

In *Farley v Skinner*,[7] Lord Steyn emphasised 'the importance, in the quest for coherent and just solutions in such cases, of simple and practical

[5] See dicta of Lord Bingham MR in *White Arrow Express Ltd v Lamey's Distribution Ltd* (1996) Trading Law Reports 69: the *Robinson v Harman* 'formulation assumes that the breach has injured [the plaintiff's] financial position; if he cannot show that it has, he will recover nominal damages only'.

[6] Along the lines of the first exception voiced in *Watts v Morrow* [1991] 1 WLR 1421, 1425.

[7] *Farley v Skinner* [2001] UKHL 49; [2002] 2 AC 732, at [1]. See to similar effect the speech of Lord Scott at [62].

rules.' Unfortunately, the desire to produce 'simple and practical rules', whilst laudable, has proved to be remarkably elusive. One reason for this may be that the cases do not in fact deal with one issue; they deal with a number of different issues, some of which overlap. It is the aim of this chapter to provide some clarification of issues bearing on the development of these rules and to suggest a simpler approach to the classification of non-pecuniary interests in contract.

The approach adopted will be first to consider three recent decisions of the House of Lords[8] and one decision of the Court of Appeal[9] which deal explicitly with the problem of non-pecuniary loss. This preliminary analysis will serve to highlight the policies at stake and, it is hoped, lend clarity to the categorisation of the cases in which the courts have allowed the recovery of damages in respect of non-pecuniary losses. The chapter will then proceed to explore the more general issue of the extent to which the law of contract provides a remedy for non-pecuniary loss. Since such a remedy remains the exception rather than the rule, it will be necessary to spell out how the boundaries of exceptional cases are being drawn and the principles behind their limitation.

The focus of our analysis is English law. The almost exclusive focus on English law may be thought to be out of place in a book devoted to a comparative analysis of remedies for breach of contract. Our response is that the issues raised by the cases which we discuss in this chapter highlight concerns that ought to be addressed in all modern legal systems. The objective therefore is simply to use the English cases as a means of illustrating the principles which are under discussion. We do not thereby wish to suggest that other legal systems ought necessarily to follow the approach which has been adopted by the English courts. But we do suggest that other legal systems can learn from the experience of the English courts. In a world where contracts are increasingly entered into for reasons other than to enhance the financial well-being of one or more of the parties to the contract, it is important that legal systems give careful consideration to the circumstances in which damages can be awarded for non-pecuniary losses suffered as a result of a breach of contract.

1 GENERAL RULE AND EXCEPTIONS

The general rule that damages are not recoverable for mental distress caused by a breach of contract is commonly traced to the decision of the House of Lords in *Addis v Gramophone Co Ltd*,[10] although the scope of the

[8] *Johnson v Gore Wood & Co* [2002] 2 AC 1; *Johnson v Unisys Ltd* [2001] UKHL 13; [2003] 1 AC 518 and *Farley v Skinner* [2001] UKHL 49; [2002] 2 AC 732.
[9] *Hatton v Sutherland* [2002] EWCA Civ 76; [2002] ICR 613.
[10] [1909] AC 488.

decision, and the precise point of law answered by the case, has been the subject of some controversy.[11] The starting point therefore remains that the law of contract does not compensate a claimant for mere disappointment or annoyance suffered as a result of the defendant's breach of contract. Contract-breaking is an 'incident of commercial life which players in the game are expected to meet with mental fortitude.'[12]

It is perhaps predictable that the rule does not come free of exceptions. The first wave of cases to challenge traditional notions of loss in this area date back to the mid-1970s.[13] At this stage the challenges might well have been interpreted as little more than evidence of a worry that the absolutism of the general rule was unsuited to modern contractual practices. Prior to the most recent decisions of the House of Lords, the leading case was that of the Court of Appeal in *Watts v Morrow*[14] where Bingham LJ, as he then was, classically expressed the two exceptional cases in which damages may be recovered in respect of non-pecuniary losses suffered by a claimant as a result of a breach of contract. The first category consists of cases where 'the very object of a contract is to provide pleasure, relaxation, peace of mind or freedom from molestation',[15] while cases in the second category allow the recovery of damages for 'physical inconvenience and discomfort caused by the breach and mental suffering directly related to that inconvenience and discomfort.'[16] These categories have been extended, and perhaps distorted beyond recognition by the courts in a line of recent cases, to which we now turn.

2 RECENT DECISIONS OF THE HOUSE OF LORDS AND COURT OF APPEAL

Johnson v Gore Wood & Co

In chronological terms, the first decision of the House of Lords is *Johnson v Gore Wood & Co.*[17] where a majority of their Lordships affirmed the general

[11] See, for example, N Enonchong 'Breach of Contract and Damages for Mental Distress' (1996) 16 *Oxford Journal of Legal Studies* 617, esp pp 619–28. It is not necessary for us to enter into this controversy for the purposes of this chapter. It suffices to note that the House of Lords in *Johnson v Unisys Ltd* [2001] UKHL 13; [2003] 1 AC 518 declined the invitation to depart from *Addis* and, as we shall see, the courts have recently affirmed the existence of the general rule that a contract-breaker cannot be liable for injured feelings or distress.

[12] Per Lord Cooke of Thorndon in *Johnson v Gore Wood & Co* [2002] 2 AC 1, 49, quoted by Lord Hutton in *Farley*, at [47].

[13] See, in particular, *Jarvis v Swan Tours Ltd* [1973] QB 233; *Jackson v Horizon Holidays Ltd* [1975] 1 WLR 1468; *Heywood v Wellers* [1976] QB 446 and *Jackson v Chrysler Acceptances Ltd* [1978] RTR 474.

[14] [1991] 1 WLR 1421.

[15] *Ibid*, at 1445.

[16] *Ibid*.

[17] [2002] 2 AC 1.

rule that damages are not recoverable for mental distress suffered as a consequence of a breach of contract. The claimant brought an action for damages against his solicitors alleging that they had been negligent in the way in which they had conducted his affairs.[18] His claim included a claim for general damages for,

> the mental distress and anxiety which he has suffered as a result of the protracted litigation process to which he has been subjected, the extreme financial embarrassment in which he and his family have found themselves, and the deterioration in his family relationships, particularly with his wife and son, as a result of the matters complained of in the re-amended statement of claim.[19]

He also brought a claim for aggravated damages 'by reason of the fact that the manner of the commission of [the defendants'] tort was such as to injure his pride and dignity.'[20] The defendants replied that damages for mental distress and anxiety did not lie for breach of a commercial contract and that this was not a class of case in which aggravated damages were in principle recoverable.

Lord Bingham of Cornhill conceded that 'some inroads'[21] had been made into the general rule that damages for breach of contract cannot include damages for mental distress, but he stated that these inroads remained 'limited'. While he recognised that it was 'undoubtedly true that many breaches of contract cause intense frustration and anxiety to the innocent party',[22] he concluded that he was not 'persuaded ... that the general applicability of *Addis v Gramophone Co Ltd* should be further restricted.'[23] Lord Goff similarly noted that there had been a 'softening' of the principle that damages cannot be recovered for mental distress but he too concluded that 'none of these developments has ... gone so far as to allow recovery on the broad grounds here pleaded.'[24] The claim for damages for mental distress and anxiety and the claim for aggravated damages were therefore struck out.[25]

[18] The claimant conducted his business through a number of companies and most of the issues before the House of Lords concerned the relationship between the claim by the companies and the claim by the claimant. We are not concerned with the latter issues.
[19] [2002] 2 AC 1, at 37.
[20] *Ibid.*
[21] *Ibid.*
[22] *Ibid*, at 38
[23] *Ibid.*
[24] *Ibid*, at 42.
[25] In *Farley v Skinner* [2001] UKHL 49; [2002] 2 AC 732, at [104]. Lord Scott of Foscote treated *Johnson* as a case where the loss claimed was too remote a consequence of the alleged breach of contract on the ground that it was not 'remotely arguable that Mr Johnson's alleged mental distress was a consequence that, at the time he retained the solicitors was reasonably in the contemplation of the parties as liable to result from a breach.'

Lord Cooke of Thorndon dissented on this issue. He accepted that the judgment of Bingham LJ in *Watts v Morrow*[26] was an authoritative statement of the law. But he was of the opinion that the exceptional cases, in which damages are recoverable, were not confined to contracts to provide 'pleasure and the like' but extended to 'breaches of contract for status such as membership of a trade union or a club.'[27] Although the case had been pleaded as a case of mental distress, he was of the view that the claim had a greater resemblance to a claim for physical inconvenience and discomfort. He concluded that 'the common law would be defective and stray too far from reality, humanity and justice if it remorselessly shut out even a restrained award under these heads.'[28] He further stated that 'a changed way of life because of poverty and damaged family relationships can be grievous forms of non-pecuniary harm' which should not be ruled out of the law's purview. As a consequence, he would have allowed the claim for damages for financial embarrassment and injury to family relationships to go to trial.[29]

Johnson v Unisys Ltd

The second decision is *Johnson v Unisys Ltd*.[30] The claimant was summarily dismissed by his employers, the defendants, in 1994. He brought an unfair dismissal claim against them. That claim was successful, although he was held to have contributed to his own dismissal. He was awarded compensation of £11,691.99. The claimant then brought an action for wrongful dismissal against the defendants. He alleged that the defendants had not informed him, prior to his dismissal, of the complaints which had been made against him. Further, he alleged that, as a result of the manner of his dismissal, he had suffered a mental breakdown and was consequently unable to resume work. The claim was for some £400,000 in damages, to compensate for the financial consequences of the psychiatric injury suffered. It was argued that the defendants had broken an implied term in the claimant's contract of employment that they would not without reasonable and proper cause conduct themselves in such a way as to damage the relationship of trust and confidence which existed between

26 [1991] 1 WLR 1421, 1445.
27 [2002] 2 AC 1, 49.
28 *Ibid.* In reaching this conclusion he drew support from *Hobbs v London and South Western Railway Co* (1875) LR 10 QB 111 and *Bailey v Bullock* [1950] 2 All ER 1167, cases which were also relied upon by Clarke LJ in his dissenting judgment in *Farley v Skinner* [2000] PNLR 441.
29 Lord Cooke (at p50) went so far as to doubt 'the permanence of *Addis* in English law'. But these are no more than the doubts of an individual judge. The majority affirmed *Addis* and refused to graft a further exception on to the rule.
30 [2001] UKHL 13; [2003] 1 AC 518, on which see the helpful case notes by H Collins (2001) 30 *Industrial Law Journal* 305 and M Freedland (2001) 30 *Industrial Law Journal* 309.

the parties. In large part the case turned on the scope of the implied term of trust and confidence in the contract of employment.[31] Their Lordships refused to imply a term that the power of dismissal would only be exercised fairly and in good faith and so dismissed the claim, essentially on the ground that the recognition of such a right of action would 'fly in the face of'[32] the limits, particularly the financial limits,[33] that Parliament has prescribed in the unfair dismissal legislation. The relationship between the common law claim and the statutory unfair dismissal claim is a fascinating issue but it is not the subject of this chapter.

Our focus is on the recovery of damages for non-pecuniary loss. At first sight *Johnson* does not seem to contribute anything to this issue because the claim was 'solely for the recovery of special damages for financial loss.'[34] The claim was not one for anxiety and mental distress resulting

[31] This is a subject which has been discussed extensively in the literature, particularly by Douglas Brodie: see further D Brodie, 'Legal Coherence and the Employment Relationship' (2001) 117 *Law Quarterly Review* 604; D Brodie, 'Mutual Trust and the Values of the Employment Contract' (2001) 30 *Industrial Law Journal* 84; D Brodie, 'Beyond Exchange: The New Contract of Employment' (1998) 27 *Industrial Law Journal* 79 and The Honourable Mr Justice Lindsay, 'The Implied Term of Trust and Confidence' (2001) 30 *Industrial Law Journal* 1. The reach of the implied term is beyond the scope of this chapter but the debate is nevertheless of significance in this context for two reasons: first, it recognises that an employee's interest in the contract of employment is not purely, even primarily, financial and secondly it has a bearing on the scope of the decision of the House of Lords in *Addis v Gramophone Co Ltd.* [1909] AC 488.

[32] [2001] UKHL 13; [2003] 1 AC 518, at [2]. This point is well made by Lord Hoffmann, extra-judicially, in his 2001 COMBAR lecture entitled 'Separation of Powers'. At para 26, he acknowledges that the House of Lords could have 'finessed or overruled' *Addis* but that what made it 'impossible' for them to take this course was that Parliament 'had introduced a statutory remedy, created a new system of tribunals to enforce it and imposed an arbitrary limit on the compensation they could award. For the courts to create a parallel common law remedy would have completely by-passed both the procedure and limitations of the statutory system. This meant that in deference to the legislature, a development in the common law which might well have taken place if Parliament had never taken an interest in the subject, was blocked off.' See also *Eastwood v Magnox Electric plc* [2004] UKHL 35, esp paras [12]–[13].

[33] The maximum sum at the time of Mr Johnson's dismissal was £11,000 so that he was given the maximum award. The limit was increased substantially by the government in October 1999 to £50,000. The award is index-linked and now stands at £51,700. The setting and the level of the upper limit has proved to be an issue of some controversy. At £400,000, Mr Johnson's claim for damages was more than 40 times the maximum award. Nevertheless, the relationship between *Johnson* and *Mahmoud v Bank of Credit and Commerce International SA* [1998] AC 20 (where the House of Lords first unequivocally recognised the existence of the implied obligation of mutual trust and confidence) is an uneasy one. This is revealed by the decision of the House of Lords in *Eastwood v Magnox Electric plc* [2004] UKHL 35, where it was recognised that *Johnson* applies in the case of dismissal but does not prevent an employee from bringing a claim in respect of a cause of action which accrued prior to his dismissal. As Lord Nicholls observed (at [32]) this has the consequence that the employer 'may be better off dismissing an employee than suspending him' because the statutory cap applies to the former claim but not to a claim for unfair suspension (an example of this phenomenon is provided by *Gogay v Hertfordshire County Council* [2000] IRLR 705). Lord Steyn in his speech bemoaned the current state of the law.

[34] [2001] UKHL 13; [2003] 1 AC 518, at [11] (Lord Steyn).

from the manner of his dismissal. Nevertheless, Lords Steyn, Hoffmann and Millett found it necessary to re-examine *Addis v Gramophone Co Ltd*[35] in some detail. It would appear that the case now stands for the proposition that 'an employee cannot recover damages for injured feelings, mental distress or damage to his reputation, arising out of the manner of his dismissal.'[36] *Addis* therefore applies to a claim for wrongful dismissal and the courts will not undo that limitation on the damages recoverable given that Parliament has now provided dismissed employees with a limited right to claim for unfair dismissal. But where the claim brought by the employee is not a claim for wrongful dismissal, then it would appear that *Addis* does not 'stand in the way'[37] of such a claim. In this respect, a claim for financial loss suffered as a result of a breach of the implied term of trust and confidence would appear to stand in a better position than a claim for damages for the distress suffered as a result of the dismissal. However the House of Lords has recently held that damages for non-pecuniary loss cannot be recovered in an unfair dismissal claim.[38]

Johnson is an important case in other respects. Both Lord Steyn[39] and Lord Millett[40] recognised that a contract of employment can no longer be equated with a commercial contract. As Iacobucci J observed in *Wallace v United Grain Growers Ltd*[41] 'work is one of the defining features of people's lives' and this must be reflected in the approach adopted by the law to the assessment of damages. Secondly, the case illustrates the significance of the hurdles presented by the doctrine of causation and the rule that the loss must not be too remote a consequence of the breach of contract. Thus Lord Steyn dismissed the claim on the ground that the losses claimed were too remote a consequence of the alleged breach of contract.[42] As we shall see, proof of the requisite causal link and the remoteness rules are likely to play a significant role in future non-pecuniary loss claims.

Farley v Skinner

The third case is *Farley v Skinner*.[43] The claimant employed the defendant surveyor to survey a house which the claimant was contemplating buying as a weekend residence. Given that the property was close to Gatwick

[35] [1909] AC 488.
[36] [2001] UKHL 13; [2003] 1 AC 518, at [44] (Lord Hoffmann).
[37] *Ibid.*
[38] *Dunnachie v Kingston upon Hull City Council* [2004] UKHL 34.
[39] [2001] UKHL 13; [2003] 1 AC 518, at [20].
[40] *Ibid*, at [77].
[41] (1997) 152 DLR (4th) 1, 33.
[42] [2001] UKHL 13; [2003] 1 AC 518, at [29].
[43] [2001] UKHL 49; [2002] 2 AC 732.

airport he expressly asked the defendant to report on whether or not aircraft noise was likely to be a problem. The defendant did so and reported that it was 'unlikely that the property will suffer greatly from such noise, although some planes will inevitably cross the area, depending on the direction of the wind and the positioning of the flight paths.' Having subsequently purchased the house and spent over £100,000 on improvements to the property, the claimant discovered that aircraft noise in the early morning and early evening was indeed a problem for him. The property was not far from Mayfield Stack where aeroplanes waiting to land at Gatwick were stacked until a landing slot became available. The claimant sued the defendant surveyor for damages, alleging that he had been negligent in carrying out his obligations to the claimant. The trial judge, Judge Peter Baker QC, held that the defendant had indeed been negligent. He could have discovered the true position by checking with Gatwick but had not taken the trouble to do so. He further found that, had the surveyor carried out his instructions properly, the claimant would not have bought the property. In relation to the claim for damages, Judge Baker concluded that there had been no diminution in the value of the property as a result of the noise but he nevertheless awarded the claimant damages of £10,000 for the distress and inconvenience which he had suffered. The defendant appealed to the Court of Appeal[44] where it was held that the claimant had not suffered any physical discomfort and inconvenience as a result of the defendant's breach of contract and that the object of the contract between the parties was not to provide enjoyment or relief from stress so that the claim did not fall within the class of case in respect of which it was appropriate to award damages for distress and inconvenience. The claimant appealed to the House of Lords where the appeal was allowed.

Their Lordships held that the claimant was entitled to recover damages on one of two grounds. The first was that it was an important term of the contract that performance should provide the claimant with peace of mind or freedom from distress. Their Lordships rejected the argument that peace of mind or freedom from distress had to be the central obligation of the contract. It sufficed that the term broken by the defendant was one which was known by both parties to be an important term of the contract: whether the contract as a whole was one to provide peace of mind was not the decisive factor. The submission that damages could only be recovered where the defendant guaranteed a particular result was similarly rejected. Damages for distress were also available where the breach by the defendant took the form of a failure to exercise reasonable care and skill. Secondly, their Lordships held that the case fell within the exceptional case

[44] [2000] Lloyd's Rep PN 516.

in which damages can be recovered for physical inconvenience. The noise from the aeroplanes was not simply a matter of disappointment. It caused the claimant 'real discomfort'[45] in that it interfered with his enjoyment of the property. That inconvenience was something for which the law afforded a remedy in damages. While their Lordships were of the view that the award of £10,000 was on the high side for an award of damages, they refused to interfere with the award.

Hatton v Sutherland

The final case is the decision of Court of Appeal in *Hatton v Sutherland*[46] where the court considered four claims brought by employees against their employers in which the employees claimed that they had suffered psychiatric illnesses caused by stress at work. In each instance, it was alleged that the employers were liable for the losses which the employees had sustained on the basis that the employers had broken their duty to take reasonable care for the safety of their employees. Three[47] of the claims failed on the ground that it was not reasonably foreseeable to the employer that the employee would suffer psychiatric illness as a result of the pressure to which the employee was subject at work. The fourth claim succeeded on the basis that the employee in that case had previously been off work suffering from depression and anxiety, with the consequence that the employer could not deny liability on the ground that it was not reasonably foreseeable that the employee would suffer psychiatric illness. On the facts of the latter case, the Court of Appeal accepted that the employers knew that the employee was being badly treated and found that they had failed to exercise reasonable care in order to prevent her from suffering psychiatric illness as a result of the pressures to which she was subject. The precise conditions which must be satisfied in order to

[45] [2001] UKHL 49; [2002] 2 AC 732, at [37].

[46] [2002] EWCA Civ 76; [2002] ICR 613. *Hatton* has itself given rise to further case-law, the details of which are beyond the scope of this chapter. One of the four cases in *Hatton* was subsequently appealed to the House of Lords and their Lordships allowed the appeal: *Barber v Somerset County Council* [2004] UKHL 13. However the appeal was largely confined to the facts of the case, in particular whether the employer had broken the duty of care imposed on it and whether the Court of Appeal was entitled to interfere with the finding of the trial judge that the employer had breached its duty of care (they concluded that they were not entitled to interfere). Their Lordships were broadly content to accept as correct the principles enunciated by the Court of Appeal in *Hatton*. These principles are likely to require further refinement but they are unlikely to need major revision. The leading post-*Hatton* cases include *Pratley v Surrey County Council* [2003] EWCA Civ 1067; *Barlow v Broxbourne Borough Council* [2003] EWHC 50 (QB); *Coxall v Goodyear Great Britain Ltd* [2002] EWCA Civ 1010; [2003] 1 WLR 536 and *Young v Post Office* [2002] EWCA Civ 661; [2002] IRLR 660.

[47] A further claim succeeded on appeal to the House of Lords: see *Barber v Somerset County Council* [2004] UKHL 13.

establish liability on the part of the employer are beyond the scope of this chapter.[48] For our purposes it suffices to note four points.

The first relates to the nature of the claims brought by the employees. The case is commonly taught and discussed in the context of the law of tort but, as Hale LJ pointed out in the judgment of the court,[49] the claims brought by the employees were in fact contractual claims. They were claims brought by 'primary victims' where 'the harm is the reasonably foreseeable product of specific breaches of a contractual duty of care towards a victim whose identity is known in advance.'[50] The analysis of the claims in contractual terms is to be contrasted with the analysis adopted by Lord Steyn in *Frost v Chief Constable of South Yorkshire Police*[51] (another case in which a claim was brought by an 'employee' against his 'employer'[52]) in which he stated:

> ... the rules to be applied when an employee brings an action against his employer for harm suffered at his workplace are the rules of the law of tort. One is therefore thrown back to the ordinary rules of the law of tort which contain restrictions on the recovery of compensation for psychiatric harm. [...] The duty of an employer to safeguard his employees from harm could also be formulated in contract. In that event, and absent relevant express provisions, a term is implied by law into the contract as an incident of a standardised contract ... But such a term could not be wider than the duty imposed by the law of tort. [53]

The analysis of Lord Steyn is not without its difficulties. Ordinarily, one would expect a court to ask whether the tortious duty of care is inconsistent with the terms of any applicable contract[54] rather than give priority to the tortious duty of care. But it is important to note that the term referred to by Lord Steyn was a term 'implied by law' and there may be no real distinction between the sources of, respectively, a term implied by law into the contract and a duty imposed by the law of tort.[55] This being

[48] They are summarised in para [43] of the judgment of the Court of Appeal.
[49] At para [21].
[50] *Ibid.*
[51] [1999] 2 AC 455.
[52] Here leaving to one side the question whether or not police constables are in fact employed under a contract of employment.
[53] [1999] 2 AC 455, 497G–498A.
[54] *Henderson v Merrett Syndicates Ltd* [1994] 3 All ER 506, 532–3; *Tai Hing Cotton Mill Ltd v Liu Chong Hing Bank Ltd* [1986] AC 80, 107. But contrast M Lunney and K Oliphant, *Tort Law: Text and Materials* 2nd edn, (OUP, 2003), p.329 where the authors argue that the employer's liability is 'primarily tortious and, though there may theoretically be a concurrent implied duty in contract, this cannot be of greater scope than the tortious duty.' The difficulty with the latter view is that it appears to stand the reasoning of the House of Lords in *Henderson* on its head.
[55] *Lister v Romford Ice and Cold Storage Co Ltd* [1957] AC 555, 587.

the case, there may be little practical difference between a claim in contract and a claim in tort.

Nevertheless, it is interesting to note the different judicial perceptions of the hierarchy that exists between the contractual claim and the tortious claim. In *Hatton* it is the language of the law of tort that predominates. Thus Hale LJ stated that

> liability in negligence depends upon three interrelated requirements: the existence of a duty to take care; a failure to take the care which can reasonably be expected in the circumstances; and damage suffered as a result of that failure.[56]

In other cases the law of tort has been very much subordinated to the claim in contract. A recent illustration of the latter phenomenon is provided by the decision of Neuberger J in *Hamilton Jones v David & Snape (a Firm)*.[57] This more recent case concerned a claim brought by a client against a solicitor in which the client alleged that, as a result of the solicitor's negligence, her former husband had been able to take her twin sons from the UK to Tunisia where he obtained custody of them. She alleged that she had suffered mental distress as a result of her solicitor's negligence. The solicitor relied by way of defence on a rule derived from the law of tort that a person cannot claim compensation for the loss of the company of a child.[58] In essence it was submitted on his behalf that the claimant could not outflank the tort law rule by resort to a claim in contract. Neuberger J rejected the submission[59] and it is suggested that he was right to do so. It is not the case that a contractual duty cannot extend beyond the duty which is imposed on the parties by the law of tort. Rather the rule works in the opposite direction: the tortious duty cannot normally extend beyond the scope of the contractual duties which the parties have, expressly or impliedly, accepted.[60] It is for the parties to define for themselves the scope of their respective contractual duties. The fact that the law of tort does not recognise the existence of a particular duty cannot of itself operate to prevent the parties from agreeing to accept such a duty as a matter of contract.

It therefore ought to follow that the line of cases represented by *Hatton* should be seen primarily in contractual terms;[61] that is to say, it is for the parties to the contract of employment to define for themselves the scope

[56] [2002] EWCA Civ 76; [2002] ICR 613 at [18].
[57] [2003] EWHC 3147 (Ch); [2004] 1 All ER 657.
[58] *F v Wirral Metropolitan Borough Council* [1991] Fam 69.
[59] [2003] EWHC 3147 (Ch); [2004] 1 All ER 657, at [51].
[60] See *Verderame v Commercial Union Assurance Co* [1993] BCLC 793, 803G–H.
[61] A reminder of the importance of the contractual terms was given by Lord Rodger in *Barber v Somerset County Council* [2004] UKHL 13 at [24]–[35].

of their respective duties and the law of tort generally cannot impose a duty on the employer which is more onerous than that to be found in the terms of the contract. The difficulty which arises on the facts of cases such as *Hatton* is that the contract of employment is commonly silent on the subject of the obligations of the employer in relation to the employee's psychiatric well-being, leaving the judge to imply an appropriate term as a matter of law into the contract. Given that, as we have noted, there may be little difference between a term implied as a matter of law into a contract and a comparable term derived from the law of tort, the practical significance of the distinction is likely to be slight.

The second point is that the claim was not for stress as such but for psychiatric illness caused by stress at work.[62] The case is therefore not an authority on the recoverability of damages for stress or anxiety which does not lead to a psychiatric illness or other stress-related physical disorder. This is not to say that it will not have an impact outside its immediate fact situation. The open recognition of 'the developing understanding ... of the nature and extent of occupational stress'[63] may induce courts in subsequent cases to relax the rules that currently restrict the recovery of damages in respect of stress which does not lead the claimant to suffer a psychiatric illness. The decision may also be influential in so far as it confirms the stance taken in *Johnson v Unisys Ltd* [64] that an employment contract cannot be equated with a commercial contract and that an employee's interest in the contract cannot be seen purely in financial terms.[65]

The third point is that a substantial component of the claims in these cases was for loss of earnings, both past and present. Thus at first instance Mrs Hatton was awarded damages of £90,675.83, of which all but £6,000 consisted of damages for loss of earnings.[66] This is an important point with regard to fears that the floodgates will be opened; it is not the stress itself which gives rise to substantial claims but the financial losses which flow from the stress.

The final point is that the threshold requirements laid down by the Court of Appeal are not easy to satisfy. In particular, employees in subsequent cases have found it difficult to prove that the employer could have reasonably foreseen that the employee would suffer a psychiatric illness.[67] As Hale LJ pointed out, psychiatric injury is, by its very nature, more difficult

[62] [2002] EWCA Civ 76; [2002] ICR 613 at [4]–[10].
[63] *Ibid* at [7].
[64] [2001] UKHL 13; [2003] 1 AC 518.
[65] That said, the decision in *Hatton* did not appear to have any influence on the decision of the Court of Appeal in *Dunnachie v Kingston upon Hull City Council* [2004] EWCA Civ 84. The latter decision was, however, overruled by the House of Lords.
[66] [2002] EWCA Civ 76; [2002] ICR 613 at [133].
[67] See, for example, *Pratley v Surrey County Council* [2003] EWCA Civ 1067 and *Barlow v Broxbourne Borough Council* [2003] EWCA 50 (QB); [2003] All ER (D) 208 (Jan).

to foresee than physical injury.[68] The difficulties of foreseeability and perhaps even more so the difficulties inherent in discerning the various (often interlinked) causes behind such injury highlight the need to consider seriously issues such a causation and remoteness when evaluating claims for non-pecuniary loss.[69]

3 THE POSSIBILITY OF CATEGORISATION?

The outcome of these cases cannot be said to be the production of 'simple and practical rules'. While the modern law continues to be based on the foundation laid in *Addis v Gramophone*,[70] the exceptions grafted on to it in *Watts v Morrow*,[71] as modified by the House of Lords in *Farley v Skinner*,[72] have left the law in a state of some complexity. In the absence of a judicial assault on *Addis* itself, the principal task that remains to be performed is to bring a greater degree of coherence to the exceptional cases in which recovery of damages for non-pecuniary loss is permitted. In our view coherence is most likely to be achieved if it is recognised that the cases are not all dealing with the same issue. The cases can in fact be divided into two principal categories, albeit that the categories are not watertight and a claimant can recover damages under both headings provided that there is no element of double recovery.

In the first category of cases the claimant seeks damages in respect of the defendant's failure to confer a promised non-pecuniary benefit on the claimant, whereas in the second category the claimant seeks damages to compensate her for the non-pecuniary loss which she has suffered as a result of the defendant's breach of contract. This classification is similar to but not identical with the distinction drawn by Lord Scott of Foscote in *Farley v Skinner*.[73] He distinguished between the case where the injured party has been 'deprived of something of value but the ordinary means of measuring the recoverable damages are inapplicable'[74] and the case where the injured party seeks to recover consequential damages in respect of the 'inconvenience or discomfort'[75] that has been suffered as a result of the breach. In our terminology the loss in the first category of case is a 'positive loss' whereas in the second category the loss is categorised as 'consequential' loss. We shall examine the cases in each category in turn.

[68] [2002] EWCA Civ 76; [2002] ICR 613, at [23].
[69] *Ibid*, at [5].
[70] [1909] AC 488.
[71] [1991] 1 WLR 1421.
[72] [2001] UKHL 49; [2002] 2 AC 732.
[73] *Ibid* at [86].
[74] *Ibid*.
[75] *Ibid*.

(a) Positive Loss: Breach of a Contractual Term Conferring Non-pecuniary Benefits

The first category consists of cases in which the defendant, expressly or impliedly, promises to confer a non-pecuniary benefit on the claimant or the effect of the breach was to deny the claimant the non-pecuniary benefit which she would have obtained from performance in accordance with the terms of the contract. The cases in this category can be sub-divided into different groups.

The first group consists of cases in which the defendant expressly promises to confer a non-pecuniary benefit upon the claimant. In general, these cases involve a promise to secure a 'state of affairs' which will bring pleasure or at least ensure peace of mind to the claimant. Explicit promises of this sort are however relatively few. It is rare (at least in reported cases) for a defendant expressly to assume such an obligation. But a variation of *Heywood v Wellers*[76] will illustrate the point. The claimant employed the defendant solicitors to take proceedings to protect her from molestation by a man with whom she had previously had a relationship. The defendants failed to take reasonable care to protect her position and she was molested by the man on three or four occasions and suffered 'much mental distress and upset'[77] as a consequence. There was no evidence to suggest that the defendants had expressly promised to take reasonable care to protect the claimant from molestation but they knew that she 'wanted to get rid of'[78] the man. Taking these facts a step further, it is not difficult to imagine a case in which a promise is made by a solicitor to take reasonable steps to ensure that a woman in the position of the claimant in *Heywood* does not suffer further molestation. Had such a promise been made, the defendants would have been liable for their failure to confer the promised non-pecuniary benefit on the claimant.[79] A claimant who wishes to recover damages in respect of a failure to provide the promised non-pecuniary benefit no longer has to prove that the object of the contract was to provide pleasure, relaxation, peace of mind or freedom from molestation;[80] it suffices that the term broken by the defendant was one which was known by both parties to be an important term of the contract.[81] Such a hurdle would not be a difficult one for the claimant to overcome in a *Heywood v Wellers* type case.

[76] [1976] QB 446.
[77] *Ibid*, at 459.
[78] *Ibid*, at 454.
[79] One would also expect there to be a liability for consequential losses suffered by the claimant provided that these losses were not too remote a consequence of the breach. We are not here concerned with a claim to recover consequential losses: we are only concerned with a claim to recover the value of the promised performance. We shall deal with consequential loss claims in more detail below.
[80] As was the case in *Watts v Morrow* [1991] 1 WLR 1421.
[81] *Farley v Skinner* [2001] UKHL 49; [2002] 2 AC 732, discussed above at 294.

Whilst many contracts are concluded with the aim of enhancing the financial position of the parties, this is not true for all contracts and, where it is not, the law ought to recognise the non-pecuniary interest of the claimant and award damages in respect of the performance to which the claimant was entitled and of which she was deprived.[82] A failure to impose liability on the defendant in such a case would effectively render the defendant's promise unenforceable. The claimant's full interest in performance of the contract would go unrecognised. As Lord Scott observed in *Farley,* quantification of the contractual promise will, 'in many cases be difficult and may often seem arbitrary.'[83] But the courts have no option but to embark on the difficult process of valuation: in many of these cases the defect cannot be cured, a replacement cannot be purchased and there is no difference in financial terms between the promised performance and the performance which has been supplied. The only loss is the failure to confer the non-pecuniary benefit and so loss of bargain damages must in these cases include in their assessment some measurement of the non-pecuniary advantages contracted for.

The second group consists of cases in which the defendant impliedly promises to confer a non-pecuniary benefit on the claimant. Examples in this category are more numerous and include the case of a contract to take photographs at a wedding[84] or to provide a holiday.[85] While the photographer or the provider of the holiday may not expressly promise to provide the client with pleasure,[86] or even to take reasonable care to provide the client with pleasure, it is clear that the 'state of affairs' contracted for is inextricably bound up with the enjoyment the claimant hopes to thereby obtain. In these cases, the law will readily imply an obligation to provide such pleasure and award the claimant damages in respect of a failure to confer the promised benefit.

The principal difficulty with this category lies in identifying the circumstances in which the law will imply an obligation on the part of the defendant to provide a non-pecuniary benefit. A contract between a prospective house purchaser and a surveyor demonstrates the difficulty. In England the practice is for potential house-buyers to have the property surveyed prior to entry into a contract to purchase. The principal reason for entry into such contract is that a survey is required by a building society or other financial institution which will typically lend the purchasers the money needed in order to enable them to purchase the property. But

[82] See generally D Friedmann, 'The Performance Interest in Contract Damages' (1995) 111 *Law Quarterly Review* 628, esp 650.
[83] [2001] UKHL 49; [2002] 2 AC 732 at [79].
[84] *Diesen v Samson* 1971 SLT (Sh Ct) 49.
[85] *Jarvis v Swans Tours Ltd* [1973] QB 233.
[86] Of course it is possible that a defendant might make such a promise. Where such a promise is made the case will fall within the scope of the first category.

the building society is not the only party who has an interest in the state of the property. The intending purchasers also have an obvious interest in the soundness of the house which they are proposing to buy. In such a case, does the surveyor promise to confer a non-pecuniary benefit on the house-purchaser? The House of Lords in *Farley v Skinner* concluded that the surveyor in an 'ordinary' surveyor contract makes no such promise and, accordingly, is not liable for the disappointment suffered by the house purchaser in the event that the house suffers from some defect which the surveyor fails to spot as a result of a failure to exercise reasonable care.[87] *Farley* was held to be distinguishable from the 'ordinary' surveyor's contract on the basis that the defendant had expressly requested the surveyor to investigate the noise levels from aircraft. This seems a somewhat formalistic approach. Is it not implicit in most contracts with surveyors that the client is seeking re-assurance or peace of mind from the surveyor? Yet *Farley* would appear to require the client expressly to stipulate her interest in the tranquil enjoyment of her property before she can recover damages in respect of the non-pecuniary losses which she suffers as a result of the loss of the expected tranquillity.[88]

There is clearly a difficulty in identifying the outer limits of this group. The issue can be stated simply but it is nevertheless difficult to resolve. The distinction that has to be drawn is between the case in which the defendant impliedly promises to confer a non-pecuniary benefit on the claimant and the case in which the defendant makes no such implied promise but the claimant nevertheless reasonably expects to obtain a non-pecuniary benefit as a consequence of performance by the defendant. While the former lies within the scope of this group, the latter does not. The problem is that the distinction between the two types of case is not easy to find, as the surveyor examples demonstrate. Does a surveyor impliedly promise to confer peace of mind on the intending house-purchasers or is it the case that the surveyor makes no such promise but the purchasers merely hope to derive peace of mind from the due performance by the surveyor of his obligation to survey the property with reasonable skill and care? The Court of Appeal in *Watts v Morrow*[89] concluded that the contract fell within the latter category, whereas the House of Lords in *Farley* decided that the particular contract in issue between the parties was in the former category. The fact that the line can be difficult to

[87] [2001] UKHL 49; [2002] 2 AC 732 at [42].

[88] We do not wish entirely to deny the relevance of the surveyor's knowledge of the client's purpose in entering into the contract. Such knowledge is clearly relevant to the question of whether or not the loss is too remote a consequence of the surveyor's breach of contract. The point with which we take issue is the apparent requirement that the client expressly inform the surveyor of her non-pecuniary interest in the performance of the contract prior to the conclusion of the contract.

[89] [1991] 1 WLR 1421.

draw in certain cases does not, however, mean that we should not attempt to draw the line at all. It simply requires us to recognise that in certain cases the line-drawing exercise will be a difficult one.

Despite these difficulties, cases can be found which clearly fall within the scope of this group; examples include contracts for the provision of a holiday,[90] contracts to provide burial services,[91] contracts to provide services at a family celebration, such as a wedding,[92] a special birthday or a christening and contracts to eradicate or reduce a source of stress in the claimant's life.[93]

The third group consists of cases in which the defendant does not promise, either expressly or impliedly, to confer a non-pecuniary benefit on the claimant but the contractual specification broken, of no intrinsic financial value, may, objectively, be accorded an 'added value'. It is reasonable to assume that the claimant expects to draw some form of additional benefit from fulfilment of the contractual term. This group of cases shades into the previous group in that, where the contractual specification objectively has an added value, a court may imply that the defendant has promised to confer a non-pecuniary benefit on the claimant. But, while there is a substantial degree of overlap between the two categories, they are not identical. In particular, in this group of cases, a court need not find that the defendant promised to confer a non-pecuniary benefit on the claimant in order to award damages: it suffices that the breach has resulted in an objective non-pecuniary loss to the claimant. In other words, in this group the emphasis is placed on the position of the claimant, whereas in the second group the focus is upon the nature of the promise that has been made by the defendant. The issue for the court here then is whether the contractual obligation broken had an objective 'added value' to the claimant which exceeded the market price of performance by the defendant.

The case of the photographer who, in breach of contract, fails to turn up at a wedding may fall into this group.[94] A court may conclude that the photographer has not impliedly promised to confer a non-pecuniary benefit on the claimants but that the breach of contract has caused an objective non-pecuniary loss to the claimants in that they have been deprived of a pictorial record of their wedding day. *Farley v Skinner* may also be said to fall into this group, in that the value of peace and quiet in the home is recognised by most 'objective' onlookers as being of value.

[90] Such as *Jarvis v Swans Tours Ltd* [1973] QB 233 and *Jackson v Horizon Holidays Ltd* [1975] 1 WLR 1468.
[91] Such as *Lamm v Shingleton* 55 SE 2d 810 (1949).
[92] Such as *Diesen v Samson* 1971 SLT (Sh Ct) 49.
[93] Such as *Heywood v Wellers* [1976] QB 446.
[94] See *Diesen v Samson* 1971 SLT (Sh Ct) 49.

The fourth group consists of cases in which the particular contractual specifications, of no intrinsic financial value, are accorded subjective 'added value' by the contracting party. In these instances, the value is not referable to any 'objective' standard. *Ruxley Electronics and Construction Ltd v Forsyth,*[95] seems most clearly to fall into this group. In *Ruxley* loss of amenity damages of £2,500 were awarded to a defendant in respect of a swimming pool which had been built to the wrong depth. The depth in no way affected the value of the swimming pool, or the defendant's use of it, but the omission was clearly of importance to the defendant. The 'added value' in *Ruxley* appears to lie in the individual tastes of Mr Ruxley; that is to say, whilst it is plain that a successful holiday is generally intended to bring added benefits beyond its financial value, it is not so clear that the exact depth of a swimming pool is integral to its value as a pool. *Ruxley* is now generally regarded as a 'loss of amenity' case. But what was this loss of amenity? One view, which has significant judicial support, is that it was a claim for 'consequential' non-pecuniary loss, with damages awarded to reflect the loss to the defendant of a pleasurable amenity (a swimming pool of a specified depth)[96] or to compensate him for the inconvenience which he suffered as a result of the breach.[97]

This interpretation of *Ruxley* has, however, been challenged by Lord Millett in *Alfred McAlpine Construction Ltd v Panatown Ltd*[98] and by Lord Scott in *Farley v Skinner.*[99] In *Panatown*, Lord Millett stated that, viewed objectively, there was no loss of amenity in *Ruxley* and that the loss could be described, more accurately, as a 'defeated expectation'.[100] Similarly, Lord Scott in *Farley* classified *Ruxley* as a case in which the claim was one to recover the value of the promised performance which had not been supplied by the party in breach. Thus he stated that *Ruxley*

> establishes ... that if a party's contractual performance has failed to provide to the other contracting party something to which that other was, under the contract, entitled, and which, if provided, would have been of value to that party, then, if there is no other way of compensating the injured party, the injured party should be compensated in damages to the extent of that value.[101]

[95] [1996] AC 344.
[96] This view was adopted by Lord Lloyd of Berwick in *Ruxley* (at 373–4) and by Lord Steyn and Lord Hutton in *Farley v Skinner* [2001] UKHL 49; [2002] 2 AC 732, at [21] and [49] respectively, although Lord Hutton did recognise (at [50]) that the principle stated in *Ruxley* 'can be of more general application.'
[97] A view adopted by Lord Clyde in *Farley v Skinner* [2001] UKHL 49; [2002] 2 AC 732, at [36]. This view is, however, difficult to defend because it seems to entail a degree of double-counting, given that Mr Forsyth was awarded damages of £750 in respect of the 'general inconvenience and disturbance' which he suffered as a result of the breach.
[98] [2001] 1 AC 518.
[99] [2001] UKHL 49; [2002] 2 AC 732.
[100] [2001] 1 AC 518, 588.
[101] [2001] UKHL 49; [2002] 2 AC 732, at [79].

This analysis of *Ruxley* gains some support from Lord Mustill's speech in *Ruxley* where he stated that the law of contract must recognise that the value of a promise can exceed the enhancement of the financial position of the promisee that will follow from performance of the promise.[102] In our submission the latter two statements constitute an explicit recognition of the fact that the conception of loss recognised by the law of contract now extends beyond purely financial losses and instead has as its focus the performance for which the claimant contracted, whether or not that performance was designed to enhance the claimant's financial well-being.

Nevertheless, it is not every case in which a claimant will be entitled to recover from the defendant the 'added value' which she attached to the contractual specification to which she is entitled but has not been given. A number of factors operate to limit the entitlement of a claimant to recover in respect of such 'added value'. One of these is the context in which the transaction was concluded. The courts are extremely unlikely to recognise the existence of any 'added value' in the case of a contract concluded between two commercial parties.[103] The reason for this is that the courts generally presume that parties to commercial contracts enter into a contract in order to make a profit, with the consequence that the aim of the award of damages is principally to entitle the innocent party to recover in respect of the financial losses which it has suffered as a result of the breach. It is true that a party to a commercial contract may have an interest in performance itself and not simply the enhancement of its financial position which performance will bring, but in such a case a court can make a specific performance order or award to the claimant damages assessed on a cost of cure basis. Either remedy will give to the claimant the performance to which it was entitled (albeit that, in the case of cost of cure damages, performance will be obtained from a third party rather than the original contracting party). In the case where a court decides not to make a specific performance order, nor to assess damages on a cost of cure basis, then it is suggested that it ought not to award damages on the basis that the claimant attached a higher value to performance than the market value of performance. The remedies of specific performance and damages assessed on a cost of cure basis can adequately protect the claimant's performance interest and there is no need to go further and recognise that a party to a commercial contract attaches an 'added value' to performance, whether that added value is ascertained on an objective or a subjective basis.

Matters are otherwise when we turn to consumer contracts. It is here that 'added value' has its principal role to play and it is to be found in the notion of the 'consumer surplus'. Consumer surplus can be defined

[102] [1996] AC 344, 360.
[103] *Hayes v James and Charles Dodd* [1990] 2 All ER 815, 823–4.

as the 'excess utility or subjective value obtained from a "good" over and above the utility associated with its market price.'[104] It is a concept more closely associated with our fourth group than our third, given the subjective emphasis contained in most definitions of the consumer surplus. 'Consumer surplus' has its academic supporters[105] and it has also received some judicial recognition.[106] For the consumer, 'profit' may well be referable to the subjective value or 'consumer surplus' she expects to obtain from performance. Take the example of a contract to decorate a house. The homeowner who enters into such a transaction is unlikely to do so with a view to enhancing her financial position. She is more likely to do so because she wishes to have her home decorated in accordance with her own taste and that taste is unlikely to be universally shared; indeed, it may be that her taste is so poor that the result of performance of the contract will be to reduce the value of her house. Thus it is that 'consumer contracts' often involve the exchange of some 'non-pecuniary advantage'[107] and this excess utility is not necessarily reflected in the market price. This notion of consumer surplus, unique to the non-commercial context, is therefore of primary importance in terms of understanding the plight of the injured party who has suffered some 'positive' non-pecuniary loss.

However it is not inevitable that the award of damages to a consumer will recognise the consumer surplus. To revert to the example of the contract to decorate a house, a consumer who is awarded damages assessed on a cost of cure basis will not be entitled to damages to reflect her consumer surplus because the effect of the award of damages assessed on a cost of cure basis will be to enable her to obtain the performance for which she contracted. To award her damages to reflect her consumer surplus would be to over-compensate her.[108] But in a case such as *Ruxley*, where the court decides not to award cost of cure damages, consideration should be given to the award of damages to reflect the claimant's consumer surplus in the case where damages awarded to compensate the claimant for the financial losses which she suffers does not provide her with full compensation.

What does the claimant have to prove in order to be entitled to recover damages assessed by reference to her consumer surplus? In our view, she has to prove that she has not been given the performance to which she was entitled and that, to award her damages in respect of her financial

[104] D Harris, A Ogus and J Phillips, 'Contract Remedies and the Consumer Surplus' (1979) 95 *Law Quarterly Review* 581, 582.

[105] *Ibid.*

[106] *Ruxley Electronics and Construction Ltd v Forsyth* [1996] AC 344, 360, *per* Lord Mustill.

[107] *Per* Oliver J in *Radford v De Froberville* [1977] 1 WLR 1262, 1271.

[108] Unless the damages are awarded to compensate the claimant for any consequential losses for any distress and physical invonvenience which she suffers while the remedial work is being carried out.

loss only, will not compensate her fully for the loss which she has, in fact, suffered. But how does a claimant prove that to award damages only in respect of her financial loss will lead to under-compensation? In answering this question no one factor is decisive. The range of factors to be taken into account by the court were identified by Lord Hutton in *Farley v Skinner* as follows:

> (1) the matter in respect of which the individual claimant seeks damages is of importance to him, and (2) the individual claimant has made clear to the other party that the matter is of importance to him, and (3) the action to be taken in relation to the matter is made a specific term of the contract. If these three conditions are satisfied, as they are in the present case, then I consider that the claim for damages should not be rejected on the ground that the other party does not receive special and specific remuneration in respect of the performance of that obligation.[109]

This list should not be regarded as exhaustive but it does give an indication of the type of factors which should be taken into account by a court when deciding whether or not to award the claimant damages assessed on the basis that she attaches a value to performance which exceeds the market value of the promised performance.

This last group represents potentially the most substantial and far-reaching recognition of the fact that a claimant need not prove that she is financially worse-off as a result of the breach in order to recover more than nominal damages. In our view, the principle now enshrined in the law is that she must prove that she has suffered a loss as a result of the breach and, while that loss will continue to be assessed purely in financial terms in most cases, the conception of loss recognised by the law is no longer confined to financial loss but may extend further. A claimant who can prove that the defendant expressly or impliedly promised to confer on her a non-pecuniary benefit or who can prove that the defendant has deprived her of a non-pecuniary benefit to which she was entitled under the contract is, in principle and subject to the usual rules of remoteness and causation,[110] entitled to recover damages for the non-pecuniary loss suffered as a result of the breach.

(b) Consequential Loss: Non-pecuniary Losses Flowing from Contractual Breach

The second category consists of cases in which the claimant has attempted to recover damages in respect of non-pecuniary losses which she has

[109] [2001] UKHL 49; [2002] 2 AC 732. at [54].
[110] On which see below, pp 315–318.

suffered as a consequence of the defendant's breach of contract. These consequential non-pecuniary losses can be divided into different categories, although, once again, the categories are not watertight. The types of consequential non-pecuniary losses that have been recognised in the cases include physical injury, psychiatric injury or illness, embarrassment and loss of reputation, (physical) inconvenience and mental distress or disappointment. It is important to note that here we are confining ourselves to a discussion of the extent to which it is possible to recover damages in respect of non-pecuniary losses suffered by the claimant. It is not our intention to discuss the separate question of the possibility of recovery in respect of pecuniary losses (in particular, loss of earnings) as a consequence of physical injury or psychiatric illness which has been inflicted on the claimant due to the defendant's breach of contract. *Hatton v Sutherland*[111] demonstrates that the latter question is a very important one, but it is one which is beyond the scope of this chapter.

The first group is the least controversial: a claim by the claimant for physical injury caused by the breach of contract. It is clear law that damages can be recovered for physical injury suffered by the claimant as a result of the defendant's breach of contract, provided that the loss is not too remote a consequence of the breach of contract.[112] In *Grant v Australian Knitting Mills Ltd*[113] the claimant purchased woollen underpants from the defendant retailer. The underpants contained excess sulphites and these caused the claimant to suffer severe dermatitis for which he was entitled to recover damages from the defendant retailers. It should be noted that liability was not based on the fault of the defendant. It sufficed for the claimant to prove that the underpants were not fit for their purpose or not of 'merchantable quality' and, once one or other of these requirements had been satisfied, the defendant was liable for the foreseeable physical injury suffered by the claimant as a result of the breach.

The second group consists of cases in which the claimant suffers psychiatric illness as a consequence of the defendant's breach of contract. Cases in this group tend to consist of professional negligence cases in which the defendant breaches a contractual duty of care and the claimant suffers psychiatric illness as a consequence.[114] An example is provided by *Cook v Swinfen*.[115] The defendant solicitor admitted that he had been negligent in the conduct on the claimant's behalf of divorce proceedings in

[111] [2002] EWCA Civ 76; [2002] ICR 613.
[112] See *Chitty on Contracts* 29th edn, (London, Sweet & Maxwell 2004), 26–073 and *McGregor on Damages* 17th edn, (London, Sweet & Maxwell, 2003), 3–017 and 20–077.
[113] [1936] AC 85. See also *Wren v Holt* [1903] 1 KB 610; *Summers v Salford Corporation* [1943] AC 283 and *Godley v Perry* [1960] 1 WLR 9.
[114] Thus liability for psychiatric illness is generally based on fault and not strict liability.
[115] [1967] 1 WLR 457. See also *Bailey v Bullock* [1950] 2 All ER 1167 and *Dickinson v Jones Alexander & Co* [1993] 2 FLR 521.

which the claimant was the respondent. One of the issues before the Court of Appeal was whether or not the claimant was entitled to recover damages for the breakdown in health which she suffered partly as a result of the negligence of the defendant. On the facts it was held that the defendant was not liable because the claimant's breakdown was too remote a consequence of the breach of duty. For present purposes, the significance of *Cook* lies in the recognition that damages can be recovered for psychiatric illness caused by a breach of contract provided that the loss is not too remote a consequence of the breach. Thus Lord Denning stated that:

> just as in the law of tort, so also in the law of contract, damages can be recovered for nervous shock or anxiety state if it is a reasonably foreseeable consequence.[116]

There are two related difficulties here. The first is that the claimant must have suffered a psychiatric illness as a result of the breach: it does not suffice for the claimant to prove that she has suffered distress or disappointment. Second the psychiatric illness must have been a reasonably foreseeable consequence of the breach and, as *Cook v Swinfen* demonstrates, it may not be easy for the claimant to prove that the psychiatric illness was reasonably foreseeable to the defendant.

The third group consists of embarrassment or loss of reputation. Once again, the general rule is that damages cannot be recovered for loss of reputation suffered as a result of a breach of contract. The decision of the House of Lords in *Addis v Gramophone Co Ltd*[117] stands in the way of the recognition of a right to recover damages in this context. A claimant who wishes to recover damages in respect of her loss of reputation must, in general, resort to a claim in defamation, with all the difficulties attendant on such a claim. However the rule that damages cannot be recovered for loss of reputation cannot be stated without qualification. The decision of the House of Lords in *Mahmoud v Bank of Credit and Commerce International SA*[118] established that employees could, in principle,[119] recover damages from their employer for the damage to their reputation caused by a breach of the employer's duty not, without reasonable and proper cause, to conduct its business in a manner likely to destroy or seriously damage the relationship of trust and confidence which existed between employer and employee. However it is vital to note that *Mahmoud* only concerned a claim to recover damages in respect of the financial losses suffered as a result of the breach of contract; it was not an attempt to recover damages

[116] *Ibid*, at 461.
[117] [1909] AC 488.
[118] [1998] AC 20.
[119] The claims failed on the facts: *Bank of Credit and Commerce International SA v Ali (No 2)* [2002] EWCA Civ 82; [2002] ICR 1258.

in respect of the embarrassment or loss of reputation *per se*. Claims in respect of the latter appear still to be governed by *Addis*, as is confirmed by the decision in *Johnson v Gore Wood & Co.*[120] Despite Lord Cooke's dissenting opinion,[121] in which he considered both financial embarrassment and damage to reputation to be comparable to physical discomfort or inconvenience,[122] the majority refused to adopt this line and dismissed the claim on this issue. Moreover, whilst *Addis* has been the subject of some criticism, the House of Lords declined to overrule it both here and subsequently in *Johnson v Unisys Ltd.*[123] It therefore remains good law.

It may nevertheless be possible to make some inroads into the general rule of no-recovery. Where the object of the contract is to enhance the reputation of the claimant, the defendant may be liable for the losses suffered by the claimant in the event that, in breach of contract, the defendant fails to enhance the reputation of the claimant.[124] However, even in this case, it may be that damages will be confined to the financial losses which flow from the failure to enhance the reputation of the claimant and will not extend to compensation for loss of reputation or embarrassment *per se*.

The fourth group consists of (physical) inconvenience. An example in this group is the decision of the Court of Appeal in *Watts v Morrow.*[125] The claimants employed the defendant to carry out a full structural survey of a large country house which they were contemplating buying as a weekend residence. They purchased the house in reliance upon the survey but, shortly after they moved into the house, they discovered that it required major repair-work. The Court of Appeal held that the claimants were not entitled to recover damages in respect of any disappointment or distress which they suffered as a consequence of the breach of contract, but that they were entitled to recover damages in respect of the 'physical discomfort or inconvenience resulting from the breach and mental suffering directly related to that inconvenience and discomfort.'[126] Instead of enjoying peaceful weekends at their country retreat, the claimants had to endure what Mr Watts described as 'quite deplorable'[127] conditions while extensive repair work was carried out to the property. For such loss, they were awarded damages of £750 each. The existence of the inconvenience can easily be discerned on the facts of *Watts* because of its physical nature; the claimants had to endure considerable physical discomfort.

[120] [2002] 2 AC 1.
[121] *Ibid* at 49.
[122] See the second exceptional category outlined by Bingham LJ in *Watts v Morrow* [1991] 1 WLR 1421, 1445 and discussed above at 290.
[123] [2001] UKHL 13; [2003] 1 AC 518, discussed in more detail above at 292–4.
[224] *Mahmoud v Bank of Credit and Commerce International SA* [1998] AC 20, 37.
[125] [1991] 1 WLR 1421. See also *Burton v Pinkerton* (1867) LR 2 Exch 340 and *Hobbs v London and South Western Railway Co* (1874) LR 10 QB 111.
[126] *Ibid* at 1445.
[127] *Ibid* at 1427.

Farley v Skinner is, in this respect, more difficult, because the inconvenience suffered by the claimant did not assume such an obviously 'physical' form. However it may be possible to accommodate the case within this group on the basis that the noise from the overflying aircraft had an impact on the claimant's senses and therefore may be said to have had a physical manifestation.[128] Similarly, the analogy drawn by Lord Steyn with nuisance cases[129] suggests that there must be a link with the senses in that the activity must consist of a noise, a smell or some other activity which has a sensory impact. However Lord Clyde appeared to adopt a wider definition of 'inconvenience.' In his opinion it covered 'the kinds of difficulty and discomfort which are more than mere matters of sentimentality'[130] and he thought that there was no 'particular magic in the word "physical."'[131] The difficulty with the latter suggestions is that they appear to extend significantly the scope of this group without providing any clear guidance as to its outer limit. It is suggested that this group consists principally of cases in which the inconvenience to the claimant assumes a physical form (such as discomfort or physical exertion) or impacts on the claimant's senses (such as noise or smells). Arguments for extending the group beyond these categories should be received with considerable caution, lest the group be extended in such a way as to encompass cases where the essence of the claim is one for mere disappointment suffered as a consequence of not getting the contractual performance to which the claimant is entitled.

The final group consists of distress, anxiety and loss of enjoyment or pleasure. Such losses are not generally recoverable in a claim for damages for breach of contract. They would appear to be recoverable only within the limits recognised by the House of Lords in *Farley v Skinner.* However it is suggested that the cases in which damages have been awarded for distress and loss of enjoyment are better seen within the first category of cases; that is to say they are 'positive loss' cases either because the defendant expressly or impliedly promised to provide the claimant with pleasure or relief from distress or the claimant was deprived, as a result of the breach, of performance to which she attached 'added value'. However it may be possible to classify them as 'consequential' loss claims in so far as the claimant is seeking to recover damages for the loss which she has suffered as a consequence of not getting the performance to which she was entitled under the contract. It is suggested that a claimant will not gain any advantage by reformulating the claim in this way as one to recover consequential losses. The rules laid down in *Farley* apply whether the

[128] See the speech of Lord Scott: [2001] UKHL 49; [2002] 2 AC 732 at [85].
[129] *Ibid* at [30]
[130] *Ibid* at [36].
[131] *Ibid*.

claim is one to recover in respect of, in our terminology, a 'positive loss' or to recover consequential losses.

(c) The Overlap

A source of difficulty in this context is the fact that these categories are not mutually exclusive and, as has been noted, it is not always easy to distinguish between the different categories of case. Thus in some cases it may not be clear whether the court is awarding damages because the claimant has been deprived of a non-pecuniary benefit which she was promised under the contract (a case of 'positive loss') or whether it is awarding the claimant damages for the consequential non-pecuniary losses which she has suffered as a result of the defendant's breach (a case of 'consequential' loss).

A case that illustrates the potential difficulty is *Hobbs v London and South Western Rly Co.*[132] In breach of contract the defendant railway company failed to transport the plaintiff and his family to Hampton Court and instead abandoned them after midnight at Esher, leaving them with a five mile walk home in the rain. The jury awarded the plaintiff damages of £8 for the inconvenience experienced as a result of having to walk home in the rain and £20 in respect of the cold which his wife suffered as a result of the incident. The defendants appealed successfully against the award of damages in respect of the wife's subsequent illness but their appeal was dismissed in relation to the award of damages for the inconvenience suffered.

In some ways the case is less than satisfactory. One major difficulty with the case is that the court did not explain the nature of the relationship that existed between the plaintiff's wife and the defendants. It is recorded that the plaintiff 'took'[133] the tickets for himself, his wife and their two children. If the plaintiff was the purchaser of the tickets and there was no contractual relationship in existence between the plaintiff's wife and the defendants, on what basis could the wife recover damages in respect of the loss which she suffered? One possible answer is that the defendants were sued for the breach of the duty which they owed to the parties as carriers. The problem with this explanation is that it would appear that the claim was one for 'breach of contract.'[134] The second difficulty with the case is that the language of the judgments is cast almost entirely in terms of remoteness. The finding of the court was, in essence, that the £20 awarded in respect of the cold suffered by Mrs Hobbs was

[132] (1875) LR 10 QB 111.
[133] *Ibid* at 112.
[134] *Ibid* at 113.

too remote a consequence of the defendants' breach of contract, whereas the £8 awarded in respect of the inconvenience suffered was not too remote a consequence of the breach.

How can we justify the award of damages of £8 in respect of the inconvenience suffered? Any straightforward answer is elusive. The first difficulty relates to the identification of the loss in respect of which the damages were awarded. Were damages awarded for the loss suffered by Mr Hobbs only, or for the loss suffered by himself and his wife? This question was not answered directly by the court. But the judgments do refer to the fact that 'the plaintiffs were put to personal inconvenience'[135] and the plaintiffs were Mr and Mrs Hobbs. This suggests that damages were awarded in respect of the losses suffered by both Mr and Mrs Hobbs.[136] A further problem relates to the measurement of the loss. Here it is difficult to be sure on what basis damages were awarded, given that the award was set by a jury and the court refused to interfere. One rationalisation is that damages were awarded to the plaintiffs to compensate them for the personal inconvenience which they suffered.[137] This puts the case in the consequential loss category and this explanation of *Hobbs* draws support from the speeches of Lord Clyde and Lord Hutton in *Farley v Skinner.*[138] An alternative explanation of *Hobbs* is that damages were awarded to reflect the fact that the plaintiffs did not obtain the performance for which they contracted. This was the explanation adopted by Lord Scott in *Farley.* Thus he stated that the 'contractual benefit' to which the plaintiff was entitled was 'the carriage of himself and his family to Hampton Court'[139] and that it was reasonable for the court to measure the lost contractual benefit by 'reference to the discomfort to the family of the walk home.'[140] The latter explanation raises problems for two reasons. First, the measure of recovery is identified in terms of the consequences of the breach and this suggests that the loss suffered by the plaintiffs was truly consequential loss. Second, the defendants conceded that they would have been liable to the plaintiffs had they incurred additional expenditure in order to complete their journey home. But the plaintiffs did not incur any such expenditure for the simple reason that no alternative means of transportation were available at such a late hour of the night. There being no *financial* consequences of the breach, the court held that the defendants were liable to the plaintiffs for the *physical* consequences of the breach.

[135] *Ibid* at 115.
[136] Albeit it is not entirely clear on what basis Mrs Hobbs was entitled to recover damages. Was she a party to a contract with the defendants and, if not, on what basis was she entitled to recover damages from the defendants?
[137] *Ibid* at 115 (Cockburn CJ), 120 (Blackburn J), 122–3 (Mellor J) and 124 (Archibald J).
[138] [2001] UKHL 49; [2002] 2 AC 732 at [35] and [57] respectively.
[139] *Ibid* at [88].
[140] *Ibid*.

This suggests that the preferable view of the case may be to classify it as a consequential loss claim.

While the line between the two categories may be difficult to draw at the margins, it is nevertheless submitted that the line ought to be retained if only because it requires the courts to articulate in clear terms the nature of the loss in respect of which damages are being awarded. There is a difference between the loss of the promised contractual performance and losses suffered as a consequence of the loss of that promised performance, albeit that the difference can, on occasion, be difficult to detect.

4 PRINCIPLES LIMITING LIABILITY

The fact that a claimant is in principle entitled to recover damages either in respect of her 'positive loss' or in respect of the consequential non-pecuniary losses which she has suffered as a result of the defendant's breach of contract does not mean that she will inevitably recover damages in respect of these losses. The courts will apply well-recognised principles in order to place limits on the liability of the defendant. Four such principles appear to be of particular significance, namely remoteness, causation, mitigation and the rules applicable to the assessment or measurement of loss. We shall give brief consideration to each principle in turn.

(a) Remoteness

Losses which are too remote a consequence of the defendant's breach of contract cannot be recovered by the claimant. It is possible to attribute an extensive role to the remoteness rules in the present context. One view is that the general rule that damages cannot be recovered for non-pecuniary losses can itself be explained as an aspect of the rules relating to remoteness of damage. Thus in *Farley v Skinner* Lord Scott stated that the 'issue can and should be resolved by applying the well-known principles laid down in *Hadley v Baxendale*.'[141] This is not a view which we share. The rule that damages are not generally recoverable in respect of non-pecuniary losses suffered as a result of a breach of contract cannot be explained satisfactorily on the basis that such losses are not a reasonably foreseeable consequence of the breach of contract. Cases can be found in which such losses were held to be irrecoverable notwithstanding the fact that they were within the reasonable contemplation of the parties at the time of

[141] At [75].

entry into the contract.[142] Indeed, as Lord Millett observed in *Johnson v Unisys Ltd*,[143] the reason that damages cannot be recovered for the ordinary feelings of anxiety, frustration and disappointment is that, far from being unforeseeable, 'they are so commonly a consequence of a breach of contract that the parties must be regarded not only as having foreseen it but as having agreed to take the risk of its occurrence.'[144] This is not to say that the rules relating to the remoteness of damage are irrelevant. They are relevant and they do have a role to play in terms of keeping liability for non-pecuniary losses within acceptable limits, but they do not contain all the answers. They must not be made to do too much work.

The remoteness rules have a greater role to play where the claim is one to recover consequential losses than they do in the case where the claim is one to recover in respect of a 'positive' loss which has been suffered by the claimant. The reason for this is that the positive loss cases have built-in rules which operate to limit the scope of liability. This is particularly so in the case where the defendant expressly promises to confer a non-pecuniary benefit on the claimant. In such a case it is likely to be extremely difficult for a defendant to contend that the non-pecuniary loss suffered by the claimant is too remote, unless the extent of the loss is very much greater than the loss which could reasonably have been foreseen.[145] Slightly more difficult is the case in which the defendant is held impliedly to have promised to confer a non-pecuniary benefit on the claimant. Here there may be more room for a remoteness rule to operate, especially if the courts are willing to imply such a promise. To date, there has been no sign of such a willingness. This being the case, it is unlikely that a defendant will succeed with a defence that the non-pecuniary loss is too remote a consequence of the breach unless, as in the case of breach of an express promise, the extent of the loss is very much greater than the loss which could reasonably have been foreseen.

There may, however, be more need for remoteness rules in the 'added value' cases, especially where the claimant accorded an 'added value' to contractual performance but that value is not referable to any 'objective' standard. That said, the cases within this category are relatively small in

[142] *Watts v Morrow* [1991] 1 WLR 1421, 1445.
[143] [2001] UKHL 13; [2003] 1 AC 518.
[144] *Ibid* at [70].
[145] Even here the defendant is likely to encounter difficulty given the general rule that the extent of the loss suffered by the claimant need not be reasonably foreseeable: see, eg, *Wroth v Tyler* [1974] Ch 30. However the proposition that the extent of the loss need not be foreseeable must be adjusted in the light of the decision of the Court of Appeal in *Victoria Laundry (Windsor) Ltd v Newman Industries Ltd* [1949] 2 KB 528 where a distinction was drawn between an ordinary loss of profits (which was recoverable) and an exceptional loss of profit (which was not). Thus in the case where the claimant suffers an extreme reaction as a result of the failure of the defendant to provide the promised non-pecuniary benefit, the defendant may be able to avoid liability for such losses on the ground that they are too remote a consequence of the breach.

number and they tend to consist of cases in which either the defendant was aware of the importance which the claimant attached to the particular contractual specification[146] or the quantum of the award was modest.[147] In both cases the defendant would find it difficult to argue that the loss was too remote a consequence of the breach. But in other cases the argument might succeed. Take a variant of the facts of *Farley v Skinner.* Suppose that the claimant had not make clear to the defendant the importance which he attached to his wish to buy a house which was not affected by aircraft noise. In such a case the claimant would probably have failed in his claim. In the first place, he would have found it extremely difficult to establish negligence on the part of the defendant given that he would then not have been subject to any particular duty to comment on the impact of overflying aircraft on the claimant's enjoyment of his property. Secondly, making the assumption that he could have established a breach of duty, he would have found it very difficult to recover in respect of his losses given that no one else in the neigbourhood appeared to be affected by the noise from the aircraft.[148] In such a case the defendant could either deny liability for the loss on the ground that liability in such subjective 'added value' cases can only arise where the defendant has knowledge of the value which the claimant attached to the broken contractual obligation or on the ground that the loss was too remote a consequence of the breach. These are two separate routes to the same result. It would appear not to matter which route is taken: both are concerned with the defendant's knowledge of the value attached by the claimant to the value of contractual performance.

When we turn to the consequential loss cases, the remoteness rules assume greater significance. Thus in *Cook v Swinfen*[149] the defendant's breakdown in health was held to be too remote a consequence of the defendant's negligence. Similarly, in the *Hatton v Sutherland* line of cases, the foreseeability of psychiatric harm has been a major issue, albeit that it has been invoked when deciding whether or not a duty of care is owed by the employer to the employee rather than in the context of the remoteness or otherwise of the loss. Unless the defendant has expressly or impliedly promised to confer a non-pecuniary benefit on the claimant, it is unlikely that non-pecuniary loss will be a 'natural' consequence of the breach. This being the case, such losses are likely to be too remote a consequence of the breach unless they were within the contemplation of both parties at the time of entry into the contract. Thus a defendant who was unaware of the possibility that the claimant would suffer psychiatric illness, loss of reputation, embarrassment or (physical) inconvenience as a consequence of the breach is likely to have a strong argument that the

[146] As was the case in *Farley v Skinner* [2001] UKHL 49; [2002] 2 AC 732.
[147] As was the case in *Ruxley Electronics and Construction Ltd v Forsyth* [1996] AC 344.
[148] [2001] UKHL 49; [2002] 2AC 732 [68].
[149] [1967] 1 WLR 457.

loss is too remote a consequence of his breach of contract. However it is important to add that the remoteness rules only come into play once the claimant has established that the loss is recoverable in the first place. As we have noted, claimants are likely to find it difficult to establish liability on the part of the defendant and, this being the case, it is more likely that liability will be kept within reasonable bounds by the rules which define the circumstances in which liability for consequential non-pecuniary losses can arise rather than by the remoteness rules themselves.

(b) Causation

Thus far causation has had a very limited role to play in the case-law because the courts have been able to deny liability on other grounds and have not generally been required to consider whether or not the claimant's loss was caused by the defendant's breach of contract. But cases will arise in which causation may prove to be crucial. The issue is most likely to crop up in the line of cases represented by *Hatton v Sutherland*.[150] For example, what is to be done in the case where the claimant employee suffers a nervous breakdown partly as a result of the defendant employer's breach of contract and partly as a result of her difficult domestic circumstances? In *Hatton* itself the Court of Appeal suggested that the defendant should be held liable for the proportion of the harm suffered by the claimant which is attributable to its breach of contract unless the harm caused to the claimant is 'truly indivisible.'[151] This is unlikely to be the last word on the issue. Difficulties are certain to arise in determining when the defendant is only liable for a proportionate share of the loss which the claimant has suffered and when the defendant must shoulder the burden for the entirety of the loss which the claimant has suffered.[152]

(c) Mitigation

Thirdly, it is necessary to consider the impact which the doctrine of mitigation may have on claims to recover damages in respect of non-pecuniary

[150] [2002] EWCA Civ 76; [2002] ICR 613.

[151] *Ibid* at [36]–[37]. But note that the rules set out by the Court of Appeal are derived from tort cases and not from cases in which the claim was one to recover in respect of a breach of contract.

[152] The relationship between *Hatton* and the subsequent decision of the House of Lords in *Fairchild v Glenhaven Funeral Services Ltd* [2002] UKHL 22; [2003] 1 AC 32 may prove to be an uneasy one. In *Hatton* liability was held to be proportionate, whereas in *Fairchild* the defendant was held liable for 100% of the claimant's losses. It may also prove to be difficult to determine when the claimant's loss is 'truly indivisible' so as to impose liability for the entire loss on the defendant.

losses. The doctrine of mitigation may be invoked by a defendant in one of two principal ways. First, the defendant may submit that the claimant ought to have sought and obtained substitute performance and, not having done so, is not entitled to be compensated in respect of her non-pecuniary loss. Alternatively, the defendant may submit that the claimant is not entitled to recover cost of cure damages and instead is confined to the recovery of loss of amenity damage to compensate her for the disappointment which she has suffered as a result of not getting the contractual performance to which she was entitled. We shall consider each alternative in turn.

The submission that the claimant ought to have sought and obtained substitute performance instead of seeking damages for her non-pecuniary loss is, in many ways, an odd one for a defendant to advance, given that the cost of obtaining alternative performance will in all probability exceed the sum likely to be awarded as compensation for non-pecuniary loss. As Clarke LJ observed in *Farley v Skinner* the claimant 'saved the defendant money' by 'not moving and putting up with the noise' instead of seeking to recover from the defendant 'the reasonable cost of buying and selling the property and of moving to a new property.'[153] Nevertheless cases can be found in which the defendant has taken the position that, while it would have been liable for the reasonable expenses incurred by the claimant, it is not liable for the non-pecuniary losses suffered by the claimant. An example is *Hobbs v London and South Western Rly Co*[154] where the defendant accepted that it would have been liable for any costs incurred by the claimants in finding alternative means of transportation to their home but submitted that it was not liable for the inconvenience which the claimants suffered as a result of having to walk home.[155] Perhaps not surprisingly, the court rejected the defendant's submission. In many ways the submission was lacking in merit. The defendant was attempting to avoid liability for a loss which the claimants had suffered (namely, inconvenience) by submitting that they ought to have incurred a different type of loss (financial loss) which they did not in fact suffer. Thus the fact that the claimant does not obtain substitute performance from elsewhere will not, of itself, operate to deny to the claimant the right to recover damages in respect of her non-pecuniary loss. But, where the cost of obtaining substitute performance is considerably lower than the damages likely to be awarded in respect of the claimant's non-pecuniary loss (which is, admittedly, likely to be a rare event[156]), mitigation may require

[153] [2000] PNLR 441, 459.
[154] (1875) LR 10 QB 111.
[155] *Ibid* at 114.
[156] *Hobbs* might have been such a case had alternative transportation been available. The claimants claimed damages of £400 which must have exceeded by an enormous margin the cost of such transportation. However the account of the facts states (at 112) that 'the plaintiff was unable to get a conveyance or accommodation at an inn, where he knocked in vain' so that the issue simply did not arise on the facts.

the claimant to seek performance from that other source rather than claim damages in respect of her non-pecuniary loss.

The source of the submission that the claimant is entitled to recover loss of amenity damages rather than cost of cure damages finds its origin in the decision of the House of Lords in *Ruxley Electronics and Construction Ltd v Forsyth*.[157] In this case, the homeowner was held not to be entitled to recover cost of cure damages because it would have been unreasonable; that is, the cost of carrying out the work was held to be out of all proportion to the benefit which the homeowner hoped to obtain from full performance. The principle upon which their Lordships relied was not the specific doctrine of mitigation but the more general concept of 'reasonableness'. On the facts it was held to be 'unreasonable' for the defendant to seek cost of cure damages and so he was confined to an award of damages for his 'loss of amenity.'

In this way reasonableness, or mitigation, may in fact widen the ambit of non-pecuniary losses, at least in the 'added value' cases. This development may be seen as a less than desirable one. It is arguable that it may weaken the commitment of the law to the protection of the claimant's performance interest. Indeed in some cases it will operate to deprive the claimant of the performance to which she was entitled under the contract and replace this instead with damages to reflect the disappointment which she experienced at not getting the promised performance.

(d) Measurement of Loss

Non-pecuniary loss is not only harder to detect and harder to prove than financial losses, but it is also notoriously difficult to measure. This point was made in robust terms by Mummery LJ in the Court of Appeal in *Farley v Skinner* when he stated:

> The incontrovertible fact is that the unobservable subjective nature and extent of intangible harm means that it is inherently difficult to prove (or to refute); that, even if properly proved, it is impossible to measure as there are no objective standards and no solid comparables; that, even if 'measured', the amount awarded is open to the trenchant criticisms that it is not truly or wholly compensatory, that it contains an impermissible punitive element and that it reflects the intrusion of an unacceptable level of subjectivity on the part of the judge; and that the whole exercise fails to satisfy a fundamental requirement of a fair and workable litigation system that the outcome of a claim should be reasonably predictable, both as to liability and

[157] [1996] AC 344, discussed in more detail above at n 95.

> *quantum*, so that the parties and their advisers can negotiate satisfactory compromises and make informed decisions on Part 36 offers and payments and their acceptance.[158]

This objection did not convince the House of Lords. Lord Steyn referred to the practice in lower courts of awarding damages on a modest scale in a wide range of contracts to compensate claimants for the loss of pleasure, relaxation and peace of mind.[159] One of the aims of the House of Lords would appear to be to legitimate this practice in the lower courts and to remind them that awards should generally be modest. Provided that lower courts follow the signals being sent to them by the House of Lords, the likelihood of unacceptable inconsistency emerging in the case-law should be low. An even greater degree of consistency may be achievable by focusing more clearly on the nature of the loss which the claimant alleges that she has suffered; in particular, whether she alleges she has suffered a 'positive' loss or whether her claim is to recover damages in respect of non-pecuniary losses suffered as a consequence of the defendant's breach.

5 CONCLUSION

The aim of this chapter is a modest one. It is not to provide a comprehensive analysis of the arguments which have been advanced for or against the award of damages in respect of non-pecuniary losses suffered as a result of a breach of contract. This chapter has taken the less ambitious route of attempting to analyse and to classify the cases in which the courts have awarded damages in respect of such non-pecuniary losses. In so doing, it has sought to distinguish between two principal groups of cases, namely those in which the claimant in a breach of contract case is seeking to recover damages on contractual breach in respect of a 'positive' loss of some non-pecuniary benefit contracted for and those in which the claimant is seeking to recover damages in respect of 'consequential' non-pecuniary losses suffered as a result of the defendant's breach. Rather than attempt to articulate an over-arching general principle which can be applied to all cases, we have sought to identify the differences between the cases and to highlight the various factors which should be taken into account by the courts when deciding cases.

The most important part of the analysis is the recognition of the 'positive' loss category of cases. It has been said that English law fails to recognise the value of the right to performance itself as opposed to the consequences of

158 [2000] PNLR 441, 454.
159 [2001] UKHL 49; [2002] 2 AC 732 at [20].

performance or the economic end-result of performance.[160] The most recent cases in this area do seem to suggest however that the courts are at least starting to take the protection of the performance interest more seriously by giving greater consideration to a range of non-pecuniary interests under the head of loss. There is growing acceptance that the claimant may be entitled not simply to the economic value of the performance, but to something which aspires to replace the promised performance itself. In practice, this aspiration is still some way from being fulfilled. At present it is confined to cases where the defendant expressly or impliedly promises to confer a non-pecuniary benefit on the claimant and, albeit more hesitantly, to cases in which the claimant makes clear that some 'added value' attaches to contractual performance. There remains room for further development. Growing recognition that consumers and employees in particular do not enter into contracts simply in order to enhance their financial position is a first tentative step in the right direction, an acknowledgment that a more expansive conception of loss is required to reflect the values of modern day society. If we are to go beyond cautious stumblings, the courts must give deeper consideration to the original 'exceptional categories' outlined by Bingham LJ in *Watts v Morrow* by drawing out the nuances which will help to infuse this area of law with the certainty currently lacking. In so doing they will be faced with the challenge of formulating a sharper definition of non-pecuniary interests, situating the limits to recovery, and setting guidelines as to the measure of damages appropriate. It is hoped that this chapter goes some way towards flagging up the task that has been embarked on and highlighting the need for further thought. Perhaps more ambitiously, this chapter attempts to make the case for some more order in the case-law and suggest a framework in which this might be done.

[160] See generally, B Coote, 'Contract Damages, *Ruxley* and the Performance Interest' [1997] *Cambridge Law Journal* 537.

Index